Adolescent Literacy Instruction
Policies AND Promising Practices

ALVERNO COLLEGE
INSTRUCTIONAL SERVICES

Jill Lewis
Gary Moorman
EDITORS

INTERNATIONAL
Reading Association
800 BARKSDALE ROAD, PO BOX 8139
NEWARK, DE 19714-8139, USA
www.reading.org

The International Reading Association attempts, through its publications, to provide a
forum for a wide spectrum of opinions on reading. This policy permits divergent viewpoints without implying the endorsement of the Association.

Executive Editor, Books   Corinne M. Mooney
Developmental Editor   Charlene M. Nichols
Developmental Editor   Tori Mello Bachman
Developmental Editor   Stacey Lynn Sharp
Editorial Production Manager   Shannon T. Fortner
Production Manager   Iona Muscella
Supervisor, Electronic Publishing   Anette Schuetz

Cover   Design: Linda Steere; Photographs (clockwise from top): PhotoDisc, Jupiter
Images/clipart.com, Jupiter Images/Fotosearch.com

The publisher would appreciate notification where errors occur so that they may be
corrected in subsequent printings and/or editions.

Library of Congress Cataloging-in-Publication Data
Adolescent literacy instruction : policies and promising practices / Jill Lewis, Gary
Moorman, editors.
    p. cm.
  Includes bibliographical references and index.
  ISBN 978-0-87207-623-5
  1. Reading (Middle school)--United States. 2. Literacy--United States. 3. Reading
comprehension--United States. I. Lewis, Jill, Ed. D. II. Moorman, Gary B.
  LB1632.A268 2007
  372.40973--dc22

                      2007013337

*We dedicate this book to those who have contributed
most to our knowledge about adolescent literacy:
the many adolescents with whom we have worked
and who have taught us so much, and our esteemed
colleagues (many of whom contributed to this book)
who have cultivated and challenged our thinking.*

CONTENTS

PART I

Adolescent Literacy Initiatives

PART II

Instructional Strategies for Adolescent Learners

CONTRIBUTORS

Donna E. Alvermann
Distinguished Research Professor
    of Language and Literacy
    Education
University of Georgia, Athens,
    Georgia, USA

Patricia L. Anders
Professor and Head of the
    Department of Language,
    Reading, and Culture
University of Arizona, Tucson,
    Arizona, USA

Thomas Bean
Professor of Literacy/Reading
University of Nevada, Las Vegas,
    Nevada, USA

William E. Blanton
Professor of Reading, Educational
    Psychology, and Reading
    Education
University of Miami, Coral
    Gables, Florida, USA

William G. Brozo
Professor of Literacy, Graduate
    School of Education
George Mason University, Fairfax,
    Virginia, USA

Doug Buehl
Adolescent Literacy Support
    Teacher
Madison Metropolitan School
    District, Madison, Wisconsin,
    USA

Kristine M. Calo
Doctoral Student in Literacy
George Mason University, Fairfax,
    Virginia, USA

A. Jonathan Eakle
Assistant Professor and Reading
    Program Director
Johns Hopkins University School
    of Education, Baltimore,
    Maryland, USA

Douglas Fisher
Professor of Language
    and Literacy Education
San Diego State University, San
    Diego, California, USA

Helen Harper
Professor of English Education
    and Cultural Studies
University of Nevada, Las Vegas,
    Nevada, USA

Julie Horton
Assistant Professor
Appalachian State University,
    Boone, North Carolina, USA

Carol Hryniuk-Adamov
Certified Reading Clinician
Winnipeg School Division,
    Winnipeg, Manitoba, Canada

Jill Lewis
Professor of Literacy Education
New Jersey City University,
    Jersey City, New Jersey, USA

David W. Moore
Professor of Education
Arizona State University, Phoenix,
    Arizona, USA

Gary Moorman
Professor of Education
Appalachian State University,
    Boone, North Carolina, USA

Karen A. Onofrey
Assistant Professor of Education
Arizona State University, Phoenix,
    Arizona, USA

Janice Pilgreen
Chair of the Graduate Reading
    Program and Director of the
    Literacy Center
University of La Verne, La Verne,
    California, USA

Paola Pilonieta
Assistant Professor
University of North Carolina at
    Charlotte, North Carolina, USA

Terry Salinger
Managing Director and Chief
    Scientist for Reading Research
American Institutes for Research,
    Washington, DC, USA

Carol M. Santa
Co-Founder and Educational
    Director
Montana Academy, Marion,
    Montana, USA

Ellen Spitler
Doctoral Student, Department
    of Language, Reading,
    and Culture
University of Arizona, Tucson,
    Arizona, USA

Nea Stewart-Dore
Adjunct Associate Professor
Central Queensland University,
    Rockhampton, Australia

Elizabeth G. Sturtevant
Associate Professor and
    Coordinator of the Literacy
    Program
George Mason University, Fairfax,
    Virginia, USA

Karen D. Wood
Professor
University of North Carolina at
    Charlotte, North Carolina, USA

Themes and Perspectives on Adolescent Literacy Instruction

This edited volume grew out of an Institute at the International Reading Association's (IRA) 2006 Annual Convention in Chicago when we had the good fortune to work with a team of the finest thinkers in the field of adolescent literacy. The focus of the Institute was on how research should inform teachers about their instruction and how teachers' experiences in providing literacy instruction to adolescents should inform the adolescent literacy research agenda; we believe that there is nothing so practical as good theory and nothing so theoretical as good practice. As we began preparing for the Institute, it was clear that the team shared a common vision of adolescent literacy instruction. The more we talked, the more it became obvious that a book that included chapters from each member of the team would be a valuable addition to the professional literature on adolescent literacy. We also sought out other authors who could write chapters that would provide an international, multilingual perspective.

As editors, we feel that we have been blessed with opportunity and good luck. Our timing could not have been better. Every year for the last decade, IRA has published *What's Hot and What's Not*, a survey of experts that lists topics of interest in the field of literacy. The hottest topic in 2007 is adolescent literacy: "The 2007 list contains one extremely hot issue—*adolescent literacy*. Not only did all our respondents agree that this was a hot issue, but they also all agreed that it should be a hot issue" (Cassidy & Cassidy, 2007, p. 1). Interestingly, adolescent literacy is a relatively new term, if not altogether a new topic. Although educators have long been concerned with reading and writing beyond the elementary school, until recently, the focus of attention was on content area reading. In this volume, Harper and Bean argue that the field of adolescent literacy can be dated to the recent publication of IRA's *Adolescent Literacy: A Position Statement* (Moore, Bean, Birdyshaw, & Rycik, 1999).

Adolescent Literacy Instruction: Policies and Promising Practices edited by Jill Lewis and Gary Moorman. © 2007 by the International Reading Association.

In the political arena, we are now witnessing a shift in perception about the need to provide literacy instruction in the upper grades. Public concern about adolescent literacy has led numerous organizations, including IRA, the National Association of State Boards of Education, and the National Governors Association (see Buehl, this volume) to issue policy statements. In the United States, the No Child Left Behind Act includes legislation aimed at secondary school literacy instruction. According to the U.S. Department of Education,

> As States and communities implement NCLB and achievement gaps are eradicated in the early grades, we can expect that many more young people will enter high school well prepared to master a rigorous curriculum. But our nation cannot afford to wait. True to its name, NCLB recognizes that change also is needed to help today's high school students catch up quickly and master both basic and advanced academic skills. (USDE, n.d., n.p.)

We are hopeful that this volume will provide insight on how such instruction can be implemented. It is divided into two parts. In Part I, issues related to policy are addressed. Policy initiatives and the rationales that support them are explored. In Part II, issues directly related to classroom instruction are investigated. Promising literacy teaching practices are identified and their implementation is explored. Throughout both parts, you will find a number of conceptual themes that thread the text together. The authors share a common perspective on learning and instructional theory, on adolescent literacy, on the importance of schoolwide and locally governed programs, and on the broad policy issues that must be addressed.

The shared theoretical perspective of the authors is derived from the rich research base on teaching and learning that has emerged over the last three decades. Our perspective has two dimensions. As John Dewey wrote over a hundred years ago, "I believe that this educational process has two sides—one psychological and one sociological; and that neither can be subordinated to the other or neglected without evil results following" (p. 77). In the psychological dimension, the concept of schema provides powerful insights on how knowledge is acquired and utilized. A schema is a knowledge structure into which new information must be assimilated before it can be understood. In turn, each schema must accommodate the new information. Through this process of accommodation and assimilation, individuals develop and enrich schemas over time. From an instructional standpoint, schema underscores the importance of building bridges between what learners already know and what they are expected to learn. Closely related to schema is the concept of metacognition—the learners' awareness of how they think and learn. A high level of metacognition results in higher levels of understanding and achievement. These two powerful psychological concepts provide the foundation for the explicit instructional practices presented in this book.

Equally powerful is the sociological concept that learning and literacy are inherently social. Vygotsky (1934/1978, 1962/1986) argues that all higher order mental activity must first appear on the interpersonal, or social, plane. Only after learners have experienced the mental activity during social activity are they able to internalize it to the intrapersonal, or psychological, plane. The key to this process is language, the tool of all tools. By using language during social activity, individuals are able to internalize the skills that guide their thinking during higher order mental activities. Instruction should take place in the Zone of Proximal Development, the difference between the learner's independent problem-solving ability and their problem-solving ability under the guidance of more knowledgeable others. In other words, by engaging in socially meaningful activity, students are able to develop independent problem-solving skills. This social view of learning suggests that classrooms should become communities of learners. Through active participation, students learn the skills, routines, practices—and most importantly—the language of the classroom community. Teachers are responsible for arranging conditions that promote use of higher order skills and for encouraging students to develop an identity as a member of the community.

Our authors also agree that the adolescents we now teach bring with them a set of background knowledge, experiences, and skills different from any other generation in history. Sometimes termed the Millennials, these adolescents have grown up in a world saturated with Information Communication Technology (ICT): They live comfortably in a digital world, with immediate access to information and communication. Their world outside of school includes computers, Internet, cell phones, e-mail, text messaging, instant messaging, cable and satellite television, and it requires its own set of literacy skills. Throughout this book, the term *multiple literacies* will be used to describe the many different forms of literacy that today's adolescents need to prosper both in their social worlds and in the school environment. The challenge for us is to build on the considerable knowledge that the Millennials have already acquired and to use these skills for developing the academic language and literacy skills necessary for success in school and the workplace. We offer instructional strategies for building these bridges.

Our volume also reflects our view that just as "it takes a village to raise a child," it takes a school community to raise the literacy levels of all students. We reject conventional thinking that in the middle and high school grades reading is a separate subject, and that it is solely the responsibility of the English/language arts teacher or the reading specialist to help adolescents increase their literacy skills. All teachers must recognize that adolescent literacy extends to literacy in specific content areas and, thus, every teacher has a significant role to assume in the literacy achievement of their adolescent students. Many chapters in this volume illustrate lessons that integrate reading and writing, as well as multimedia, across content disciplines.

Expanding adolescents' literacies for success in school also requires schoolwide staff development efforts that are comprehensive, ongoing, and locally controlled. We believe that this book can serve as a primary resource for developing such programs. Chapters within this volume provide examples of effective secondary reading programs that benefit greatly from supportive and knowledgeable leadership. Although such leadership begins with the principal, we believe a full-time and highly trained certified reading specialist should be in charge. We are optimistic about the emergence of the concept of literacy coaches and the Standards that have been developed for this position by IRA, along with others (see http://www.reading.org/resources/issues/reports/coaching.html). We illustrate how literacy coaches embedded in the school are able to assume a collaborative, supportive role with content area teachers.

Our passion for improving adolescents' literacy must be coupled with policies aligned to this goal. Toward this end, policymakers must consider the entire in- and out-of-school context as they draft positions and set legislation for improving literacy skills of our youth. Our volume speaks to resources, teacher expertise, school leadership, school conditions, community and parental involvement, and the role of the business community in this enterprise. And we prepare our readers to challenge policymakers who believe that adolescent literacy can be improved solely by imposing accountability measures on schools and teachers. Our book emphasizes the need for policymakers to provide the resources needed and to take a comprehensive look at the challenges faced by those working in schools who are committed to improving the futures of our youth through education and enhanced literacy achievement.

We believe this book is rich in terms of both its strong theoretical perspective and practical instructional suggestions. The credit for this clearly goes to the 24 chapter authors. We are grateful to them for the insights we have gained on the topic of adolescent literacy. We hope you find reading the book as enjoyable and educational as we have.

Jill Lewis, Gary Moorman
March 2007

REFERENCES

Cassidy, J., & Cassidy, D. (2007, February/March). What's hot, what's not for 2007. *Reading Today, 24*, 1, 11–12.

Dewey, J. (1897). *My pedagogic creed.* Retrieved March 23, 2007, from http://www.rjgeib.com/biography/credo/dewey.html

Moore, D.W., Bean, T.W., Birdyshaw, D., & Rycik, J.A. (1999). *Adolescent literacy: A position statement for the Commission on Adolescent Literacy of the International Reading Association.* Newark, DE: International Reading Association.

U.S. Department of Education. (n.d.). *No Child Left Behind: Transforming America's high schools.* Retrieved February 23, 2006, from http://www.ed.gov/about/offices/list/ovae/pi/hsinit/papers/nclb.pdf

Vygotsky, L.S. (1978). *Mind and society: The development of higher mental processes* (M. Cole, V. John-Steiner, S. Scribner, & E. Souberman, Eds. & Trans.). Cambridge, MA: Harvard University Press. (Original work published 1934)

Vygotsky, L.S. (1986). *Thought and language* (A. Kozalin, Trans.). Cambridge, MA: The MIT Press. (Original work published 1962)

PART I

Adolescent Literacy Initiatives

CHAPTER 1

Setting the Agenda for Adolescent Literacy

Terry Salinger

HIGHLIGHTS

- A national agenda for adolescent literacy is still at a formative stage as policymakers look for policy actors who advocate for ideas and approaches.
- National responses to the perceived crisis in early reading achievement do not necessarily offer the best approaches to meeting the needs of adolescent struggling readers.

According to John Kingdon's (1995) study of policymaking, the process of setting an agenda involves the work of one or more prominent policy actors who have identified a condition that merits attention, based on analysis of various indicators, some buzz or another, and often even data. When the condition changes precipitously, the policy actors ensure that stakeholders—and the public—begin to recognize the condition as a problem that must be solved. This chapter considers the current national interest in adolescent literacy in terms of the situation that Kingdon described. That there is some condition regarding adolescents has become widely accepted, but the question remains open as to whether a viable agenda for dealing with it has yet emerged.

Recognizing that there is a problem is really only the start because the magnitude of the issues and their causes and potential effects all contribute to whether the problem is deemed salient, immediate, and ultimately fixable through some level of human effort. According to Kingdon

---

Adolescent Literacy Instruction: Policies and Promising Practices edited by Jill Lewis and Gary Moorman. © 2007 by the International Reading Association.

(1995), it takes strong policy actors to move an agenda forward—one or more individuals who attend to the problem and are ready to bring it to prominence so that an agenda can be established and acted on at the local and national levels.

Reading professionals are all too familiar with this phenomenon, having witnessed the reaction of education policymakers and the general public most recently to publication of *Becoming a Nation of Readers* (Anderson, Hiebert, Scott, & Wilkinson, 1985), *Preventing Reading Difficulties* (Snow, Burns, & Griffin, 1998), and the *Report of the National Reading Panel* (National Institute of Child Health and Human Development, 2000). Even though Allington (2000) maintained that every 30 years a "very public yet personal debate about the nature of appropriate reading instruction emerges in the media and in the policy talk in legislative venues" (p. 24), it seems as though the reading debate is actually ongoing.

New Attention to Reading Achievement

Changes in the National Assessment of Educational Progress (NAEP) reading test drew attention to reading and advanced the reading agenda played out since the late 1980s (Allington, 2000). These changes were very important from a measurement and conceptual perspective. Test development began to reflect a constructivist perspective on reading that resulted in items asking for more than low-level inferences and searches for information embedded, however obscurely, in the text itself. Newer items required a written response, rather than selecting from multiple-choice options. Additionally, the introduction of NAEP achievement levels—below basic, basic, proficient, and advanced—gave educators and the media a new way to talk about how students were doing in reading and in all subjects. The new terminology, especially "basic" and "below basic," seemed clearer to a public that hadn't understood the meaning of earlier descriptors, especially reading "on grade level," "below grade level," or "above grade level." It didn't matter that the achievement-setting process was found to be faulty (Pellegrino, Jones, & Mitchell, 1999); the new descriptors stuck and became part of the policy vernacular. Following the lead of NAEP and states such as Michigan and Illinois, state reading tests began to change too, and many adopted the new achievement-level language as their reporting mechanism.

The newly designed state tests showed unanticipated results as well: The tests were more challenging, and students didn't do as well as they seemed to be doing on other measures, including international comparative assessments. The availability after 1990 of state comparisons on NAEP—first for grade 4 reading, then for grade 8 reading and mathematics—provided even more fuel for the policy debates. State NAEP comparisons also enabled a very potent force for policy change. State-by-state comparative data were circulated widely, precipitating comparisons across states and also within states as policymakers compared glowing results on state reading tests with considerably lower results on NAEP. The ability to disaggregate NAEP data highlighted the discrepancy between scores of white students and students of color, dramatically pointing out that an achievement gap existed, even though students in the aggregate often seemed to be doing fine.

What happened in California, where NAEP scores were very low, dramatically illustrates how rapidly policy actors can bring attention to a problem and begin a change process. The State Board of Education, influenced by then member Marion Joseph and others, lobbied for a change from the existing kindergarten to grade 12 literature-based curriculum to one that was strongly grounded in phonics and systematic instruction (Song, in press). State standards were changed to reflect this shift; credentials of professional development providers were tightly regulated; and systematic instruction using core reading programs was mandated in the state's elementary schools. Numerous policy actors hit their stride, including native Californians and "outsiders." The publishing giants watched carefully because California, like Texas, has statewide adoption of textbooks.

A new policy agenda for early reading was emerging on the national level too, within what Kingdon (1995) would call a "policy window": an opening that becomes available when numerous forces and conditions converge to such an extent that policy actors or even "policy entrepreneurs" focusing on recognized problems can propel their solutions to prominence. The policy window in early reading resulted in state standards for reading being developed in every state except Iowa, and standards-based assessments followed quickly. Panels were established to investigate the issue of poor early reading achievement, resulting in reports that shaped first the Reading Excellence Act, then No Child Left Behind and the multibillion-dollar Reading First program. Although we might want to think about these events as being merely part of the background for the current attention to adolescents' literacy needs, they are far more important. It is not so much that a new policy window is opening for adolescent readers as that the general reading window is opening a little wider. There is a cautionary tale in how early reading policy has evolved.

Early Reading Policy's Repercussions

The best chronicle of the emergence of current policy for early reading is the work initiated at the University of Michigan in 1998 with support from the Center for the Improvement of Early Reading Achievement, the Department of Education, and the Spencer Foundation (Miskel et al., 2003). These researchers sought to identify the elite actors shaping policy in the reading arena by studying archival records and contemporary media sources, conducting interviews, and analyzing their data at the national and state levels to get a sense of what was going on. Referring to the transition from the Reading Excellence Act to Reading First, Song (in press) wrote, "Across virtually all 50 states, reading became an area of passionate interest and policy activities, and very often a source of intense controversy about teaching methods, curriculum standards, and assessments." The data suggested that it was the Department of Education, the American Federation of Teachers, and the National Institute of Child Health and Human Development that led to opening the policy window in early reading at the national level. Only two individuals rated a place in the list of top 20 policy actors; both are affiliated with private commercial firms, not universities. The International Reading Association was ranked 6th, and interestingly, the Office of the President, although strongly influenced by Reid Lyon, came in near the bottom, at 17th. The discussion will return to Lyon later.

Continuing the metaphor, into the policy window bounded large commercial publishers that could market basal or core reading programs as the primary vehicle for offering systematic, phonics-based instruction grounded in scientific research. The prominence of comprehensive, commercial reading programs had been minimized by the trend toward using trade or leveled books as primary material, which was one indicator of whole-language or balanced-reading instruction. Now the use of such programs has seen a huge resurgence. Although there is no definitive list of federally approved publishers, the guidance for instruction in Reading First schools mandates use of a core reading program. Further, the consumer's guide (Simmons & Kame'enui, 2003) to core reading programs developed at the University of Oregon and its offshoots have all but eliminated programs not developed by five or six major publishers from use in Reading First schools. In their attempts to demonstrate that they are scientifically based, the developers of the most common core reading programs have adopted similar instructional models, leading to standardization in early reading instruction.

If the window for reading policy is just opening a bit wider for adolescents, the important question is whether policy for adolescent literacy will take the same trajectory toward systematic instruction provided by scientifically based commercial materials that are all very similar in approach.

Of course early reading connotes specific grade levels, a circumscribed period of grades and ages. Adolescent literacy is a more ambiguous concept, and there is far less clarity about its conceptual boundaries or its definition. Sorting through the ambiguity involves answering questions such as, What constitutes adolescence? What defines adolescent literacy? What are the problems here? Who is working on solutions? These questions are considered next.

What Constitutes Adolescence?

Putting some boundaries around adolescence is a difficult task because it involves more than just calculating age or number of years of school attendance. At two workshops on adolescent literacy sponsored by the National Institute for Literacy and the National Institute of Child Health and Human Development (2002), the definition covered middle school and high school students. This is a logical categorization, except that entry into middle school can occur at fifth grade or later. Fourth graders are often left in a sort of limbo, at least in terms of instructional policymaking. Yet they—and often fifth and sixth graders—may be tottering on the brink of sophisticated literacy skills. Their skills may not be completely set, so they quickly fall farther and farther behind academically because they can't really read to learn. Alexander (2005/06) has proposed a more salient life-span interpretation of literacy growth. According to her, literacy evolves and matures over time in ways that are not governed by grade-level designations.

What Defines Adolescent Literacy?

Adolescent literacy—as an outcome of schooling—is perhaps most frequently (and simplistically) defined by achievement levels on state reading tests or on NAEP. Such definitions may appear to be policy relevant, but the inconsistency of these measures makes them a questionable metric.

NAEP provides the single most dependable measure of aggregate reading levels of students in grades 4 and 8 at the national and state levels and nationally at grade 12. NAEP sets national goals for literacy, and they are indeed demanding. Many states have used NAEP as the model for state tests, but local standard-setting processes mean that the actual results for students may differ widely when state tests and students' scores on them are compared to NAEP state data. Many states have also adopted the terms "basic," "proficient," and "advanced" to categorize students' scores, but they haven't necessarily adopted NAEP's rigorous criteria for classifying test results into one or another category. SchoolMatters (2005) published a comparison of results on state tests and NAEP scores for students in South Carolina and Texas, focusing specifically on students at grade 4. On the state tests, 31.4% of the South Carolina students were deemed to be reading at proficiency; in Texas, 85% of the students were categorized in this way. However, scores for students in both states on grade 4 NAEP were about the same—27% proficient in Texas and 26% in South Carolina. Another study (McCombs, Kirby, Barney, Darilek, & Magee, 2005) presented a similar comparison of discrepancies in state reading test passing rates and results on the NAEP reading test at grade 8. A study commissioned by the National Research Council compared state tests in reading and other subjects nationwide to determine equivalency of these tests. The title of the report succinctly expresses the findings: *Uncommon Measures* (Feuer, Holland, Green, Bertenthal, & Hemphill, 1999).

What Are the Problems?

At least three factors define the problem in adolescent literacy: poor achievement, especially as noted in the achievement gap between racial and ethnic groups; perceived deficits in students' preparation for post-secondary work and study; and dropout rates. The three are all problems on their own, and, of course, they are also related to literacy.

Students' poor achievement, as measured on state and national tests, has already been discussed. Even though we may be skeptical about what test results actually mean, the discrepancy across sub-groups—the achievement gap—continues as students move beyond the early grades. Students' needs for literacy skills to make sense of content area subjects only exacerbate the problem. NAEP consistently points out the achievement discrepancies, and much of the impetus behind the No Child Left Behind legislation has been to close the gap. At the same time, data collected by the National Center for Education Statistics,

Public Agenda, and other sources, and compiled by the American Diploma Project (Achieve & American Diploma Project, 2004) show that most high school graduates need remedial help if they enter college and most college students never attain a degree. Additionally, most employers claim that high school graduates lack basic skills, including in mathematics, and most workers question the preparation their high schools provided. The extent to which literacy skills per se have shaped these findings and perceptions has not been quantified, but literacy professionals can easily imagine the close connections that must exist.

Next there are the students who drop out of high school, often within sight of their graduation day. The Alliance for Excellent Education (http://www.all4ed.org) has been at the forefront of bringing the dropout issues to public attention. Also powerful is the Bill and Melinda Gates Foundation, one of the supporters of a new website called StandUp.org that includes tool kits for parents and community groups to address the dropout issue. The website is a marvel in proactive social marketing; it features a dramatic little ticker that counts off the seconds until the next student drops out of high school and tallies the number of students who have dropped out since the beginning of the calendar year.

Dropouts don't cite literacy as motivation for leaving high school, but their major reasons all suggest literacy-related issues. Uninteresting classes was a reason named by 47% of the students included in a recent study (Bridgeland, Dilulio, & Morison, 2006), followed by missing too many classes (43%), spending too much time with peers who weren't interested in school (42%), and having too much freedom (38%). Only 35% of the students said that they left because they were failing. Interestingly, the reasons are almost identical to those provided in a study conducted over a decade earlier by Education Testing Service (Corley, 1995).

The literature on dropouts has also introduced the concept of students who are pushed out of school, perhaps because they can't keep up and also because they are bored or find school irrelevant (Achieve & American Diploma Project, 2004; Bridgeland et al., 2006). Here again, literacy skills probably factor into many students' decisions to leave before obtaining a degree. As literacy professionals, we can recognize that many of these factors may be caused or exacerbated by reading issues.

Who Is Working on Solutions?

This question asks who or what has emerged as the policy actors try to shape the adolescent literacy agenda. Who or what is trying to open the policy window for adolescent literacy? And here the discussion becomes very interesting. It is far easier to name the entities—both governmental and nongovernmental—that are working toward a solution than to identify individual policy actors. Certainly, Carnegie Corporation of New York and the Alliance for Excellent Education work tirelessly toward improvement in adolescent literacy and in the quality of schools for middle and high school students. *Reading Next* (Biancarosa & Snow, 2004) is their joint publication; it lays out clear criteria for sound adolescent literacy instruction.

The International Reading Association (IRA, 2006) and other member groups (IRA & National Middle School Association, 2002) have made strong statements about literacy, suggesting, for example, that middle schools and high schools can benefit from the services of qualified, well-trained literacy coaches who work with content area teachers. The National Governors Association (Achieve & National Governors Association, 2005; National Governors Association Center for Best Practices, 2005) has urged its members to recognize the importance of literacy issues and has recently funded eight states in their efforts to develop adolescent literacy plans. Unfortunately, many of the funded states think that they will be able to piggyback their plans on their work in Reading First. The National Conference of State Legislatures (Walton, 2005) has focused attention on improving high schools because of the economic advantages of advanced schooling, and the Southern Regional Education Board (n.d.) has likewise urged its membership to attend to high school reform. The National Assessment Governing Board (National Commission on NAEP 12th Grade Assessment and Reporting, 2004) has called for a redesign of grade 12 NAEP as a wake-up call about poor achievement in high schools. What is not obvious is whether any of these entities can play a role as powerful as that played by the major policy actors who shaped the early reading agenda.

Many of the strong, well-regarded researchers in adolescent literacy are contributing to the knowledge base about this age group. Some, like Judith Langer (n.d., 2000), have developed what might be called programmatic approaches to change—not formal programs neatly packaged with lesson plans and teacher resources, but ways of thinking about how to approach and choreograph instruction for this age group. The WestEd Strategic Literacy Initiative, often referred to as Reading Apprenticeship (Fielding, Schoenbach, & Jordan, 2003), is another example of an approach rather than a program. It involves intense professional development to get teachers to think differently about their students, the texts they present, and their own literacy skills. By understanding the metacognitive aspects of successful reading comprehension, teachers gain strategies to help their students improve their reading in all content areas. Work by Don Deshler (Deshler, Schumaker, & Woodruff, 2004), Mary Beth Curtis (Curtis & Longo, 1999), and others is backed by years of research as well. In this volume, Alvermann and Eakle's study of students' out-of-school literacy has shed new light on what it means to be a literate adolescent (see chapter 4).

Research Limitations

Two elements are missing from much of this excellent research. The first is the idea of scalability and sustainability. Can programs be implemented on a large scale? If so, will whatever remains in place be sustained when the researchers' training and technical assistance are withdrawn and implementation is passed on to various successions of new teachers and administrators? Another issue is often referred to as "scientific rigor." It calls for validation of effectiveness through research conducted using experimental or quasi-experimental methodology, ideally randomized field trials, and large samples of students. For the workshops on adolescent literacy sponsored by the National Institute for Literacy and the National Institute of Child Health and Human Development (2002), Curtis (2002) identified 155 research studies published between 1990 and 2002. She found many of them methodologically lacking but did classify 90 of them as descriptive and 65 as impact studies that used some kind of experimental design. They were spread pretty evenly across four subject categories: print (accuracy and fluency), language (word meaning and discourse processing), cognition, and situation (motivation and interests). Interestingly, nearly 25% of the articles had been published in journals related to special education or learning disabilities. Curtis acknowledged that the database does not constitute the kind of scientific base put forth for early reading, even though many of us would argue that descriptive work can tell far more about students' learning than the controlled studies that are so highly valued. The perceived lack of scientific rigor is currently being addressed, both by commercial publishers who need to bolster claims of program effectiveness with randomized field trials and by the Department of Education.

What About the Department of Education?

The Department of Education ranked first in the list of influential policy actors in early reading (Miskel & Song, 2004), but it is too early to tell if its ranking will be the same for adolescent literacy. Nonetheless, the department is trying to build a database of scientific research in adolescent literacy. Certainly attention is being placed on relevant issues through the Striving Readers program (http://www.ed.gov/programs/strivingreaders/index.html). Eight sites were recently funded to conduct randomized field trials to evaluate the effectiveness of intensive literacy interventions for struggling readers when used in conjunction with schoolwide reading-in-the-content-area professional development for teachers. Four of the recipients (the Ohio Department of Youth Services; Newark, New Jersey; Memphis, Tennessee; and Springfield/Chicopee, Massachusetts) will use Scholastic's Read 180.

The department is also funding the Enhanced Reading Opportunities (ERO) study, in which yearlong, intensive intervention is offered to ninth-grade students who are reading two or more years below grade. The ERO study, also using randomized field trials, is currently underway in 34 schools in 10 districts nationwide. The two programs being studied are variations of the Reading Apprenticeship Strategic Literacy Model developed by WestEd and the Strategic Instruction Model developed at the Center for Research on Learning at the University of Kansas. Both programs have been modified from their whole-school approach to become self-contained intervention programs.

No data are yet available from either study, and release of reports of findings is a long way off. Still, the requirement for randomized field trials emphasizes that the same kind of scientific base will be prerequisite for program validation and wide-scale acceptance.

Commercial publishers need randomized field trials too—or at least rigorous experimental studies—in order to publicize their scientific base and to gain recognition by the federally funded What Works Clearinghouse (http://whatworks.ed.gov). The clearinghouse has not tackled adolescent literacy yet, but many of the programs submitted for possible inclusion in the ERO project were simply programs for younger students that had been quickly modified for use in high schools.

Finally, the new Center for Instruction, created with federal funds, will be investigating the research base further. The RMC Research Corporation established the center, a consortium of the Florida Center for Reading Research at Florida State; the RC Research Group; Texas Institute for Measurement, Evaluation, and Statistics at the University of Houston; and Vaughn Gross Center for Reading and Language Arts at the University of Texas at Austin. These entities were powerful in shaping the early reading agenda, with strong researchers such as Joe Torgesen (Torgesen et al., 2006), Sharon Vaughn, and David Francis. But there may be a particular slant to their investigations of adolescent literacy because they have a particular sense of how reading problems should be addressed. Key terms in their vernacular include high-level decoding, fluency, core programs, intensive intervention—and, of course, randomized field trials to see "what works." As the center builds a scientific research base for adolescent literacy, it remains to be seen how inclusive that base will be in terms of honoring qualitative as well as quantitative research.

Policy Actors or Policy Entrepreneurs?

The Michigan researchers who studied the policy networks swirling around Reading First used the term "policy entrepreneur" for those people who can persistently and opportunistically play in the policy arena. Song and her colleagues (Song, Coggshall, & Miskel, 2004) wrote, "Like surfers, [policy entrepreneurs] wait for the perfect wave and then paddle like mad when they sense that those forces beyond their control (e.g., a swing in the national mood, a change of administration) will propel their proposals forward" (p. 451). These folks know how to use research, even if they are not researchers themselves. Sometimes they are the funders of research who recognize the value of supporting an agenda with data; they will back research to investigate questions they consider significant. The most important aspect of these entrepreneurs is that they are in the inner circles or at least are working their way inside; they have specific tactics that help them win trust and influence decisions. The two most often cited tactics for influencing national early reading policy seemed to be presentation of research findings and making direct contact with government officials. Here "officials" does not mean specific project officers within the Department of Education; instead it means those within the government who can influence policy by the sheer breadth of their connections and the power of their words.

To illustrate, the two most important actors in early reading were both researchers but were affiliated with commercial companies, not universities (Miskel et al., 2003). But it was Reid Lyon whom the Michigan researchers found to be the premier policy entrepreneur (Song et al., 2004). Lyon contributed to the debate about early reading instruction and to the policy setting that guided subsequent legislation, and he had overarching influence on direct changes in how reading was in fact taught in many schools. All these factors remain part of the policy-building record of the past few years. Lyon's influence has ensured that Reading First "guidance" is more than merely guidelines; Reading First has achieved a measure of scalability that has perhaps never been seen in educational change processes in the past.

What About Adolescent Literacy?

We don't have anyone near Reid Lyon's clout in adolescent literacy, and we don't come close to having a model to scale up to ensure good instructional practice for adolescent literacy learners at all stages of the developmental continuum. So that leaves literacy professionals who are committed to adolescents at an interesting point in time.

What we do have is the Striving Readers and ERO studies, which are investigating models of intervention grounded in the use of specific, comprehensive instructional programs. Striving Readers grants require following a particular model: Use of an intervention for students who are at least two years behind grade level in reading and a schoolwide intervention to make teachers in all subjects aware of literacy issues and able (ideally also willing) to incorporate strategies into their instruction that would enable all students, regardless of reading levels, to access the content in the subjects they teach. The evaluation of the intervention through rigorous randomization of statistically powerful samples of students can validate the programs that seem to be making a difference—essentially labeling them as scientifically based.

One of the inherent—and valuable—research questions in the Striving Readers and ERO studies is whether use of a carefully designed intervention will make more of a difference for the struggling adolescent readers in the treatment group than will business as usual for the similar students in the control group. But the danger of this research is that it can reify programmatic solutions to complex problems without providing the insight needed to understand the conditions under which the program worked. These conditions include not just students' entry-level reading scores as a baseline determinant of the skill level but also teacher, school, community, and complex inter- and intrastudent variables. And not the least of these is the extent to which students feel safe and open to learning within their school environment (Osher & Dwyer, 2006).

Programmatic solutions are the foundation of Reading First: a comprehensive core reading; aligned supplemental and intervention programs; and the Dynamic Indicators of Basic Early Literacy Skills, or DIBELS, as the primary assessment procedure. Professional development and coaching are also parts of Reading First that can build classroom teachers' capacity, but essentially the system is designed to be teacher proof. This model of comprehensive, systematic, programmatic answers to students' reading problems could easily migrate from early reading to adolescent literacy, rendering commercial publishers and the research paradigms that contribute to a narrowly defined scientific base the policy entrepreneurs driving the adolescent literacy agenda. This is not the venue in which to debate the apparent one-size-fits-all programmatic approach of the early reading agenda, but it is the place to reiterate the obvious: There's a world of difference between beginning readers and adolescents. Trying to force an early childhood model and early childhood research onto the issues of middle and high school struggling readers simply will not work (see Salinger, this volume, chapter 3; Salinger & Bacevich, 2006).

If this is the direction toward which agenda setting for adolescent literacy is taken, it means that the work of power elites has already been done. There is an answer to the question of how to address adolescents' literacy needs, and the answer has a solid research base. The answer has taken shape in Reading First with its three-tier model of addressing students' needs—commercial core/basal textbooks, intervention, and supplementary programs—focusing on scientifically based reading research and a dedicated block of time that must be spent on systematic instruction. Ratchet up the model for older students, hang a few adolescent features on existing programs, and off we go, ready to fix the problems that underlie the adolescent literacy agenda.

Of course, packaged programs or semipackaged programs emanating from a university setting aren't going to address student boredom, teacher attitudes or inertia, or poorly resourced schools. And they aren't necessarily going to address the huge variety of needs of students across the entire span called adolescence (Alexander, 2005/2006). Such programs look at a period of time through a lens of academic struggle as they seek to address students' reading difficulties. This is their purpose, of course; that's why they were developed and what schools and districts pay money to get. But this is a simplistic way to look at adolescent struggling readers because they are just so much more complicated than younger struggling readers. They bring more experience, both positive and negative, to literacy learning. Looking through a lens focused on the problem makes it hard to separate reading difficulties from whatever compensatory skills students have developed or whatever motivation they have for using literacy in out-of-school settings.

So Is There an Agenda for Adolescent Literacy?

The answer to this question is "probably not yet." But a model exists for setting the agenda, and indeed a "solution" to the reading "problem" also exists in Reading First. The real problem, however, might be that this solution is not the right one for adolescents.

Questions for Reflection

1. What aspects of the agenda-setting process for early literacy seem to provide positive recommendations for educators interested in establishing a proactive agenda for adolescent struggling readers?

2. What are some of the ways in which university-based researchers and school-based educators can work together to influence the agenda for adolescent literacy?

3. The early literacy agenda has focused primarily on young struggling readers. Is this the right focus for adolescents or is there a need to focus more broadly, that is, on the literacy needs of all adolescents?

Terry Salinger is Managing Director and Chief Scientist for Reading Research at the American Institutes for Research (AIR) in Washington, DC. Prior to joining AIR, she was the director of research at the International Reading Association. She has been a university professor and spent the first 10 years of her professional life as a teacher in the New York City public schools. She also headed a study of the secondary component of the Alabama Reading Initiative, and is the project director for an IES study of the effectiveness of reading interventions for struggling adolescent readers, the ERO study mentioned in this chapter. Although her specific areas of focus are reading and literacy research and assessment, she provides content expertise on studies investigating preservice teachers' preparation to teach beginning reading, developing a curriculum for adult ESL learners, and monitoring the implementation of the Reading First program. She can be reached at TSalinger@air.org.

REFERENCES

Achieve & American Diploma Project. (2004). *Ready or not: Creating a high school diploma that counts.* Washington, DC: Authors.

Achieve & National Governors Association. (2005). *An action agenda for improving America's high schools.* Washington, DC: Authors.

Alexander, P. (2005/2006). The path to competence: A lifespan developmental perspective on reading. *JLR: Journal of Literacy Research, 37,* 413–436.

Allington, R.L. (2000). *Effects of reading policy on classroom instruction and student achievement* (Report No. 13011). Albany, NY: National Research Center on English Learning and Achievement. Retrieved March 28, 2006, from http://cela.albany.edu/reports.htm

Anderson, R.C., Hiebert, E.H., Scott, J.A., & Wilkinson, I.A.G. (1985). *Becoming a nation of readers: The report of the Commission on Reading.* Champaign-Urbana, IL: Center for the Study of Reading & the National Academy of Education.

Biancarosa, G., & Snow, C. (2004). *Reading next: A vision for action and research in middle and high school literacy* (A report to Carnegie Corporation of New York). Washington, DC: Alliance for Excellent Education.

Bridgeland, J.M., Dilulio, J.J., Jr., & Morison, K.B. (2006). *The silent epidemic: Perspectives of high school dropouts.* Washington, DC: Civic Enterprises.

Corley, R.J. (1995). *Dreams deferred: High school dropouts in the United States.* Princeton, NJ: Policy Information Center, Educational Testing Service.

Curtis, M.E. (2002). *Adolescent literacy—state of the science* (National Institute of Child Health and Human Development & National Institute for Literacy Adolescent Literacy Workshop II). Retrieved April 24, 2006, from http://www.nifl.gov/partnershipforreading/adolescent/summaryIIa.html

Curtis, M.E., & Longo, A.M. (1999). *When adolescents can't read: Methods and materials that work.* Cambridge, MA: Brookline Books.

Deshler, D.D., Schumaker, J.B., & Woodruff, S.K. (2004). Improving literacy skills of at-risk adolescents: A school wide response. In D.S. Strickland & D.E. Alvermann (Eds.), *Bridging the literacy achievement gap grades 4–12* (pp. 86–104). New York: Teachers College Press.

Feuer, M.J., Holland, P.W., Green, B.F., Bertenthal, M.W., & Hemphill, F.C. (Eds.). (1999). *Uncommon measures: Equivalence and linkage among educational tests.* Washington, DC: National Academy Press.

Fielding, A., Schoenbach, R., & Jordan, M. (Eds.). (2003). *Building academic literacy: Lessons from reading apprenticeship classrooms, grades 6–12.* San Francisco: Jossey-Bass.

International Reading Association. (2006). *Standards for middle and high school literacy coaches.* Newark, DE: Author. Retrieved April 10, 2007, from http://www.reading.org/downloads/resources/597coaching_standards.pdf

International Reading Association & National Middle School Association. (2002). *Supporting young adolescents' literacy learning: A joint position statement.* Newark, DE; Westerville, OH: Authors. Retrieved April 10, 2007, from http://www.reading.org/downloads/positions/ps1052_supporting.pdf

Kingdon, J.W. (1995). *Agendas, alternatives, and public policies* (2nd ed.). New York: HarperCollins.

Langer, J.A. (n.d.). *Guidelines for teaching middle and high school students to read and write well: Six features of effective instruction.* Albany, NY: Center on English Learning and Instruction.

Langer, J.A. (2000). *Beating the odds: Teaching middle and high school students to read and write well* (2nd ed., Rev., Report No. 12014). Albany, NY: National Research Center on English Learning and Achievement. Retrieved February 9, 2007, from http://cela.albany.edu/reports/langer/langerbeating12014.pdf

McCombs, J.S., Kirby, S.N., Barney, H., Darilek, H., & Magee, S.J. (2005). *Achieving state and national literacy goals: A long uphill road: A report to Carnegie Corporation of New York.* Santa Monica, CA: RAND.

Miskel, C., Coggshall, J.G., DeYoung, D.A., Osguthorpe, R.D., Song, M., & Young, T.V. (2003). *Reading policy in the states: Interests and processes* (Final report for the Field Initiated Studies Grant PR/Award No. R305T990369, Office of Educational Research and Improvement, U.S. Department of Education and the Spencer Foundation Major Research Grants Program Award No. 200000269). Ann Arbor: University of Michigan.

Miskel, C., & Song, M. (2004). Passing Reading First: Prominence and processes in an elite policy network. *Educational Evaluation and Policy Analysis, 26*(2), 89–109.

National Commission on NAEP 12th Grade Assessment and Reporting. (2004). *12th grade student achievement in America: A new vision for NAEP: A report to the National Assessment Governing Board.* Washington, DC: National Assessment Governing Board.

National Governors Association Center for Best Practices. (2005). *Reading to achieve: A governor's guide to adolescent literacy.* Washington, DC: Author.

National Institute for Literacy & National Institute of Child Health and Human Development. (2002). *Adolescent literacy—research informing practice: A series of workshops.* Retrieved April 24, 2006, from http://www.nifl.gov/partnership forreading/adolescent/overview.html

National Institute of Child Health and Human Development. (2000). *Report of the National Reading Panel: Teaching children to read: An evidence-based assessment of the scientific research literature on reading and its implications for reading instruction* (NIH Publication No. 00-4769). Washington, DC: U.S. Government Printing Office.

Osher, D., & Dwyer, K. (2006). *Safeguarding our children: An action guide.* Longmont, CO: Sopris West.

Pellegrino, J.W., Jones, L.R., & Mitchell, K.J. (Eds.). (1999). *Grading the Nation's Report Card: Evaluating NAEP and transforming the assessment of educational progress.* Washington, DC: National Academy Press.

Salinger, T., & Bacevich, A. (2006). *Lessons and recommendations from the Alabama Reading Initiative: Sustaining focus on secondary reading* (Prepared for Carnegie Corporation of New York). Washington, DC: American Institutes for Research.

SchoolMatters. (2005, Fall). *The National Assessment of Educational Progress and state assessments: What do differing student proficiency rates tell us?* Retrieved March 1, 2006, from http://www.schoolmatters.com/pdf/naep_schoolmatters.pdf

Simmons, D.C., & Kame'enui, E.J. (2003, March). *A consumer's guide to evaluating a core reading program, grades K–3: A critical elements analysis* (Rev. ed.). Eugene: University of Oregon.

Snow, C.E., Burns, M.S., & Griffin, P. (Eds.). (1998). *Preventing reading difficulties in young children*. Washington, DC: National Academy Press.

Song, M. (in press). Reading from the top: State impact on reading curriculum and instruction. In B. Cooper, L. Fusarelli, & B. Fusarelli (Eds.), *The rising power of the state in education*. New York: State University of New York Press.

Song, M., Coggshall, J.G., & Miskel, C.G. (2004). Where does policy usually come from and why should we care? In P. McCardle & V. Chhabra (Eds.), *The voice of evidence in reading research* (pp. 445–461). Baltimore: Paul Brookes.

Southern Regional Education Board. (n.d.). *High schools that work: Key practices.* Retrieved February 10, 2007, from http://www.sreb.org/programs/hstw/background/keypractices.asp

Torgesen, J., Myers, D., Schirm, A., Stuart, E., Vartivarian, S., Mansfield, W., et al. (2006, February). *National assessment of Title I interim report: Volume II: Closing the reading gap: First year findings from a randomized trial of four reading interventions for striving readers*. Washington, DC: Institute of Education Sciences, U.S. Department of Education.

Walton, C. (2005, July). *State legislation and high school reform. Redesigning high schools: A primer for policymakers*. Washington, DC: National Conference of State Legislatures.

CHAPTER 2

Federal and International Reading Association Policies and Initiatives for Adolescent Literacy

Jill Lewis

HIGHLIGHTS

- The International Reading Association (IRA) engages in broad-based advocacy to ensure that its members' views are part of significant policy deliberations, especially at the federal level.
- A committee of IRA's Board of Directors reviews the Association's policies on adolescent literacy as stated in its position papers and resolutions.
- These policies are compared to existing federal law to identify gaps between what IRA wants and what exists in the law.
- The committee proposes an action plan to disseminate and promote its views on adolescent literacy and to inform members about model initiatives that align with IRA's views.

The mission of IRA is "to teach the world to read." This mission is pursued through several avenues, one of which is advocacy. IRA has always worked to influence federal education policies related to literacy education, and its advocacy is guided by membership interests and concerns. The organization pursues its advocacy goal in a variety of ways. To disseminate the organization's points of view, members work with IRA's Government Relations Division to write position papers that are widely distributed to policymakers. The Delegates Assembly of IRA

Adolescent Literacy Instruction: Policies and Promising Practices edited by Jill Lewis and Gary Moorman. © 2007 by the International Reading Association.

passes resolutions on specific topics of immediate concern, such as adolescent literacy. The director of government relations, Richard Long, and other staff from that office visit members of Congress throughout the year to discuss literacy issues that affect students and teachers, including new policies Congress is considering, the federal budget for education, and bills that are up for authorization or reauthorization. Members of IRA are invited to offer testimony at federal and state-level education policy hearings. Moreover, members of the press frequently contact the Government Relations Office to hear IRA's position on policy matters.

IRA also hosts a Government Relations Workshop each year to give members an update on policy developments and an opportunity to visit their Congressional representatives' offices on the Hill to share some talking points that explain IRA's position on pending legislation and key issues. A state-level initiative, the Legislative Action Team (LAT), includes IRA members from every state who alert their state IRA affiliate reading association members to policy developments that may affect their students, their schools, or their profession. LAT members also alert the Government Relations staff to state developments and seek the staff's assistance with state issues. The IRA website (http://www.reading.org) further explains that "The Legislative Action Team is a grassroots network of IRA members from across the United States who have volunteered to participate in advocacy efforts in favor of legislation that promotes quality instruction."

IRA also ensures its views reach a wide audience by being part of coalitions that address issues that have a wider scope, such as the Alliance for Excellent Education and the National Joint Committee on Learning Disabilities. But literacy is certainly a part of the discussion, and IRA's views carry import at these coalition meetings. IRA stays abreast of current literacy research, monitors voting trends, and anticipates new directions for literacy policy. Coupled with its advocacy initiatives, the organization remains a formidable policy player. Many recognize the quality of IRA's policymaking and advocacy, and as Salinger notes (see chapter 1) it ranked sixth among key policymakers identified by Miskel et al. (2003).

Adolescent literacy has been a key focus of the International Reading Association, and recently this topic has gained the attention of policymakers and the public. This chapter describes the evolution and outcomes of a plan by the International Reading Association to conduct a review of IRA's literacy policies pertaining to adolescent literacy that are stated in the organization's resolutions and position papers vis-à-vis existing federal policy. Through this effort, IRA would be able to purposefully plan future advocacy activities and additional position statements. The process IRA used for implementing that plan is also described here, along with the outcomes of the policy review, and the proposed action plan intended to benefit IRA's members and, ultimately, struggling adolescent readers.

In 2004, largely because of the No Child Left Behind (NCLB) legislation and the unintended consequences resulting from its regulations (Lewis & Moorman, in press), IRA's membership increased its interest in the organization's advocacy work. With regard to NCLB, the membership wanted to know from Board members, all of whom visited many state reading councils, (1) What is IRA's position? (2) Is a similar position reflected in any federal legislation? (3) If it isn't, what can we do to make this happen? These were critical questions; their answers might suggest new directions for IRA's advocacy initiatives. Much attention had been focused on grades K–3 in NCLB, but all grades were affected by the legislation. IRA could consider these questions within the context of adolescent literacy. To consider them, IRA would take a self-reflective stance, something that IRA does on a continuing basis, but now it would be focused specifically on IRA's advocacy vis-à-vis NCLB and adolescent literacy.

A self-reflective organization is likely to stay mindful of its mission and goals in order to ensure that its actions are achieving the intended outcomes. Lucas (1991) defines reflection as "systematic enquiry into one's own practice to improve that practice and to deepen one's understanding of it" (p. 84). Once the picture of current performance is clear, the self-reflective organization can draw conclusions about its current status and act on these by developing strategies for areas identified as in need of improvement (Braskamp & Ory, 1994). Accurate self-assessment requires introspection and realistic self-perception (Wilson & Pearson, 1995). The results can mobilize an organization and suggest directions that will help it realize its intentions.

As Braskamp and Ory (1994) point out in their discussion of self-analysis, raters who rate themselves may be the most important source of information about their own performance. No one knows the work, the thought behind it, and personal goals better than they do. IRA's Executive Committee thought similarly and, rather than looking for external raters, in March 2005 appointed a Policy Review Committee composed of IRA Board of Directors members. The committee's charge was twofold: (1) to conduct annual reviews of IRA's policies in relation to U.S. governmental policies to improve reading achievement, and (2) to better highlight and align IRA policies with current issues and needs

(IRA, 2005a). This chapter reviews the work of this committee, especially as it relates to adolescent literacy.

Planning for Self-Assessment

The committee planned to eventually look at many areas that affect our members, such as instruction for English-language learners, teacher training, special education, and early childhood education. However, the initial focus of the review was adolescent literacy because of the recent emphasis on high school reform, especially NCLB's mandates for all teachers, testing in grade 8 and once in high school (in addition to grade 3), and the new Striving Readers grants for adolescent literacy that were first awarded for the 2005–2006 academic year (U.S. Department of Education, n.d.). Five years had passed since the organization's last position statement on this topic, and it was now time to undertake a review and consider updating the material that is disseminated by IRA on adolescent literacy.

Although IRA has more than 50 publications on adolescent literacy, most of these could not be considered as reflective of IRA's position on this subject because they were individually authored and were often teacher education texts, not policy or position statements. However, the Policy Review Committee identified two documents that were clearly statements of IRA's positions, namely, (1) *Adolescent Literacy: A Position Statement for the Commission on Adolescent Literacy of the International Reading Association* (Moore, Bean, Birdyshaw, & Rycik, 1999), and (2) *Supporting Young Adolescents' Literacy Learning: A Joint Position Statement of the International Reading Association and the National Middle School Association* (IRA & NMSA, 2002). A resolution on adolescent literacy was also passed by the Delegates Assembly (IRA, 1999) that reiterates the essential ideas of the 1999 position paper. Thus, using the two position papers, the committee began the self-analysis to answer the question "What do IRA's position papers have to say about what is important in adolescent literacy instruction?"

To further define its task, the committee decided to focus on four target areas for its analysis of adolescent literacy:

1. curriculum issues, specifically content and materials;

2. instruction;

3. high-quality teachers and professional development; and

4. student assessment.

We realized that these target areas might require some modification in the future for the other areas of investigation.

This fact-finding mission for purposes of self-analysis was instructive. By creating a side-by-side table illustrating IRA's views alongside those reflected in federal legislation, it was easy to see similarities and differences in perspectives. Figure 2.1 illustrates some of the findings; key phrases in federal material that parallel IRA language are boldfaced.

The numbering system is probably unfamiliar to most readers. Wherever the number 20 appears (for example, 20 U.S.C. § 6311), it means the legislation has to do with education. U.S.C. refers to United States Code. The code results from an effort to make finding relevant and effective statutes simpler by reorganizing them by subject matter, and eliminating expired and amended sections. The number following the code is the section number in which a particular statute appears. The explanation for anything appearing as PL is a little different. For instance, PL 107-110 NCLB refers to Public Law, and these numbers are assigned chronologically. When a bill is signed into law by the president it is sent to the Office of the Federal Register to be assigned a law number and paginated for the United States Statutes at Large. Afterward, a List of Public Laws is created, posted online, and then published in the Federal Register.

Findings

Curriculum: Content

After reviewing the chart entries (as shown in Figure 2.1), the committee drew conclusions about similarities and differences between IRA's viewpoints and the federal government's perspectives on what is needed for adolescent literacy achievement. One very important conclusion is that, not surprisingly, the federal government's education legislation has made few specific statements about adolescent literacy. This was disappointing in several respects. First, because there were few specifics, the government had free reign to incorporate whatever it wished into the Striving Readers grant application in 2005. This is the federal government's most recent initiative in adolescent literacy. As stated in the Federal Register (2005), the purpose of this program is, "to raise the reading achievement levels of middle and high school-aged students in Title I-eligible schools with significant numbers of students reading

Figure 2.1. Comparison of IRA and Federal Policy Perspectives

IRA's Viewpoint	Federal Policy and Legislation
Curriculum: Content	
• Adolescents need well-developed repertoires of reading comprehension and study strategies. (CAL, 5)	**Striving Readers (2005)—No Child Left Behind Act (NCLB), 2001, Public Law 107-110. CFDA Number: 84.371A**. Intensive, targeted intervention for struggling readers. "Of particular concern with adolescent struggling readers are vocabulary, fluency and comprehension" (47816 A Federal Register, Vol. 70, No. 156, Monday, Aug. 15, 2005)
• Integrate literacy throughout the curriculum. (SYA, 3)	**Striving Readers (2005)—NCLB Act, 2001, Public Law 107-110. CFDA Number: 84.371A**. Providing professional development aligned with scientifically based reading research or integrating comprehension and literacy skills in the classroom across subject areas.
Curriculum: Materials	**P. L. 107-110 NCLB**, January 8, 2002, 20 U.S.C. § 6383, Subpart 4, Improving Literacy Through School Libraries. "Increased access to up-to-date school library materials"; **"provide students with access** to school libraries during non-school hours." (115 Stat. 1567, Sec. 1251)
• Adolescents deserve access to a wide variety of reading material that they can and want to read. (CAL, 4; SYA, 3)	
• Need age-appropriate materials they can manage and topics and genres they prefer. (CAL, 5)	
• Include material that will appeal to linguistically and culturally diverse students. (SYA, 3)	20 U.S.C. § 7251—Reading Is Fundamental—distribution of inexpensive books to school-age children that **motivate children to read**. (Subpart 5, Section 5451, 115 Stat. 1824)
Instruction	**P. L. 107-110 NCLB**
• Time spent in reading is associated with attitudes toward additional reading. (CAL, 5)	20 U.S.C. § 6315—Targeted Assistance Schools. "Use **effective methods and instructional strategies**

(continued)

CAL = *Adolescent Literacy: A Position Statement for the Commission on Adolescent Literacy of the International Reading Association* (Moore, Bean, Birdyshaw, & Rycik, 1999)
SYA = *Supporting Young Adolescents' Literacy Learning: A Joint Position Statement of the International Reading Association and the National Middle School Association* (2002)

Figure 2.1. Comparison of IRA and Federal Policy Perspectives (continued)

IRA's Viewpoint	Federal Policy and Legislation
• All adolescents, and especially those who struggle with reading, deserve opportunities to select age-appropriate materials they can manage and topics and genres they prefer. (CAL, 5) • Adolescents deserve reading specialists who assist individual students having difficulty learning how to read. (CAL, 7) • Adolescents' personal identities, academic achievement, and future aspirations mix with ongoing difficulties with reading. (CAL, 7) • It is during the middle school years that most students refine their reading preferences; become sophisticated readers of informational text; and lay the groundwork for the lifelong reading habits they will use in their personal, professional, and civic lives. (SYA, 2) • Language arts teachers often have sole responsibility for guiding students' reading growth. (CAL, 4) • Many teachers come to believe teaching students how to effectively read and write is not their responsibility. (CAL, 4)	**that are based on scientifically based research** that strengthens the core academic program of the school." **P. L. 105-332**, Carl D. Perkins Vocational and Technical Education Act of 1998, <u>20 U.S.C. § 2301</u> et seq., <u>20 U.S.C. § 2342</u>—State Plan. "Improve academic and technical skills of students participating in vocational education." School Dropout Prevention Initiative, <u>20 U.S.C. § 6561</u>, Subpart 2, Section 1825, 1615 Stat. 191. "Public schools that serve students in **grades 6 through 12** and that have annual school dropout rates that are above the State average annual school dropout rate, to enable those schools, or the middle schools that feed students into those schools, to implement effective, sustainable, and coordinated school dropout prevention and reentry programs that involve activities such as— **(D) planning and research;** **(E) remedial education;** **(F) reducing pupil-to-teacher ratios;** **(G) efforts to meet State student academic achievement standards;** **(H) counseling and mentoring for at-risk students;**
High Quality Teachers and Professional Development • Every teacher must possess the knowledge and skills to integrate reading instruction across the curriculum. (SYA, 2) • Adolescents deserve expert teachers who model and provide explicit instruction in reading comprehension and study strategies across the curriculum. (CAL, 7)	**P. L. 107-110 NCLB**, <u>20 U.S.C. § 6314</u>—Schoolwide Programs. "Provide for high quality and ongoing professional development." <u>20 U.S.C. § 6315</u>—Targeted Assistance Schools. "Provide for high quality and ongoing professional development." **P. L. 105-244** Higher Education Act of 1998, <u>20 U.S.C. § 1021</u>. "Improve the quality of the current and future

(continued)

Figure 2.1. Comparison of IRA and Federal Policy Perspectives (continued)

IRA's Viewpoint	Federal Policy and Legislation
• Adolescents deserve teachers who understand the complexities of individual...readers, respect their differences, and respond to their characteristics. (CAL, 8)	teaching force by improving the preparation of prospective teachers and enhancing professional development activities."

Student Assessment

• Adolescents deserve assessments that are regular extensions of instruction; provide usable feedback based on clear, attainable, and worthwhile standards; exemplify quality standards; performances illustrating the standards and position students as partners with teachers evaluating progress and setting goals. (CAL, 7)

• Adolescents deserve classroom assessments that bridge the gap between what they know and are able to do and relevant curriculum standards. (CAL, 6)

• Using tests simply to determine which students will graduate or which type of diploma students will receive especially disadvantages adolescents from homes where English is not the first language or where poverty endures. (CAL, 6)

P. L. 107-110 NCLB

20 U.S.C. § 6311—State Plans— Annual LEA Report Cards. "Information that shows how the school's students' achievement on the statewide academic assessments and other indicators of adequate yearly progress compared to students in the local educational agency and the State as a whole."

20 U.S.C. § 6314—Schoolwide Programs. "**Measures to include teachers in the decisions regarding the use of academic assessments**...in order to improve information on and to improve the achievement of individual students and the overall instructional program."

"Activities to ensure that students who experience difficulty mastering the proficient or advanced levels of academic achievement standards...shall be provided with effective, timely additional assistance which shall include measures to ensure that students' **difficulties are identified on a timely basis** and to provide sufficient information on which to base effective assistance."

Striving Readers, **P. L. 107-110 NCLB**, 20 U.S.C. § 6311—State Plans—Academic Assessments. "**Involve multiple up-to-date measures...including higher-order thinking skills and understanding.**" "Produce individual student interpretive, descriptive and diagnostic reports...allows parents, teachers and principals to understand and address the specific academic needs of students."

below grade level" (Funding Opportunity Description section, ¶1). In fact, insofar as curriculum content, the Striving Readers grant application (U.S. Department of Education, 2005) opens the door to the same kind of highly prescriptive teaching that IRA found many lower grade teachers objecting to since NCLB was implemented (IRA, 2005b). The grant application states,

> The basic skills adolescent readers need are the same foundational skills we expect younger students to master as they learn to read. Scientifically based reading research identifies explicit and systematic instruction in five essential components of reading: *phonemic awareness* (the ability to hear, identify and manipulate individual sounds in spoken words), *phonics* (the understanding that there is a predictable relationship between phonemes and graphemes), *vocabulary* (development of stored information about the meanings and pronunciation of words), *reading fluency* (the ability to read text accurately and quickly) and *reading comprehension* (understanding, remembering, and communicating with others about what has been read). Of particular concern with adolescent struggling readers are vocabulary, fluency and comprehension, as well as issues such as motivation and access to age appropriate reading materials. (U.S. Department of Education, 2005, p. 2)

This sounds very much like the Reading First guidelines with only minor tweaking and looks quite different from IRA's curriculum position, which calls for "well developed repertoires of reading comprehension and study strategies" (Moore et al., 1999, p. 5).

The second disappointment is how little attention the federal government has heretofore paid to struggling adolescent readers. On the brighter side, however, this failing has opened an opportunity for IRA to press hard at the federal level for the members' interests and concerns about these students. The review identified areas where IRA could use the federal government's own language to bring home the organization's point of view. For instance, in some cases, the language used by IRA and the federal government was strikingly similar, such as use of the term *access*. *Access* is a term that IRA uses in its position paper when speaking about curriculum, and that appears in the Curriculum: Content section of the chart (Figure 2.1). For IRA, *access* means availability of books in classrooms and school and community libraries (IRA & NMSA, 2002, p. 3; Moore et al., 1999, p. 4). It is unclear, however, how the federal government defines *access*. Where it is used in the previous excerpt from the Striving Readers grant application (U.S. Department of Education, 2005), it might refer to availability of books only in school libraries. This possibility is reinforced by the language used in the No Child Left Behind section titled Improving Literacy Through School Libraries (20 U.S.C. § 6383), which specifically calls for "increased access to up-to-date school library materials" and designates that funding will "provide students with access to school libraries during non-school hours" (Sec. 1251). The lack of clarity in NCLB leaves the door open for IRA to inform legislators and other policymakers about the important contribution classroom libraries make to student achievement, and to get the language in future grant applications or federal legislation on adolescent literacy modified to reflect IRA's definition.

Another aspect of curriculum content that the committee reviewed concerned the teacher's preparation for developing adolescent literacy, especially in content subjects. IRA might be encouraged by the federal government's call for "professional development aligned with scientifically based reading research or integrating comprehension and literacy skills in the classroom across subject areas" (U.S. Department of Education, 2005, p. 4). Unfortunately, though, the individual hired to provide this professional development might not have the requisite expertise. Many of IRAs members are reading specialists, individuals who have received specialized training to help struggling readers and whose expertise has been certified by their state. Specialists are referred to in the Striving Readers grant application, but it only indicates that grant funds may be used for "employment of a reading specialist or coach" (U.S. Department of Education, 2005, p. 4). Although grant applicants had to include the coach's requisite qualifications, the government sets no clear criteria for that position. For IRA, teacher and reading specialist expertise in reading is critical to adolescents' reading achievement, and IRA has established standards for the coach positions (IRA, 2004). This is an area where IRA will continue to recommend strongly that the reading coach have specialist certification.

Curriculum: Materials

As the Curriculum: Materials section of the chart (Figure 2.1) notes, IRA believes that reading materials adolescents are assigned must be age appropriate and reflect genres and topics that adolescents prefer (Moore et al., 1999, p. 5) and offer "a wide variety of reading material that they can and want to read" (IRA & NMSA, 2002, p. 3; Moore et al., 1999, p. 4). There is only the briefest mention of student interest in the federal legislation, within the Reading Is Fundamental section of

NCLB (2002) that explains that this program provides for "distribution of inexpensive books to school-age children that motivate children to read" (20 U.S.C. § 7251). The committee also found that although IRA speaks of the need to consider linguistic and cultural diversity when selecting materials and designing curriculum for adolescents, the federal government does not address this issue in NCLB.

Members of the public most directly affected by NCLB echo IRA's concerns. The Public Education Network held hearings between September 2005 and January 2006, allowing students, parents, and community members to testify about their experiences with NCLB. According to the Public Education Network (2006) hearings summary, students commented that although teachers might have the necessary certification, they were often not able to "reach students with a variety of learning styles and needs in a culturally sensitive manner" (p. 4).

Instruction

The committee found similar concerns and omissions from the federal laws when it compared them with IRA's position on instruction. For instance, IRA specifically mentioned that "Adolescents deserve reading specialists who assist individual students having difficulty learning how to read" (Moore et al., 1999, p. 7) and further noted that adolescents' personal identities and academic achievements are affected by their reading achievements. IRA also called attention to language arts teachers' central role in developing adolescent literacy, largely because "Many teachers come to believe teaching students how to effectively read and write is not their responsibility" (Moore et al., 1999, p. 4). As noted on the chart (Figure 2.1), however, the federal law (NCLB, 2002) focuses only on the need to "use effective methods and instructional strategies that are based on scientifically based research that strengthens the core academic program of the school" (20 U.S.C. § 6315). IRA also points out the larger role informational text plays in adolescents' academic lives (IRA & NMSA, 2002, p. 2). Federal law comes closest to recognizing the need to develop academic literacy in the Carl Perkins Vocational Technical Act (1998) where it mentions that state plans should be organized to "improve academic and technical skills of students participating in vocational education" (20 U.S.C. § 2342-State Plan). But this is hardly recognition of the changing nature of texts adolescents must comprehend as compared with literacy requirements in earlier grades.

High school graduation and the dropout rate receive attention in the federal laws, including in the School Dropout Prevention Initiative (2002), and the views evident in this legislation are noted in the Instruction section on the chart (Figure 2.1). Neither high school graduation nor the dropout rate is directly addressed in IRA's position statements and resolutions for adolescent literacy. As of yet there is no evidence for a direct causal relationship between high school graduation and literacy levels, but low achievement in reading is characteristic of students who drop out of high school. For instance, in her study of Chicago's public schools, Roderick (2006) found that "students who were on-track by the end of their freshman year were more than three and one-half times more likely to graduate in four years than off-track students" (p. 15). The complexity of the relationship is noted by Swanson (2004) at the Urban Institute's Education Policy Center, who commented, "high poverty districts may attract less qualified teachers, which results in less effective and less engaging instruction, producing lower levels of academic achievement, which in turn may lead students to drop out of high school at higher rates" (p. 35).

High Quality Teachers—Professional Development

The committee partially addressed quality teaching within the Instruction section. Here, however, the focus is on federal law pertaining to high-quality teachers, specifically on the subsection of NCLB that deals with this area and has had tremendous effect on teachers and paraprofessionals nationwide. When NCLB was passed on January 8, 2002, it required that all students be taught the core subjects by a "highly qualified teacher" (HQT). The definition of HQT set forth in the law was that the teacher has a bachelor's degree, has obtained full state certification, and has demonstrated knowledge in the core academic subjects he or she teaches (U.S. Department of Education, 2004, p. 9). Special education teachers were held to the same standard as regular classroom teachers. Originally, states were given until the 2005–2006 year to meet the HQT goal, but the deadline has been extended if there is demonstrable evidence that a state is implementing the law and making "a good-faith effort to reach the HQT goal in NCLB as soon as possible" (Spellings, 2005, ¶3). The issue of teacher quality and what makes an effective teacher is hotly debated. Whether a teacher needs to be certified is also an area of differing opinions. Some reports claim that certified teachers are no better in practice than uncertified instructors (Walsh, 2001), and others assert that certification is an important step in ensuring quality teaching (Darling-Hammond, 2002).

IRA's views are clear. The organization certainly agrees that all students should be taught by HQTs, but to IRA being qualified includes expertise in teaching reading (IRA & NMSA, 2002, p. 2; Moore et al., 1999, pp. 7–8). This expertise can best be acknowledged through teacher certification for any of the grades kindergarten through 12 that includes ample preparation in developing students' literacy. The federal government does not mention the need for this expertise. It is mystifying how teachers can be held accountable for student achievement in reading while not being required to have received training in teaching reading prior to entering the classroom. The high-quality and ongoing professional development called for in federal law suggests that in the federal government's view state certification requirements will satisfy whatever prospective teachers might need to address literacy issues. Unfortunately the variability in certification across the states suggests this should not be a given. And although the Higher Education Act (1998) calls on states to "improve the quality of the current and future teaching force by improving the preparation of prospective teachers" (Title II, Sect. 201[a], Purpose 2), it fails to suggest that learning how to teach reading would be a critical component of that preparation. If federal law can mandate, and it does, that teachers must have knowledge in the core subjects they teach, can it not also mandate knowledge of how to develop students' literacy?

Assessment

The committee also noted the wide disparity in views of assessment. IRA's position is that assessment should inform instruction and to do so it must provide information that is useful to the classroom teacher. In his discussion of audiences for assessment, Roger Farr (1992) makes a distinction between different assessment frameworks, their different intended audiences, their different purposes, and the different procedures each uses to collect information. The type of assessment required by NCLB is clearly for an audience well beyond the school level. Students, parents, entire school districts and states, and the federal government are all to be informed by statewide assessments mandated by NCLB. In addition, the criteria IRA members would use to determine reading achievement would entail greater breadth than that evident on statewide assessments. These statewide tests are designed to compare large-scale educational programs and to provide accountability to public stakeholders (Murphy, 1997), not to help teachers make instructional decisions. They do not consider the specific learning context and are created by external agencies far removed from particular schools. These differences in viewpoints toward assessment suggest that we cannot sacrifice authentic classroom assessment for statewide tests; they serve different purposes. Many public stakeholders are also critical of NCLB assessments, and the Public Education Network (2006) reported that those who testified often spoke of the anxiety that students felt as a result of the high-stakes testing NCLB requires (p. 2).

The analysis of these issues has afforded IRA another opportunity to target its advocacy to specific areas where there are discrepancies between IRA's views and those of the federal government as expressed in federal law.

IRA's Next Steps for Adolescent Literacy

For nearly a year the IRA Board Policy Review Committee reviewed documents and conducted self-analysis regarding adolescent literacy policies. IRA's position as an elite policy actor for adolescent literacy is well deserved. Position papers and resolutions make a compelling case for the need for additional resources and teacher preparation that will lead to adolescent literacy achievement. As noted in the analysis, in some cases IRA's views align with federal legislation. The committee also reflected on some additional strategies that IRA might pursue to strengthen its advocacy even further, reaching an even wider audience at a time when concerns about adolescent literacy are receiving increased national attention. Toward that end, in January 2005 the committee presented its findings and recommendations to the Board of Directors. A set of recommended action steps were provided to IRA's Government Relations Division for consideration, as that division planned for additional advocacy to address issues surrounding adolescent literacy. IRA has always engaged in thoughtful and productive advocacy. Since January 2005, when the committee's work on adolescent literacy was completed, developments within the federal government prompted actions by IRA that align well with the committee's recommendations. Additionally, the organization has made some changes internally that are in concert with these recommendations. The recommendations are noted here, along with recent, relevant IRA and federal actions.

1. IRA needs to develop a mechanism to provide ongoing recommendations for action after IRA develops policy statements that allow general IRA recommendations to be amended in response to specific legislative or regulatory proposals. The LAT described at the beginning of this chapter is one such mechanism that can be used to further advance IRA's views on adolescent literacy. The LAT can be expanded to include representatives from each state's local councils. Other response mechanisms could include designated sections of the IRA website and advocacy blasts on IRA's homepage as new federal issues emerge, in order to encourage members to speak to their representatives in Congress about pending legislation or funding issues that pertain to adolescent literacy, such as increased funding for Striving Readers or dropout prevention. Currently, the webpage links members to the LAT coordinator and to the Government Relations Workshop, as well as to IRA's position papers. Members can also join a listserv to receive monthly updates on what is happening in Congress. As of now, this listserv does not provide a mechanism for discussing these issues, or how potential legislation would affect members, and this addition should be considered. During the past year, IRA's Government Relations Division has held phone conferences with members to provide updated information. Before these calls take place, PowerPoint slides are sent to those who have signed up for the call, and members are taken through these during the conference. It thus appears that members are being provided critical information, and these activities could be expanded to opportunities that would promote specific recommendations for action.

2. Build membership awareness of what legislation permits. Recent attention to and funding for early childhood literacy initiatives have overshadowed literacy needs in other grades. Despite the unevenness of funding for adolescent literacy vis-à-vis the early grades, some funding is available and increases—especially through programs such as Striving Readers—are anticipated. IRA can use its publications and other mechanisms to inform its members about funding sources for adolescent literacy, including those that are embedded in legislation and that, on the surface, appear limited to lower grades. Providing a set of questions or guidelines for reviewing policies could assist members as they look at proposed policies. Review guidelines would help members determine what else they need to know for their specific situation or what their state's members need to know. These could be sent to all members and not just those who visit IRA's website or who are already developing advocacy expertise.

3. Produce adolescent literacy instructional models for dissemination. To obtain evidence of the efficacy for the ideas it advances for improving adolescent literacy, IRA can reach out to the membership for models of real adolescent students in real classrooms with effective teachers who implement what IRA proposes and where students achieve high levels of literacy. Each model should be complete in its presentation, and should include appropriateness or suggested modifications for urban schools and English-language learners. Some models might be designed to provide evidence for a causal link between dropouts and reading achievement that would strengthen the government's concerns about students completing high school and IRA's advocacy for more funding for adolescent literacy initiatives. IRA has contacted states that have received Striving Readers grants to identify models that might now be available. The Publications Division of IRA is also seeking more professional development materials that would assist teachers who work with struggling adolescents. In addition to its Five Star Policy Recognition Program honoring states and councils that have adopted and implemented policies supporting effective literacy instruction for all children, IRA is currently working with a member task force on the Quality Undergraduate Elementary & Secondary Teacher Education in Reading, or QUESTER, project. This task force will develop a certificate of distinction for initial preparation in reading and will provide models for secondary teacher preparation as well as for elementary teachers. Recently IRA has invested in developing a complete literacy research database for analyzing and disseminating descriptive data related to reading instruction. These new initiatives certainly will provide significant models for developing adolescent literacy.

4. Play watchdog on models held up by the U.S. Department of Education as examples. As NCLB has unfolded, questions have arisen about some of the relationships between the Education Department and publishers, professional developers, and awards granted. On September 22, 2006, the Education Department Inspector General's Office (U.S. Department of Education, 2006a) released one report about these relationships, and others are forthcoming, including one from the General Accounting Office, Congress's independent audit agency. IRA's (2006a) press release about this is quite clear about the Association's position that it will hold the Education Department accountable to high standards:

> The U.S. Department of Education Office of the Inspector General's (IG) report on Reading First outlines unethical actions by several individuals who violated the intent and spirit of the Reading First statute in an ongoing and systematic manner. These actions have damaged the integrity of the Department. It is to its credit that they have issued this report. Now it is time to implement its findings.
>
> The IG's report directly quotes individual communications to establish that there was a plan to direct the outcomes of independent panels, stack those panels with those who already had formed a bias, and promote specific reading programs while eliminating others. (¶2–3)

IRA's (2006b) Board of Directors recently passed a position statement on Reading First. Although the statement commended the teachers and administrators who have worked diligently to provide for the literacy needs of children, the paper opens with this strong admonishment:

> The Board of Directors of the International Reading Association (IRA) deplores the intentional mismanagement that occurred in the administration of the Reading First program by the U.S. Department of Education as detailed in the Final Inspection Report issued by the Office of the Inspector General. It is essential that all laws and regulations be closely adhered to in the administration of this program in order to implement it successfully, to protect its integrity among educators, and to ensure its continued public support. (¶1)

Based on these recent responses to federal actions, there is every reason to believe that IRA will hold the Education Department to the same standards IRA imposes on its own models of success and will be critical should the Education Department models fall short of these.

5. Call for more grants for a wide range of school types. As IRA seeks effective adolescent literacy models, it should explore not only the curriculum that a program uses but also the context in which it is delivered. Large and small; urban, rural, and suburban; charter and traditional public schools that teach adolescents should be included in the mix. Funding for adolescent literacy initiatives is scarce. Currently only 5% of Title I funds go to high schools. The Striving Readers program in its first year of funding awarded only eight grants (U.S. Department of Education, n.d.). Although President Bush's budget for FY2007 proposed increasing Striving Readers (U.S. Department of Education 2006b), the FY2007 budget is a Continuing Resolution of the FY2006 budget, and no new grants will be awarded. Further, the restrictions previously mentioned in this chapter limit the kinds of models that might emerge from this program. It should also be noted that a number of the recipients are using the same instructional programs, READ 180 and the SIM Content Literacy Curriculum, further preventing a real exploration of alternative instructional models for adolescent literacy. Working with such alliances as the Committee for Education Funding, of which IRA is already a member, IRA can call greater attention to the need for grants to develop and implement such models.

6. Develop a white paper on the importance of professional development for all teachers. The committee noted that many national recommendations for adolescent literacy policy call for content area teachers to integrate literacy development in their curriculum. The National Governors Association's (2006) policy position, for instance, includes support for "expanded flexibility to increase professional development opportunities for secondary school teachers and school leaders, in particular those individuals working in hard-to-serve schools or critical shortage areas, such as math, science, reading, and special education" (Section 13.3.3). Unfortunately, teacher certification programs, traditional or otherwise, seldom include strategies for integrating reading instruction in their content fields.

The Learning First Alliance (2000) discussed the value of professional development in teacher growth in the following comment:

> An expert teacher possesses a broad set of techniques for addressing the learning needs of each student in a class, the ability to determine rapidly which technique is needed at a given time for each particular student, and the ability to integrate these techniques effectively while teaching a diverse classroom. Therefore, a novice teacher may require extended focus on selected aspects of reading or writing before the fluent integration of practices characteristic of proficient teachers can be expected. (¶6)

Thus it is imperative that IRA advocate for additional funding to provide professional development in adolescent literacy for all teachers with responsibilities for these students.

7. Provide more information on contributions literacy makes to vocational education subjects. Adolescent literacy for vocational and technical education has received scant attention in the organization's publications, position statements, and resolutions. The Carl Perkins Vocational Technical Act (1998) calls for a program that "builds student competence in mathematics, science, reading, writing, communications...in a coherent sequence of courses" (20 U.S.C. § 2371—Tech-Prep Education). IRA can use this language as an opportunity to address the relationship between vocational competence and literacy.

New attention has been drawn to this particular piece of legislation because President Bush's FY2006 budget request proposed elimination of funding for the Vocational Education State Grants and National programs, authorized by the Perkins Act. Congress, however, did not concur with the president's recommendation and the FY2006 final appropriations put $1.3 billion into it. A similar scenario has occurred for FY2007. In August 2006, $1.3 billion was approved by the House for this program for FY2007. The Continuing Resolution for FY2007 retains this program. Reading professionals and teachers concerned about their students' futures might be pleased with a new provision it contains. It permits for the first time both basic grantees and Tech Prep grantees to use funds to develop personal graduation and career plans for students participating in career and technical education programs. This provision could positively affect adolescent literacy because students might realize the need to increase their literacy skills in order to achieve their personal goals. Motivation for learning could increase.

Additional Observations

Although the committee's goal was to analyze IRA's resolutions and position papers on adolescent literacy vis-à-vis federal legislation, some interesting observations were made based on informal comments about NCLB and adolescent literacy that Board members had heard from IRA's members during visits to state councils.

The committee members felt that with some laws there might be misinterpretation or lack of information at the state or district level and that this could disadvantage IRA members who are involved with adolescent literacy programs. For instance, Schoolwide Programs (2007) is part of the Title I legislation. However, members had frequently commented to Board members that all Title I funds were for the elementary grades. It is true that as of now only 5% of Title I funds reach high schools, but IRA members who work with adolescents need to be aware that there is nothing in the federal laws that prohibits Title I funds being used for adolescent learners. If a school building serves grades K–8, then the eighth graders can be included in any schoolwide program. The same holds true for a K–12 building. If state departments of education or district-level administrative offices have a different impression of this legislation, then IRA's members need to be able to provide them with the correct information so that adolescents can benefit from this funding source. This highlights the committee's conclusion that IRA members need more information about decision points in legislation so they can influence the use of those funds in the school building and school district and understand other features of legislation that can positively affect adolescent literacy programs and teachers who deliver them.

The transitory nature of federal funding also concerned the committee, and the possibility of short-lived opportunities for adolescent literacy requires IRA's continued vigilance in its advocacy for retaining those federal programs that yield positive benefits for our members and those whom they teach. For example, one key component piece of legislation, the Dropout Prevention Program, has unfortunately been written out of the 2007 federal education budget. In FY2004 it received less than half of the $10.9 million it had received the previous year, and between 2004 and 2006 its budget remained just under $5 million. Although supporting only a few small programs, this funding could have made an important contribution to adolescent literacy development; its monies included support for remedial education as well as for efforts to meet state student academic achievement standards and to provide mentoring and professional development. IRA's resolution and position statements for adolescent literacy certainly support these activities. President Bush claims that dropout prevention is addressed in several other programs and hence is not needed. But Striving Readers, suggested as one such program, is much narrower in scope than the Dropout Prevention Program. Striving Readers also has greater federal oversight and more stringent requirements for evaluation. Salinger (see chapter 1) offers additional information on this program.

The Executive Office of the federal government does appear to recognize the need for improving instruction at the high school level. In fact, in its report about the FY2007 budget for education, it noted the following:

There is a growing need for expanding NCLB principles to high schools and for improving secondary education, as nearly one-third of incoming ninth-graders do not make it to Graduation Day within four years and less than one-third of high school graduates are prepared for college. In addition, international assessments show that our high school students score well behind those of many other nations in key subjects like mathematics. In response, the 2007 request includes a $1.7 billion comprehensive proposal to improve the quality of secondary education and ensure that every student not only graduates from high school, but is prepared to enter college or the workforce with the skills to succeed. (U.S. Office of Management and Budget, 2007, ¶16)

However, although the education budget for FY2007 does include $1.7 billion for secondary education, a significant part of that funding will need to go to the additional testing that is being required. The budget report states that the High School Reform proposal "creates a new, flexible $1.5 billion grant program to help states implement tests in language arts and math in high schools and to support a wide range of effective interventions" (U.S. Office of Management and Budget, 2007, ¶17). It is unclear how many dollars will be left for adolescent literacy programs once the cost of testing and mathematics programs are deducted.

Continuing Prospects for Influence

Although the federal government's recent involvement in public education has been extensive, its participation in the affairs of schools is not new. The founding fathers of the United States, particularly Thomas Jefferson, saw education as necessary for realizing the nation's goals, whether the basis be religious, political, or economic. The General Court of Massachusetts passed one of the first public education laws in 1647. However, in the last forty years, the federal government has assumed a larger role in identifying literacy issues, crafting legislation to address these, and, at least for a while, increasing support for literacy initiatives. Tied to this support, however, are a growing number of federal laws that limit local control of education in several respects (Lewis & Moorman, in press).

IRA has always been concerned with *how* children learn to read; the federal government has typically been concerned with *that* they learn. What has shifted recently and what most concerns many of IRA's members is the federal government's increased specificity in what should happen in classrooms. As reported by the Center on Education Policy (2003),

> the requirements for scientifically based research have generated controversy as educators have raised concerns that the provisions will be interpreted in a way that imposes a specific ideology on public schools, will yield just a small number of acceptable practices, will give the federal government too much control over curriculum and instruction, and other issues. (p. 105)

This situation has created a decline in teacher morale. In a study conducted by IRA (2005b), a random sample of 4,000 members was sent a survey about NCLB. From that sample, 1,557 usable surveys were returned. One item asked respondents to rate whether they agreed strongly, agreed, disagreed, or disagreed strongly with the statement that teacher morale has improved as a result of NCLB. More than 3 out of 4 respondents (78.2%) disagreed or disagreed strongly.

Although teacher morale is not a policy issue that IRA currently addresses in position papers or resolutions, it is one that can be affected by the response the professional teacher community makes to teachers' concerns. As a self-reflective organization engaged in advocacy, IRA has had a positive influence on federal legislation that affects IRA's membership and children's literacy development throughout the world. Edmondson (2005) studied the influence of various professional organizations on federal policy. With regard to IRA's influence on the Reading Excellence Act, she remarked,

> Because of the influence IRA could exert, some of the language in the House version of the bill was changed in the Senate version. Further, IRA has frequently been able to form strategic alliances with other professional organizations to reinforce its positions. (p. 7)

This suggests a very powerful presence that IRA, as an elite policy actor, will continue to refine and strengthen as it works toward influencing literacy policies that impact communities, schools, teachers, and children.

Questions for Reflection

1. What might have been the outcome had the committee reviewed books and journal articles published by IRA for this self-reflection?

2. What features of the federal laws that concern adolescent literacy were new to you?

3. What additional recommendations for action items would you make based on the information the committee found?

Activities

1. Review the commission's position statement that was used for this self-reflection. What other aspects of adolescent literacy would you now include if this statement were to be revised?

2. What are some changes or additions to federal legislation for adolescent literacy that are under consideration at this time? What do you think of these ideas?

3. What has occurred with the FY2008 education budget since this chapter was written and has a bearing on adolescent literacy programs in your school and your state?

Jill Lewis is Professor of Literacy Education at New Jersey City University, Jersey City, New Jersey, USA. She has served on the Board of Directors of the International Reading Association (2004–2007), on the Board of Directors for the American Reading Forum (2003–2005), and on IRA's and New Jersey Reading Association's Governmental Relations Committees. She has also served on several literacy task forces for New Jersey and received NJRA's Distinguished Service Award. She has also worked in Macedonia, Kazakhstan, and Albania for the Reading and Writing for Critical Thinking Project, and currently serves as a volunteer consultant for the Secondary Education Reform Activity program in Macedonia. Her areas of expertise include adolescent literacy, content literacy, literacy policy and advocacy, reading across the curriculum, classroom research, and leadership development. She can be contacted at jlewis@njcu.edu.

REFERENCES

Braskamp, L.A., & Ory, J.C. (1994). *Assessing faculty work: Enhancing individual and institutional performance*. San Francisco: Jossey-Bass.

Carl Perkins Vocational Technical Act, 20 U.S.C. § 2301 et seq. (1998 & Updated 2006).

Center on Education Policy. (2003, January). *From the capital to the classroom: State and federal efforts to implement the No Child Left Behind Act*. Washington, DC: Author.

Darling-Hammond, L. (2002). Research and rhetoric on teacher certification: A response to "Teacher certification reconsidered." *Education Policy Analysis Archives, 10*(36). Retrieved February 1, 2007, from http://epaa.asu.edu/epaa/v10n36.html

Edmondson, J. (2005, February 3). Policymaking in education: Understanding influences on the Reading Excellence Act. *Education Policy Analysis Archives, 13*(11). Retrieved February 23, 2007, from http://epaa.asu.edu/epaa/v13n11/v13n11.pdf

Farr, R. (1992). Putting it all together: Solving the reading assessment puzzle. *The Reading Teacher, 46*(1), 26–37.

Federal Register Online. (2005, August 15). Department of Education, Office of Elementary and Secondary Education; overview information, Striving Readers; notice inviting applications for new awards for fiscal year (FY) 2005. In *Federal Register Online*. Retrieved October 18, 2006, from http://a257.g.akamaitech.net/7/257/2422/01jan20051800/edocket.access.gpo.gov/2005/05-16135.htm

Higher Education Act of 1965, P.L. 105-244 (Amended 1998). Retrieved February 24, 2007, from http://www.ed.gov/policy/highered/leg/hea98/index.html

International Reading Association. (1999, May). *Resolution on adolescent literacy*. Retrieved February 23, 2007, from http://www.reading.org/downloads/resolutions/resolution99_adolescent_literacy.pdf

International Reading Association. (2004). *Standards for reading professionals—Revised 2003*. Newark, DE: Author.

International Reading Association. (2005a, March 16–17). *Executive Committee meeting summary*. Newark, DE: Author.

International Reading Association. (2005b, February). Mixed reactions to NCLB. *Reading Today, 22*(4), 1, 4.

International Reading Association. (2006a, September 25). *IRA responds to Reading First report*. Retrieved February 22, 2007, from http://blog.reading.org/archives/002015.html

International Reading Association. (2006b, November). *Position statement on Reading First*. Retrieved February 22, 2007, from http://www.reading.org/resources/issues/positions_reading_first.html

International Reading Association & National Middle School Association. (2002). *Supporting young adolescents' literacy learning: A joint position statement*. Newark, DE; Westerville, OH: Authors. Retrieved February 23, 2007, from http://www.reading.org/downloads/positions/ps1052_supporting.pdf

Learning First Alliance. (2000, November). Conclusion. In *Every child reading: A professional development guide*. Retrieved February 2, 2007, from http://learningfirst.org/publications/reading/guide/conclusion.html

Lewis, J., & Moorman, G. (in press). Federal and state literacy mandates for secondary schools: Responding to unintended consequences. In L.S. Rush, A.J. Eakle, & A. Berger (Eds.), *Secondary school literacy: What research reveals for classroom practice*. Urbana, IL: National Council of Teachers of English.

Lucas, P. (1991). Reflection, new practices and the need for flexibility in supervising student teachers. *Journal of Further and Higher Education, 15*(2), 84–93.

Miskel, C., Coggshall, J.G., DeYoung, D.A., Osguthorpe, R.D., Song, M., & Young, T.V. (2003). *Reading policy in the states: Interests and processes* (Final report for the Field Initiated Studies Grant PR/Award No. R305T990369, Office of Educational Research and Improvement, U.S. Department of Education and the Spencer Foundation Major Research Grants Program Award No. 200000269). Ann Arbor: University of Michigan.

Moore, D.W., Bean, T.W., Birdyshaw, D., & Rycik, J.A. (1999). *Adolescent literacy: A position statement for the Commission on Adolescent Literacy of the International Reading Association*. Newark, DE: International Reading Association.

Murphy, S. (1997). Literacy assessment and the politics of identities. *Reading and Writing Quarterly, 13*, 261–277.

National Governors Association. (2006, August 10). *Policy position: ECW-13. High school reform to lifelong learning: Aligning secondary and postsecondary education*. Retrieved October 18, 2006, from http://www.nga.org/portal/site/nga/menu item.616f0cf559d998d18a278110501010a0/?vgnextoid=2aea9e2f1b091010V gnVCM1000001a01010aRCRD&vgnextchannel=00bd6eb58fda0010VgnVC M1000001a01010aRCRD&vgnextfmt=print

No Child Left Behind Act of 2001, 20 U.S.C. § 6315 et seq. (2002).

Public Education Network. (May, 2006). *Open to the public: The public speaks out on No Child Left Behind*. Retrieved January 31, 2007, from http://www.publicedu cation.org/2006_NCLB/main/2006_NCLB_National_Report.pdf

Roderick, M. (2006, April). *Closing the aspirations-attainment gap: Implications for high school reform*. Retrieved February 1, 2007, from http://www.mdrc.org/pub lications/427/full.pdf

School Dropout Prevention Initiative, 20 U.S.C. § 6561 (2002).

Schoolwide Programs, 20 U.S.C. § 6314 (OSCN, 2007).

Spellings, M. (2005, October 21). *Key policy letters signed by the education secretary or deputy secretary*. Retrieved January 15, 2007, from http://www.ed.gov/policy/ elsec/guid/secletter/051021.html

Swanson, C.B. (2004). *Who graduates? Who doesn't? A statistical portrait of public high school graduation, class of 2001*. Retrieved February 23, 2007, from http:// www.urban.org/url.cfm?ID=410934

U.S. Department of Education. (n.d.) *Striving Readers: Awards: 2005–06*. Retrieved February 23, 2007, from http://www.ed.gov/programs/strivingreaders/ awards.html

U.S. Department of Education. (2004, May). *No Child Left Behind: A toolkit for teach- ers* (Rev. ed.). Retrieved February 22, 2007, from http://www.ed.gov/teach ers/nclbguide/nclb-teachers-toolkit.pdf

U.S. Department of Education. (2005). *Fiscal year 2005 application for new grants for the Striving Readers Program*. Retrieved January 26, 2007, from http:// www.ed.gov/programs/strivingreaders/2005-371a.pdf

U.S. Department of Education, Office of the Inspector General. (2006a, September). *The Reading First Program's grant application process*. Retrieved January 31, 2007, from http://www.ed.gov/about/offices/list/oig/aireports/i13f0017.pdf

U.S. Department of Education. (2006b, March 22). *$30 million in Striving Readers grants awarded to help struggling readers: First grants to support president's Striving Readers program*. Retrieved June 28, 2006, from http://www.ed.gov/news/press releases/2006/03/03222006.html

U.S. Office of Management and Budget. (2007). Focusing on the nation's priori- ties: Department of Education. In *Budget of the United States Government: Fiscal Year 2007*. Retrieved February 1, 2007, from http://www.whitehouse.gov/omb/ budget/fy2007/education.html

Walsh, K. (2001). *Teacher certification reconsidered: Stumbling for quality.* Baltimore: Abell Foundation.

Wilson, P.F., & Pearson, R.D. (1995). *Performance-based assessments: External, internal, and self-assessment tools for total quality management.* Milwaukee, WI: ASQC Quality Press.

CHAPTER 3

Emergence of a Secondary Reading Initiative in Alabama

Terry Salinger

HIGHLIGHTS

- Secondary teachers created their own version of a statewide reading reform effort to meet the requirements of their content areas and the needs of their students.
- Certain conditions—not all positive—enabled the initiative to take root and survive at the local level when state support faded.
- Improvement in reading instruction in secondary schools is best encouraged when teachers receive support from coaches and trainers who are knowledgeable about middle and high school teaching and learning.

As part of its focus on adolescent literacy, Carnegie Corporation of New York commissioned a descriptive study (Salinger & Bacevich, 2006) of the secondary component of the Alabama Reading Initiative (ARI). ARI is a kindergarten to grade 12 reading reform effort directed toward changes in teacher instruction and student achievement. Carnegie wanted to know what was working among secondary teachers as they tried to implement ARI, what inhibited full implementation, and what seemed to sustain the initiative in the face of minimal state funding. The study involved interviewing more than 100 teachers, administrators, and other stakeholders. Students participated in focus groups at their schools, and about 1,200 Alabama middle and high school teachers completed surveys (Salinger & Bacevich, 2006).

Adolescent Literacy Instruction: Policies and Promising Practices edited by Jill Lewis and Gary Moorman. © 2007 by the International Reading Association.

Data confirmed the role of ARI in Alabama middle and high schools as an agent for positive change and as a challenge to implement.

This chapter reports on the study and illustrates its findings with quotations from many of the Alabama educators and stakeholders who were interviewed. A comment from a high school teacher, however, captures much of the findings. This comment represents an essential point of view for all content area teachers—the perspective on teaching and learning without which adolescent learners' needs cannot be fully addressed:

> What's changed with me since being involved in ARI is it's made me realize reading is not a separate subject. When I went to school, it was an isolated subject. It's got me bringing reading into my math class, making me realize reading is an integral part of any subject.

Background of the Alabama Reading Initiative

Alabama schools have long been considered among the weakest in the nation. Many students qualify for free or reduced-cost lunch, and many schools receive low scores on the National Assessment of Educational Progress, have high dropout rates, and are poorly resourced. To illustrate, in 1998, the first year of ARI, National Assessment of Educational Progress (NAEP) scores for Alabama indicated that just 24% of fourth graders were reading at or above the proficient level on the reading test and that 21% of eighth graders scored at or above proficient. State test results were not much better. One Alabama policymaker who participated in developing ARI said that students were not necessarily failing state tests, but their scores were low enough to suggest students could not read at grade level, think deeply about what they were reading, and use their skills in content area learning. Their barely passing test scores were being achieved through what she called "coping and masking skills," essentially, compensatory abilities that allowed them to pass tests but that did not serve them well in content area coursework. A respondent to a 2002 report on reading policy in Alabama (Coggshall, 2003) said the problem was "cumulative, and it catches up with people as they get to high school. Every year the deficit gets bigger and bigger."

Leaders of the A+ Foundation, a Montgomery-based nonprofit organization dedicated to improving K–12 education in Alabama, and Katherine Mitchell of the Alabama State Department of Education worked to secure the funds, the energy, and the collective human resources to take action. A panel of teachers, higher education faculty, State Department of Education staff, business leaders, and representatives of educational organizations as diverse as the Alabama chapter of the National Education Association and the Alabama Eagle Forum met during the summer of 1997 for a two-week working session. Together, they envisioned a statewide effort to achieve the common goal of 100% literacy for students at ARI sites. Participants referred to the session as a kind of think tank for solving literacy problems in the state.

This formative study group conceptualized ARI as a K–12 research-based professional development program for teachers and administrators. At interested schools, 85% of the faculty would have to commit to using research-based practices and to working toward 100% literacy as a schoolwide goal. Teachers and administrators would have to attend a two-week summer program and additional monthly professional development sessions, and schools would have to employ reading coaches, who would in turn be supported by regional reading coaches. All participants would receive substantial professional resources about improving instruction and assessment. The recommendations derived from a concept of students as actively involved in their reading process. The initial 1998 cohort of 16 schools swelled each year as more and more elementary and secondary schools sought to participate. Eventually, the state Department of Education had to slow the growth curve because of lack of capacity to meet schools' needs for support. Approximately 25% of the ARI schools across the state now serve middle or high school students.

Initial funding was relatively bountiful, but as the years progressed, funding sources shrank, especially for secondary schools. One secondary teacher commented that funding was a "real special challenge for the entire state. We lost most of our funding, all of our technology funding, our library enhancement funding." The Reading Excellence Act and then Reading First provided windfalls that allowed ARI to flourish in the early grades, but secondary schools have had to struggle. One state administrator commented, perhaps a bit defensively, "[I'm not saying we've provided the] very best infrastructure or leadership to our secondary folks, but ARI should be commended for including secondary at least in theory, on paper, and with [some] budget." The state Department of Education has continued to have a few staff focused at least in part on secondary ARI, but its continuation as a viable secondary initiative has resulted far more from local efforts and the sheer energy and dedication of teachers and administrators to bring about change.

Secondary ARI as an Agent
for Positive Change

Secondary ARI has proven to be an agent for change at numerous levels, with positive outcomes for students and teachers. Of course, improvements in achievement test scores are often considered to be the most important indicator of positive change resulting from a reform initiative, and this outcome of reform has not been exemplary in all ARI schools.

In Alabama, secondary students must take the SAT-10 and also pass a high school exit test. Quantitative evaluations of ARI (Moscovitch, 2004) have shown some improvements in test scores but not dramatic gains. The 2004 evaluation of ARI concluded,

> While ARI schools outperformed non-ARI schools in 2003 for all students [on the SAT-10], the ARI makes more of a difference for non-poor White or Asian students than for minorities and/or students living in poverty.... In middle school grades, the ARI advantage is 6 percentiles for majority students and 1 percentile for minorities or students in poverty. (p. 3)

Thus the benefits of ARI are clearly stronger in the schools that already have the most advantaged students—this in a state where approximately 25% of the close to 750,000 students live at or below the poverty line.

But test scores show only part of the picture, and teachers and others reported very positive results from ARI in terms of overall student achievement and other factors. An official from the A+ Foundation commented on the complexity of school improvement:

> We're seeing chronically underperforming schools have amazing results. This just has such a huge impact that they double their efforts and keep wanting to achieve more and more. We're not seeing rapid gains in the SAT-10 scores, but we are seeing huge gains in the writing assessments. And it will be interesting to see future writing assessment scores at the high school level. With high schools, you look to the high school graduation exam, but are changes in these and the writing assessment scores due to other things [than ARI]?

Teachers and administrators often credited ARI for increases in test scores. One high school principal said that since ARI was introduced, his school "got a higher percent of [students] passing the graduation exam. That's the most notable thing." A teacher said, "Kids are now passing reading portions of the high school exam when they never could before."

A regional reading coach commented on several of the schools she serves:

> Now our scores went up at [one high school], and they have continued to. Last year 100% of the seniors passed. [Another high school] got an A on high school graduation scores. Writing scores have gone up. When you look at statistics across the state, ARI schools outperform non-ARI schools as far as testing is concerned.

However, not all ARI schools have seen dramatic or consistent increases in test scores. One school reading coach explained, "Students are now trained to deal with unfamiliar vocabulary and reading problems on their own with ARI reading strategies, [but] there has not been improvement consistently on assessments." This slow progress may be partly attributable to changes in the student population, as one middle school teacher explained,

> I wish I could see lots more success. At the same time, our SES level has been continually dropping, too. We're very transitory, so we have a lot of students that we have for two years and don't see in eighth grade, or come in eighth grade only.

Indeed, shifting demographics in Alabama schools seem to mitigate the ARI impact. The 2004 quantitative evaluation (Moscovitch, 2004) reported, "There are examples where [ARI] schools raise the scores of both their Black students and their White students but nonetheless see a drop in overall scores as racial composition changes" (p. 14).

Fortunately, thoughtful educators recognize that test scores are not the only sign of successful reform initiatives. Our study of ARI implementation found other signs of change, and many of them are such that they can form the foundation of future improvements. Some of the changes—or outcomes—are related to students and others to teachers.

Student Outcomes

Teachers and administrators responded enthusiastically to questions about ARI outcomes for students. They said that students seemed to be demonstrating increased engagement with reading and were more confident than before about themselves as readers. One teacher explained that before ARI, students "would forget their books, or not bring them, and now they're ready on Monday mornings with the books and ready to go to the library. It's important to them now." Another teacher noted that students seemed "more open to reading, don't mind reading [and] may bring books to class to read when they finish; now they pull out books, tote books around school with them." A third teacher explained that when she provides daily newspapers for her students, they "are excited and want to look at the headlines—they search out reading." A high school reading coach concurred:

> Students have become *much* more excited about reading and read so much more...voluntarily! Children can read without being nerds. Everyone reads, not just smart kids. Children's excitement has been a measure of effectiveness [of ARI].

Many interviewees commented on students' improved attitudes toward school and learning. One state administrator noted that ARI schools generally seemed to have "fewer [students] with belligerent attitudes toward reading. Many students have truly developed a love for reading." Interviewees stressed that more students had begun to think of themselves as competent readers, capable of gaining something from reading in and out of school. A middle school teacher said,

> The students are simply reading more. Just to see students who are sitting and reading, that's unusual. They come to me all the time, [asking] how can I be "reader of the week"? They're seeking the recognition that comes with reading. I kind of feel like we got away from that for a while. The big push was technology. Then with all the standardized tests that they have to take, the most important thing is, what are your test scores? But a truly educated person is a well-read person. Our students are becoming aware of this.

Further, ARI may have enabled some students to take the bold step of asking for assistance with their learning. One teacher told of students who

> will come after school and ask for help with reading. When you get popular basketball players doing that, or other students who are struggling, you keep that information confidential. You are really surprised that they can't read, but you are more surprised that they came and asked for help.

Many interviewees also noted that since implementing ARI, they had observed decreases in discipline problems and referrals for special services. A junior high school principal referred to the ARI-related changes in his school as a "rebirth," adding that the school seemed to be meeting its goal of decreased discipline referrals because "the more engaged they are, the less time [students have] to get into trouble." A regional reading coach observed "a decrease in referrals in most of these schools. Even in the inner cities, even in schools where [implementation] is just scraping the surface, you see the difference in those classes."

A reading coach reported that although she had observed only small changes in referrals, "One thing that jumped dramatically was library circulation." School libraries and media centers often had poor resources, although some principals had tried to provide high-interest books and magazines with ARI funds, and the reading coaches in some schools had set up their own lending libraries. Regardless of the resources, students seemed interested in leisure-time reading. As one teacher said,

> Before [ARI], students never wanted to read. They were always tired of reading. Now they have been given time in the library; they enjoy reading, and they are upset when they don't have a chance to go to the library.

Additionally, a regional reading coach indicated that even public libraries had been influenced by ARI, saying, "I think outside reading is increasing.... Public libraries are branching out and supplementing materials from the schools. Lots of efforts like that—I see [this] in the communities."

One possible explanation for these changes is increased awareness on the part of students about what it means to be a reader and what they themselves can do to improve their skills. Teachers reported that students were using the reading comprehension strategies that are the core of ARI. These include, among others, careful use of context clues and attention to content-specific vocabulary and text structure; and use of mnemonic devices, graphic organizers, K-W-L charts, and content-area word walls. In many ARI schools, students participate in schoolwide Drop Everything And Read time or Sustained Silent Reading, cooperative learning groups, and other activities that challenge them to reinforce their skills. These strategies—presented in the professional development workshops, illustrated in a huge resource notebook, and reinforced by the reading coaches—enhanced students' comprehension, engaged them intellectually, and gave them power over their reading. Teachers reported observing students using these strategies to read independently and to study. One regional reading coach said,

I went to one of my schools, and all of them were doing reciprocal teaching. It was obvious that these kids had done this before; they were comfortable with their roles, and they were talking to each other and not at each other.

A school reading coach commented,

One change [was noted] when the children were taking their graduation exams and when they were doing their work in class. There are certain strategies affiliated with note-taking, and you can see them using that note-taking when you walk around. You see them taking notes, [making] circles. So that is positive to me. The kids may or may not care about ARI. They are not making the [entire] connection; they are making the connection to the strategy. They don't care that our school is an ARI school. They are children, [and] that is not what they are thinking about, [but] I can see the children using the strategies.

Talking about her students' reactions to ARI strategies, a high school teacher admitted that some students "have accepted [ARI], although begrudgingly because it requires new skills and brainwork and has no busywork. I find throughout their work, even in other classes...that they are using [reading strategies]." To gain this acceptance, some schools avidly promoted their connection to ARI, displaying an ARI wall banner or an ARI logo on the school website and promoting schoolwide activities that celebrated ARI and reading. Other schools took a more subtle approach, implementing the initiative without referring explicitly to ARI. The ways in which schools adopted the ARI methods and perspective may have differed, but interview data strongly suggested that students benefited from ARI implementation. Test scores per se may not indicate huge advancements, but signs of better behavior, engagement, and actual strategy noted by teachers suggest positive changes for secondary schools.

Teacher Outcomes

There were many positive outcomes for teachers as well. Certainly, as indicated previously, teachers had become knowledgeable about strategies to increase students' comprehension of what they read and to further their understanding of content as well. But the outcomes were not just superficial adoption of some reading-in-the-content-area strategies. It is not an exaggeration to say that teachers' philosophies changed as a result of their involvement in ARI training and their use of ARI approaches. Many teachers and other interviewees used the term "awareness" to characterize the changes brought about by ARI—awareness not just of the importance of reading but also of the impact teachers can have on students' reading performance. One teacher noted, "Because of ARI, reading is a foundation to everything, so I think ARI is giving teachers a way to get their point across in their subject matter." Another teacher explained that

> [ARI] has changed the way we approach material with our classes. It has made us aware of the need to read and monitor reading. It has been good for everyone. It has still changed our approach because we are so aware of it. We are encouraged to make [students] dig more, spoon-feed less, make students aware of the importance of reading. Since before ARI the focus has definitely changed, that goes without saying.

Some teachers acknowledged that they had previously wanted to blame elementary schools for students' poor preparation or to accept that their students couldn't read. This attitude has changed. One reading coach quoted her school's principal, who told the faculty, "We can't focus on what they didn't get in elementary. They're here now."

Many teachers' comments reflected this "they're here now" attitude. One teacher noted that in her school, "The vast majority of teachers are looking to improve their abilities" to address students' reading difficulties. Another teacher explained, "I've had a realization within myself that if a student cannot read, that he/she is very limited in what they can absorb from my class since so much is printed text." Still another teacher who attributed changes in philosophy to ARI explained,

> I've learned that ARI is the most important thing in the class and in teaching. I've learned to understand that there are multiple learning strategies and methods, and have been able to think about the whole classroom environment and focus on making it kid friendly so they aren't afraid to open their minds up.

Teachers had high expectations for students' reading that translated to awareness of strategies and also to personal responsibility for helping students achieve. Of those surveyed, 83% of middle school teachers and 80% of high school teachers agreed with the statement "ARI raised my expectations for the level and amount of reading students can handle." A middle school assistant principal observed, "Even our below-grade-level students realize that our teachers care, that they can be successful too."

In addition to knowledge of strategies and a sense of responsibility, teachers became much more acutely aware of struggling readers as individuals with specific needs and patterns of reading deficiencies. One regional reading coach explained that much of the change

> was about frame of reference. A lot of teachers weren't identifying students as struggling readers because they were comparing them to other classmates, and they were *all* poor readers. And we had to raise awareness and let them compare them to national levels and stuff like that.

In this way, ARI was more strategic than simply incorporating new activities into instruction; many teachers learned how to recognize the reading difficulties that might be impeding their students' learning and to change instruction accordingly. One teacher explained,

> First of all, I think that every teacher [in this school] has become a diagnostic teacher, which before, we were not. They know how to tackle and intervene in those interferences that are causing them not to comprehend text. They are using so much more data as a result. We as a faculty at this school are a much more humane faculty. We don't have to hide, any of us that have reading deficiencies.

One key to being such a diagnostic teacher is using data to inform instructional decisions, a hallmark of ARI. A principal commented on the increased use of data in one school:

> The biggest thing...that ARI has done for us is to make us look at the research and the data that is available to us and structure our teaching around the data that is available to us and [note] our strengths and weaknesses. As long as we continue to do that, we'll be successful. This year, the ARI people, actually the regional [reading coach], she was able to get me a printout of our student scores, a breakdown.... Those are the kinds of things that ARI has made us do. It's made us analyze the data to cover where our weaknesses are.

Teachers seemed to change in terms of their skill levels and their attitudes and sense of efficacy for meeting students' needs. These shifts implied positive changes within individual teachers, but the study data also indicated growth in teachers' sense of professionalism and identification with a proactive community. A principal noted that collaboration grew and helped teachers discover ways to use data to inform instructional choices:

> An unintended benefit is the bringing together of faculty in ways that never happened before. You have whole faculties that are now looking at assessments rather than bunches of useless data, but are looking at it

and reflecting on it, and realizing where groups of students and individual students have shortcomings, and how that reflects on their instruction. That may have been born of the reading initiative—and where ARI initiated these kinds of conversations, the best practices center also works with the ARI schools, teaching them how to do self-assessments and reflections and how to facilitate powerful conversations in schools. It's allowed teachers to learn how to have conversations about practices, and kids, and growth, without being judgmental.

Collaboration became more common than it had been in many schools; in some schools, teachers reported that they had never had content-area or grade-level meetings before ARI. Teachers worked together to find the most effective and efficient ways to incorporate ARI strategies into instruction. A junior high school teacher explained how she and her colleagues eased the ARI implementation process:

> Teachers have responded well. If they aren't sure in one [ARI] area, they talk to coworkers—have they tried it? How does it work? Teachers [are] talking a lot about what they've tried and what works. At first it took some getting used to. It was a little difficult choosing what would work for you. But now everyone is used to implementing the strategies, and they've seen how they help in a lot of different areas.

An assistant principal agreed, indicating that teachers in her school "talk about a particular student and how they can work toward eradicating those interferences that the student is having. Those powerful conversations are taking place all over the building all day. The collaboration is so much more."

The development of professional community, spurred by ARI, seemed an especially rewarding outcome for teachers. A regional reading coach noted, "Yes, I'm seeing collaboration. They are seeing that they can help students make the connections across the content levels and then they can't stop; they keep working together." Another regional reading coach agreed:

> It didn't occur with all, but the teachers [in some schools] that were receptive to change couldn't get enough.... Their doors were more open, and they made the children more proud of what they produced. Everything became more community oriented. Teachers started covering each other's classes so that they could do guided reading while the teachers got to meet with the reading coach.

Professional community, a sense of shared ability to address the needs of students, and awareness that students were in fact applying the ARI strategies were all positive outcomes for teachers. These outcomes can be considered part of the foundation needed for improved teacher performance and measurable academic advancement. Secondary teachers who are willing to overlook poor reading skills and feel that they either can't or don't have to deal with these skills will inevitably not be able to motivate students to do the work needed to improve. The cycle of failure continues, with few students escaping and few teachers finally realizing that they can make a difference. ARI seemed to break this cycle for many Alabama secondary teachers.

Secondary ARI as a Challenge to Implementation

One goal of the descriptive study was to identify challenges to implementation and ways in which schools had overcome them. Among the challenges revealed in the data were the initial one-size-fits-all model for ARI, lack of expertise and credibility in secondary issues, competition for attention from literacy programs for the early grades, and overall funding shortfalls. Data also showed how a genuinely secondary ARI emerged as teachers tried to make the initiative work for them.

Recommendations from the formative reading panel for ARI had not distinguished between early and later grades. The initial plan had somewhat of a one-size-fits-all feel to it, with the assumption that strategies for beginning reading instruction would work with minor modifications as students progressed through school. This view was undoubtedly influenced by the vast amount of "scientifically based research" on early reading that the formative panel reviewed, but it became the first challenge to be overcome in creating an ARI that would work well in secondary schools.

After a year or two of professional development, secondary teachers began to complain that ARI strategies and materials, as well as the approach to professional development, were not appropriate for their work with middle and high school students. The director of an inservice center said, "The bad thing in the beginning is that it was one size fits all. The presentation styles were the same for both groups. Elementary school teachers accept materials and will play with you, whereas secondary teachers won't." One state administrator admitted, "It's a challenge at the state level to learn the subtle differences about what we need to be doing at the elementary versus the secondary levels." Gradually, state staff responded by revising and tailoring some aspects of the professional development and materials to accommodate a secondary-specific perspective.

However, shortage of staff at the Department of Education with real knowledge of secondary teaching and learning was another challenge. A state administrator told interviewers,

> Even though there is a secondary person at the state department, many times that secondary person is in dual roles, supporting the elementary as well as trying to keep the secondary going.... As you know, we have 134 schools right now in the secondary.... [State-funded support staff] are spread very thinly.

At the time of the interviews, there were only two regional reading coaches supporting the school-based reading coaches and teachers in the secondary ARI schools.

A related obstacle to implementation was lack of knowledge of secondary issues among school-based reading coaches, many of whom had "moved up" to middle or high school after working as elementary reading specialists. One high school principal explained his frustration with ARI professional development:

> This has been a real weak link from the beginning. The [school reading coaches] will tell the secondary principals, "I don't know about secondary." Well, you can't expect a principal to take their time away from school and go to a meeting where they preface the conversation with, "Well, I'm not sure about secondary."

Secondary teachers often responded in the same way to their schools' coaches, but in many places teachers' emerging sense of collaboration and professionalism enabled them to craft their own vision for ARI in spite of what was perceived to be inappropriate coaching.

Issues of early reading instruction often set the direction for educational agendas and may draw attention away from concerns about older students. In Alabama, this was certainly the case. The state has been widely recognized for the quality of its implementation of Reading First, and many educators in the state have felt that spending money on programs in the early grades was far more beneficial than spending it on older students, especially as the state has experienced several years of fiscal difficulties. Reading First funding has been used in ARI sites and has allowed the number of sites to grow. However, little funding has been available for secondary ARI. A district administrator explained this persistent problem for secondary schools:

> There are many big differences [between elementary and secondary ARI], and funding is one. I don't think that there's a category within the budget to support secondary. I think that secondary just sort of falls into the overall budget, and whatever can be taken out is used.... We wish that we had a budget to work from and that we could make long term plans, but it's...very short-term. This is what's available now.

Signs of Sustainability

In spite of significant challenges, secondary ARI has continued to emerge as a vehicle for change in secondary schools. The descriptive data suggest many reasons why this has happened. Even though many people mentioned fiscal issues as a major problem, their comments never implied that insufficient funding per se was the primary obstacle to implementation in schools that were truly committed to ARI. Perhaps it was the school teacher mentality that so many educators have—they can hold things together to create something positive for their students.

Certainly, the outcomes for students and teachers motivated secondary educators to keep working to tailor ARI to their needs. But there were definitive precursor factors that supported emergence of secondary ARI. One was what the literature refers to as "sensemaking" (Coburn, 2001, 2005). The secondary ARI teachers constructed a shared understanding of the initiative and of its implications for their students and their teaching. Without undergoing this process of "sensemaking," teachers might have been inclined to marginalize ARI and continue with "business as usual."

Leadership was also an important factor, and leaders can take many forms and assume many jobs. It is not just the principal who needs to provide leadership; and indeed in some ARI schools principals had enough to do to keep the building quiet, productive, and peaceful. The regional reading coaches were often cited as the real leaders, people whom the teachers and principals respected and wanted in their schools more often. Interestingly, one of the coaches came to his role through social studies and had acquired his extensive knowledge of reading on his own. The school reading coaches were less frequently named as leaders, and some school administrators suggested that the coaches needed to be trained and encouraged to assume leadership roles in their own ways. Sometimes teachers became leaders among their colleagues. In one school, for example, teachers spoke about "the data guy," who had taken it upon himself to demystify assessment data for his colleagues so that they could better understand their students' strengths and weaknesses. In so doing, he helped accomplish the ARI goal of data-driven instructional decision making.

Of course, additional funding would have made it easier for secondary schools to implement ARI. The teacher who said, "The thing that has affected us more here at the local level is the loss of professional learning money," was not alone in focusing on professional development opportunities rather than materials and supplies. Somehow the schools that were dedicated to the initiative found ways to carry on. Some principals moved funds around, for example, using Title I funds to purchase extra books. Others wrote grants. One principal said, "We wanted a Saturday Academy, and wrote a grant for it, but didn't get the funds for it. We're willing to give up Saturday mornings to get students that extra dose of reading or math."

Without minimizing the need for funding to carry on materials- and training-intensive initiatives such as ARI, secondary schools that seemed to be successful in the face of state fiscal challenges demonstrated high degrees of local ownership. Administrators and teachers felt a commitment to bringing about change, and students responded to the commitment of those around them. The professional communities and sense of efficacy that emerged in such places gave birth to local experts who sought to ensure continuation of the changes the initiative had begun. In many places, ownership was directed toward a local model, a way of implementing ARI that teachers' and administrators' collective sense had deemed right for their school and their students. One teacher captured the confluence of factors that can make ARI work:

> You have to have administration supporting you, and they have to be involved. They have to lead the school, they have to be that instructional leadership. [You need an] administrator who is concerned with academics of the school, and have to have a good reading coach, one who can work really well with the teachers.... I think as long as you have a really strong administrator and an adequate reading coach or a really strong reading coach and an adequate administrator, you'll be fine. But a lot of schools don't have either, and just have some strong faculty members trying to make it happen. I think it can work in any school as long as they are willing to effect change.

Recommendations for Sustainability

Carnegie Corporation was interested not only in what was going on in Alabama but what recommendations our data could offer to other districts and states contemplating a secondary reading initiative. Interview data suggested many ways the emerging secondary ARI could be strengthened and made more durable, and from the data emerged five primary recommendations. The first is that any model adopted for a kindergarten to grade 12 initiative must be flexible enough that teachers at different levels can adapt it to their instructional needs and the needs of their students. That a secondary ARI emerged at all means that the original model did in fact possess hidden flexibility.

The second recommendation is that initiatives should focus, as ARI did, primarily on comprehension. Such a focus does not preclude meticulous attention to other skills, and certainly Alabama Reading First demonstrates this kind of attention. But if teachers of older students are to see the value of an initiative and if the initiative is to make students better able to read to learn, then comprehension must be front and center in the design.

Third, many interviewees at the school and state level mentioned that secondary ARI lacked one important dimension: a procedure for identifying the students who are most at risk for reading failure and diagnosing their needs. It was clear that students' reading skills were deficient, but there were no diagnostic data on and no intervention programs for students with the severest difficulties. Reading First provided a mechanism for kindergarten to grade 3, but there was nothing beyond that point, and many interviewees said it was needed in secondary classes too.

The final recommendations concern funding and leadership. Descriptive data suggested that dedicated, resourceful secondary educators managed—somehow—to keep ARI going in their schools even as state funding decreased. The fourth recommendation follows from what interviewees said they had done: Educators need to be creative in the use of local monies and also to be vigilant for sources of external funding.

Planning a comprehensive and ambitious initiative such as ARI begins with centralized, sophisticated leadership from dedicated individuals who have a vision for change and the wherewithal to bring it about. But centralized leadership must also encourage the development of local leaders who share the vision and high expectations inherent in the primary model and can shape the model to meet local needs. One state administrator captured the process of devolving leadership and vision to local educators that was the hallmark of the most committed, successful ARI secondary schools:

And I think we need more buy-in at the local level. Give full support the first year, and half the second. Then you will have developed this local expert. The state cannot sustain the thing; we have got to pass it on to the [local education agencies].

There may be some bureaucratic defensiveness in this administrator's comment because state secondary ARI funding was cut so dramatically, but the message remains important. A flexible model focused on comprehension as an ultimate goal and capable of identifying and helping struggling readers can be so attractive to secondary educators that they make it their own, tailor it to their needs, and allow local leadership to flourish. Students and teachers are the ultimate winners in such a situation, and secondary ARI demonstrates this clearly.

Hopeful Signs for Secondary ARI

In fall 2005, the Alabama Department of Education decided against requesting a grant for funding from the federal Striving Readers program. The grant, which could have totaled $5 million each year for five years, would have helped refine a secondary model of ARI, but state administrators were reluctant to ask districts and schools to enter into the lottery that the grant's random assignment requirement imposed. Cynics probably assumed that the initiative would languish, but this has not been the case. A small number of staff at the state level have continued to work toward a distinct secondary ARI, and in the meantime, test scores in ARI secondary schools seem to be inching upward. As reported in the *Birmingham News* (Leech, 2006), more schools are expressing interest in adopting the initiative, and the state Department of Education is not only acknowledging the importance of reading instruction in secondary schools but also working actively with schools that want to bring about change.

Questions for Reflection

1. The chapter discusses outcomes—or changes—in teachers and students. Which changes seem to be the most significant and why are they important?

2. Not all ARI schools experienced improved scores on standardized assessments, yet many teachers perceived their students as being better prepared for such tests because of ARI strategies. In what ways might these teachers be right about their students?

3. What different roles did leadership play as secondary teachers sought to tailor ARI to their needs?

Terry Salinger is Managing Director and Chief Scientist for Reading Research at the American Institutes for Research (AIR) in Washington, DC. Prior to joining AIR, she was the director of research at the International Reading Association. She has been a university professor and spent the first 10 years of her professional life as a teacher in the New York City public schools. She also headed a study of the secondary component of the Alabama Reading Initiative, and is the project director for an IES study of the effectiveness of reading interventions for struggling adolescent readers. Although her specific areas of focus are reading and literacy research and assessment, she provides content expertise on studies investigating pre-service teachers' preparation to teach beginning reading, developing a curriculum for adult ESL learners, and monitoring the implementation of the Reading First program. She can be reached at TSalinger@air.org.

REFERENCES

Coburn, C.E. (2001). Collective sensemaking about reading: How teachers mediate reading policy in their professional communities. *Educational Evaluation and Policy Analysis, 23,* 145–170.

Coburn, C.E. (2005). Shaping teacher sensemaking: School leaders and the enactment of reading policy. *Education Policy, 19,* 476–509.

Coggshall, J.G. (2003). *Alabama reading policy: Problems, processes, and participants.* Ann Arbor: University of Michigan School of Education.

Leech, M. (2006, October 12). State reading initiative may spread. *Birmingham News.* Retrieved October 14, 2006, from http://www.al.com/news/birminghamnews/index.ssf?/base/news/11606446104380.xml&coll=2

Moscovitch, E. (2004). *Evaluation of the Alabama Reading Initiative.* Gloucester, MA: Cape Ann Economics.

Salinger, T., & Bacevich, A. (2006). *Lessons and recommendations from the Alabama Reading Initiative: Sustaining focus on secondary reading* (Prepared for Carnegie Corporation of New York). Washington, DC: American Institutes for Research.

CHAPTER 4

Challenging Literacy Theories and Practices From the Outside

Donna E. Alvermann and A. Jonathan Eakle

HIGHLIGHTS

- Designating adolescent literacy practices as either school-based or outside of school is too restrictive and suggests that there are few if any relations between the two.

- Young people's engagement with multiple forms of text is achieved with little, if any, regard for space and time constraints.

- Where boundaries do exist, youth find ways of grafting elements of popular culture one upon another to escape (if even temporarily and partially) various attempts at partitioning their literacy practices into in-school and out-of-school spaces.

> There is no Frigate like a Book
> To take us Lands away
> Nor any Coursers like a Page
> Of prancing Poetry—
> This Traverse may the poorest take
> Without oppress of Toll—
> How frugal is the Chariot
> That bears the Human soul.
>
> Emily Dickinson, 1894/2004 (PoetryX.com)

On a México City rooftop, in a Baltimore harbor shopping mall, and along a remote stretch of beach on a Georgia island, invisible WiFi waves drift like warm summer breezes over an ocean; these waves carry literacies that include print, pictures, video,

---

Adolescent Literacy Instruction: Policies and Promising Practices edited by Jill Lewis and Gary Moorman. © 2007 by the International Reading Association.

music, library catalogs, and maps, all broadcasted from free or low-cost digital wireless networks that are fast becoming part of an archive from which seemingly endless texts pour out. These literacies can be intercepted with various technologies that are increasingly affordable. We think these new "chariots" of literacies would bring a smile to Emily Dickinson as they do to many of us who today engage and find pleasure in variations of texts, imageries, and literacy practices.

We open this chapter with an interface of Emily Dickinson and wireless communication technologies (WiFi) because it provides a particularly salient example of how traditional print literacies, new and old technologies, and textual aesthetics can come together in various and sometimes unlikely spaces. Such instances support the growing body of literature that questions a strict division between in-school and out-of-school literacy practices (e.g., Hull & Schultz, 2002). WiFi points to many students' literacy practices in a world increasingly blurred by technologies and practices that are not confined to what takes place during school hours and within school walls.

Glossary

Imageries:	The creation of mental or material references that involve problem solving, aesthetics, and so forth.
Lines of escape:	A term coined by Deleuze and Guattari. Rather than oppose or resist social practices, such as categorizations by race, gender, class, struggling reader, and so forth, people or groups may simply turn their back on those practices. Also known as "lines of flight."
Literacy practices:	Literacy does not simply involve a set of discrete skills, such as reading and writing. The practice of literacy involves the uses of all communication resources, such as film and drama, that overlap other points of communication resources, such as books.
Textual aesthetics:	Forms of communication that appeal to sensations, such as pleasure, joy, sorrow, disgust, and so forth.
The outside:	A term borrowed from Deleuze's (1986/2000) analysis of Foucault's project. The space that exists beyond what is usually accepted by dominant social groups or institutions, such as those of education that prescribe step-by-step formulas for teaching reading.

Our interest here is in exploring how data we gathered on young people's literacy practices in outside-school spaces such as museums (Eakle, 2005) and a public library that housed an after-school media club (Alvermann et al., 2001) suggest new possibilities that challenge prevailing theories about literacy teaching and learning. Specifically, we argue that through the literacies practiced in out-of-school settings, young people are able to show through their actions and projects how engagement with texts of various kinds is achieved with little, if any, regard to space and time constraints. Literacy teaching and learning can be as boundless and fluid as the invisible WiFi waves that surround us.

Framing Perspectives

What exactly do we mean by the *outside*? In one sense, we use this term to simply illustrate that literacy learning is not confined to the traditional boundaries of classroom walls. To restrict literacies to those that are either school-based or that take place outside of school would suggest that there are few if any relations between the two. In most schools, strict classifications of spaces and practices have a history in literacy education—with written texts being privileged over texts passed on through oral practices, such as storytelling (Collins & Blot, 2003). However, it is also the case that multiple communication systems, especially those involving art forms such as music, poetry, and drama, are readily available to, and used by, youth in and out of school.

Youth who grew up using these multiple literacies are now reaching young adulthood. For example, while teaching conventional methods to young beginning teachers, Jonathan (coauthor) invited students to clarify questions that they had generated while reading a text by using any resources at hand. Rather than using traditional resources (e.g., accessible printed texts), they WiFied using various new technologies and in short order had impressive data to critically analyze their questions. Based on the success of that lesson, in another class the same choices were offered to experienced teachers. They remained in their seats and discussed the text among themselves. In the end, their work was far less rich than that of their junior counterparts who had ventured outside the boundaries of the classroom using digital resources.

Nonetheless, traditional forms of literacy instruction in which knowledgeable elders dispense book knowledge to less-adept youth are not located exclusively in schools, as we will illustrate in this chapter. Regardless of whether one's point of reference is in or out of school, most young people have at their disposal a wide range of texts and nonlinguistic resources from which to choose. Indeed, we live in times when notions of multiple forms of literacies are the rule, and not the exception, among youth.

Second, we use the word *outside* in another related way. We live in an era of high-stakes reading tests and an increasing concern that too many U.S. schools are failing to demonstrate adequate yearly progress. It is a time when outcome measures that assess primarily print-centric forms of knowledge go largely unchallenged as markers of what is deemed proof of literacy achievement. Such measures place constraints on, or boundaries around, what counts as literacy, primarily by attempting to control or discipline teachers and students to make them compliant with national, state, and local expectations (e.g., No Child Left Behind Act, 2002). In other instances, strategies of control are more subtly embedded in the general attitudes and values of a school and community. Yet, however real or palpable these boundaries may be, they are unlikely to eclipse the multiple forms of literacy at play in our highly technological world—one in which relations of power are malleable and ever changing. We argue subsequently that youth are increasingly finding ways to be outside or escape these boundaries, which is a notion involving relations of power.

Michel Foucault (1975/1977), a French philosopher, rarely used the word *power* by itself, preferring instead to write about *relations of power*. He perceived such relations to be mobile and capable of being modified or reversed. From this perspective, exercising power is not simply about dominating, resisting, or accepting a practice, such as the teaching of conventional reading strategies. Power also involves those who find a way to be outside conventions, sometimes by simply turning their back on those who try to impose conventional standards or rules (e.g., No Child Left Behind directives). That, in part, is why we wrote this chapter—to illustrate how young people's engagement with multiple forms of text is often achieved with little, if any, regard for the traditional boundaries deemed important by many current literacy programs and government mandates.

Although it is arguably the case that young people are caught up to some extent by globalizing trends in media consumption, it is also the case that they know how to form their own groups as knowledgeable, productive audiences. Guattari (1989/2000), in fact, has pointed out that youth groups that form around particular trends in popular culture—such as transnational popular music—continuously form, dissolve, and reform around certain centers of knowledge and practices. One such center that has received notable attention recently is MySpace, an online community that may have more active "citizens" than the population of México (Fisch, 2006). As teacher educators we wonder if collective groups of youth and teachers could or will form around new technologies in ways that lie outside prevailing theories about literacy teaching and learning. For that to happen, what boundaries would they need to escape? More to the point, are they escapable? Although our data sources gathered in out-of-school settings allow for only tentative answers, we share them here as first steps toward a larger agenda of pointing to new possibilities that are outside prevailing theories about literacy teaching and learning.

How Escapable Are the Boundaries?

Museum Boundaries

Multiple literacy practices are the rule in museums. Experts in a variety of communication modes, particularly the plastic arts (e.g., architecture, painting, and sculpture), create and oversee museum space. In some cases museum walls are like textbook displays, where print and graphics coexist to present particular concepts, percepts, and feelings (Eakle, in press). At other times, museums incorporate moving objects, audio and video technologies, and interactive digital devices into their instruction. These approaches and practices have been described as museum literacies (Eakle, 2005). Uses of museum literacies are especially apparent in art museums, where Jonathan studied adolescent literacy practices during museum events in Marthasville, a southeastern U.S. metropolitan area (names and places in this chapter are altered to maintain participant privacy). School groups were studied during guided tours, as well as other groups and individuals visiting the museums with minimal supervision. In addition, museum administrators, designers, artists, and educators were observed and interviewed during the investigation (Eakle, 2005).

To many educators, museums are known as informal learning environments that encourage exploration and engaged learning (Paris, 2002). Although free from some common boundaries found in schools, such as relying mostly on classrooms with similar layouts for literacy instruction, much museum education operates with practices that are akin to those of formal education. This notion is borne out in the following comments of

Meredith Polk, the education director of the Bedford Museum, one of the museums investigated that displays African art objects:

> Karen, our [education program] manager, has been looking at Howard Gardner's…types of learning, intelligences, not about the kids that are coming in, but about the docents. What kind of learner are you and how does that affect the kind of tour that you give? And it was great to see groups of docents that realized that they were kinesthetic learners and they're the ones that are like this [gestures wildly] and they have got kids doing poses and they've got kids acting out plays and stuff like that.

Indeed, at the Bedford Museum, directors, docents, and other educators promoted multiple pedagogies of knowing and acting. Part of this multiplicity involved print text sources describing displayed objects, which were very much a part of the museum's design and strategies to engage its visitors. In fact, a sizeable amount of time and money was spent by the museum creating various printed texts, such as museum guides, illustrated brochures, descriptive wall labels, and laminated information sheets. Consistent with the education manager's interest in multiple intelligences, these texts were made available, according to Meredith, to accommodate particular learning styles:

> I think it's important to have them [print texts] for the people who do want to read. But educational studies tell us that people either learn visually or they learn by doing, or they learn aurally. And it's only recently with the increase in technology that we can really address those other two learning styles…it's not really a question of whether people *like* to read, it's that some people just don't learn that way.

As shown through Meredith's words, the ubiquitous educational study governed this museum's pedagogy alongside its mission of meeting individual learning styles. Although on the surface such concepts suggest a freedom that is not always found within formal school boundaries, the museum's strategies of engagement were nonetheless bounded by a particular progressive worldview. These strategies of engagement seemed to work well for some of its elementary-aged visitors as they acted out various object-centered scenarios; for instance, hands-on explorations of an authentic museum object while taking on the role of a junior archeologist. However, it is important to note that although the print reading style of learning was made available by the museum, very rarely did museum educators and their patrons use printed texts. This was especially true of adolescent visitors who at times laughed at the very notion of reading in a museum. On the few occasions when adolescents read printed text in the museum, the act ended with comments such as one made by Periwinkle, an adolescent in Jonathan's investigation: "Oil on hmmm, *whatever*."

Notably, more often than not transmission style education practices slipped into the instruction of the Bedford Museum. For example, consider the following exchange that took place in an Egyptian art gallery between Maggie, a Bedford docent, and Bishop, an adolescent visiting the museum during a school fieldtrip:

Maggie: Is there anything that you've learned that you would like to see, that you'd like to talk about, various gods or so forth that you'd like to talk about?

Bishop: Isis?

Maggie: [pointing to an artifact] All right that's the wife of this guy Osiris. [Quickly turning to another object in a glass case] Look the artists that decorated the tombs, the beautiful tombs, they didn't have scrap paper so they would use a bit of limestone and put it on there and then practice on a bit of old limestone and then go into the tombs and do their graph, grids. [Turning to another student] You look like a mathematician, are you a mathematician?

Bishop: [interjecting] Was Osiris the first pharaoh?

Maggie: No, he was the lord of the underworld, but he was, had these kinglike qualities. [Turning to another Egyptian tomb object] Here are the canopic jars where they would put the liver, the lungs, the stomach, the um, intestines. And there's the salt, that they would wrap, smother the body in so it would dry out, so it would not get smelly diseased, with bacteria set in. It would be preserved. That was the whole point of the mummification.

This typical exchange is far from the visitor-centered multiple-learning-style philosophies put forth by the museum and its educators. In fact, docent–teachers usually moved from object to object dispensing expert knowledge that was repeated, usually in rote fashion, from museum tour to museum tour. Their scripts often originated in docent training sessions where print texts were distributed and explained to docents by museum curators and directors, and Maggie carried such printed scripts for reference as she performed her oral texts to museum visitors. Importantly, when young people disrupted the docents' oral text scripts, such as when Bishop asked questions, often the response from docents was short and of little relevance to the museum visitor. Apparently, educator-dominated talk—a subtle, everyday, and powerful means of drawing boundaries around what is deemed important to learn by elders—is part and parcel of how many people inside and outside school walls think that learning commences.

Escaping Museum Boundaries

Unlike many younger patrons of the Bedford Museum, adolescent visitors were not so easily engaged by the multiple learning strategies used, such as having them act out kinesthetic scenarios. For example, standing around a museum object depicting a shaman transforming into a jaguar, middle school students stared blankly into space or giggled and poked fun at a docent who was attempting to involve them in a mock transformation. In this case, which was far from an isolated one, the adolescents escaped the museum education practices by simply turning their attention away from the docent, and perhaps most interesting given the scenario, by transforming the situation into one in which they were in control of the mockery. In this vein, later Lakesha, their teacher, remarked,

> I think that the docent got a little discouraged in the beginning [laughs]. They did this whole meditative thing, when they were supposed to be, to try to pretend like they were turning into some kind of animal. And it didn't work out for them [laughs].

Indeed, the docents' expectations of capturing adolescents' interest in an object by having them perform dramatic simulations seemed rather ridiculous to the savvy youth and their teacher. Nonetheless, when the same transformation museum object was encountered without the docent-led engagement strategy by Bishop and Flo aka Mic, another adolescent participant in the study, their transaction was different, giving a hint of what might engage some adolescent museum visitors:

> Flo aka Mic: [with excitement] That looks like Kurtis, the curly dog! It reminds me of CatDog on Nickelodeon. Or he looks like Stitch from that movie.
>
> Bishop: It's weird; it looks like a cheetah and something else. A man behind it, like a sorcerer type.

As shown in this brief example, when adolescents were outside the purview of the museum educators and teachers, they often created meaning from their observations that made sense in their worlds of popular culture. During the study, this was borne out in other instances in which adolescents touring the museum outside the auspices of teachers and docents connected Bedford museum objects to anime, Harry Potter, and computer games. In fact, this is but a small instance of how participants in the study attempted to create new possibilities and connections that escape the typical confines of being receptacles of expert knowledge. It is no small point that when Flo aka Mic returned to school, he carefully sketched what had captured his attention in the museum: an image of the transformation object that he labeled "CatDog."

To be sure, creating from the everyday and the familiar was a principal strategy of escape both in and out of school for the adolescents in the investigation, as they crafted images, raps, rhymes, and projects that drew in large part from youth popular culture, such as Flo aka Mic's CatDog. It was this very act of creation from the mundane, an approach quite familiar to many contemporary artists, that seemed to capture many of the adolescent participants' attention instead of the museum objects dubbed by Bedford Museum educators as "sparkling" and "glorious." For instance, after the museum tour Flo aka Mic reflected,

> The museum was kinda weird and at the same time it was kinda boring. At the same time it was kinda interesting too. The interesting part is how creative they were—the people who lived in Egypt, in Africa, and West Africa and South Africa. And how they did the things they did, the way they used the different symbols instead of depending on someone else. How they spread their minds, they spread their minds as Africans, and they show people that they're not afraid; to show people they're not ashamed of what they do.

A Public Library's Subtle Boundaries

Museums and public libraries share a common goal in their efforts to entice young people to explore multiple forms of literacy in rather informal learning environments—informal at least when compared to school libraries. Unlike time spent in school libraries, public libraries and museums do not regulate adolescents' passage from one room to another through the ringing of bells. Nor do public libraries and museums attempt to regulate what adolescents read, at least not to the extent that school libraries do (Dressman, 1997). Moreover, it is rare in public libraries and museums to see "no talking" signs posted or strict dress codes enforced. Young people are well aware of the relaxed norms operating in both of these outside spaces, particularly in those that cater to youth groups through specially trained docents or youth librarians.

Because public libraries are community settings where interactions with adults are not governed by the same set of conditions operating in the more formal institution of schooling, one might expect to find youth treated not as separate from the adult world (e.g., not as less knowledgeable or as having less discerning tastes than their elders) but as individuals valued for knowing and desiring certain things relevant to their particular situations and surroundings (Amit-Talai & Wulff, 1995). Not so, or at least this was not the case in the public library where Donna (coauthor) and her colleagues (Alvermann et al., 2001) worked as facilitators and researchers of a weekly media club project, which was designed to engage reluctant adolescent readers in multimodal literacies that spanned a range of texts (print, visual, aural, and digital). Assisting on the project were Cathy, the young adult (YA) librarian, and her assistant, Joan.

Although welcoming young people's use of the YA section of the public library, Cathy held certain views pertaining to such use that differed in subtle but important ways from the preferred literacy practices of the youth who frequented her library's boundaries. For example, during an interview conducted halfway through the study, Cathy explained that she appreciated fully why young people needed to socialize, particularly because she was the mother of a very sociable high school student. Cathy pointed out that socializing in the YA section of the library was fine as long as it was "appropriate" socializing, that is, "kids hanging out and talking with friends in a way that would lead them to read a book they might have seen [hanging] on a wall while they were conversing."

That she had not communicated her definition of appropriate socializing to the participants in our media club was somewhat puzzling, especially given her clearly stated policy on e-mailing and instant messaging: Two people seated side by side in the library were not to use the YA section's new bank of computers for e-mailing or instant messaging one another. When queried about the reason for this policy, Cathy explained that she wanted her young patrons to think of computers as tools for completing homework assignments or researching a topic. A subtle but important point in both of these related instances is that reading and school literacy can be isolated from young people's larger set of literacy practices.

Equally subtle was Cathy's approach to handling issues of censorship. Although she stated that she was personally offended by rap lyrics that were uncomplimentary of young women, she also noted that her training as a librarian made her hesitant to censor what young people read on the Web. Citing literature on the ineffectiveness of Cyber Patrol, an Internet censorship filter that students across the country know how to disable without any difficulty, Cathy noted,

> So because it's part—because I know rap music's part of the culture, it would be pretty silly if I were to say, "I'm sorry, there's no rap music." I mean I could say that but it would be pretty silly because if they weren't getting the lyrics off the library [computers]...they'd certainly [still] be listening. If it's a cultural kind of thing, then I'm not going to say something.

Cathy's antidote for combating offensive Web lyrics involved her assistant, Joan, in the development of a home page on the YA section's computers:

> What we're working on in the library...and it's hard 'cause we're incredibly understaffed...but it's just critical that we develop our own website suggestions on our YA home page. The trick there is...if you give them too many websites to choose from, then they're not going to choose any. So the trick is to have just enough websites to get into homework, to get into entertainment, to get into things. But again, you know, you go into an appropriate website and then they've got links to third party websites that you can't vet.

That we observed the young people in our media club project rarely if ever using the YA homepage will come as no surprise. When it was suggested to Joan that the origami links and the book display nearby that featured some origami artwork were not tapping young people's interests, but that links to DragonBall Z and Pokémon might be welcomed, she replied that she had plans to build a young adult CD collection (though by the time the project ended several months later, there was no sign of the collection).

Joan also indicated that most of her energy was going into a poetry and coffee night to celebrate National Poetry Month in April, an event at which young people would read their poetry. She added that, unfortunately, none of the youth in the media club project were participating because "they were not too much into reading." When the researchers mentioned that Peaches and Lorraine (the self-chosen pseudonyms of two girls in the media club) were interested in writing poetry, Joan seemed incredulous but thanked them for the information and said she would talk to the girls about it. To the knowledge of Donna and colleagues, Peaches and Lorraine did not participate in poetry night. Again, the YA staff gave a subtle but persistent message that only certain kinds of literacy practices, such as reading self-authored poetry, counted when it came to the time they spent planning and preparing materials for young people's use.

Escaping a Public Library's Subtle Boundaries

The potential for socializing in the YA section of the public library that played host to Donna and her colleagues' media club project opened up new social spaces, especially for youth who were known to be reluctant readers and who did not always fit comfortably in more structured learning environments. It was a site at which officially sanctioned literacy practices could be negotiated and even redefined from time to time. Although such lines of escape were transitory and largely accomplished without the YA librarian's knowledge, this was not always the case. For example, one escape in particular (captured in Donna's field notes) stands out:

> Seymour Butts (a self-chosen pseudonym) was sitting at a computer engaged in instant messaging with several online friends. This was considered a taboo activity in the YA section of the library on the first floor, though not in the adult section on the second floor. With his legs draped over the side of a chair, Seymour seemed oblivious to all that surrounded him with one exception: the messages flowing constantly across the computer screen. Occasionally, he would laugh out loud as he continued to keyboard in his responses. Interestingly, his computer screen faced where Cathy, the YA librarian, was sitting at the reference desk less than 15 feet away. She never said a thing despite the fact that when the four new computers had arrived earlier in the month she had put in a request for four computer carrels that formed an L-shape around her desk.

Censorship plagued the media club project from the start. Although Cathy had said at the start of the media club project that she opposed censorship generally, six months later during an interview with Donna she qualified her earlier statement, saying that "parents do not monitor what kids are doing at the library so [I have] to." Joan agreed, saying that if she (Joan) did not step in she would feel as if she would be morally violating her responsibilities as an adult in the YA section. It was Seymour, with his choice of pseudonyms, who once again tested the waters. When he told Margaret Hagood, one of the facilitators of the media club project, that he wanted to be called Seymour Butts, he fell over laughing. Margaret told him that she couldn't see us talking about this with others, but he was adamant, claiming that the name was from *The Simpsons* television program and made sense to him because "the whole media club project was about stuff they like." When Margaret told him we could go with just plain Seymour within the media club environment, he said that was fine. But more to the point (and in retrospect), was it the case that Seymour Butts had cleverly engineered an escape from one of the more subtle boundaries (soft censorship) at work in the YA library space? By providing Margaret with a rationale she found difficult to refute, had he indeed stood the "moral responsibility of adults" issue on its head? We believe so, and the fact that neither Cathy nor Joan ever questioned him about his choice of pseudonyms supports our thinking on this point.

One final escape story is worth telling. As noted earlier, Peaches and Lorraine were not on Joan's invited list for the poetry and coffee night scheduled in honor of National Poetry Month. That didn't stop Margaret, however, from encouraging the two girls to continue their interest in writing poetry. In an e-mail with the subject header "How is your poetry book coming?" Margaret wrote,

> Hi Peaches, I have a couple of poems to give to you. They reminded me of the poetry you write. I was looking through a book of poetry and came across a poem by Nikki Giovanni and a poem by Langston Hughes. I thought that they would be interesting to share together because they both express different emotions about how the authors feel. I would like to know what you think of them. Do you think that these two poets think like you? Do you have any poems that you would like to share? Write back. :) Margaret

Margaret's e-mail was posted on Wednesday at 8:46 p.m. At 4:41 p.m. the next day, while sitting at a computer in the YA section of the library, Peaches wrote,

> Dear Margaret,
> I didn't read the poems but I know it was good

That was it: a one-sentence response to an eight-sentence query. Nothing more was ever said or written about the two poems. Another clever escape engineered this time by a young girl who indeed "was not too much into reading"? We think so.

How Our Data *May* Inform School Literacy Practices

The tentativeness in the wording of this section's heading is deliberate. The amount and kind of data that we could present in a chapter with restrictions on its length do not fully warrant the implications we draw here. Yet we do draw them in the spirit of hoping to start a conversation motivated in part by the questions that appear at the end of the chapter.

Connecting With Popular Culture

Flo aka Mic's engagement with the museum object when no educators were present and Seymour's ability to relax while instant messaging with friends, though in full view of the YA librarian's monitoring station, suggest to us the importance of valuing young people's expressions of independence through the use of commonly shared knowledge about popular culture. The connections that Flo aka Mic and Bishop made between a museum art object and popular culture might seem on first appearance rather unrelated and inconsequential to literacy teaching and learning, especially given the No Child Left Behind era in which we live. Yet we submit that it is exactly in times such as the present—when state and national policymakers are attempting to constrain literacy practices to particular boundaries of strategies and academic performance standards—that literacy educators and researchers need grounding in what counts as relevant literacy practices from a student perspective.

Borrowing from Flo aka Mic and Seymour, rather than be afraid and ashamed of local, everyday literacies associated with popular culture, we should look to young people for clues of escape, similar to those Guattari (1989/2000) identified in youth groups that embrace transnational trends for resisting and transforming certain aspects of their worlds. Such local, frugal chariots of literacy (Dickinson, 1894/2004) over time have "pranced" through various forms and deliveries, such as scripted reading programs. By noticing the attitudes and practices of artists and the media that capture local attention, we think that there are opportunities for educators, as well as youth, to escape (at times) highly regulated pedagogies and the boundaries they create. For instance, some portion of a school week might be deregulated so that young people could independently engage with texts that lead to creative literacy productions deemed so vital in some corners of society, and yet sorely missing in many schools.

Complicating, Not Simplifying

Although some who read the previous paragraphs may dismiss them out of hand, claiming perhaps that this approach is too progressively oriented or student centered, even bordering on the romantic, we would argue otherwise. Our experiences in working with youth outside school have taught us the importance of complicating what we view as overly simplistic theories about reading and writing that get taken up in the name of advancing literacy achievement and high school graduation rates. Although we do not intend to diminish the importance of academic literacy, at the same time we stand firm in our conviction that studying young people's literacy practices from the outside can produce new kinds of evidence that are potentially useful to teachers, supervisors, administrators, and other educators working within the school literacy environment. Such evidence may serve as an invitation to explore the boundaries within which teachers operate, as well as to point out escape routes available to them and the students placed in their care. By viewing relations of power as pliable and answerable in many respects to local constituencies, teachers and school administrators might consider looking to parents for support of literacy practices that their youngsters value and engage in outside of school.

"Doing" Museum, Library, and School Literacies

In negotiating the various patterns associated with being a particular kind of museum docent or a particular kind of YA librarian, Meredith and Cathy, respectively, called attention to the typically unmarked and invisible ways of displaying (Goffman, 1976) or "doing" (West & Zimmerman, 1987, p. 137) particular kinds of museum and public library literacies. The negotiation processes in which these two women engaged as authority figures responsible for the education of young visitors who were ostensibly dependent on their services also called attention to several existing and shifting relations of power. For example, when Cathy expressed to Donna her expectation that "appropriate socializing" among youth in the YA section of the library should in some way relate to reading books, she was marking a subtle boundary to which participants in the media club project seemed oblivious. For whatever reason, she had not communicated this expectation to them.

On the other hand, Cathy made explicit her policy of forbidding two friends sitting side by side in the library from e-mailing or instant messaging one another, but she did not enforce it on a regular basis. In fact, the tacit agreement between Cathy and Seymour Butts regarding instant messaging provided an easy escape, one that on the surface at least seemed akin to the various arrangements worked out between Meredith and the student visitors who resisted engaging in what they deemed childish dramatic play in the museum. With or without Meredith's approval, the young people in Jonathan's study simply wandered off to pursue their own interests. That escapes such as these are less likely tolerated in schools goes without saying. What is worth commenting on, however, is this: "Doing" school literacies is in no way superior to "doing" literacies in other settings. Rather, what we have tried to show through our separate studies is the futility of partitioning youth's literacy practices into in-school and out-of-school spaces.

For as we have written elsewhere (Alvermann & Eakle, 2007), to reify distinctions between in-school and out-of-school literacies serves mainly to separate these literacies from the very spaces that give them meaning and make them worth pursuing. It also limits what teachers and researchers can learn from students' literacy experiences, at least to the extent that students are willing to share their perceptions of those experiences. Listening to and observing youth as they communicate their familiarity with multiple texts across space, place, and time can provide valuable insights into how to approach both instruction and research—insights that might otherwise be lost or taken for granted in our rush to categorize literacy practices as either in-school or out-of-school and thus either worthy of our attention or not.

Questions for Reflection

1. How might studies such as the two described here produce evidence that will be useful to teachers, supervisors, administrators, and other educators working within a school literacy environment?

2. What are the power relations operating when attempts are made to partition adolescents' literacy practices into in- and out-of-school spaces?

3. To what extent should elements of popular culture that youth deem important be used in literacy education in and out of school?

Donna E. Alvermann is university-appointed Distinguished Research Professor of Language and Literacy Education at the University of Georgia, Athens, Georgia, USA. Her research focuses on adolescent literacy, especially as it intersects with young people's interests in digital media and popular culture. She can be reached at dalverma@uga.edu. A. Jonathan Eakle is Assistant Professor and Reading Program Director at Johns Hopkins University School of Education, Baltimore, Maryland, USA, where he teaches cross-cultural studies and literacy courses. His research addresses how young people use multiple literacies for learning, pleasure, and resistance in classrooms and out-of-school settings. He may be contacted at jeakle@jhu.edu.

REFERENCES

Alvermann, D.E., & Eakle, A.J. (2007). Dissolving learning boundaries: The doing, re-doing, and undoing of school. In D. Thiessen & A. Cook-Sather (Eds.), *International handbook of student experience in elementary and secondary school* (pp. 143–166). New York: Springer.

Alvermann, D.E., Hagood, M.C., Heron, A., Hughes, P., Williams, K., & Yoon, J.C. (2001, April 14). *Looking at the "critical" in critical media literacy: Are adolescents critical?* Paper presented at the annual meeting of the American Educational Research Association, Seattle, WA.

Amit-Talai, V., & Wulff, H. (Eds.). (1995). *Youth cultures: A cross-cultural perspective.* New York: Routledge.

Collins, J., & Blot, R.K. (2003). *Literacy and literacies: Texts, power, and identity.* Cambridge, England: Cambridge University Press.

Deleuze, G. (2000). *Foucault* (S. Hand, Ed. & Trans.). Minneapolis: University of Minnesota Press. (Original work published 1986)

Dickinson, E. (2004). There is no frigate like a book [online]. In J. Dempsey (Ed.), *Poetry X.* (Original work published 1894) Retrieved July 23, 2006, from http://poetry.poetryx.com/poets/45

Dressman, M. (1997). Congruence, resistance, liminality: Reading and ideology in three school libraries. *Curriculum Inquiry, 27,* 267–316.

Eakle, A.J. (2005). *Literacy in the art museum: A theatre of values.* Unpublished doctoral dissertation, University of Georgia, Athens.

Eakle, A.J. (in press). Museum literacy, art, and space study. In D. Lapp, S.B. Heath, & J. Flood (Eds.), *Handbook of research on teaching literacy through the communicative and visual arts* (Vol. 2). Mahwah, NJ: Erlbaum.

Fisch, K. (2006, August 15). *Did you know?* [digital online multimedia]. Retrieved February 14, 2007, from http://thefischbowl.blogspot.com/2006/08/did-you-know.html

Foucault, M. (1977). *Discipline and punish* (A.M. Sheridan Smith, Trans.). New York: Vintage Books. (Original work published 1975)

Goffman, E. (1976). Gender display. *Studies in the Anthropology of Visual Communication, 3,* 69–77.

Guattari, F. (2000). *The three ecologies*. New Brunswick, NJ: Athlone Press. (Original work published 1989)

Hull, G.A., & Schultz, K. (2002). *School's out! Bridging out-of-school literacies with classroom practice*. New York: Teachers College Press.

No Child Left Behind Act of 2001, Pub. L. No. 107-110, 115 Stat. 1425 (2002). Retrieved June 25, 2006, from http://www.ed.gov/policy/elsec/leg/esea02/index. html

Paris, S.G. (Ed.). (2002). *Perspectives on object-centered learning in museums*. Mahwah, NJ: Erlbaum.

West, C., & Zimmerman, D.H. (1987). Doing gender. *Gender & Society, 1,* 125–151.

CHAPTER 5

Immaturity and the Struggling Teen

Carol M. Santa

HIGHLIGHTS

- Beyond the broad spectrum of clinical and pedagogical diagnosis, the root problem with many struggling adolescent learners is personal immaturity.
- Too many strategies for helping struggling adolescent learners address the symptoms of immaturity but not the condition itself.
- Real strides can be made by pedagogical approaches that entail the following:
  - Containment and structure
  - Adult–child relationships and adequate recognition
  - A theoretical framework and strategies for learning

Ten years ago my husband and I, along with another professional couple, started a school for struggling teenagers. We remortgaged our nearly paid off house, bought a run-down cattle ranch 40 miles out of town, and started Montana Academy, a boarding school for defiant, shut-down adolescents.

Students enter our school with 3-inch-thick files of educational tests documenting their academic failures and inabilities to "do" school, as well as evaluations specifying various psychiatric disorders. They have been labeled with a myriad of diagnoses such as Asperger's syndrome, bipolar disorders, anxiety, attention deficit, and oppositional defiant disorders. Many have been classified as dyslexic or learning disabled. They have received a plethora of diverse treatments—stimulants, antidepressants, mood stabilizers, individualized education programs, special

Adolescent Literacy Instruction: Policies and Promising Practices edited by Jill Lewis and Gary Moorman. © 2007 by the International Reading Association.

education classes, tutors, and therapy. Although these symptoms are often real and at times require pharmacological interventions, we have come to believe that treating the symptomatic manifestations is not all that is required to get these kids back on track.

Instead, we consider struggling teens as expressing a global failure of personality development. Across all symptomatic diagnoses, they exhibit a general immaturity that extends along multiple dimensions—emotional, social, cognitive/academic, and even moral. In brief, we have a large percentage of adolescents who are simply not ready to take on the tasks required of youngsters at the cusp of becoming adults. From what we have observed, the gap between internal maturation and external demands of school and society leads directly to many of the diagnoses and symptom clusters exhibited in struggling adolescents. Appropriate treatment both in school and society requires not simply addressing the symptoms, but also repairing the gap in maturation.

The Immature Adolescent

The floundering teens who come to Montana Academy have failed to develop an internal solidity and confidence. They are easily overwhelmed and avoid challenges. They have difficulty delaying gratification and lack frustration tolerance. They are distractible, impulsive, and self-centered. Moral issues of right and wrong are a matter of whether or not they will get caught or offend a primitive loyalty to friends, even though such friendships are superficial and ever-changing. The world revolves around them. They have a childlike sense of the future, reflecting a quality of magical thinking. They talk about far-flung goals—"I wanna be a physicist or a rock star"—without any thought that their current behavior has anything to do with a future goal. In other words, they think and act more like toddlers than successful adolescents.

We also find that their approach to school lacks maturity. If they don't like their teacher, they won't try. They have difficulty turning in assignments and tend to blame others for their lack of success. They shut down, functioning far below their intellectual potential. They are disengaged and bored in class. They exhibit profound deficiencies of executive functioning such as planning, organizing, and self-monitoring. These dysfunctional social, psychological, and educational behaviors camouflage the underlying problem of general immaturity.

Many of our students have difficulties with reading comprehension and learning strategies. They are unaware of how text is organized and don't know how to organize information while reading. In addition, they have difficulty distinguishing essential from nonessential information. Moreover, they seem unaware of their inability to comprehend, and they lack a repertoire of strategies for fixing up any perceived comprehension problems. These readers typically become frustrated and give up. They lack task persistence and knowledge about how to go about learning. The learning behaviors of our immature 15- and 16-year-olds are more typical of third and fourth graders displaying a younger child's nonstrategic approach.

Meeting the Needs of the Immature Adolescent

Montana Academy offers many advantages for helping adolescents mature that cannot be duplicated in the public school system. Our academic classes are small—from 4 to 10 students. Our schedule is organized around 12-week blocks with students only taking three academic classes and a study hall. We have highly competent teachers with exceptional content backgrounds and, perhaps even more important, the ability to connect with our students. With two psychiatrists and six doctoral-level clinical psychologists on staff, our students receive in-depth individual and group therapy. We have specialized groups for students dealing with adoption, divorce, grief, trauma, and substance abuse. Students also participate in experiential education—they ride horses, fish, play hockey, canoe, mountain climb, and ski.

We have a system of student accountability and structure that I would have envied as a public school teacher. If students don't perform in our school, they do not get free time. Instead of riding horses, they are required to take additional tutorial classes. Rather than skiing or hiking in Glacier Park, they might be restricted to the campus on the weekends, or in severe cases they might not get to go home for the winter holiday.

Along with accountability is an increase in structure. Students have a predictable and relatively simple life schedule that helps them organize and accomplish priority tasks. Many dangerous distractions such as television, cell phones, cars, and drugs are not available. Reading hour occurs nightly with everyone on campus—including staff—reading books of choice. Students have access only to healthy food, participate in daily sports programs, and are in bed by 10 p.m. Phone time is limited to weekly calls to families. Finally, the entire program of care is integrated:

teachers, therapists, parents, and supervisory staff communicate regularly, and what happens in one domain of life is addressed in all areas.

Even though many of these contextual advantages are difficult to replicate in the daily lives of adolescents in public school settings, we have learned some general principles about helping teens grow up that apply beyond the cattle guard marking the entrance to our school. Although these principles are relevant for anyone dealing with teens, they become even more important for helping struggling teens mature and develop a view of themselves more congruent with the tasks of a successful adolescent. These principles involve (1) containment and structure, (2) adult–child relationships and accurate recognition, and (3) strategies for learning.

Containment and Structure

Struggling teens lack an internal personality structure to manage their lives. Adolescence is the time for students to get ready to run their own lives. But if students' internal structures are insufficient, they feel overwhelmed and out of control emotionally and behaviorally. In most situations, they are too immature to manage school tasks. Their grades are poor; they don't do homework; they act as if they don't care.

Students must first be contained so they are safe to deal with tasks necessary for growing up. Structure produces predictability and simplifies the distractions intruding on their ability to organize themselves internally. Demuth and Brown (2004) have shown that the degree of parental involvement, supervision, monitoring, and closeness are each independent preventive factors for delinquent behavior. Simplifying and structuring their world aids teens in doing cognitive and emotional tasks.

Similarly, consistent classroom procedures and routines provide security, particularly for struggling, immature teenagers. For example, Wang, Haertel, and Walberg (1993) in a comprehensive review of literature examining factors related to student achievement found that classroom management had a pronounced effect on success. Students do better in classrooms where instructional routines are explicit and where expectations and consequences are clear. Struggling, immature teens can't manage chaotic, unstructured school situations.

Creating containment means establishing clear and consistent routines for behavior in the hallways, in the classroom, and in the lunchroom. It means explicit rules for respecting one another, for turning in class assignments, for earning grades, for doing homework, and so on.

Having consistent expectations and consequences across classrooms and all facets of the school creates an envelope of safety and containment.

We have learned some other commonsense notions about containment and structure that have general applicability to any school situation. For example, keep routines and rules simple, straightforward, and limited to critical factors. Too many regulations and procedures dealing with every aspect of school life become overwhelming, and consequently students won't take them seriously. Decide what rules are critical and communicate these to every part of the school community. Determine clear, consistent, and publicly understood consequences for infringements. When students break rules, keep anger and disapproval at a minimum. Don't attempt to shame, instill guilt, and make kids feel like bad kids. Instead, apply the consequence: "I feel badly about what you did, but you understand the consequence for this is.... It's the rule."

Dufour and Eaker (1998) talk about the "loose-tight" leadership style. Tight means having clear routines, expectations, and consequences, but the approach is loose in terms of allowing students to make appropriate choices. Students need opportunities to make appropriate and inappropriate choices within an environment where they feel safe to learn from mistakes.

Adult–Child Relationships and Accurate Recognition

Nurturing the development of immature teenagers begins with positive human relationships. The most important lesson we have learned from our students now seems so obvious. Positive human relationships are as important or perhaps even more important for immature teens as for the chronologically young child. Even though struggling teens often appear indifferent to adult attention or recognition, this attitude is simply a defense that camouflages a deep need for adult mentorship and modeling.

In our school, therapy involves sorting out past issues and teaching specific skills, but primarily entails an accurate mirroring relationship where students begin to understand who they are. Students learn skills for dealing with and managing emotions, along with direct instruction on practical coping skills. Therapy depends not only on specific ideas and issues that are uncovered, but also on engaging the student in a relationship. Therapy is a process that involves teaching skills but also creates a laboratory for exploring oneself. Students discover new concepts about themselves and apply these new emotional skills in the context of a relationship, a relationship based on accurate recognition and unconditional acceptance. In this relationship students are encouraged to develop more accurate ideas of who they are.

The academic part of our school involves the same mixture as therapy. The student learns specific content and process in the context of a relationship with a teacher. This relationship is less important when a child is emotionally stable, secure, and mature enough to understand the need to acquire present knowledge for future purposes. High school students are expected to read their assignments, take notes from lectures, and participate in learning information. But many students lack the maturity and strategic skills to perform these learning tasks. They depend on the holding context of a personal relationship with a teacher and the explicit teaching of skills and strategies for being a successful student. As part of the process of growing up, young children perform in order to please others. Then as they attain a more sophisticated self, they begin to perform for their own self-satisfaction.

Recognition must be accurate as opposed to cheerleading. We don't tell students they are doing well if they aren't. We're honest. An example of what I mean happened recently at Montana Academy in Phil Jones's Writing Workshop class. Students do formal presentations of their weekly writing assignments. Lila never felt comfortable presenting her ideas. Each week Phil invited her to present, but she always refused. At the beginning of class, Phil decided to read excerpts of two student papers displaying exceptional imagery. Lila's paper was one of them. When she realized that Phil was reading her work, she pulled her sweatshirt up over her head. Phil read her paper aloud, talked about why the imagery worked, chuckling at the humorous content. He recognized her work specifically and honestly. He didn't cheerlead with global statements about doing a nice job. The next week Lila stepped to the front of the class and presented her own work. Instead of making a big deal out of it, Phil quietly nodded his head, listened, and again commented on specifics in her paper that worked. His recognition was honest. He does not do backflips over less than adequate papers or when a student finally turns in a late assignment. Instead, he notes the specific accomplishments and also gives gentle, clear feedback on specific ways to improve.

Accurate recognition is more than just providing students with feedback about schoolwork. It has to do with students knowing they are being understood. For example, recently Sam slouched into Jenny Stone's art class and pressed his head down on his desk, refusing to engage with anyone in class. Instead of making an issue out of it during class, Jenny asked him to stay for a few minutes afterward. She initiated a conversation: "What's going on? Obviously something is happening with you right now that keeps you from doing class today. Help me understand." Sam spent the next five minutes talking about the events and feelings in his life that led to his behavior. Jenny closed the conversation with a remark: "Well, I get it and hear how you are working through this. But disengaging from class is not going to make life easier for you. I want the best for you and need for you to pay attention tomorrow. In the meantime, let me know how I might be helpful." Jenny recognized what led to his behavior, but also let him know her expectations. The next day Sam turned in his first drawing.

These examples fit exactly what researchers have documented about the effects of teacher–student relationships. In a meta-analysis of more than 100 studies, Marzano and Marzano (2003) found that teacher–student relationships are key to effective classroom management. Teachers who had strong relationships with their students had far fewer discipline problems and related issues than those not having high-quality relationships. Wentzel (1997, 1998) has shown that perceived positive support and caring from teachers is directly related to positive attitudes toward school, academic effort, and achievement.

A challenge for public schools is to create situations in which students have opportunities to build relationships with significant adults. A study panel from the National Research Council (2004) has identified key features conducive to building student connectedness. Some of these are ensuring that every student has an advisor, forming multidisciplinary teacher and student teams, developing mentoring programs, providing service learning and community service projects, and using a variety of instructional methods. Districts can offer some inservice support to staff, emphasizing the importance of structure and containment as well as clinical help in understanding constructive ways to recognize students so they begin to imagine themselves as successful and competent.

Strategies for Learning

Struggling students don't do well in classrooms where learning expectations are vague and when assigning is synonymous with teaching. Students having difficulty in school need to know what they are expected to learn and the learning tools for meeting these expectations. The traditional telling and assigning approach works if a student has already acquired the ability to form abstractions, relate new information to previous knowledge, organize, and communicate effectively. But when students are immature and have a long history of school failure, they must be explicitly taught the skills that facilitate learning.

Most of our students start to become successful in school within a few months of being at Montana Academy. Although this shift in academic performance can be attributed to a mixture of factors—an integrated therapeutic and academic program, teacher competence, the building of student–teacher relationships, small classes, and the limited number of courses students take simultaneously—it also has to do with how we teach. Several features that define our classroom practices have general application. Students know what they are expected to learn, and assessment targets are clearly defined. Students internalize a theoretical framework so they understand why learning strategies are essential to their own success, and learning how to learn occurs in every class—including music and art.

Clear Learning Targets and Assessments

We make the purposes and the assessments of our lessons clear so that students know what they are to accomplish. When teaching a single lesson or a unit of study, teachers begin by explaining the deep understandings they hope students take away from the lesson. They post these essential learnings as questions visibly displayed in the room. Teachers also let students know at the beginning of the lesson the content of the assessment used to measure deep understandings. Posting assessments is even more effective when teachers also engage students in a discussion about the criteria for succeeding with an assessment. This is particularly true with essay tests. Knowing what to expect and what the assessments are before beginning a unit of study can help struggling teens attain a sense of control of their own learning.

Theoretical Framework for Learning

For the past 20 years I have worked with a number of talented secondary teachers to create a staff development program (http://www.project criss.com) to help students become better readers, writers, and learners (Santa, Havens, & Valdes, 2004). We have learned that strategic teaching is more than just showing students how to employ learning strategies. Students also need to develop a framework for understanding themselves as learners. Just as in the therapeutic program where students learn how a developmental model of human behavior helps to explain and change their behavior, a theoretical model about what it means to be a mature learner provides struggling teens with the foundation to examine and change their own learning.

The framework centers on the concept of metacognition. Students begin to see that metacognition, or the process by which individuals assess and understand their own learning, provides the overarching, executive process underlying the active process of comprehension.

We incorporate information about metacognition as part of regular content instruction, and teachers have developed instructional approaches to make this esoteric concept accessible to their students. They begin by explaining that metacognition can be thought of as having two key elements: self-awareness about the state of one's learning and strategy knowledge. Then they help students through modeling and reflection to understand why these two elements are fundamental to their success as learners.

Teachers show students how to watch over their learning as part of content instruction. They explain that metacognition involves self-checking one's learning—it's about becoming more aware of how one's learning is progressing. This awareness aspect of metacognition is critical because many immature learners don't realize the need to self-check their own learning. They unconsciously see the job of monitoring learning as belonging to someone outside of themselves, such as a teacher or parent. The mature learner has taken on this self-monitoring responsibility.

Class discussions then focus on the second part of being metacognitive—the strategies for going after meaning and for repairing comprehension breakdowns. Not only do mature learners self-monitor, but they have a repertoire of deliberate strategies to ensure their understanding and learning.

To help students with self-awareness and strategy knowledge, teachers demonstrate and talk about the underlying processes characterizing mature learners. Successful learners engage their background knowledge, set learning purposes, and are actively persistent. They don't give up when learning becomes challenging. They understand the importance of writing and discussion, and know how to impose structure on information so that it becomes memorable. As a staff we identified these as component processes of being metacognitive, and we include practical ways to address these processes in every class.

Background knowledge. For example, teachers help their students understand how information becomes memorable and useful in relation to what an individual knows. They show students how to "prime" background knowledge and build goals or purposes for reading. For example, Rick Stern launched a social studies unit on the 1930s with the following type of questions and comments: "What do you know about the Great Depression? Develop questions or predictions based on the title and what you already know. Page through the assignment and think about what you might learn about this era of history. Why is it important to consider your background knowledge before reading?"

Imposing structure. We teach students about the importance of organizing or transforming information. Teachers model flexible ways to structure information. Students learn how to take notes, to underline selectively, and to transform information into hierarchies of meaning. Teachers remind their students, "How are you going to organize this information to make it more meaningful to you? What organizing format makes the most sense—a chart, two-column notes, a concept map, picture notes? Why do we need to impose structure on information to remember it?"

Active persistence. We help students understand that learning takes work. Most immature learners don't know what it means to work, to be actively persistent. They think that learning means glossing through a text or passively viewing a video.

Teachers model what active engagement and learning effort looks and feels like. During a lecture, Jack Cesarone stops and instructs his biology students to turn to a partner and ask a question about what they have heard. His students read scientific articles and respond by drawing, developing oral and written summaries, and writing study questions. Throughout he engages his students in conversations: "How are you going to persist in learning this information? Why does learning take work?"

Discussion. Discussion comes naturally to adolescents, but few realize it can provide the basis for learning and understanding. We help students internalize the value of discussion through demonstrations. They might read several paragraphs and then talk about what they have just read to a partner. They learn to develop thoughtful questions to lead their own discussions. Students become aware that talking and communicating lead to deeper understanding. Talking helps learners become more aware of what they know.

Writing. Teachers help students understand why writing is essential to learning. For example, students keep daily journals in science classes. After listening to a brief lecture, students write about what they have learned or describe a specimen viewed through a microscope. Students share their writing in pairs or with the whole class. They talk about what writing does for them as a learner.

We help students become more metacognitive by demonstrating and talking about learning processes as part of teaching and learning: "Have you brought your background knowledge to this learning situation? What strategies are you using to organize information? Do they work? How are you going to check your own comprehension to make sure you are getting it? Are you able to communicate clearly through writing and talking about what you are learning?" Our goal is for students to become more responsible learners and to extend their knowledge about learning to new situations.

Closing Comments

Poor school performance characterizes many struggling teens. They arrive not knowing how to learn and with emotional blocks that keep them from succeeding. The various symptoms that adolescents exhibit are often related to a broad immaturity that leaves them unable to function appropriately in middle or high school, where instruction begins to focus on content. Unfortunately, the general assumption is that students are both mature enough and have the executive skills required to delay gratification, control impulses, plan, organize information, and have a realistic future orientation. In short, these children lack the emotional, psychological, and educational skills required of successful adolescents.

Our job at Montana Academy is the same as in schools everywhere: create environments that allow students to change their sense of self and begin to feel competent and empowered. We don't treat school failure as a primary underlying problem, but rather as a complex symptom that requires an integrated approach. All schools must focus first on containment and building a safe learning environment that entails supportive alliances with parents. Containment requires predictable structure, accountability, and communication. Second, we must establish caring, supportive adult teacher–student relationships to support students' emotional needs and develop a sense of belonging and commitment to school. Finally, we can improve academic competence and foster a new sense of capability by providing students with clear learning expectations and a theoretical framework for learning, and by directly teaching efficient skills for learning throughout the curriculum.

Questions for Reflection

1. Given the importance of adult–child relationships in addressing teenagers' immaturity, how might schools be structured to ensure that students have opportunities to build significant relationships with teachers and other staff?

2. How can schools use containment strategies without becoming too autocratic and controlling?

3. Why is the concept of metacognition so central to interventions designed to further the personal development of teenage students with pervasive immaturity problems?

Carol M. Santa is Co-Founder and Educational Director of Montana Academy, Marion, Montana, USA, a private residential school for troubled teenagers. She has been an elementary teacher, reading specialist, language arts coordinator, and university professor. She currently is Co-Director of Project CRISS, a program that focuses on reading, writing, and studying across the curriculum. Carol has authored more than 50 articles in professional journals and has either edited or authored a half dozen other professional books. In 1999–2000 she served as President of the International Reading Association. You may contact her at carols@montanaacademy.com.

REFERENCES

Demuth, S., & Brown, S. (2004). Family structure, family processes, and adolescent delinquency: The significance of parental absence versus parental gender. *Journal of Research in Crime and Delinquency, 41*(1), 58–81.

Dufour, R., & Eaker, R. (1998). *Professional learning communities at work: Best practices for enhancing student achievement*. Alexandria VA: Association for Supervision and Curriculum Development.

Marzano, R.J., & Marzano, J.S. (2003). The key to classroom management. *Educational Leadership, 61*(1), 6–13.

National Research Council. (2004). *Engaging schools: Fostering high school students' motivation to learn*. Washington DC: National Academies Press. Retrieved March 1, 2007, from http://www.nap.edu/books/0309084350/html

Santa, C., Havens, L., & Valdes, B. (2004). *Project CRISS: Creating independence through student-owned strategies* (3rd ed.). Dubuque, IA: Kendall-Hunt.

Wang, M.C., Haertel, G.D., & Walberg, H.J. (1993). Toward a knowledge base for school learning. *Review of Educational Research, 63,* 249–294.

Wentzel, K. (1997). Student motivation in middle school: The role of perceived pedagogical caring. *Journal of Educational Psychology, 89,* 411–419.

Wentzel, K. (1998). Social relationships and motivation in middle school: The role of parents, teachers, and peers. *Journal of Educational Psychology, 90,* 202–209.

CHAPTER 6

Creating a Schoolwide Literacy Initiative

Douglas Fisher

HIGHLIGHTS

- Schoolwide literacy initiatives are increasingly common in secondary schools.
- The seven basic components of an effective schoolwide literacy initiative are vision and mission, a literacy leadership team, opportunities for wide reading, systematic and consistent strategies, data-derived instruction, professional development, and administrative accountability.
- Engaging the entire faculty and staff is critical in getting a schoolwide literacy initiative started.

---

lvaro is a 16-year-old high school student who arrived illegally from rural Mexico when he was 13. He left his mother and father, grandparents, and some siblings behind. His family decided to send two of their children to the United States for a chance at a better education. Alvaro and his sister live in a garage off a one-bedroom house owned by his uncle. When he arrived, Alvaro spoke no English and his formal Spanish was limited. During the spring of his sophomore year, he learned that his grandmother had died. A short time later, in English class he wrote the poem in Figure 6.1.

How did Alvaro develop this level of language? What did his teachers and school do to advance him from English-language learner to a student who could participate in academic discourse? The answer may

---

Adolescent Literacy Instruction: Policies and Promising Practices edited by Jill Lewis and Gary Moorman. © 2007 by the International Reading Association.

Figure 6.1. Alvaro's Poem to His Grandmother

My Grandmother

Ooh my grandma, we share moments
Of pure love together, day and night
You stand by me; my size doesn't matter
What is going to happen in the future?
I know you are on heaven
I miss you, Grandma, more that I can say
By my side, I just wish to see you one last time
But you were in Mexico and I was in the U.S. when you died
I just wanted to hug you, kiss you
And have you say "I love you so much"
I make a promise for you
I will get a diploma for you
An outstanding student award in your name
And when I go back to Mexico,
I will put that diploma
On your tombstone and know we will be together
One more time
Not in a physical way, in an emotional way
It doesn't matter if you are in heaven and I'm here
Some day I will enjoy you in heaven
Then will be together for the rest of our days.

surprise you. Alvaro's school, Hoover High in San Diego, is part of growing network of secondary schools that have created schoolwide plans to address the literacy needs of their students.

A few years ago, schoolwide literacy initiatives at the secondary level were limited. For example, the California Department of Education's document *Strategic Teaching and Learning* (2000) contained just a single page on the subject. Today, however, ample journal articles and books are available that describe successful schoolwide literacy initiatives and provide guidance in creating them. The National Association of Secondary School Principals (2005), for instance, published a guide for middle and high school leaders that focuses on assessment, professional development, highly effective teachers, and intervention. The Association for Supervision and Curriculum Development also published a book, *Creating Literacy-Rich Schools for Adolescents* (Ivey & Fisher, 2006), which addresses the role of the English teacher, the role of the content teacher, wide reading, intervention, and schoolwide supports. Similarly, a report from the Carnegie Corporation of New York, published by the Alliance for Excellent Education (Biancarosa & Snow, 2004), identified teacher teams, leadership, and a comprehensive and coordinated literacy program as key components for improving adolescent literacy achievement.

Moreover, recent research has shown that schoolwide literacy initiatives have had a demonstrable impact on students in urban, suburban, and rural middle and high schools (Brozo & Hargis, 2003; Fisher, Frey, & Williams, 2002). In her three-year study of a 23,000-student district that implemented a literacy plan, Frey (2006) documented significant changes in student achievement. These results were realized during a period when the district grew in size and became increasingly diverse. Every middle and high school in this district was able to meet Adequate Yearly Progress (AYP) targets for all significant subgroups by the third year of implementation.

Components of Effective Schoolwide Literacy Initiatives

An effective schoolwide literacy initiative requires attention to a number of factors, including vision and mission, literacy leadership teams, opportunities for wide reading, systematic and consistent strategies, data-driven instruction, professional development, and administrative accountability.

Vision and Mission

But first, let's consider which middle and high schools might need a schoolwide literacy initiative. Would a school not meeting accountability targets benefit from a schoolwide focus on literacy? Would a school where the majority of students read at or above grade level also benefit? What about a school that educates large numbers of English-language learners, students living in poverty, or students with disabilities? And what about Lake Wobegon—a school where all students are above average? Given the evidence that literacy learning and achievement occurs on a continuum (Flood, Lapp, Squire, & Jensen, 2003), it seems reasonable to suggest that each of these schools would benefit from a schoolwide focus on literacy. As Farnan, Flood, and Lapp (1994) note, "there is no point on the continuum that denotes too much literacy or, for that matter, not enough. There are no good or bad places to be, only places informed by children's previous knowledge and construction of literacy concepts" (p. 136). As such, every middle and high school has the opportunity to facilitate increased literacy learning and achievement for their students.

For example, the director of secondary education in the district that Frey (2006) studied engaged faculty members with the comment, "We know that our students can read; the problem is they *don't* read" (p. 44). At Hoover High, the principal and teachers agreed that they wanted to be the "model school for all schools," not just a model for urban schools. To attain such a goal, they had to radically increase literacy achievement, attendance, and professional development opportunities.

Literacy Leadership Team

When the majority of teachers in a school agree on a vision that includes a schoolwide focus on literacy, the school is ready for action. A lot of work will then need to be done—plans developed, professional development organized, and peer coaching implemented, to name just a few (Cobb, 2005). The literacy leadership team, preferably an elected group of teachers from each department or unit within the school, becomes the "conscience of literacy leadership," as noted by one of the teacher leaders at Hoover High. The literacy leadership team needs regular access to the administration. The team also needs to establish itself as a group with leadership qualities, credibility, and clout. Literacy leadership teams typically meet at least bimonthly to accomplish their work. Team members continually remind teachers in the school that "it takes us all" (Fisher & Frey, 2006). They also develop systems of support to ensure that every teacher has the resources and skills necessary to realize the school's vision and mission for literacy.

Opportunities for Wide Reading

As an important part of the schoolwide plan, students need significant opportunities for self-selected reading. A time should be set aside each day for free, voluntary reading such as Silent Sustained Reading (e.g., Fisher, 2004; Ivey & Broaddus, 2001). Opportunities for reading may also be infused into every class, as in the form of independent reading time (Allen, 2000; Ivey, 2002). In this case, students are provided time to read widely from a list of books related to the topic under investigation. For example, during a unit of study on the eye in a biology classroom, Hoover's Mr. Bonine had students read a variety of sources, including those found in Table 6.1. These texts are diverse in many aspects— reading difficulty, topical focus, required background knowledge—but

Table 6.1. Texts About Eyes

Ballard, C. (2003). *Eyes: Injury, illness, and health.* Portsmouth, NH: Heinemann.

Biello, D. (2006, April 4). Scientists build liquid crystal bifocals. *Scientific American.* Retrieved November 23, 2006, from http://www.sciam.com/article.cfm?chanID=sa003&articleID=00099837-91AB-1431-91AB83414B7F0000

Cobb, V. (2002). *Open your eyes: Discover your sense of sight.* Brookfield, CN: Millbrook Press.

The human eye cannot spot the offside rule. (2004, December 30). *Science Daily.* Retrieved November 22 from http://www.sciencedaily.com/releases/2004/12/041219161332.htm

KidInfo Website: http://www.kidinfo.com/Health/Human_Body.html

Parker, S. (1991). *The eye and seeing.* New York: Franklin Watts.

Silverstein, A., Silverstein, V.B., & Nunn, L.S. (2001). *Seeing: Senses and sensors.* Brookfield, CT: Twenty-First Century Books.

Viegas, J. (2002). *The eye: Learning how we see.* New York: Rosen Publishing.

all contain key content vocabulary and allow his students to expand their knowledge of the process of seeing.

As noted by Fisher and Ivey (in press), opportunities for wide reading should not be limited to students who read at or above grade level. Reading intervention programs for students who struggle with reading and writing must also include opportunities for students to engage in real reading. Simply attending to basic skills or providing isolated skills instruction will not ensure that these students will read. They need occasions where they can apply what they learn to texts that they have chosen to read.

Systematic and Consistent Strategies

Across the country there are excellent content teachers who use evidence-based literacy strategies. Although such strategies differ when applied to science content versus art content, a general consistency must be maintained. Many students experience little or no consistency in the application of the strategies across the curriculum and thus do not develop habits for routinely using them.

As part of their schoolwide literacy focus, the teachers at Hoover High identified seven instructional strategies that they all agreed to implement (Fisher, Frey, & Williams, 2002). The goal was to ensure that these strategies became ingrained learning habits that students were able to use across the school day. Table 6.2 contains a list of the strategies selected by the staff at Hoover as well as a brief description of each.

It is important to note that these specific strategies are probably not the only reason for the increases in student achievement. Each of the strategies selected by the Hoover teachers has a research base, but the teachers could have chosen seven (or five or ten, for that matter) different strategies and achieved similar results. The key is that all of the teachers agreed to implement these seven strategies and to ensure that all students could apply these approaches to texts.

Table 6.2. Schoolwide Content Literacy Strategies

Anticipatory Activities	Strategies such as bellwork, anticipation guides, and KWL charts designed to activate background knowledge and make connections between what students already know and what they are learning. These strategies also help students see the relevance of the curriculum.
Cornell Note-Taking	Using split pages in which students take notes on the right side and identify key ideas on the left and write a summary at the bottom, this strategy improves listening comprehension as well as provides students with a study tool.
Graphic Organizers	Any number of tools for displaying information in visual form. Common graphic organizers include semantic webs, cause/effect charts, Venn diagrams, matrices, and flow charts.
Read-Alouds and Shared Readings	On a daily basis, the teacher reads aloud material connected with the content standards being taught. This short, 3- to 5-minute reading provides students with a context for learning, builds their background knowledge, improves vocabulary, and provides them with a fluent reading model.
Reciprocal Teaching	In groups of four, students read a piece of text and engage in a structured conversation in which they summarize, clarify, question, and predict. In doing so, they learn to use strategies that good readers use while reading for information.
Vocabulary Development	In addition to the incidental vocabulary learning that is done through read-alouds and anticipatory activities, students are taught specific content vocabulary words required of the discipline.

(continued)

Table 6.2. Schoolwide Content Literacy Strategies (continued)

Writing to Learn	These brief writing prompts provide students an opportunity clarify their understanding of the content as well as provide the teacher a glimpse into students thinking. As such, teachers know when reteaching or clarifications are necessary.

Source: Fisher, D., & Frey, N. (2006). Majority rules: A schoolwide literacy success. *Principal Leadership, 6*(7), 16–21. Used with permission.

Data-Driven Instruction

Linking the curriculum and instruction to assessment systems provides teachers with evidence that students are mastering content, as well as with information about the need for intervention or reteaching (Langer, Colton, & Goff, 2003). Highly effective schools, schools that beat the odds, use assessment information to guide instruction (Reeves, 2000).

There is evidence that students need regular test format practice if they are to perform well on state assessments (Langer, 2001). This stands to reason if you consider "tests" as a genre that students must learn, in the same way that biographies, historical fiction, or travelogues are considered genres. Such an assessment-to-instruction approach has been successfully used at an Albuquerque, New Mexico, middle school by teachers who give students a 10-question assessment and a writing prompt on a monthly basis (Fisher, 2005). Teachers at each grade level spend part of their professional development time discussing the item analysis from the common assessment, planning intervention groups, and determining reteaching needs.

The key to successful linking of curriculum, instruction, and assessment seems to involve the frequency with which teachers engage in this process of creating assessment items. It provides teachers an opportunity to clarify their thinking about content standards and the role that language plays in learning, as well as an occasion for teacher teams to discuss aggregate and disaggregate data and to plan instruction.

Professional Development

As part of the schoolwide literacy plan, the literacy leadership team and the site administrators will likely realize that all teachers can benefit from continuing professional development. But the professional development plan needs to be coherent and coordinated. Not all professional development opportunities are created equally. One-shot, isolated events are less likely to affect teacher behavior or student performance (National Staff Development Council, 2001). "Seagull consulting"—when someone flies in, drops something off, and flies back out—is also not going to change achievement. What all teachers need and deserve is a comprehensive professional development plan, differentiated based on their current knowledge and expected performance, and aligned with the overall goals of the school. One of the best ways to meet this need is through professional learning communities (e.g., DuFour & Eaker, 1998).

The Ball Foundation—in partnership with several school districts including Springfield, Illinois; Northview, Michigan; and Chula Vista, California—has used professional learning communities, called communities of practice, to engage teachers in discussions about teaching and learning. In these communities of practice, teachers select topics, meet regularly, engage one another about teaching and learning, and grow as professionals. Importantly, communities of practice are not top down. As Rogers and Ricci (n.d.) note,

> A **community of practice** (CoP) is a group of practitioners dedicated to learning with and from one another in pursuit of promising instructional, organizational and leadership practices that support increased student achievement. Communities of practice can exist among peers within a school, across a district and across partnerships. Communities of practice are not the latest organizational fad, but recognition of how knowledge and learning get transferred, developed and evolved in any social system by those doing the work. (¶1)

A graphic representation of the benefits of communities of practice, as outlined by the staff of the Ball Foundation, can be found in Figure 6.2. It is interesting to note that the data from their partnerships suggest that these communities of practice not only transform teachers' behaviors, but also their assumptions, beliefs, humility, and compassion.

Administrative Accountability

Many of us have been part of a schoolwide effort that failed. For example, a school may decide to institute a "no hats" policy. Over time, however, some teachers implement the plan and others ignore it. Students know this and believe that the implementers are strict or worse yet, ogres. Students' perspectives of those not implementing a school policy range from "they don't care" to "she's cool; she lets us get away with it."

Figure 6.2. Ball Foundation's Benefits of Communities of Practice

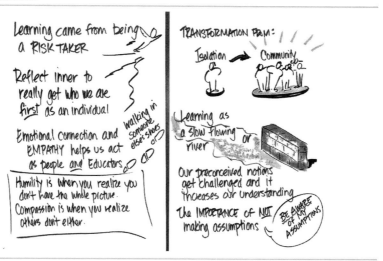

Learning came from being a RISK TAKER

Reflect inner to really get who we are first as an individual

Emotional connection and EMPATHY helps us act as people and Educators

walking in someone else's shoes or...

Humility is when you realize you don't have the whole picture. Compassion is when you realize others don't either.

TRANSFORMATION FROM:

Isolation → Community

Learning as a slow flowing river

Our preconceived notions get challenged and it increases our understanding

The IMPORTANCE of NOT making assumptions

BE AWARE OF MY ASSUMPTIONS

Reprinted with permission from Rogers and Ricci (n.d.), found at the Ball Foundation website: http://www.ballfoundation.org/ei/work/cop-intro.html

Without a plan, contingencies, conversations, and such, the implementation of the policy wanes. Strong leadership for ensuring policy adherence is essential, as is the teacher buy-in that comes from shared conversation before the policy is implemented.

Schoolwide literacy plans face the same risk. They need cultivation, attention, and monitoring to be effective. Although many aspects of schoolwide literacy plans can be implemented and monitored by teachers, there are certain things that require administrative support. Teachers are more likely to give the plan a try if they know that their administrators are ensuring schoolwide implementation of the agreed-upon plan.

Doug Williams, the Principal of Hoover High, provides a glimpse into the role of an effective administrator who leads school change and improvement. Mr. Williams is regularly in classrooms, interacting with students and teachers. When he sees opportunities for teachers to use content literacy strategies, he talks with them about it. He also asks students he sees in the hallways about teachers' instructional strategies, such as read-alouds. Walking down the hall one afternoon, he stopped Jamar and said, "Heard a good book lately?" Jamar was quick with his response, "Yeah, Ms. Dahlin read this tight poem about cancer and then cut off some of her hair to donate!"

Figure 6.3. Doug's Challenge

Challenge
- Identify 10 students—Your Students
- Monitor achievement in your class.
- Ask them about achievement in their other classes.
- Encourage them to perform at their personal best.
- Encourage them to attend Synergy or other support programs.
- Offer support as an adult friend, a mentor, or a caring individual.
- Encourage students to remain at Hoover through graduation.

A B C
A. Accept the challenge to support 10 students.
B. Believe in them. Make them believe they can excel in school and on standardized testing.
C. Commit to focusing on these students throughout the school year.

Begin to identify your students today.
Start the process by next week.

Mr. Williams also attends all staff development sessions, participates in common assessment meetings, and publicly recognizes teachers who successfully facilitate their students' use of reading and writing. Mr. Williams is also known for his challenges to the staff during monthly learning community meetings. In February 2003, for instance, Mr. Williams challenged each teacher or staff member to choose 10 students they would get to know well. He wanted each of the school employees to mentor, coach, and guide 10 students toward success. The challenge, as he presented it, can be found in Figure 6.3. This simple appeal changed the culture of the school. Teachers began talking with each other about the needs of their students and how to solve those needs. The result was better coordination of services.

Getting Started: A Schoolwide Literacy Initiative in Hawaii

Waianae High School educates more than 2,000 students, the vast majority of whom are Hawaiian or of Hawaiian ancestry. Of these more than 2,000 students, over 60% qualify for free lunch and 23% have been identified as having a disability. The school has entered program improvement for failure to make AYP. On the 2005 state assessment only 23% of the students were proficient in reading (the target was 30%), only 3% of the students were proficient in math (the target was 28%), and only 67% of the students graduated (the target was 75%). However, as Principal Joann Kumasaka notes, Waianae also has a number of significant accomplishments that are overlooked in the aggregate numbers alone. First, Waianae students continue to increase in their literacy performance. For example, in 2002 only 12% of their students were proficient in reading on the Hawaii State Assessment, or HAS. This has nearly doubled in three years. Second, there is a core group of teachers who have remained at the school, despite the pressure of restructuring under NCLB. In addition, Waianae students have received a number of awards, including awards for their superior video productions, news casting, a business and marketing student presentation, sports, and community engagement.

The staff and administration at Waianae have clarified their vision—they consistently report that they want their students to "read the world." To this end, a literacy leadership team called the Literacy Cadre was formed. This team has identified specific schoolwide structures and instructional strategies to be implemented, including the following:

- **Dedicated reading time through daily Sustained Silent Reading.** The faculty and staff voted to change the bell schedule and allocate time for "just reading" so that their students increase their reading volume. They see this as part of reading the world—using books to find information and for pleasure.

- **Read-alouds and shared readings.** The Literacy Cadre and administrative team identified reading comprehension as a need for the students at Waianae. As such, they decided to focus on teacher modeling through think-alouds connected to daily read-alouds and shared readings in all classrooms.

- **Writing to learn.** In addition to reading comprehension, the Literacy Cadre members knew that students needed to spend more time thinking. They recognized that thinking occurs as students write. Thus they decided to focus on the use of daily writing prompts in each classroom.

- **Cornell note-taking.** As their final schoolwide initiative for the first year of implementation, the Literacy Cadre members focused their efforts on teaching students to store information externally. They want to ensure that their students are college-ready and that they have systems for studying the content information required in the Hawaii standards.

The teachers at Waianae are regularly provided with student assessment information, and the administrators are investigating the use of teacher-created assessments to complement the work already being done in this area. Further, the Literacy Cadre was provided with two full days of release time to write a professional development plan for the school.

Waianae operates on a 4-by-4 block schedule, and teachers have between 75 and 90 minutes of planning time per day. As part of the schoolwide literacy plan, teachers will attend one professional development seminar of 60 minutes every week. The Literacy Cadre formed committees on each of the four components of the literacy plan, and these committees were charged with developing specific professional development activities, using teacher demonstrations and videos. Finally, Waianae staff members are working to revise their intervention supports and services for students who read significantly below grade level. The principal already spends considerable time with teachers and students and has clearly communicated her expectations for the implementation of the plan to the faculty.

Conclusion

The components of an effective schoolwide adolescent literacy initiative are fairly straightforward. Adolescents of all types need teachers who engage them, access to books that they can and want to read, and instruction that builds their confidence and competence. Although the components are easy to enumerate, the implementation is often challenging. There are still too many schools that cannot create the critical mass among teachers that is necessary to improve student achievement. There are still too many secondary school teachers who see themselves as teachers of content and not teachers of students who have vastly different needs and skills (Moje, 1996).

Proponents of schoolwide literacy initiatives know that all learning is based in language—not that all teachers are teachers of reading—and then provide professional development and coaching for all content teachers. When a chemistry teacher, for example, is asked to explain how students learn, he or she is most likely to talk about reading texts, completing experiments and writing lab reports, listening to lectures, watching films, talking with peers, and being generally engaged with the big ideas of the content area. Proponents of schoolwide approaches to literacy instruction note that these are literacy strategies that can be used to help students learn chemistry, and a host of other content areas.

Unfortunately, the attempt to create a comprehensive plan often results in no plan ever being adopted. As seen in the beginnings of a schoolwide literacy plan from the school in Hawaii, it's best to just get started. The Waianae plan is expected to evolve over time, becoming more sophisticated, complex, and robust. The adage "hope is not a plan" reminds us of the urgent need adolescents have for their teachers to do something—and to do something together that allows students to use language to learn.

Remember Alvaro? He would likely not be writing poems, in English, for his grandmother had his school not launched a schoolwide initiative. Nor would he be standing outside the school as I write, picketing the proposed immigration policies that he read about in the newspaper. Literacy has opened the world to him. His teachers have ensured that he has a repertoire of reading, writing, speaking, listening, and viewing habits that he can use to understand and shape his world.

Questions for Reflection

1. Which components of a schoolwide literacy plan are evident in your school?

2. Which could become defining features of your school's plan?

3. Do you believe that the plan for Waianae High School will result in increased student achievement? Explain your reasoning.

4. What else would you recommend for Waianae High School to effect positive change?

Activity

Follow a student for a day. How fractured is this student's experience? How many different types of instruction interventions are used? Where can this student find consistency?

Douglas Fisher is Professor of Language and Literacy Education in the Department of Teacher Education at San Diego State University (San Diego, California, USA), Co-Director for the Center for the Advancement of Reading at the California State University Chancellor's office, and past Director of Professional Development for the City Heights Educational Collaborative. He has published numerous articles and books on reading and literacy, differentiated instruction, and curriculum design. An early intervention and language development specialist, he has taught high school English, writing, and literacy development, and has taught courses in SDSU's teacher-credentialing program and graduate-level courses on English language development and literacy. He can be reached at dfisher@mail.sdsu.edu.

REFERENCES

Allen, J. (2000). *Yellow brick roads: Shared and guided paths to independent reading 4–12*. York, ME: Stenhouse.

Biancarosa, G., & Snow, C. (2004). *Reading next: A vision for action and research in middle and high school literacy* (A report to Carnegie Corporation of New York). Washington, DC: Alliance for Excellent Education.

Brozo, W.G., & Hargis, C. (2003). Taking seriously the idea of reform: One high school's efforts to make reading more responsive to all students. *Journal of Adolescent & Adult Literacy, 47*, 14–23.

California Department of Education. (2000). *Strategic teaching and learning: Standards-based instruction to promote content literacy in grades four through twelve*. Sacramento: CDE Press.

Cobb, C. (2005). Literacy teams: Sharing leadership to improve student learning. *The Reading Teacher, 58*, 472–474.

DuFour, R., & Eaker, R. (1998). *Professional learning communities at work: Best practices for enhancing student achievement*. Bloomington, IN: National Education Service.

Farnan, N., Flood, J., & Lapp, D. (1994). Comprehending through reading and writing: Six research-based instructional strategies. In K. Spangenberg-Urbschat & R. Pritchard (Eds.), *Kids come in all languages: Reading instruction for ESL students* (pp. 135–157). Newark: DE: International Reading Association.

Fisher, D. (2004). Setting the "opportunity to read" standard: Resuscitating the SSR program in an urban high school. *Journal of Adolescent & Adult Literacy, 48*, 138–150.

Fisher, D. (2005). The missing link: Standards, assessment, and instruction. *Voices From the Middle, 13*(2), 8–11.

Fisher, D., & Frey, N. (2006). Majority rules: A schoolwide literacy success. *Principal Leadership, 6*(7), 16–21.

Fisher, D., Frey, N., & Williams, D. (2002). Seven literacy strategies that work. *Educational Leadership, 60*(3), 70–73.

Fisher, D., & Ivey, G. (in press). Evaluating the interventions for struggling adolescent readers. *Journal of Adolescent & Adult Literacy*.

Flood, J., Lapp, D., Squire, J.R., & Jensen, J.M. (Eds.). (2003). *Handbook of research on teaching the English language arts* (2nd ed.). Mahwah, NJ: Erlbaum.

Frey, N. (2006). "We can't afford to rest on our laurels": Creating a district-wide content literacy instructional plan. *NASSP Bulletin, 90*(1), 37–48.

Ivey, G. (2002). Getting started: Manageable literacy practices. *Educational Leadership, 60*(3), 20–23.

Ivey, G., & Broaddus, K. (2001). "Just plain reading": A survey of what makes students want to read in middle school classrooms. *Reading Research Quarterly, 36,* 350–377.

Ivey, G., & Fisher, D. (2006). *Creating literacy-rich schools for adolescents.* Alexandria, VA: Association for Supervision and Curriculum Development.

Langer, G.M., Colton, A.B., & Goff, L.S. (2003). *Collaborative analysis of student work: Improving teaching and learning.* Alexandria, VA: Association for Supervision and Curriculum Development.

Langer, J.A. (2001). Beating the odds: Teaching middle and high school students to read and write well. *American Educational Research Journal, 38,* 837–880.

Moje, E.B. (1996). "I teach students, not subjects": Teacher-student relationships as contexts for secondary literacy. *Reading Research Quarterly, 31,* 172–195.

National Association of Secondary School Principals. (2005). *Creating a culture of literacy: A guide for middle and high school principals.* Reston, VA: Author.

National Staff Development Council. (2001). *Standards for staff development.* Oxford, OH: Author.

Reeves, D. (2000). *Accountability in action: A blueprint for learning organizations.* Denver: Advanced Learning Press.

Rogers, M., & Ricci, J. (n.d.). *The practice of communities of practice in school districts.* Retrieved November 21, 2006, from http://www.ballfoundation.org/ei/work/cop-intro.html

Crafting Successful Roles for Literacy Coaches in Secondary Schools (Remember Chocolate)

Elizabeth G. Sturtevant and Kristine M. Calo

HIGHLIGHTS

- Middle and high schools across the country are hiring literacy coaches who work with teachers to improve instruction.

- Professional organizations and educational publications suggest a wide variety of roles for literacy coaches; however, the potential for individual coaches to feel overwhelmed and ineffective is high.

- School leaders should take steps to help literacy coaches experience acceptance and success; in particular, they must ensure that coaches are seen as peer support rather than as supervisors.

- Strategies are available to help literacy coaches learn about schools and work with others to build an effective program.

- Districts should provide continuing support and professional development for literacy coaches.

Across North America and beyond, school districts are increasing their focus on the needs of adolescent literacy learners, in part through increased staff development efforts for content teachers. A literacy coach, or teacher who works primarily to assist other teachers in improving literacy instruction, is increasingly a central feature of these efforts. Literacy educators who may have once worked primarily with small groups or whole classes of students are being

Adolescent Literacy Instruction: Policies and Promising Practices edited by Jill Lewis and Gary Moorman. © 2007 by the International Reading Association.

asked to move into new roles, sometimes for more than one school. In some cases, elementary reading specialists are finding themselves in middle or high school settings for the first time. Some middle and high school English language arts teachers or content area teachers are taking additional coursework in reading in order to serve their own schools as literacy coaches. The roles and responsibilities of literacy coaches are multifaceted and important, but can sometimes be unclear. Coaches, teachers, and school leaders can work together to define and shape the role of the coach so that together they can build an effective literacy program.

In this chapter, we first explore the need for secondary literacy coaches and their potential role in the middle and high school. We then discuss strategies coaches can use to be successful in their work.

The Need for Coaches in the Secondary School

Since the implementation of the 2001 No Child Left Behind Act, and, in particular, Reading First, federal funding for literacy programs in the United States has centered primarily on kindergarten through third grade (Vacca, 2006). This is not surprising given the great need for strong programs to ensure that all children get off to a good start in reading and writing development. However, concern for the literacy needs of adolescent learners goes back at least to the early part of the 20th century (Moore, Readence, & Rickelman, 1983). Federal funding available in the 1960s and 1970s enabled secondary schools in many parts of the United States to hire literacy educators (variously called reading specialists, reading teachers, and reading resource teachers) who were assigned to work with students and other teachers (Anders, 2002). In most states, preservice secondary teachers have been required to take courses in content area reading since at least the 1980s (Farrell & Cirrincione, 1986). Moreover, districts across North America have offered inservice programs related to reading and writing in the content areas for many years. However, over the past two decades numerous researchers have expressed concern about whether schools have adequately supported the secondary content teachers who have made efforts to infuse literacy into their instruction (e.g., O'Brien, Stewart, & Moje, 1995). Roadblocks to improved literacy programs for adolescents have included issues such as the factory-like context of secondary schools—especially high schools—which remained largely unchanged over a century (Cuban, 1993), as well as a reliance on short-term staff development.

More recently, the 2005 Striving Readers discretionary federal grant program has provided money to fund literacy professionals in some secondary schools in the United States. Provincial and state governments, school districts, and private funding agencies such as foundations are also showing a greatly increased concern for the needs of adolescent learners. Professional organizations such as the International Reading Association's Commission on Adolescent Literacy (Moore, Bean, Birdyshaw, & Rycik, 1999; Vacca, 2006) and policy groups such as the Alliance for Excellent Education (Kamil, 2003; Sturtevant, 2003) have helped to inspire this rising national interest in the needs of adolescent literacy learners. State and federal mandates for high stakes graduation requirements have also made the public more keenly aware that adolescents have learning and literacy needs that must be addressed.

With new interest in adolescent literacy has come a realization that improved student learning requires knowledgeable teachers across content areas who are able to link content with literacy and motivate and engage adolescent learners (Strickland & Alvermann, 2004). *Reading Next* (Biancarosa & Snow, 2004), a report commissioned by the Alliance for Excellent Education, recommends 15 elements leaders should be aware of when building effective adolescent literacy programs. One critical element is strong, substantive professional development. The report notes that effective professional development experiences are systematic, frequent, long-term, and ongoing. The minimal success of staff development for secondary teachers that has depended on intermittent workshops with limited follow-up has given way to coaching models that embed educators knowledgeable in secondary literacy in schools where they can work with teachers on an ongoing basis. When content area teachers have the support they need to effectively reach adolescents and help them become more effective learners, students and teachers benefit.

The Coach's Role

Even though some middle and high schools have had literacy educators serving in a variety of roles for many years, the expectations of literacy professionals working as literacy coaches are often poorly defined (Darwin, 2002; Toll, 2005). Schools may receive funding and subsequently hire literacy coaches without clear plans for exactly what coaches will be asked to do and expected to accomplish. Conversely, some districts have such strict guidelines for coaches that little room is left for school-level decision making on what would make the most sense in a given context (e.g., Darwin, 2002). Anecdotal and published evidence indicates that coaches' roles may be widely different in different settings. This situation obviously raises dilemmas for literacy coaches, who report problems in defining their roles, communicating with administrators, and gaining acceptance from the teachers with whom they are asked to work.

In recognition of the need to further define the role and responsibilities of the secondary literacy coach, the International Reading Association (2006), in a unique collaboration with professional education organizations representing science, social studies, mathematics, and English language arts educators, created *Standards for Middle and High School Literacy Coaches*. This document identifies what these organizations concur are essential roles and responsibilities of middle and high school literacy coaches. Suggested roles include assisting content teachers in learning new teaching strategies by modeling and observing in individual classrooms, facilitating inquiry groups, and disseminating information within departments or teams. The document also suggests that coaches can act as liaisons among teachers and administrators and provide leadership in creating schoolwide literacy plans.

Other writers concur with the suggestions of this document, noting the value of one-to-one mentoring, small group book clubs, study groups, and whole-faculty experiences. Walpole and McKenna (2004), for example, explain the value of coaches working with small groups of teachers:

> Book clubs and study groups are important because they establish a collegial climate for teaching and learning; all participants are reflecting together on ideas expressed in text, and all are making connections to their prior knowledge and experience and to the building's reading program. (p. 197)

Another key factor in the success of coaching lies in meeting the needs of teachers within a particular context and encouraging reflective practice (Carr, Herman, & Harris, 2005; Sweeney, 2003). In addition, many experts agree that the role of the literacy coach is highly collaborative (e.g., Guth & Pettengill, 2005). For example, in her report related to the San Francisco Bay area, Symonds (2003) noted, in schools where teachers work with coaches regularly, teachers, coaches, and administrators report a growth of collaborative teacher culture marked by increased teacher willingness and ability to collaborate, peer accountability, individual teacher knowledge about other teachers' classrooms; increased levels and quality of implementation of new instructional strategies, and support for new teachers. (p. 4)

Along with offering professional development for individuals and groups of teachers, Neufeld and Roper (2003) recommend that literacy coaches play an instrumental role in the creation and implementation of a schoolwide literacy plan that provides a structure for moving the school forward in addressing students' literacy needs. Literacy plans can be developed through a systematic look at the student achievement patterns, school resources, required curriculum, teachers' skills and interests, community resources, and other factors (National Association of Secondary School Principals [NASSP], 2005). Overall, the plan should help the school to establish and maintain a risk-taking environment in which teachers feel willing and able to improve their classroom practice. Getting teachers involved in dialogue about instructional practices can help establish a sense of community that enables teachers to share their successes and struggles. Effective literacy plans can also ensure that schools are making data-supported decisions that will successfully address important issues concerning the literacy learning of all students. By focusing on student achievement across all content areas and for all populations served by the school, literacy coaches help to ensure that all students are equipped with the tools they need to be motivated and strategic readers, writers, and learners.

Keys to Success as a Coach

At a recent International Reading Association symposium (Sturtevant, 2006), a group of middle and high school literacy coaches from several countries was discussing common dilemmas. "My biggest problem is *time*," said a literacy coach from Wisconsin, "I never have enough time to plan with teachers or to read professional resources." A coach from Michigan concurred, "Time is a big issue for me, too, but what I need is access to teachers' planning time—they are so busy they never have time to meet with me!" A coach from Florida brought up a related issue, "Time is a problem, but my biggest dilemma is how to get the teachers to invite me to their classrooms. How can I help them if they don't let me observe?" Coaches from Illinois and British Columbia concurred, with one adding, "It's a struggle to figure out how to get content teachers to trust us so we can discuss teaching with them." Agreement was heard around the group. Finally, a high school literacy coach from Bermuda shared her secret: "What I do is buy chocolate," she said. Heads turned. "Yes," she went on, "I buy it in bulk. Always have chocolate in your office. Teachers always need chocolate. Then they visit you more often and you get more opportunities to interact and discuss issues with them. It decreases isolation and resistance."

As this scenario illustrates, when coaches gather there is much talk about their role and responsibilities. Some stress that the coach's multifaceted role can quickly become unrealistic and overwhelming; others note that their job is only manageable with the support of strong principals who understand students' literacy needs and the culture of their particular school. Yet, the promise of literacy coaching is great. For example, Neufeld and Roper (2003) noted that

> coaching, thoughtfully developed and implemented within a district's coherent professional development plan, will provide teachers with real opportunities to improve their instruction, principals with real opportunities to improve their leadership, and districts with real opportunities to improve their schools. (p. 26)

For this prediction to become reality, literacy coaches in middle and high schools need a variety of types of support and need to be strategic about how they use their time and energy.

Strategies Coaches Can Use to Increase Their Effectiveness

Table 7.1 lists seven strategies coaches can use to increase their effectiveness. This list, built from conversation with coaches as well as advice found in books and articles, is not meant to be comprehensive. Rather, we hope to encourage brainstorming among coaches, faculty, and administrators about the best ways for a coach to work at their school.

Work With School Leaders

Numerous reports on literacy coaching stress the value of understanding and discussion between school leaders and literacy coaches (e.g., Guth

Table 7.1. Strategies for Literacy Coaches

Strategy 1: Work with school leaders
Strategy 2: Organize a literacy council or literacy leadership team
Strategy 3: Learn the curriculum
Strategy 4: Work with teachers outside their classrooms
Strategy 5: Work with teachers within their classrooms
Strategy 6: Get to know students, families, and the community
Strategy 7: Avoid isolation

& Pettengill, 2005). A literacy coach can be a valuable asset to a school, but the role is new to many schools. While this unfamiliarity can cause difficulties, it also is an opportunity to build a role definition that fits into a school's context. School administrators can meet with a new coach to have an open discussion of the role and responsibilities each of them envision. Principals and coaches may both wish to read documents that help to define the coach's role, such as the recent report on adolescent literacy published by the National Association of Secondary School Principals (NASSP, 2005) as well as the new middle and high school coaching standards (International Reading Association, 2006). Monthly meetings between a coach and school administrator are also valuable for keeping communication open.

Depending on the size of the school, there may also be other leadership meetings that would be beneficial for coaches to attend. For example, some schools have monthly meetings of department chairpersons or interdisciplinary team leaders. By attending these meetings, coaches can learn a great deal about their school's culture and needs. The coach can get to know a range of school-based leaders at these meetings and can gain their trust over time. These discussions can also set the stage for the development of a school literacy council and various coach-led activities such as student groups.

The school principal and other leaders can do much to ensure the success of the coach by making appropriate introductions in large and small groups, clarifying the role of the coach at meetings of teachers, and helping coaches develop relationships with departments, teams, and individual teachers. As noted earlier, teachers need to see coaches as valued advisors rather than as supervisors, and the principal can play an important role in clarifying this distinction.

Organize a Literacy Council or Literacy Leadership Team

Working toward improved literacy in a middle or high school should be a whole-school effort. A literacy council, sometimes called a literacy leadership team (NASSP, 2005), can be extremely helpful in building concern about literacy and creating and implementing a school literacy plan. A literacy coach can assist a school administrator in organizing this type of team, which often consists of key administrators, the literacy coach, and representatives from different departments and grade levels. Some schools also invite students and parents to join the literacy team. This group can first conduct an assessment of the needs of school. This process might include a review of student assessment data; an anonymous survey of teachers' attitudes and knowledge related to using reading and writing strategies in their instruction; and focus groups of students, parents, and teachers from various grade levels or content areas. The leadership team can then work with the literacy coach to plan and monitor staff development efforts and other activities to support literacy in the school.

Learn the Curriculum

Coaches entering a school have a lot to learn. One common concern at the middle or high school level is that the curriculum is vast, including not only the core content areas but also numerous elective subjects. It is important for coaches to make a strong effort to learn about different curriculum areas by reviewing curriculum guides, textbooks, and the testing program in different subject areas. However, it is not possible for a coach to become expert in every field. Coaches will likely have one or two curriculum areas in which they are most comfortable, if they have taught in the middle or high school level before. Coaches can work collaboratively with teachers of other subjects, asking them about their curriculum goals and working with the teachers to design lessons that help students read, write, and learn more effectively.

It is also very important for coaches to gain an understanding of factors that influence teachers' instructional decisions at their school. Do teachers feel that constraints related to curriculum, budget, high-stakes testing, or other issues get in the way of using literacy strategies? Often, for example, high school history teachers mention that their curriculum requires them to go very quickly over content, which gets in the way of giving in-depth reading assignments of original sources. Many teachers, in fact, have learned content literacy strategies in courses and workshops that they would like to use, but have experienced difficulty in adapting the strategies to the contexts of their own teaching situations (Sturtevant, 1996). Coaches and teachers can work together to brainstorm ways around these constraints.

Work With Teachers Outside Their Classrooms

Secondary schools are often large, and coaches sometimes report finding it difficult to break into the culture and gain acceptance. The teacher quoted earlier who suggested chocolate was touching on one way to establish trust and community. Similarly, coaches might try holding a weekly open house in their office or a central location such as the school media center. This could occur either after school or during teachers' planning periods or lunch period. Providing snacks and allowing teachers to borrow professional books and materials can help establish rapport. Also, coaches should let teachers know they are ready to hear their concerns and ideas. Even if few teachers initially attend, it helps to be patient and persistent. Also, it is important to include teachers of English to speakers of other languages, special education, and electives.

A second strategy for working with teachers outside classrooms is to organize interest-based study groups on a choice of topics. Coaches might gain input from teachers in different subject areas through informal discussions or a survey conducted by the literacy team. Topics could cross content areas (such as teaching vocabulary or working with English-language learners) or could be pertinent to teachers in a particular content area or course (such as how to integrate writing with mathematics instruction). Study groups can enable teachers to informally learn about a new topic and at the same time get to know the literacy coach. Coaches, in turn, can offer valuable professional development and also gain a deeper understanding of the issues the teachers are facing.

Study group attendance should be voluntary and schedules should be mutually convenient. Nothing squelches a teacher study group more than required attendance. Coaches can facilitate the group but may also wish to invite participants to act as facilitators so they can all feel they are contributing to the study group's success. Together, the group members can decide what they will read before coming to each meeting. At the first session, open-ended questions—What did you think about what we read? or How do you see this connecting to your classroom?—can get the discussion started. After the group has begun to gel, coaches can encourage group members to try new strategies found in the readings in their classrooms. People can try things out, then talk about their successes and challenges in the subsequent group meeting. This approach will help to establish a collegial atmosphere and encourage risk taking.

Administrators can encourage study groups by providing a budget for books and refreshments as well as by giving recognition to study group members in newsletters or by other means. In addition, some districts are able to offer teachers benefits such as points toward recertification for this type of professional development.

Work With Teachers Within Their Classrooms

A typical responsibility of coaches is to work with teachers in their classes by modeling strategies or observing instruction and offering feedback. However, this role is sometimes difficult for a coach to enact because teachers are often reluctant to invite a stranger into their room, and many are understandably anxious that a coach may actually be sent to evaluate their work. First, as noted earlier, it is essential for principals to help teachers understand the role of the coach. In addition, coaches can make progress in gaining access to classrooms by patiently working with teachers outside the classroom and gradually working in the classrooms of teachers with whom they make contact.

After getting to know a few teachers, it is often possible for coaches to ask to come into teachers' classrooms to try out strategies they have just learned or that they wish to adapt to new subject areas. This is a nonthreatening way to let teachers see a strategy in action and to show that the coach is willing to take risks and try new things. Request that the teacher observe you and give you feedback on how the students responded. Reverse the process when teachers are comfortable. Coaches can also offer to mentor a new teacher or one who is interested in making changes in instruction. Be sure to ask the teacher to identify his or her needs, and work from there.

Get to Know Students, Families, and the Community

Although the role of the coach is primarily to work with teachers on various professional development activities, as a literacy leader in the school it is important that the coach make an effort to know the students and their families and understand the community. One middle school coach we know says that every year she learns the names of every sixth-grade student and every new student in the school (quite a task!) because then, over time, she will know all of the students. She does this partly by modeling lessons in sixth-grade classrooms and observing regularly at this grade level. Of course, in larger schools this would not be possible, but coaches can get to know students through various student activities, such as reading or technology clubs, and through work in classrooms. Coaches also can make efforts to reach parents through workshops or discussion groups for parents on a variety of topics and attendance at community events.

Avoid Isolation

In order to be effective, coaches need support. Some districts have included formal biweekly or monthly meetings for their coaches across the district to get together as a literacy coaching team. This provides coaches an important avenue to build a cohesive and supportive network. At these meetings, coaches have a chance to talk about their successes and their challenges. They can get advice and feedback from one another that they can bring back to their own work environments. Districts also can use technology to help coaches build a support network. For example, coaches can use online discussion boards to post questions and ideas for one another.

Another support for coaches is ongoing professional development—not just for the teachers in their schools but for themselves. By having coaches attend professional conferences such as the annual conference of the International Reading Association or the National Middle School Association conference, coaches can stay current with how to support content literacy in their schools. (For a list of relevant organizations, see Table 7.2.) Coaches also can run their own book study groups at their district

Table 7.2. Helpful Websites for Secondary Literacy Coaches

Alliance for Excellent Education	http://www.all4ed.org
International Reading Association	http://www.reading.org
National Association of Secondary School Principals	http://www.principals.org
National Council for the Social Studies	http://www.ncss.org
National Council of Teachers of English	http://www.ncte.org (see also the section devoted to literacy coaching: http://www.ncte.org/collections/literacycoach)
National Council of Teachers of Mathematics	http://www.nctm.org
National Middle School Association	http://www.nmsa.org
National Reading Conference	http://www.nrconline.org
National Science Teachers Association	http://www.nsta.org

meetings. This gives coaches a chance to extend their professional knowledge about literacy and also to gain experience in facilitating discussions and managing study groups. Each can then try a book study in his or her own school with interested staff.

Local universities can be another support for literacy coaches. In a district in Arizona, literacy specialists worked with local university staff to implement a course for teachers held in the district for university credit. This helped further establish the literacy specialists' credibility with other teachers in the district and also gave them an additional network of teachers interested in literacy learning to rely on.

Conclusion

The role of the literacy coach at the middle or high school is an important one. Coaches can have great impact on a school's literacy program and on teachers' professional development and students' learning. However, the possibilities for the coach's role are so numerous that coaches can easily feel overwhelmed and ineffective. School leaders, in consultation with literacy coaches, need to develop long-term plans that do not attempt to accomplish everything in the first year or two. With thoughtful planning and solid support, literacy coaches can help schools and teachers create learning environments that support, motivate, and guide adolescent literacy learners.

Questions for Reflection

1. How do you think teachers in your content area would respond to a literacy coach in their school? Why?

2. What do you think a literacy coach would need to learn about a school before he or she could work there successfully?

Activities

1. Visit a middle or high school and observe a teacher's class. Ask the teacher to discuss with you what types of reading and writing students are asked to complete for this class, and why these are required.

2. Interview a middle or high school literacy coach, reading teacher, or reading specialist. Ask them to describe what they do over the course of a week, and which activities they find most valuable.

3. Interview an adolescent. Ask him or her to describe the types of reading and writing regularly done for school. Also discuss other reading and writing he or she does that is not for school, for example, writing on e-mail or recreational reading.

Elizabeth G. Sturtevant is Associate Professor and Coordinator of the Literacy Program at George Mason University, Fairfax, Virginia, USA. She is co-editor for the *Journal of Literacy Research* and previously co-chaired the IRA Commission on Adolescent Literacy. A former secondary social studies teacher, reading specialist, and literacy coach, Sturtevant has authored numerous articles, book chapters, and books, and has worked extensively on programs to improve adolescent literacy in urban, suburban, and rural settings in the United States and southeastern Europe. You can reach her at esturtev@gmu.edu. **Kristine M. Calo** is a doctoral student in literacy at George Mason University, Fairfax, Virginia, USA. Her research interests include comprehension and informational texts. In her former roles as a middle school reading/language arts teacher in Illinois and Arizona, a school administrator at a K–5 Title I school in Arizona, and as the Assistant Director of Curriculum and Professional Development for a public school district in Arizona, she focused on literacy in the content areas and the professional development of teachers and administrators. In addition to working on her doctorate, she also freelances and is an educational consultant. She may be contacted at kcalo@gmu.edu.

REFERENCES

Anders, P.L. (2002). Secondary reading programs: A story of what was. In D.L. Schallert, C.M. Fairbanks, J. Worthy, B. Maloch, & J.V. Hoffman (Eds.), *51st Yearbook of the National Reading Conference* (pp. 82–93). Oak Creek, WI: National Reading Conference.

Biancarosa, G., & Snow, C. (2004). *Reading next: A vision for action and research in middle and high school literacy* (A report to Carnegie Corporation of New York). Washington, DC: Alliance for Excellent Education.

Carr, J.F., Herman, N., & Harris, D.E. (2005). *Creating dynamic schools through mentoring, coaching, and collaboration.* Alexandria, VA: Association for Supervision and Curriculum Development.

Cuban, L. (1993). *How teachers taught: Constancy and change in American classrooms, 1890–1990* (2nd ed.). New York: Teachers College Press.

Darwin, M.J. (2002). *Delving into the role of the high school reading specialist.* Unpublished dissertation, George Mason University, Fairfax, VA.

Farrell, R.T., & Cirrincione, J.M. (1986). The introductory developmental reading course for content area teachers: A state of the art survey. *Journal of Reading, 29,* 717–723.

Guth, N.D., & Pettengill, S.S. (2005). *Leading a successful reading program: Administrators and reading specialists working together to make it happen.* Newark, DE: International Reading Association.

International Reading Association. (2006). *Standards for middle and high school literacy coaches*. Newark, DE: Author. Retrieved March 1, 2006, from http://www.reading.org/downloads/resources/597coaching_standards.pdf

Kamil, M.L. (2003). *Adolescents and literacy: Reading for the 21st century*. Washington, DC: Alliance for Excellent Education.

Moore, D.W., Bean, T.W., Birdyshaw, D., & Rycik, J.A. (1999). *Adolescent literacy: A position statement for the Commission on Adolescent Literacy of the International Reading Association*. Newark, DE: International Reading Association.

Moore, D.W., Readence, J.E., & Rickelman, R.J. (1983). An historical exploration of content area reading instruction. *Reading Research Quarterly, 18*, 419–438.

National Association of Secondary School Principals. (2005). *Creating a culture of literacy: A guide for middle and high school principals*. Retrieved March 30, 2006, from http://www.principals.org/s_nassp/sec.asp?TRACKID=&SID=1&VID=1&CID=62&DID=62&RTID=0&CIDQS=&Taxonomy=False&specialSearch=False

Neufeld, B., & Roper, D. (2003). *Coaching: A strategy for developing instructional capacity: Promises and practicalities*. Retrieved March 30, 2006, from http://www.aspeninstitute.org/atf/cf/%7BDEB6F227-659B-4EC8-8F84-8DF23CA704F5%7D/ECSCOACHINGPAPERJULY03.PDF

O'Brien, D.G., Stewart, R.A., & Moje, E.B. (1995). Why content literacy is difficult to infuse into the secondary school: Complexities of curriculum, pedagogy, and school culture. *Reading Research Quarterly, 30*, 442–463.

Strickland, D.S., & Alvermann, D.E. (Eds.). (2004). *Bridging the literacy achievement gap, grades 4–12*. New York: Teachers College Press.

Sturtevant, E.G. (1996). Lifetime influences on the literacy-related instructional beliefs of experienced high school history teachers: Two comparative case studies. *Journal of Literacy Research, 28*, 227–257.

Sturtevant, E.G. (2003). *The literacy coach: A key to improving teaching and learning in secondary schools*. Washington, DC: Alliance for Excellent Education.

Sturtevant, E.G. (2006, April). *Dilemmas of the literacy coach: Negotiating your way in the secondary school*. Paper presented at the Institute for Adolescent Literacy, International Reading Association, Chicago, IL.

Sweeney, D. (2003). *Learning along the way: Professional development by and for teachers*. Portland, ME: Stenhouse.

Symonds, K.W. (2003). *Literacy coaching: How school districts can support a long-term strategy in a short-term world*. Oakland, CA: Bay Area School Reform Collaborative.

Toll, C.A. (2005). *The literacy coach's survival guide: Essential questions and practical answers*. Newark, DE: International Reading Association.

Vacca, R.T. (2006). Foreword. In E.G. Sturtevant, F.B. Boyd, W.G. Brozo, K.A. Hinchman, D.W. Moore, & D.E. Alvermann, *Principled practices for adolescent literacy: A framework for instruction and policy* (pp. ix–xi). Mahwah, NJ: Erlbaum.

Walpole, S., & McKenna, M.C. (2004). *The literacy coach's handbook: A guide to research-based practice*. New York: Guilford Press.

CHAPTER 8

An International Perspective on the State of Adolescent Initiatives

Carol Hryniuk-Adamov

HIGHLIGHTS

- An unprecedented collaboration among provinces and territories strengthens literacy instruction in Western and Northern Canada.
- Manitoba's approach to curriculum development promotes leadership among adolescent literacy educators.
- The International Reading Association fosters adolescent literacy initiatives and professional development in Canada.
- Literacy coaches are often challenged by inadequate support systems.

In this chapter I share a Canadian perspective on the development of adolescent literacy initiatives. I reflect on this work from the context of Manitoba, my home province, which had the lead responsibility for the collaborative development of the English language arts curriculum framework for the four western provinces and two northern territories. I will focus on the impact of *The Common Curriculum Framework for English Language Arts, Kindergarten to Grade 12* on adolescent literacy, discuss the role of curriculum development in Manitoba, explore adolescent literacy initiatives, reflect on the role of the literacy coach, and conclude with remarks about the future.

Adolescent Literacy Instruction: Policies and Promising Practices edited by Jill Lewis and Gary Moorman. © 2007 by the International Reading Association.

The Common Curriculum Framework
for English Language Arts

In chapter 1 of this volume, Terry Salinger raises important questions on how an agenda is set for adolescent literacy. In western and northern Canada, it was the provincial and territorial ministers of education, deputy ministers, and assistant deputy ministers who set the agenda for adolescent curriculum development and literacy education in the last decade. Some of these leaders were insightful educators who understood the importance of involving teachers meaningfully in all phases of the curriculum development and implementation process.

There were also several important historic and educational implications for the signing of the Western and Northern Canadian Protocol (WNCP). Education is a provincial responsibility in Canada. Therefore collaboration among the provinces and territories had many positive implications for adolescent literacy development. The Western provinces of Manitoba, Saskatchewan, Alberta, British Columbia, the Northwest Territories, Yukon, and later Nunavut agreed they would collaborate on the development of common curriculum projects. The agreement, the WNCP common curriculum frameworks (WNCP, 1998), and the WNCP assessment document, *Rethinking Classroom Assessment With Purpose in Mind* (WNCP, 2006), can be viewed at http://www.wncp.ca.

This initiative was the first time in Canadian history provincial and territorial governments mandated that exemplary early, middle, and senior year educators from these jurisdictions collaborate to develop a common framework for the English language arts curriculum. The final document included 56 specific learning outcomes for each grade level from kindergarten to grade 12. It became *The Common Curriculum Framework for English Language Arts* (WNCP, 1998), hereinafter referred to as the ELA Framework document.

There were many unique aspects of this historic document. Throughout its development, early years teachers consulted and collaborated with teachers of middle and senior years in various configurations to write the specific learning outcomes. This approach led to greater curriculum continuity and stronger emphasis on the reading process. The document integrated six language arts, including viewing and representing, and it expanded the notion of text to include oral, print, and other media. Although *adolescent literacy* was not defined in the document, *adolescence* would encompass both the middle and senior years from grades 5–12.

The ELA Framework document also emphasized that language learning was not the sole responsibility of English language arts teachers, but rather was a shared responsibility of all K–12 subject area teachers. This mandate began new discussions about teaching the six strands of language arts across the curriculum. Each province and territory's curriculum developers were given permission to use the document and adapt it to meet the unique needs of their teachers and students in developing jurisdictional curriculum frameworks and support materials. At http://www.wncp.ca readers can navigate to each jurisdiction's website to view all the provincial and territorial curricula with online teacher support documents for instructional and assessment strategies.

The significance of the ELA Framework document increased when it became the basis for the development and selection of common learning resources for the four western provinces and two northern territories. This document signaled a new era in the development of curriculum-congruent learning resources in Canada. There were formal interjurisdictional calls to the Canadian publishing industry to develop teaching and learning resources to match the specific learning outcomes of the ELA Framework document. The Canadian publishing industry responded favorably and provided many exemplary curriculum congruent teaching and learning resources for western and northern Canada. Thus, for the first time, Canadian publishers were directed by these governments who received recommendations from leading educators.

Interjurisdictional learning resource review teams met in Saskatchewan to review the submitted resources for curriculum congruency. The educators who participated in these sessions became very influential. The criteria they developed, detailed annotated bibliographies, and information on the WNCP learning resource review process can be viewed at http://www.wncp.ca. Teachers were given the choice of several recommended integrated learning resources for use in their classrooms, including the option to maintain their literature-based or resource-based learning focus with multiple trade books. Teachers, in consultation with their principals, also had the option not to use any reading program as this is often a school-based decision.

Curriculum Development in Manitoba

One example of flexibility and adaptation was evident in Manitoba where the development teams for framework documents maintained the wording of the specific learning outcomes, added detail, and developed standards for assessment at grades 3, 6, 9, and 12. Variations of the collaborative process model were used to develop all subsequent Manitoba curriculum documents and materials. Several teams of educators developed strategy-rich curriculum supports called Foundations for Implementation. They provided detailed suggestions for instruction and classroom-based assessment of the 56 specific learning outcomes at every grade level K–12. The development of strong curriculum and support materials had many positive implications for adolescent literacy educators. Subsequent subject area curriculum writing teams integrated literacy strategies from the English language arts documents across curricula.

In Manitoba, an agenda for adolescent literacy based on the new curriculum has been evolving for some time. Literacy, differentiated instruction, assessment, a new information technology literacy continuum, and meeting the needs of struggling or striving learners have been made high priorities. Government consultants have provided direction through significant, collaborative curriculum development, implementation workshops, assessment projects, comprehensive learning resource reviews, mentoring, and literacy across the curriculum institutes, as well as through specific subject area summer institutes at no cost to teachers. Although the government's direction was top down with a clear political agenda, those educators in leadership roles made sure that there was significant and meaningful involvement of Manitoba educators in all initiatives.

New models of collaborative development of all curriculum projects involved large teams of exemplary educators at all levels in active, meaningful participation and professional development. Usually, these educators were nominated in a top-down approach by their superintendents or selected through civil-service competitions. The involvement of many practicing educators allowed for a great deal of direction to come from the bottom up. This built upon a longtime Manitoba tradition of some teacher involvement in curriculum development. The collegiality and ongoing mentoring in teams strengthened the educational community by creating a culture of cooperation and collaboration.

Many of these development team members were recognized as potential literacy leaders in their schools, districts, or the profession, and as having some links to the national and international literacy community as well. New literacy leaders emerged as a result of their intense participation in professional dialogue and collaborative writing. A decade of this kind of adolescent literacy curriculum development has resulted in a significant expansion of strong literacy leadership among secondary teachers across the province. Many former team members have become consultants, administrators in school districts, instructors in various universities in the province, graduate students, reviewers, and writers of teaching and learning resources for Canadian publishers.

We have had exemplary educators serve as "policy actors" and "elite actors" (Salinger, chapter 1) in branches of our provincial governments. Manitoba and other western and northern jurisdictions have had the benefit of significant teacher input and direction during this decade of curriculum and assessment reform by the provincial ministry of education.

But, as in the United States, the approach of an election could quickly change the direction, philosophy, and actions of policymakers in Canada. A new political party in provincial power might switch the emphasis to high-stakes large-scale assessment. Then the large-scale assessment expert teams, which also include Manitoba teachers, would become the lead policy actors and elite actors.

Canadian educators wonder about how our adolescent literacy initiatives in curriculum and assessment affect student performance. What has been the impact of the ELA Framework on Canadian adolescents' literacy achievement? In the past, Canadians have done fairly well in international literacy assessments such as the Programme for International Student Achievement (PISA). Within several years of the release of *The Common Curriculum Framework for English Language Arts*, a sample of 15-year-old Canadian adolescents was tested during the PISA assessments in 2000 and 2003 (Bussiere, Cartwright, Knighton, & Rogers, 2004). In 2000, reading was a major focus. In 2003, mathematics was a major focus with reading science and problem-solving being minor domains.

Many variables can affect students' test results. The western provinces were all at various stages of implementation of the new ELA Framework at the time the PISA was administered. In general, Canadian students did fairly well in these international assessments in 2000 and 2003. Only Finland outperformed Canada in the results of PISA reading assessments. In 2003, students in Quebec, Ontario, Manitoba, and British Columbia performed at the Canadian average in all the minor domains. Some provinces did have scores less than the national average. As middle and senior years Canadian literacy educators, we have much to do collectively to strengthen literacy skills and strategies for all adolescents across the country.

Students from the province of Alberta did significantly better than the Canadian average. Alberta is the western province that conducts the most large scale assessment of students at grades 3, 6, 9, and 12.

Their provincial assessments are based on outcomes from their provincial Program of Studies for English Language Arts. The program of studies includes many of the outcomes of the ELA Framework document.

It is too early to determine the extent of full implementation of innovative curriculum development initiatives on delivered curriculum and the actual academic achievement of Canadian students in the western provinces at the times the PISA was administered. The next Pan-Canadian Assessment Program (PCAP) will be administered in 2007 to a representative sample of 13-year-olds in the provinces and territories. This national assessment may yield more information to understand the impact of the curriculum initiatives on western and northern Canadian adolescents' reading performance. We wait to see the nature and the results of the PCAP being conducted by the Council of Ministers of Education. We continue to explore multiple initiatives in our ongoing professional development to improve adolescent literacy instruction and assessment.

In Manitoba, the provincial grade 12 English language arts tests are based on the outcomes and standards of the ELA Framework. Our framework incorporates all of the general and specific outcomes set out in the WNCP document. You may view examples of assessment at the province of Manitoba education website. The passing rate is encouraging. The large-scale assessment is an innovative English language arts process standards test that is conducted over several days and incorporates significant specific learning outcomes that may be assessed in paper-and-pencil tasks, given the limitations of large-scale assessment, and honors the before, during and after phases of the reading process and a variety of genres. The preparation for writing the test necessitates class or group discussion based on the readings of both transactional and literary texts. Students are required to respond personally, analytically, and critically. In classrooms across the province, students examine sample rubrics, test formats, and test items prior to the provincial administration of the test; consequently, students are well aware of the criteria and expectations. Teachers are trained to mark student papers using provincially set criteria and exemplars. After each administration a representative sample of papers are scored centrally using a double-blind process to provide feedback to local school and division authorities so that they can adjust their marking processes.

In time the impact of the common curriculum development may be seen on adolescent student performance. The first class to follow the ELA Framework since kindergarten is now in grade 10. It will be important for the province and teachers to do an intensive curriculum evaluation and analysis of the impact of the curriculum on academic performance after 12 years of implementation and in preparation for future curriculum renewal.

The most notable effect of this collaborative initiative is the ongoing collaboration among teachers who were involved in writing and implementation teams. This has spread to other subject areas. There is a strong provincial government directive to continue to apply the literacy, communication, inquiry, and research strategies from the English language arts documents to other content areas by subsequent subject area development teams. Some members from the ELA teams have also served on other development teams to provide continuity. In addition, there has been a strong interest in literacy across the curriculum initiatives and schoolwide literacy plans, sometimes as part of general school improvement plans. In Manitoba, grade 8 classroom-based assessments were administered in 2006 for expository writing and will occur this year in reading. These assessments will provide more information to teachers, parents, students, and the province.

Because of the common literacy curriculum, major cross-curricular literacy initiatives are emanating from Manitoba. The provincial literacy across the curriculum summer institute model for teachers of students in grades 5–12 is in its fourth year of implementation. It has been adapted for presentations in the Northwest Territories and Yukon. Major presentations of these core strategies have occurred at IRA regional and provincial conferences in each of the jurisdictions in the western and northern Canadian protocol as well as in Ontario. More teachers of all subjects see the benefit of shared literacy strategies from a common curriculum framework to improve academic literacy in every content area subject. Literacy across the curriculum is one of the most popular topics for districtwide in-service workshops in Manitoba. School-based psychologists are required as part of their university training to study the ELA teacher support documents in order to develop curriculum-based recommendations that encourage effective strategy use to develop language and communication across the curricula. Educators in Manitoba have made a strong case for the importance of increasing the momentum for literacy across the curriculum with the involvement of school officials at all levels—province, division, school, and classroom—and parents. More research needs to be done to assess the impact of teaching literacy skills and strategies across the curricula in Canada.

Many of these adolescent literacy initiatives in Manitoba would not have occurred without strong multipronged professional development and support for decades from the International Reading Association. Our local Reading Council of Greater Winnipeg, formed in 1956 and one of the first Canadian councils, has always provided accessible and affordable, high-quality professional development for Manitoba educators. We are also supported by our provincial reading association, several local councils, and a special-interest council of reading clinicians.

Adolescent Literacy: A Canadian Perspective

After reading and then reflecting on each of the previous chapters, I recognized that Canadian teachers have major challenges ahead of us in implementing our curricula and in developing new adolescent literacy initiatives. We are learning to understand and teach the new multiliteracies and information technology as foundation skills to prepare students more effectively to read and comprehend their digital world. We look to the work of Alvermann and Eakle (see chapter 4) to help us understand our students and our new roles in a growing digital divide. We are committed to teaching oral, print, and other media text in all subject areas, but more support is needed to implement our new provincial Information Technology Literacy Continuum for Manitoba (Manitoba Education, Citizenship, and Youth, 2006), posted at http://www.edu. gov.mb.ca/k12/docs/support/tfs/appendixa.html.

More secondary teachers are assuming that they have a role in adolescent literacy instruction. They previously thought that this was the responsibility of elementary teachers. But literacy and communication have been mandated by the province as foundation skills in all provincial curricula in some parts of the country. The range of reading levels is wider than ever in many regular classes. Secondary subject area teachers are asking for more ongoing support as they develop their repertoires of strategies for teaching reading across the curriculum.

Districts are creating new professional learning opportunities, including job-embedded sessions to improve our middle and senior high schools. School districts have offered content area reading courses at no cost to teachers after school to meet the need for professional development. At both the district and school levels, innovative literacy across the curriculum professional development projects are being developed and implemented by teams of educators both formally and informally in Lunch and Learn or Literacy Cafe sessions.

In chapter 2 of this volume, Jill Lewis, IRA Board member (2004–2007), gives the reader insight into the process of self-reflection that the IRA board has undertaken in an effort to remain mindful of its mission and committed to attain its goals. This process is a model for our provincial and territorial councils. Her excellent summary of U.S. federal policies that affect the literacy education of adolescents, IRA's viewpoints, and various responses is very helpful. Canadians follow American federal education policies and processes with interest because these may, in turn, affect our politicians and our profession. Fortunately, as of now, education remains a provincial and territorial matter rather than a federal one in Canada.

Over the years, IRA's divisions have been especially responsive to Canadian members who were seeking more professional development to meet the needs of adolescent students and their teachers. This international support has fostered new approaches and initiatives to improve adolescent literacy at a critical time in our professional journey. IRA has become a premier professional organization for Canadian leaders in adolescent literacy.

Lewis cites the influential IRA position statements on adolescent literacy formulated by members of the Adolescent Literacy Commission, or ALC (Moore, Bean, Birdyshaw, & Rycik, 1999), as well as the joint position statement issued with the National Middle School Association. These resources have been critical supports for advocating for more attention to adolescent literacy in Canada. The ALC position statement provided a powerful springboard for a discussion of the complex issues that needed to be addressed in planning comprehensive adolescent initiatives.

There are a growing number of teachers at this level who realize the need to teach language and literacy across the curriculum, and who are now looking to IRA for more resources. The historic Canadian IRA Forum on Adolescent Literacy, held in Winnipeg in 2002, featured Donna Ogle and Carol Santa as well as local experts in adolescent literacy. Leaders attended from other provinces and territories. This forum initiated major momentum in setting the agenda for future Canadian adolescent literacy institutes and conferences. It significantly raised the profile of IRA as a source of high-quality professional development and publications for our middle and high school educators. It also provided a model for future partnerships with our IRA councils to develop adolescent literacy programs and to undertake joint planning with consultants from the provincial government.

Moreover, it led to Manitoba's annual three-day adolescent literacy institute, Literacy across the Curriculum. This event has been held for three years sponsored by our provincial department of Manitoba

Education, Citizenship, and Youth. Successful versions of these institutes have also been delivered by Manitoba educators in the Yukon and Northwest Territories at the request of their literacy leaders.

In Canada, we are exploring new models for professional development and innovative post-baccalaureate course delivery for content literacy or literacy across the curriculum. There is a growing demand for innovation and flexibility from secondary educators. For two years, for instance, we established a partnership with one of our universities and offered unique post-baccalaureate courses in our own high schools and in conjunction with the provincial government's adolescent literacy summer institute.

These courses and institutes were intense group experiences and have demonstrated some long-term benefits. They helped spark the creation of a new professional learning community of 180 secondary educators across Manitoba. This, in turn, created more momentum to develop creative school-based adolescent literacy initiatives. For two consecutive years, two groups of 15 teachers who had attended the three-day institute in August also elected to spend three Saturdays to complete the university's post-baccalaureate course requirements. The special course was offered over three months, in order to provide teachers with sufficient time to experiment with the strategies and materials and get important specific corrective feedback from their students, school colleagues, and classmates in peer assessment. The transformations were noteworthy.

At subsequent summer literacy institutes, former institute and course participants from across the province shared the strategies they had implemented and spoke about their personal literacy journeys and transformations. The carousel presentations created a celebratory atmosphere. Participants heard many unique presentations about creative initiatives around the province. Many left feeling more connected to a provincial learning community and empowered with strategies and the supportive virtual network of new colleagues to help them to overcome local obstacles.

Secondary teachers who attended the summer institute and course have found new voices as adolescent literacy advocates and literacy leaders in their schools. Principals are asking them to share strategies at staff meetings, and at school professional development days. Several teachers have continued their consultations electronically via e-mail. Because of the ongoing support of classmates, they are becoming more actively persistent in their efforts to bring their more reluctant colleagues on board. Teachers are publishing successful projects in the provincial teachers' journals and are also making presentations in each others' school districts.

Developing Canadian Adolescent Literacy Initiatives

Canadian policymakers and adolescent literacy advocates are looking for major large-scale initiatives to increase engagement, actual reading skill, and strategy use throughout the jurisdiction, and know they must look beyond test scores for determining success. Alabama's increased emphasis on improving reading comprehension, as described by Salinger (see chapter 3), is similar to the direction we have taken to target improving reading skills and strategies across all curricula. In Manitoba, for instance, we have been focused on improving comprehension instruction by teaching strategies in the three phases of the reading process—before, during, and after reading in English language arts—and across the curricula.

We can learn from the challenges identified in the Alabama Reading Initiative (ARI) data, such as the inadequacies of the "initial one-size-fits-all model for ARI, lack of expertise and credibility in secondary issues, competition for attention from literacy programs for the early grades, and overall funding shortfalls" (Salinger, chapter 3). Similar problems exist in Canada. The ARI experiences provide precedents and cautions to consider in planning new Canadian projects.

In undertaking future initiatives, Salinger provides sound advice:

- Any model we adopt needs to be flexible so teachers can adapt it to their students' instructional needs. Flexibility is also key in implementing any adolescent literacy initiative with our secondary teachers.

- In choosing a priority, we must focus on comprehension because it is the basis for learning in all content areas. This affirms our current direction as we focus our efforts to show how comprehension instruction can be embedded in the daily routines of teaching all content area subjects. All students need ongoing comprehension strategy instruction.

- There is a need to develop a procedure for identifying and diagnosing the students who are most at risk for reading failure in the secondary school.

- Creative use of local funds and vigilance in seeking external funding are important elements. Clearly, we need more funding for ongoing curriculum-based adolescent literacy interventions and initiatives.

Salinger underscores the important factor of shared leadership in this study. The Alabama administrators emphasized the need for personal leadership development for the school-based literacy coaches. Effective development of local capacity with homegrown experts and local leaders is essential to sustain adolescent literacy initiatives. The profession is currently in a state of flux with many skilled teachers retiring and new, inexperienced teachers starting their careers. To respond, we need new mechanisms to mentor and coach literacy leaders at the school, district, and provincial levels.

Salinger recommends the process of "devolving leadership," which we also affirmed in our Manitoba curriculum development experiences. We found that effective literacy leadership develops both from the top down and the bottom up.

School-Based Initiatives

Many educators at the secondary level in Canada are ready to focus on schoolwide initiatives and eagerly await further development of whole-school models such as the one undertaken at Herbert Hoover High School and described by Doug Fisher in chapter 6. Fisher helps readers envision a schoolwide plan at the secondary level that comprises exemplary team efforts led by a principal who is a strong instructional leader, and a staff who serve as role models, in collaboration with university professors. This schoolwide approach has enormous potential in Canada and other countries.

Nevertheless, reading Fisher's chapter prompted several important questions. How do the teachers and students feel now about their school being touted as the model school for all schools? How has the positive attention affected the school? How does the literacy leadership team keep up the spirit that "it takes us all" (Fisher & Frey, 2006) throughout the year? What types of formative assessment tools and strategies do teachers use to inform their instruction?

Fisher's chapter on the school model in San Diego follows discussion of a very special school setting in Montana. Santa's chapter in this volume (see chapter 5) calls for an integrated and holistic approach to address the complex needs of adolescents whose delay in literacy may affect their emotional, social, cognitive, and academic needs. She stresses that there are therapeutic principles as well as academic and learning principles that must be addressed, including the following:

- "containment and structure,"
- the development of a meaningful adult–child relationship and "accurate recognition," and
- explicit teaching of basic principles of learning and strategies in order for students to develop stronger ownership as they take charge and direct their own learning (Santa, chapter 5).

Santa suggests that containment and structure are essential. But the term *containment* may be problematic in Manitoba; it may sound too clinical or restrictive for some educators in our province who do not work in the closed therapeutic and academic setting of Montana Academy. We are certainly conscious of classroom management's pronounced impact on student achievement (Wang, Haertel, & Walberg, 1993). Classrooms are microcosms of our culturally diverse communities. In our experience, it is impossible to teach learning strategies if the class is in chaos. Classroom management with structure, rules, and routines must be fostered through ongoing, respectful, and culturally sensitive communication with students, families, caregivers, and their larger communities.

Our documents encourage building safe and caring school communities so that all learners feel they are valued and belong, enabling them to develop the confidence to take the inevitable risks that accompany learning. We need to foster positive relationships among classmates in the school community and increase student engagement that will hopefully translate into regular attendance. Accordingly, the fifth general outcome of our ELA Framework stresses the need to build and celebrate community, and recognizes that language and literacy are critical elements in developing and fostering an understanding of diversity in our democratic learning communities.

Santa's explicit links between ongoing self-assessment and metacognition are the direction Canadians have been moving. In Manitoba's school districts, we have collaborated with parent councils to provide more evening workshops for parents and adolescent students. The goal of these sessions is to teach many of the key learning principles that Santa has outlined and to help parents understand assessment processes.

These evening workshops have been very successful. Parents welcome practical suggestions for supporting the development of study strategies, positive attitudes toward school, and a work ethic in the home. The belief that hard work, over time, pays off remains a value extolled by many immigrants in our countries but needs some reinforcement with a new generation. Powerful discussions at these sessions have served to strengthen family communication and home–school partnerships to improve adolescent literacy.

The Role of Literacy Coach

Chapter 7 in this volume provides an overview of the need for literacy coaches, their potential roles and inherent challenges, and practical strategies for thriving and surviving as a coach. Authors Elizabeth Sturtevant and Kristine Calo remind readers of the need for balance between task and maintenance functions in coaching. The authors' cautions about the coaches' lack of support, role definition, and feelings of being overwhelmed are familiar complaints that we hear in Canada. These are sobering reminders of the dilemmas and fragmentation that the best trained literacy coaches and literacy leaders may experience as they multitask with inadequate support systems. Michael Fullan (2002), our Canadian expert on teacher change, has warned us about the deleterious effects of fragmentation, lack of coherence, and feeling overwhelmed. Sturtevant and Calo also highlight excellent resources that are available to provide the necessary support that literacy coaches require.

There is some caution in Canada about the role of literacy coaches. Several years ago the certification requirement for resource teachers was lifted in some jurisdictions. This change resulted in some untrained teachers being given resource responsibilities, such as diagnostic assessment and writing individual education plans and special education funding proposals without sufficient training and support. The promise of on-the-job instruction did not always materialize. Consequently, a concern has arisen that some individuals designated as literacy coaches have not completed the necessary educational requirements or been given the necessary supports for success. An untrained or unqualified literacy coach may have a detrimental impact on educators, students, and staff, as well as a negative effect on future adolescent literacy initiatives, which would lead to new cynicism at the secondary level.

Challenges faced by literacy coaches, according to Sturtevant and Calo, may include "lack of role definition, restrictive guidelines, communication with administration, gaining acceptance from the teachers," as well as the usual issues of time, trust, isolation, and resistance that all consultants face. In a coaching role, literacy leaders collaborate with teachers to build a common vision and belief system, a culture of collaboration and a sense of professional learning community. At the same time, they must overcome a fear of change and a culture of resistance in some high schools. In Manitoba, resource teachers and reading clinicians often take on these roles in addition to their diagnostic, teaching and programming roles. The effect can be overwhelming, especially if one is assigned to multiple schools.

The authors suggest that when teachers establish a sense of community they are better able to share successes and struggles. This insight resonates loudly with our collaborative curriculum development team experiences of the last decade in Manitoba. There is great potential with effective coaching to implement the most promising practices to support students, teachers, and administrators in their initiatives to improve adolescent literacy.

Conclusion

It is encouraging to know that so many dedicated researchers and practitioners are collaborating to improve adolescent literacy at this time. From the highest levels of nations, provinces, states, and territories where policies must be set and resources allocated, to our local middle schools and high schools, we are translating solid theories and research into promising practices and effective adolescent literacy initiatives. We can transform adolescent literacy globally with this intensive and comprehensive, collaborative approach.

Never have we defined more clearly what constitutes solid theory, research-based evidence, effective practices and strategies for instruction, and assessment of adolescent literacy in Canada. We have a professional and collective responsibility to deliver our intended curricula so that all students can achieve their literacy learning potential. We also know that differentiating instruction and improving assessment will be perpetual tasks in our diverse classrooms.

We continue to reflect on why it so difficult to infuse content literacy strategies in our secondary schools (O'Brien, Stewart, & Moje, 1995). We need to create a culture that welcomes change and supports the strategic teaching and research-based strategies mandated in our curricula. We need more dialogue with our colleagues as we critically reflect on our pedagogical practice, test new theories, conduct action and formal research, and practice strategies. We need to schedule more time for coaching and mentoring. Canadian educators know that we are part of a growing worldwide community of secondary teachers committed to improving adolescent literacy.

Supported by our administrators and department heads, we are finding new ways to team with our colleagues from all subject areas in our schools. We are coordinating our efforts to use common strategies and develop schoolwide literacy plans. In professional learning communities, we are discovering a new collective energy, a renewed sense of purpose and direction for adolescent literacy endeavors. In a dynamic global learning community supported through our IRA network of colleagues and resources, we can engage and empower each other to transform ourselves and to create safe and caring democratic learning communities in our world.

Questions for Reflection

1. What do you think are priorities for adolescent literacy initiatives where you teach?

2. Compare your perspectives and experiences regarding adolescent literacy initiatives with the international experiences and perspectives expressed in this chapter. What are key similarities and differences?

Carol Hryniuk-Adamov is a Certified Reading Clinician at the Child Guidance Clinic, serving in six schools of Winnipeg School Division in Winnipeg, Manitoba, Canada. She is a doctoral student at the University of Manitoba, Winnipeg, Manitoba. She has taught at the Universities of Manitoba and Winnipeg. Her main areas of research interest include translating literacy research into instructional and assessment practice, and promoting parental involvement, school literacy plans, leadership development, assessment for learning, and literacy across the curriculum throughout western and northern Canada. She is extremely active in the International Reading Association and in her local and provincial IRA councils. You can contact her at cadamov@shaw.ca.

REFERENCES

Bussiere, P., Cartwright, F., Knighton, T., & Rogers, T. (2004). *Measuring up: Canadian results of the OECD PISA study: The performance of Canada's youth in mathematics, reading, science, and problem solving: 2003 first findings for Canadians aged 15.* Ottawa, ON: Statistics Canada.

Fisher, D., & Frey, N. (2006). Majority rules: A schoolwide literacy success. *Principal Leadership, 6*(7), 16–21.

Fullan, M. (2002). The change leader. *Educational Leadership, 59*(8), 16–20.

Manitoba Education, Citizenship, and Youth. (2006). *Information technology literacy continuum.* Winnipeg: Manitoba Education, Citizenship, and Youth. Retrieved December 1, 2006, from http://www.edu.gov.mb.ca/k12/docs/support/tfs/appendixa.html

Moore, D.W., Bean, T.W., Birdyshaw, D., & Rycik, J.A. (1999). *Adolescent literacy: A position statement for the Commission on Adolescent Literacy of the International Reading Association.* Newark, DE: International Reading Association.

O'Brien, D.G., Stewart, R.A., & Moje, E.B. (1995). Why content literacy is difficult to infuse into the secondary school: Complexities of curriculum, pedagogy, and school culture. *Reading Research Quarterly, 30*, 442–463.

Wang, M.C., Haertel, G.D., & Walberg, H.J. (1993). Toward a knowledge base for learning. *Review of Educational Research, 63*, 249–294.

Western and Northern Canadian Protocol (WNCP) for Collaboration in Basic Education. (1998). *The common curriculum framework for English language arts, kindergarten to grade 12.* Winnipeg: Manitoba Education and Training. Retrieved March 4, 2007, from http://www.wncp.ca

Western and Northern Canadian Protocol (WNCP) for Collaboration in Education. (2006). *Rethinking classroom assessment with purpose in mind.* Retrieved July 31, 2006, from http://www.wncp.ca/assessment/rethink.pdf

PART II

Instructional Strategies for Adolescent Learners

CHAPTER 9

Academic Literacy: Principles and Learning Opportunities for Adolescent Readers

Jill Lewis

HIGHLIGHTS

- Academic literacy involves skills, dispositions, language, and relationships adolescents rarely experience in their out-of-school Discourse communities.

- Evidence suggests that students' academic literacy is not as well developed as their other literacies.

- Ten principles can guide curriculum development for adolescents' academic literacy.

- There are learning opportunities that integrate these principles and that encourage collaborative, reflective classrooms that promote academic literacy.

I t's the first day of the fall semester. Fifteen college freshmen reluctantly enter my classroom, none with the course text that was available at the bookstore, and few with notebooks or other materials suggesting a readiness to learn. Most students have something (an iPod?) plugged into their ears. It's a diverse group of students: Hispanic, Asian, African American, Middle Eastern, and Caucasian; they range in age from 18 to mid-30s, some having waited until their children entered school to begin college. This is my Reading for College course, a class that underprepared college freshmen at my university are required to take at the

Adolescent Literacy Instruction: Policies and Promising Practices edited by Jill Lewis and Gary Moorman. © 2007 by the International Reading Association.

beginning of their college career. Regardless of their differences, as discussion and introduction to the course begins, it is clear that all of the students resent having to take this course. No one ever told them they had reading difficulties; their recent college admissions test revealed the deficiencies. This is a noncredit course, and students are angry that they have to pay tuition for it while not receiving anything that will count toward graduation requirements. I don't blame them, but they are not alone.

These students represent only a small fraction of the more than 60% of the freshmen at my university who need at least one remedial course at the time of their entrance to college, a typical number according to a study by ACT (2004a.). In 2004, 1.2 million high school graduates took the ACT Assessment, but only 22% achieved scores that would deem them ready for college in all three basic academic areas— English, math, and science. A similar report released by ACT in March 2006 found that only 51% were prepared for college-level reading (ACT, 2006a). A snapshot of universities across the country provides support for ACT's findings. According to the Ohio Board of Regents, one quarter of the 39,395 first-year college students at the state's 13 public universities during the 2003–2004 school year took at least one remedial course (Fields, 2006). In fall 1997, 65% of all New York City Board of Education (BOE) graduates who entered bachelor's programs (BA or BS) and 86% of all BOE graduates who entered associate's programs (AA or AS) failed one or more of the City University of New York's Freshman Skills Assessment Tests in the basic reading, writing, and mathematics skills. Fifty percent of those entering the City University of New York placed into remedial reading and 61% placed into remedial writing (Cilo & Cooper, 2000). Nearly a third of Colorado graduates who enrolled in the state's public colleges in fall 2004 needed remedial classes in mathematics, writing, or reading, according to the Colorado Commission on Higher Education (Gose, 2006). Is adolescent literacy achievement in the United States really as bad as these data suggest?

Some have remarked that this is a false picture. They say that politicians, industrialists, and media pundits have manufactured a crisis about public education and that when we look at the data more carefully we will see that students are doing at least as well now as they have always done (Berliner & Biddle, 1995; Bracey, 2006). Some argue that our students actually have higher levels of achievement than previous generations but that we are not using the right tools for assessment to gauge students' "new literacy" proficiencies. Consequently, we deem our students deficient. Kist (2003) visited a number of new literacy classrooms and describes the assessment system he found:

> Students are assessed on their product achievement and their process achievement and complete a portfolio of their work in multimedia form, essentially creating a kind of electronic portfolio system. Such an electronic portfolio can include scanned photos of student work in multimedia; checklists of student behaviors as they collaborate; video footage of each student working collaboratively; examples of "think-alouds" as students describe their processes of creating a product in some medium; and letters in which students self-reflect on how they believe they have reached their goals. (pp. 11–12)

He concludes, "Traditional paper/pencil achievement tests, which are taken in isolation and use print-based formats, are not going to assess the achievements needed by students as they move deep into the 21st century" (p. 12).

An equally compelling argument is that our students are truly falling behind when compared internationally, that our schools are failing our children, and that if this trend continues the United States will not be able to successfully compete in the international marketplace. This argument is bolstered by some interpretations of national and international test results. When compared internationally on the reading Program for International Student Assessment (PISA) tests, the U.S. 15-year-olds scored slightly below the international average (National Center for Education Statistics, 2004). These tests ask students to apply reading skills to reading materials that they are likely to encounter as young adults, including magazines and government forms. Our own national tests yield similar results. The Harvard Civil Rights Project (Lee, 2006) found that the average reading score gain on NAEP from 2002 to 2005 (post-NCLB) was null for grade 4 and minus 3 points for grade 8. In 8th grade, 29% of students tested below basic achievement levels. African American and Latino 17-year-olds were reading as well as white 13-year-olds by the end of 11th grade. The picture could be even more dismal, considering that 35% of the students who fail to graduate drop out between 9th and 10th grade and thus are not included in the data for 17-year-olds. Concern about student achievement on these assessments and about our nation's future has spawned such federal initiatives as the America Reads Act, No Child Left Behind, and Striving Readers.

Can either of these two views serve as the basis for our education policies and instructional decisions for adolescent literacy? Should we agree that schools and adolescents are doing just fine, thank you, and ignore naysayers whose real intention might just be to put a negative spin on public education? Or should we refute those who suggest it is the new literacies that we should use as the yardstick for measuring student achievement, and join the chorus of public education critics who push for an overhaul of our public schools?

I suggest that neither position is completely satisfactory or accurate. Adolescents have multiple literacies; they use different ones in different communities, including peer groups, church, and family. Literacies are always situated within specific social practices within specific Discourses (Gee, 1996, 2000). Some of these literacies are better developed than others, and competence is relative to specific contexts, communities, and practices (Kern & Schultz, 2005). Today's adolescents communicate well with their peers and, in fact, develop innovative uses of language, such as rap. There is evidence, however, that middle grade and high school students are not as accomplished in academic literacy, the kind of literacy needed for achievement on traditional school tasks and standardized assessments (Lewis, 1996). Reconciling this kind of literacy with other forms that students use in other contexts is challenging. Kist (2003) reports that for many of the new literacies teachers struggle with their own definitions of achievement. As these teachers attempt to create classrooms that honor and feature multiliteracies, they also see a widening divide between their own definitions of achievement and the official state or provincial definitions of achievement, ones that tend to promote print literacy exclusively.

Defining Academic Literacy

Bourdieu (1977b) explains that cultural capital derives from one's "habitus," which he defines as "a system of lasting, transposable dispositions which, integrating past experiences, functions at every moment as a matrix of perceptions, appreciations, and actions" (pp. 82–83). It consists of those cultural signals, dispositions, attitudes, skills, references, formal knowledge, behaviors, goals, and competencies that are rewarded within particular contexts, such as school, to achieve particular outcomes, such as high achievement or high aspirations (Bourdieu, 1977a). The culture of schooling requires academic literacy. It includes particular student–student and teacher–student interactions; formal skills and knowledge, including academic vocabulary and linguistic patterns; expectations for attention and participation; and a reward structure for academic success. Influences outside of school, especially an adolescent's peers and family, will affect a student's habitus and shape that person's approach to schooling.

When our students come face-to-face with more traditional forms of learning (e.g. school learning), they need to use specialized academic literacy skills to comprehend and communicate about texts that are often decontextualized and disconnected from many students' experiences. Marzano (2004) considers academic knowledge as having a more narrow scope than an individual's general knowledge. Depending on students' prior experiences, including subjects taken in school and the quality of teaching experienced in those subjects, students may or may not have the topic and domain knowledge (Alexander & Jetton, 2000) needed for success in a particular academic environment.

Academic literacy is needed not only for college. According to Achieve, Inc., and the American Diploma Project (2004) and ACT (2004b), the skills required for workforce training beyond high school are similar to those expected of a first-year college student. In addition, it has been estimated that 85% of all jobs are now classified as "skilled," meaning that they require some education beyond high school. There does not appear to be support for the proposition that those not going to college need to be qualified to enter college credit courses in order to enter the workforce. However, Barton (2006) makes a strong case for advancing the academic skills of a high proportion of those high school graduates if they are to compete successfully for the higher paying jobs available to those without a college degree and to advance in such jobs. Thus when we design curricula to promote academic literacy, we may be moving students out of their comfort zones, but moving them to a place that is necessary for personally rewarding futures. Not to do so is a disservice to our students.

How Did We Arrive at This Place?

Minimally it appears there is a disconnect between literacies students use outside of school and the academic literacy they must demonstrate in school. Varied explanations are offered for this situation, including inadequate teacher preparation (Darling-Hammond, 2000; National Center for Education Statistics, 1999); failure of the teaching profession to attract the best and brightest (Rossi & Grossman, 2001); limited prior knowledge, experience, and motivation of students (Boldt, 2006); and the changing demographics, specifically that approximately 40 million people in the United States speak a maternal language that is not English (King & Goodwin, 2002).

There is also the issue of role clarification. Whose job is it to teach adolescents to read? Content area teachers believe they should be teaching their content, not literacy (Kamil, 2003). This attitude is exacerbated by the recent mantra that all children will be reading by the end of 3rd grade and the definition of high-quality teachers as those who have majored in the subjects they teach.

A very compelling explanation of weak student performance on state or standardized assessments is that many teachers' expectations of adolescents are too low and do not sufficiently challenge adolescents, especially those who struggle with academic literacy. Since Rosenthal and Jacobson's now classic research (1968), *Pygmalion in the Classroom*, an extensive body of research has been developed that describes how teachers' expectations can influence student performance. The effect of such behavior is cumulative, and over time teachers' predictions of student achievement may in fact become true. My own students tell stories of how their high school teachers didn't give homework, use textbooks, or provide much direct instruction. According to the students, the teachers "didn't think we could or would do it, so we just didn't try."

All of these explanations are reasonable and suggest multifaceted causality. But none offers a concrete on-the-ground solution. For this we need to look into classrooms, identify the literacy skills students need for academic success, and then integrate learning opportunities in our daily teaching to ensure that students learn and are able to apply them in learning events that are meaningful and worthwhile for adolescents' futures.

Guiding Principles for Developing Academic Literacy

Middle grades and high school students need ample opportunity to develop the reading and study skills needed for academic success. To this end, I recommend 10 principles that serve as a framework for designing instructional opportunities aimed at improving adolescents' academic literacy (Lewis, 1996, 2007). These principles apply regardless of whether we teach a content field, perhaps social studies, physics, business, mathematics, or literature, or have students in what is sometimes referred to as a basic-skills class in middle grades or high school. These principles assume that content teachers understand the role literacy plays in comprehension of the content and students' construction of meaning and that integrated literacy instruction should be part of what occurs in the content class.

Principle 1. Students need high-interest and challenging reading material, with models, practice material, and longer selections drawn from sources that are commonly found in academic text. Each text we use should add to the knowledge base students will bring to other academic situations. Further, challenging materials will promote high expectations and give students a reality-based context in which to practice their increasing comprehension of sophisticated text. The positive impact of academically challenging high school programs is significant among African-American and Hispanic students (Adelman, 1999).

This principle is supported by research from ACT (2006b), which found that the ability to read complex texts is the clearest differentiator between students who are more likely to be ready for college-level reading and those who are less likely to be ready. Although most states don't define the types of reading materials to which high school students in each specific grade should be exposed or define complex texts, ACT (2006b) recommends a useful set of criteria, referred to as RSVP, for these materials.

- Relationships—Interactions among ideas or characters in the text are subtle, involved, or deeply embedded.
- Richness—The text possesses a sizable amount of highly sophisticated information conveyed through data or literary devices.
- Structure—The text is organized in ways that are elaborate and sometimes unconventional.
- Style—The author's tone and use of language are often intricate.
- Vocabulary—The author's choice of words is demanding and highly dependent on context.
- Purpose—The author's intent in writing the text is implicit and sometimes ambiguous.

We do not help students gain proficiency with academic texts if we avoid using them because we think students won't or can't read them. We need to scaffold with explicit instruction that guides students through comprehension of the text and construction of meaning. This principle applies equally well to all media.

Principle 2. Students need learning opportunities that develop critical thinking. It is our ability to engage in critical thinking that determines the extent to which we make assumptions, contemplate, question, and anticipate the implications of the decisions we make. Adolescents will need to problem solve and think critically whether in the workforce or at college. It is essential that they have opportunities to justify personal viewpoints, evaluate and modify their responses after discussion and review, and critique the responses of others. The results of ACT's National Curriculum Survey, completed by thousands of high school teachers across the country in 2003, suggest that high school teachers are more likely to teach higher-order critical reading skills to classes of students they perceive to be college bound than to classes of students they assume are not going to college (ACT, 2004b). This decision about who needs what ignores the reality that effective decision making and the ability to understand diverse points of view and meet literacy challenges are essential in all aspects of life.

Principle 3. Students need to experience process-oriented instructional approaches that encourage development of self-monitoring and metacognitive habits. Adolescents' comprehension will deepen when they have opportunities for self-monitoring in order to plan, implement, and evaluate their literacy, and to reflect on the thinking processes they use for constructing meaning. They will develop the habit of thinking about how they are processing and responding to ideas while they are reading, viewing, or listening to texts. Such opportunities will promote continuous self-assessment and flexible approaches to comprehending texts whereby students can adapt their strategies to accommodate the demands of the tasks and their purposes. In their synthesis of the literature on metacognition, Collins, Dickson, Simmons, and Kame'enui (1996) found four areas of convergence in the research: (1) Metacognitive knowledge facilitates reading comprehension. (2) Self-regulation facilitates reading comprehension. (3) Motivation may mediate students' use and benefit from metacognitive knowledge and self-regulation strategies. (4) Metacognitive instruction facilitates reading comprehension.

Principle 4. Students need learning opportunities that promote use of prior knowledge to facilitate prediction and comprehension. By preparing students for the texts they will encounter, students are helped to recall and organize what they already know about the topic and to anticipate the content and focus of the material. Readers who possess rich prior knowledge about the topic of a reading almost always understand the reading better than classmates with low prior knowledge (Anderson & Pearson, 1984). But "when readers process text containing new factual information, they do not automatically relate that information to their prior knowledge, even if they have a wealth of knowledge that could be related. In many cases, more is needed for prior knowledge to be beneficial in reading comprehension" (Pressley, 2001, World knowledge section, ¶3). Our teaching must begin where the students are but demonstrate how to move beyond their existing knowledge to formulate new understandings.

Principle 5. Students need to have learning opportunities for integrating reading and writing. The processes of reading and writing are mutually supportive and interactive. Good readers tend to be good writers, and good writers tend to do well in reading (Strickland, 1991; Teale & Sulzby, 1986). Langer and Flihan (2000) provide this explanation:

> Due to their different beginnings, research traditionally approached writing and reading as distinct areas of exploration. The 1980s marked a change in focus. Research began to examine the relationships between writing and reading as cognitive and social processes.... Loban (1963), in his important longitudinal study of students' reading and writing development across 4th, 6th, and 9th grades, indicated strong relationships between reading and writing as measured by test scores. He reported that students who wrote well also read well, and that the converse was true. Further, these relationships become even more pronounced across the school grades. (A Brief History of Writing and Reading Research section, ¶5; Writing and Reading Relationships section, ¶2)

Our instruction needs to help students learn to use writing as a complement to their reading and other text experiences so they are able to clarify meaning for themselves.

Principle 6. Students need learning opportunities that provide for partnership and collaboration. Peer relations are critically important during adolescence. We can use their need for connection to instructional advantage by engaging students in collaborative projects. Even single text assignments with follow-up activities can provide several stopping points at which students can compare their responses with those of a peer or a group, modify answers, and consider alternative solutions. Such practice offers students the chance to think about their comprehension processes and to understand their personal responses to the text, as well as to understand different perspectives. Johnson and Johnson (1986) found persuasive evidence that cooperative teams achieve at higher levels of thought and retain information longer than students who work quietly as individuals. Students are capable of performing at higher intellectual levels when asked to work in collaborative situations than when asked to work individually (Vygotsky, 1978). Equally, cooperative work can provide the means for developing leadership, building relationships, and enhancing communication skills.

Principle 7. Students need opportunities to learn that support a variety of learning-style preferences. Research has yet to provide a satisfactory scientific basis for teaching to specific learning styles. Nevertheless, we do know that individuals have preferences insofar as how they learn, and our questions and activities throughout our instruction should be varied to appeal to a range of these. We should include many visual models to accompany explanations of concepts, and we should offer multiple opportunities for discussing concepts and developing interpretations with peers to provide another avenue for learning. As students use the language of the text, they gain confidence in the use of new discourse patterns, concepts, sentence structures, and vocabulary that are common in academic settings.

Principle 8. Students need learning opportunities that allow them to assume responsibility for their own learning. To promote adolescents' control of their developing academic literacy, we need to encourage them to create their own summaries and graphic organizers that represent key ideas from academic texts. This process encourages students to take ownership of the ideas and to think about their wider application. Placing the locus of control within students enables them to realize that their own efforts make a difference in learning. Giving students this responsibility implies trust and confidence in them. Adolescents respond well to such respect and it generally promotes their enthusiasm for learning.

Principle 9. Students need learning opportunities that measure success using a variety of authentic assessments. Authentic assessments give teachers and students a more complete picture of student progress than do traditional assessments such as multiple-choice, short answer, essay, and standardized tests. Wiggins (1990) reminds us that "Traditional assessment, by contract, relies on indirect or proxy 'items'—

efficient, simplistic substitutes from which we think valid inferences can be made about the student's performance at those valued challenges" (¶1), and in contrast to the drill-type questions asked on traditional tests, "Authentic tasks involve 'ill-structured' challenges and roles that help students rehearse for the complex ambiguities of the 'game' of adult and professional life" (¶3, bulleted item 6). Authentic assessments inform teaching as well as learning. Thus the types of assessments Kist (2003) witnessed in the new-literacy classrooms and described previously would provide the kind of feedback that is needed for students and teachers. These assessments allow students multiple forms of representation of knowledge: film, music, and art. This would demonstrate teachers' respect for and celebration of individual diversity and learning.

Principle 10. Students need opportunities to use technology as a learning tool, not as an end in itself. Electronic technology and the Internet are transforming the way we organize and seek knowledge, replacing linear models with hypertext links that disregard disciplinary boundaries. When used properly, technology can support learning by providing opportunities for teachers to expand teaching approaches and it can engage students in new ways of learning. It is tempting to spice up instruction with video, PowerPoint presentations, and Web interactions, but how we use technology and encourage students to use it can determine whether this means for learning is productive and worthwhile. It must be relevant and interactive to the course work and help students learn how to be discriminating in their use of technology, especially the Internet.

Learning Opportunities to Address the Principles

With these principles in mind, we can begin to develop learning opportunities that integrate several principles simultaneously and that will increase students' academic literacy. All of the descriptions in other chapters of this book that describe ways to engage adolescents in literacy incorporate some of these principles. One difference in this chapter is that the learning opportunities I offer are designed specifically to address academic literacy, using a variety of texts. Further, many are tools for explicit instruction that would serve as adjuncts to popular techniques for developing adolescent literacy that may already be familiar, such as QAR, SQ3R, K-W-L, reciprocal teaching, guided reading, questioning the author, graphic organizers, and think-alouds. The purpose for each learning opportunity is provided, along with the recommended procedure and the principles addressed.

1. Learning Opportunity: Survey of Academic Self-Esteem

Purpose: By completing this survey (see Figure 9.1), students can analyze their literacy strengths in academic settings and identify areas where they feel they might improve. Students can set goals for themselves and revisit this survey throughout the year to self-assess improvements and set new goals (Lewis, 1993).

Procedure: Administer this survey and ask students to be completely honest about themselves. Inform them that they will not be graded on this; it is a tool for self-development. Students might want to share what they have learned about themselves by doing this survey and discuss individual items more in depth. The class should take the lead on this.

Principles addressed: 8, 9

2. Learning Opportunity: Look Who's Talking

Purpose: To teach students to view texts from multiple perspectives and to comprehend what they contribute to an author's focus and conclusions. When students are given an opportunity to consider the multiple perspectives that could be taken on a particular event, they become more sensitive to the view that their ideas are not necessarily the only ones possible.

Procedure: Ask students to consider the following situation: A neighbor purchases a shiny, new, red BMW convertible. Ask students what might be an initial reaction of each of the following individuals to this purchase: a psychologist, a historian, an economist, an author, a teenager, an artist, an environmentalist, and a mathematician. Students easily recognize that each might think quite differently about this event. The artist, for instance, might notice the car's sleek lines, the shade of red, and the interior design. An economist might wonder how much the car cost and whether it was a good investment. The psychologist might be curious about the individual's motivation for this purchase, and so on. Ask students to then identify other situations in which there might be multiple perspectives. These might include reactions to objects, world events, and scientific discoveries. Once the idea of multiple perspectives is established, students can locate readings, videos, news stories, and other texts and identify possible perspectives for each.

Principles addressed: 2, 3, 7, 8, 10

Figure 9.1. Survey of Academic Self-Esteem

Directions: The survey that follows asks a series of questions that you should answer based on your experiences and your knowledge of yourself. Think for a few minutes about each question before you rate yourself. Be as truthful as possible. The information you obtain is to be used for your own benefit. It is not a test! You will not be graded on your answers.

Survey of Academic Self-Esteem

(Adapted from "The Effects of a Precollege Reading Course on the Academic Self-Esteem of Urban College Students," by J. Lewis, Fall 1993, *Inquiries in Literacy Learning and Instruction* [College Reading Association Yearbook, pp. 47–55].)

Directions: For each item, circle the number that you feel best describes you as you are now. (1 = not true of me at all; 4 = very true of me)

1. I can successfully prepare to take exams.	1	2	3	4
2. I can figure out what will be asked on tests.	1	2	3	4
3. I have successful strategies for taking notes on lectures and reading assignments.	1	2	3	4
4. I know how to preview my textbooks.	1	2	3	4
5. I know how to come prepared for class.	1	2	3	4
6. I know how to mark and underline reading material for review purposes.	1	2	3	4
7. I know how to make predictions when I read.	1	2	3	4
8. I am able to answer questions in a classroom.	1	2	3	4
9. I am able to read a textbook with understanding.	1	2	3	4
10. I know when to slow down my reading rate for better comprehension.	1	2	3	4
11. I know how to use context to get the meaning of unknown words in academic material.	1	2	3	4
12. I have good strategies for thinking critically about things I have read.	1	2	3	4
13. I am able to figure out the main ideas of academic reading materials (for example, literature, business, social studies, science).	1	2	3	4

(continued)

Figure 9.1. Survey of Academic Self-Esteem (continued)

14. I am able to set purposes for my reading.	1	2	3	4
15. I can read and interpret maps, graphs, and charts.	1	2	3	4
16. I know how to create summaries and visual aids to help me remember what I have read.	1	2	3	4
17. I know how to distinguish between important and unimportant details when I read.	1	2	3	4
18. I am able to participate successfully in a classroom.	1	2	3	4
19. I am able to ask a teacher for help when I have a question.	1	2	3	4
20. I believe I will be admitted to the college of my choice.	1	2	3	4
21. I believe I have a lot of knowledge to share with others.	1	2	3	4
22. I believe I will graduate from college.	1	2	3	4
23. I believe I will have a successful future.	1	2	3	4

Survey Analysis

Let's analyze the results of your survey. The following chart shows the category into which different items fall. Place your ratings on the chart. Then respond to the questions that follow the chart.

Category	Question Nos.							
Study Skills	1	2	3	4	6	14	16	
Your Ratings	—	—	—	—	—	—	—	
Reading Skills	7	9	10	11	12	13	15	17
Your Ratings	—	—	—	—	—	—	—	—
Participating in Classrooms	5	8	18	19	21			
Your Ratings	—	—	—	—	—			
Expecting a Successful Future	20	22	23					
Your Ratings	—	—	—					

Assessing Your Academic Self-Esteem

1. Based on the information you've obtained from this survey, what are your area(s) of greatest confidence? _____

2. In a few sentences, describe the academic self-esteem goals you would like to achieve this year. _____

3. Learning Opportunity: In My Own Words

Purpose: To prepare students for summarizing lengthy pieces of text; to help students understand the meaning of ownership of an idea and to accomplish this with texts that have complex language (Lewis, 2007).

Procedure: Choose written text that contains complex ideas and language. Select two or three key sentences from the text that students will need to rewrite in their own words after they have read the text. They may do this with a partner or a small group. The class should compare responses to (1) confirm comprehension of complex ideas, (2) recognize multiple ways the same idea can be expressed, and (3) develop new academic vocabulary. If students have changed the meaning of the text, discuss where the confusion may have occurred and have students revise their original rewritten sentence. Students can partner to create sentences or to compare their writing prior to class review. After working with single sentences that contain complex ideas, students should be able to transition to creating summaries of texts of increasing complexity and length.

Principles addressed: 1, 2, 5, 6

4. Learning Opportunity: Visually Speaking

Purpose: To develop students' abilities to interpret visual messages accurately and to create and respond to such messages.

Procedure: This is more of a series of lessons, rather than a single learning opportunity. Analyze the visuals students will encounter in their textbooks or other materials you plan to use. These might include bar charts, pie charts (or circle graphs), flowcharts, timelines, tables, line graphs, diagrams, photographs, maps, and artwork (Lewis, 2007). Identify the key features of the visual that you want to share with students. Based on the visual's features, ask students some of these questions that will direct them to closer inspection of the visual and facilitate comprehension: (1) Provide a quote from another source and ask, Does the visual support this quote? Why or why not? (2) Add to the visual another detail from this text. (3) What is your personal response to this visual? (4) Find two visuals on the same topic and ask, What differences do you see in the ways information on the same topic is portrayed on the two visuals shown here? (5) With another two visuals on the same topic ask, How do the purposes of these two visuals on the same topic differ? (6) How does this visual help you to better understand your world? (7) How does this visual help you to comprehend the text? (8) Leave off some information from a visual of a table and ask, for example, What percentages do you predict will complete the last two columns? (9) What inferences can you draw from this visual? (10) What conclusions can you draw from this visual? (11) Paraphrase or summarize this visual. (12) How are the different parts of this visual related to each other? (13) Use this visual to create questions for a quiz. (14) Draw a sketch, graph, chart, or table for the information here. (15) Select two visuals from the same text where similar information is displayed differently and ask, What two things does Visual A tell you more easily than Visual B? What does Visual B tell you more easily?

Principles addressed: 2, 4, 6, 7, 8

5. Learning Opportunity: Websites for Me

Purpose: To teach students how to critically analyze websites for purpose, authenticity, authoritativeness/accuracy, author's assumptions and biases, recency, links to other sources, grammar and spelling, and visual content.

Procedure: Provide students with a set of websites they would find if they did a search on a particular topic. Ask a series of questions that involve students in identifying the purposes, biases, and authenticity of the sites (Lewis, 2007). Once students have worked with the sites you have provided, ask them to do a similar activity with sites they select on a topic of their choice (see Figure 9.2).

Principles addressed: 2, 4, 6, 7, 9

6. Learning Opportunity: Who Says So?

Purpose: To develop students' critical thinking about text, encourage an appreciation for levels of expertise, and discourage students from accepting only evidence that confirms their current beliefs or from ignoring evidence that does not agree with their current ideas.

Figure 9.2. Websites for Me

A. Below are examples of sites you might find if you did a search on the topic WOMEN IN THE MILITARY. Consider the point of view that each site might reflect as well as the authoritativeness of the information that each might provide. Then answer the questions below the list.

a. American Women in Uniform, Veterans Too!
   Military women—a history of military women from the Revolutionary War to present day. Information about combat issues, current women veterans issues, and extensive information about military women, past and present...ramblings of a self-appointed distaff critic who will continue to remind you that women are veterans too...and support for our young men and women in the military.
   http://coelacanth.aug.com/captbarb

b. Women in Vietnam
   Interviews, articles, first-person accounts, and announcements of events of interest and research requests.
   http://www.illyria.com/vnwomen.html

c. Women in the United States Military
   Women make up about 20 percent of today's military. Information and resources concerning women in the U.S. military, both in the past and the present.... Higher Positions for Women in the Military. Women are rising to increasingly higher levels in the Defense ...show that officer and enlisted women on active duty increased from 13....
   http://usmilitary.about.com/od/womeninthemilitary/index_r.htm

d. Center for Women Veterans
   Women Veterans Comprehensive Health Centers.... Women in the Military.... VA Benefits and Services.... Gains made by women in the military continue through the 1970s and that trend remains....
   http://www1.va.gov/womenvet

e. Hot Topics—visionforum.org
   If certain federal lawmakers have their way, your 18-year-old daughters will be registered for selective service and drafted for combat by the next war.... Christians have long since abandoned the issue of women in the military. Sadly, far too many pastors and...by permitting and perpetuating the practice of women in the military.
   http://www.visionforumministries.org/issues/women_in_the_military

f. GenderGap: Women & the Military
   This is one woman's study of women around the world who have gone into combat during the last 6,000 years—now available online. Site includes a section on American Women and the....
   http://www.gendergap.com/military.htm

g. Linda Chavez: Sexual tension in the military. Townhall.com.
   $200,239 as of 2:15 PM Monday. More on National Security. Today's Opinion. Monday. Sexual tension in the military. Linda Chavez (archive) May 5, 2004.... Admit it, the increased presence of women in the military

(continued)

Figure 9.2. Websites for Me (continued)

serving in integrated units has made military.... While some advocates of women in the military have argued that women's...
http://www.townhall.com/columnists/LindaChavez/2004/05/05/sexual_tension_in_the_military

h. Military Resources: Women in the Military
Access to information on American history and government, archival administration, information management, and government documents to NARA staff, archives and records management professionals, and the general public.... Military Resources: Women in the Military. African-American Women in Military History. From the Air University Library...World War II. Women in Military Service for America Memorial
http://www.archives.gov/research/alic/reference/military/women.html

i. Untitled Document
Their Own Self. FRED Columns. Women in the Military. More Letters from the Field. About our policy of putting women into military jobs for which they are not suited: It isn't working. It isn't coming close...telling the politicians what they want to hear: that women in the military are working out....
http://www.fredoneverything.net/MoreWomenLetters.shtml

Your Ideas About These Websites

Carefully read each question below, and then circle all of the websites that you think apply. Be sure you are prepared to justify your answers.

1. Which of the websites listed above might include very positive remarks about women serving in the military?
   a.   b.   c.   d.   e.   f.   g.   h.   i.
2. Which of the websites listed above will probably contain more opinion than fact?
   a.   b.   c.   d.   e.   f.   g.   h.   i.
3. Which of the websites listed above will probably contain a good deal of statistical information?
   a.   b.   c.   d.   e.   f.   g.   h.   i.
4. Which of the websites listed above will probably give primarily historical information about women in the military as well as information about this issue in the present?
   a.   b.   c.   d.   e.   f.   g.   h.   i.
5. Which of the websites listed above are most likely to be representative of the U.S. government's view about women in the military?
   a.   b.   c.   d.   e.   f.   g.   h.   i.
6. Which of the websites listed above will most likely limit its content to one war?
   a.   b.   c.   d.   e.   f.   g.   h.   i.

B. Visit two of the websites listed above and, for each, comment on the following:

Links to other sources
Grammar and spelling
Visual content

Procedure: Provide students with characteristics of expert, informed, and unsupported opinions (see Lewis, 2007): (1) Expert opinion: Often firsthand research, for example, a music historian on the influence of the Beatles, or a paleontologist on animal extinction. (2) Informed opinion: References to data sources, historical references, use of visual aids. (3) Unsupported opinion: Sweeping generalizations, stereotypes, unsupported claims. Provide examples for each. Then give students statements and ask them to explain what would be needed to make the statement an expert, informed, or unsupported opinion. For example, you could provide the statement, "Teenagers who do chores at home will get better grades in school than those who don't do chores." Students might suggest for expert opinion, "I interviewed and examined the report cards of 50 students at my school and found that those who had to do chores at home got better grades." For informed opinion they could create a sentence such as "A report in *Time* magazine reported that students had better grades in high school when they had responsibilities at home for such things as taking out the garbage." An unsupported opinion might be, "I don't think teenagers will do better in school if they have to do chores at home." When students work with texts, encourage continued application of these distinctions.

Principles addressed: 1, 2, 3, 4, 5

7. Learning Opportunity: Drill Down

Purpose: This is a management tool used to help an individual or group analyze a problem by breaking it down into its component parts (Manktelow, n.d.). It can be usefully adapted for developing students' academic literacy.

Procedure: Students might consider such problems as music piracy, illegal immigration, relationships in a novel or play, or global warming. Students write a statement of the problem on the left-hand side of a large sheet of paper. The problem might have appeared in written text, in a film, or in a talk students heard. Then, a little to the right of the statement, students write down the points that make up the next level of detail on the problem. These may be factors contributing to the problem, information relating to it, or questions it raises. Students can next create a semantic web to illustrate the component parts. This process of breaking the problem down into its component parts is called drilling down. As students work with the problem, they can conduct research on the nature of the problem, its causes, effects, solutions tried (and why they may not have succeeded), and their own solutions.

Principles addressed: 1, 2, 4, 5, 6, 7, 8, 10

Conclusion

Our personal goals for teaching adolescents are varied, but the idea of teaching implies that those whom we teach will learn. For adolescents to develop mature understanding and to think critically and compassionately about their lives and those of others, we must commit to moving them beyond their present knowledge, skills, dispositions, and interactions to new ideas, attitudes, and experiences. A focus on academic literacy can provide this momentum and simultaneously build for each student a positive sense of self and possibility. As teachers, we should do no less.

Questions for Reflection

1. Reflect on your own experiences as a middle grades or high school student. Which teachers did you most admire? Why? What did these teachers expect of you? Which principles of instruction described in this chapter did you experience as a student?

2. Which of the learning opportunity lessons described do you think would be most difficult to implement in your classroom? Why? What might you do to make teaching this learning opportunity possible?

Activities

1. Interview two teachers, one who teaches a middle grades content subject and one who teaches a content subject in high school, to learn their attitudes about incorporating literacy-based instruction into their content teaching.

2. Observe a middle grades or high school content teacher. What do you notice about the expectations the teacher has for students? Which principles of instruction described in this chapter did you observe during the lesson?

3. Search the Internet for another learning opportunity for adolescent literacy development that you believe incorporates some of the

instructional principles described in this chapter. Explain the ways in which you feel the learning opportunity accomplishes this. Also discuss how you might need to modify this learning opportunity to use it with your students.

Jill Lewis is Professor of Literacy Education at New Jersey City University, Jersey City, New Jersey, USA. She has served on the Board of Directors of the International Reading Association (2004–2007), on the Board of Directors for the American Reading Forum (2003–2005), and on IRA's and New Jersey Reading Association's Governmental Relations Committees. She has also served on several literacy task forces for New Jersey and received NJRA's Distinguished Service Award. She has also worked in Macedonia, Kazakhstan, and Albania for the Reading and Writing for Critical Thinking Project, and currently serves as a volunteer consultant for the Secondary Education Reform Activity program in Macedonia. Her areas of expertise include adolescent literacy, content literacy, literacy policy and advocacy, reading across the curriculum, classroom research, and leadership development. She can be contacted at jlewis@njcu.edu.

REFERENCES

Achieve & American Diploma Project. (2004). *Ready or not: Creating a high school diploma that counts*. Washington, DC: Authors.

ACT. (2004a). *Crisis at the core: Preparing all students for college and work*. Iowa City, IA: Author. Retrieved May 31, 2006, from http://www.act.org/path/policy/reports/crisis.html

ACT. (2004b). *Ready for college and ready for work: Same or different?* Iowa City, IA: Author. Retrieved June 5, 2006, from http://www.act.org/path/policy/pdf/ReadinessBrief.pdf

ACT. (2006a, March 1). *High school reading not challenging enough, says ACT* [Press release]. Retrieved May 31, 2006, from http://www.act.org/news/releases/2006/03-01-06.html

ACT. (2006b). *Reading between the lines: What the ACT reveals about college readiness in reading*. Iowa City, IA: Author. Retrieved May 31, 2006, from http://www.act.org/path/policy/pdf/reading_report.pdf

Adelman, C. (1999). *Answers in the tool box: Academic intensity, attendance patterns, and bachelor's degree attainment*. Washington, DC: Office of Education Research and Improvement, U.S. Department of Education.

Alexander, P., & Jetton, T. (2000). Learning from text: A multidimensional and developmental perspective. In M. Kamil, P. Mosenthal, P.D. Pearson, & R. Barr (Eds.), *Handbook of reading research* (Vol. 3, pp. 285–310). Mahwah, NJ: Erlbaum.

Anderson, R.C., & Pearson, P.D. (1984). A schema-theoretic view of basic processes in reading comprehension. In P.D. Pearson (Ed.), *Handbook of reading research* (pp. 255–291). New York: Longman.

Barton, P.E. (2006). *High school reform and work: Facing labor market realities.* Princeton, NJ: Educational Testing Service.

Berliner, D.C., & Biddle, B.J. (1995). *The manufactured crisis: Myths, fraud, and the attack on America's public schools.* Reading, MA: Addison-Wesley.

Boldt, M. (2006, June 19). Pawlenty: Schools in "silent crisis." *St. Paul Pioneer Press.* Retrieved March 12, 2007, from http://www.accessmylibrary.com/com site5/bin/pdinventory.pl?pdlanding=1&referid=2930&purchase_type=ITM& item_id=0286-15653510

Bourdieu, P. (1977a). Cultural reproduction and social reproduction. In J. Karabel & A.H. Halsey (Eds.), *Power and ideology in education* (pp. 487–511). New York: Oxford University Press.

Bourdieu, P. (1977b). *Outline of a theory of practice* (R. Nice, Trans.). Cambridge, England: Cambridge University Press.

Bracey, G.W. (2006). *Reading educational research: How to avoid getting statistically snookered.* Portsmouth, NH: Heinemann.

Cilo, M.R., & Cooper, B.S. (2000). *Bridging the gap between school and college: An analysis of K–16 education in New York City.* New York: Mayor's Advisory Task Force on the City, University of New York.

Collins, V.L., Dickson, S.V., Simmons, D.C., & Kame'enui, E.J. (1996). *Metacognition and its relation to reading comprehension: A synthesis of the research* (Tech. Rep. No. 23). Eugene, OR: National Center to Improve the Tools of Educators. Retrieved June 30, 2006, from http://idea.uoregon.edu/~ncite/documents/techrep/tech23.html

Darling-Hammond, L. (2000, January 1). Teacher quality and student achievement: A review of state policy evidence. *Education Policy Analysis Archives, 8*(1). Retrieved February 14, 2007, from http://epaa.asu.edu/epaa/v8n1

Fields, R. (2006, June 18). Plan to groom grads for college gets "incomplete." *Plain Dealer Bureau.* Retrieved March 12, 2007, from http://www.kidsohio.org/NewsMediaArticlePF.asp?ID=64

Gee, J.P. (1996). *Social linguistics and literacies: Ideology in discourses.* New York: Routledge.

Gee, J.P. (2000). Discourse and sociocultural studies in reading. *Reading Online, 4*(3). Retrieved April 10, 2007, from http://www.readingonline.org/articles/art_index.asp?HREF=handbook/gee/index.html.

Gose, B. (2006, March 10). Colorado debates how to send more at-risk students to college. *The Chronicle of Higher Education.* Retrieved October 16, 2006, from http://chronicle.com/free/v52/i27/27b01601.htm

Johnson, R.T., & Johnson, D.W. (1986). Action research: Cooperative learning in the science classroom. *Science and Children, 24,* 31–32.

Kamil, M.L. (2003). *Adolescents and literacy: Reading for the 21st century.* Washington, DC: Alliance for Excellent Education.

Kern, R., & Schultz, J.M. (2005). Beyond orality: Investigating literacy and the literary in second and foreign language instruction. *The Modern Language Journal, 89,* 381–392.

King, S.H., & Goodwin, A.L. (2002). *Culturally responsive parental involvement: Concrete understandings and basic strategies.* Washington, DC: American

Association of Colleges for Teacher Education. Retrieved May 31, 2006, from http://www.aacte.org/Publications/kinggoodwin.pdf

Kist, W. (2003, September). Student achievement in new literacies for the 21st century. *Middle School Journal, 35*(1), 6–13. Retrieved June 24, 2006, from http://www.nmsa.org/Publications/MiddleSchoolJournal/September2003/Article1/tabid/141/Default.aspx

Langer, J., & Flihan, S. (2000). Writing and reading relationships: Constructive tasks. In R. Indrisano & J.R. Squire (Eds.), *Perspectives on writing: Research, theory, and practice* (pp. 112–139). Newark, DE: International Reading Association. Retrieved June 8, 2006, from http://cela.albany.edu/publication/article/writeread.htm

Lee, J. (2006). *Tracking achievement gaps and assessing the impact of NCLB on the gaps: An in-depth look into national and state reading and math outcome trends.* Cambridge, MA: The Civil Rights Project at Harvard University. Retrieved February 14, 2007, from http://www.civilrightsproject.harvard.edu/research/esea/nclb_naep_lee.pdf

Lewis, J. (1993, Fall). The effects of a precollege reading course on the academic self-esteem of urban college students. In *Inquiries in literacy learning and instruction, the fifteenth yearbook of the College Reading Association* (pp. 47–55). Logan, UT: College Reading Association.

Lewis, J. (1996). *Academic literacy: Readings and strategies.* Boston: Houghton Mifflin.

Lewis, J. (2007). *Academic literacy: Readings and strategies* (Rev. 4th ed.). Boston: Houghton Mifflin.

Manktelow, J. (n.d.). *Drill down: Breaking problems down into manageable parts.* Retrieved June 22, 2006, from http://www.mindtools.com/pages/article/newTMC_02.htm

Marzano, R.J. (2004). *Building background knowledge for academic achievement: Research on what works in schools.* Alexandria, VA: Association for Supervision and Curriculum Development.

National Center for Education Statistics. (1999). *Teacher quality: A report on the preparation and qualifications of public school teachers.* Retrieved April 15, 2006, from http://nces.ed.gov/surveys/frss/publications/1999080/7.asp

National Center for Education Statistics. (2004). *Digest of education statistics.* Washington, DC: Author. Retrieved May 12, 2006, from http://nces.ed.gov/programs/digest/d04

Pressley, M. (2001, September). Comprehension instruction: What makes sense now, what might make sense soon. *Reading Online, 5.* Retrieved May 29, 2006, from http://www.readingonline.org/articles/art_index.asp?HREF=handbook/pressley/index.html

Rosenthal, R., & Jacobson, L. (1968). *Pygmalian in the classroom: Teacher expectation and pupils' intellectual development.* New York: Holt Rinehart & Winston.

Rossi, R., & Grossman, K.N. (2001, September 24). Substandard teachers under the microscope. *Chicago Sun-Times.* Retrieved March 12, 2007, from http://findarticles.com/p/articles/mi_qn4155/is_20010924/ai_n13915531

Strickland, D.S. (1991). Emerging literacy: How young children learn to read. In B. Persky & L.H. Golubchick (Eds.), *Early childhood education* (2nd ed., pp. 337–344). Lanham, MD: University Press of America.

Teale, W.H., & Sulzby, E. (1986). *Emergent literacy: Writing and reading.* Norwood, NJ: Ablex.

Vygotsky, L.S. (1978). *Mind in society: The development of higher psychological processes* (M. Cole, V. John-Steiner, S. Scribner, & E. Souberman, Eds. & Trans.). Cambridge, MA: Harvard University Press. (Original work published 1934)

Wiggins, G. (1990). The case for authentic assessment. *Practical Assessment, Research & Evaluation,* 2(2). Retrieved January 26, 2007, from http://PARE online.net/getvn.asp?v=2&n=2

CHAPTER 10

Reinventing Comprehension Instruction for Adolescents

Patricia L. Anders and Ellen Spitler

HIGHLIGHTS

- Certain selected vintage reading comprehension theories and instructional strategies have stood the test of time and are key to providing valuable insights for adolescent literacy instruction.
- Sociocultural perspectives, integrated with vintage theories and strategies, provide for the reinvention of adolescent literacy instruction that is relevant and meaningful.
- An example is provided of reinventing classroom norms to create a discourse community that thrives on comprehension and discussion strategies designed to enhance students' metacognition.

The purpose of this chapter is to review reading comprehension instruction research and strategies that have stood the test of time and to integrate them with current socioculturally based literacy perspectives. We do this to provide clarification of what may seem to many as a confusing array of advice from reading comprehension experts. Does adapting new perspectives suggest discarding the old? We think not and invite our readers to entertain these suggestions as possibilities for adolescent reading comprehension instruction. Moreover, we offer a firsthand account by a high school teacher who transformed her English class into an exciting venue for identity-changing literacy instruction.

Adolescent Literacy Instruction: Policies and Promising Practices edited by Jill Lewis and Gary Moorman. © 2007 by the International Reading Association.

Vintage Reading Comprehension Theory and Instruction

A Brief History of Theory and Research

The 1970s–1980s were a remarkable period of theory development and research about reading comprehension. One program of research, particular to adolescent literacy, was the work of Hal Herber's research team at Syracuse University. That team's work was the basis of Herber's first book on content-area reading, *Teaching Reading in Content Areas* (1970). Herber, Frank Smith (1971), and Ken Goodman (1976) each theorized that reading was a unitary act, meaning that the psycholinguistic processes involved were all engaged simultaneously. This perspective was counter to the prevailing view at the time, as well as to the view currently promoted by federal policymakers. As this chapter is being written, federal policymakers define reading as the acquisition of skills independent of the ideas in the materials students are being asked to read. Herber and his colleagues maintained, and we concur, that reading instruction should be provided to help students engage ideas and concepts. Hence, content area teachers are advised to consider the content being read by students and to select instructional strategies that engage students in that content.

Following Goodman and Smith's landmark publications, a federally funded research center called the National Center for the Study of Reading (CSR) was established at the University of Illinois. Cognitive psychologists and teacher educators joined to conduct research into the reading comprehension process and the teaching of reading comprehension. CSR's impact on the field was tremendous, not only because of its research productivity, but also because it intellectually supported scholars apart from the center who carried out their own reading comprehension research. Much was learned about how to teach reading comprehension, and those lessons are an integral part of the history of reading research. We consider the center's work vintage in that it has stood the test of time and provides much of the theoretical and research basis for commonly accepted content-area literacy instruction.

CSR's research was based on schema theory, which was first suggested by Bartlett (1932) and Piaget (1985) and then elaborated on by the researchers at the CSR (Anderson & Pearson, 1984; Schallert, 2002). Schema theory can be thought of as a metaphor for how the brain stores knowledge and experience in nodes that are organized and interconnected. A schema is not a particular memory, rather it is "the abstracted residue that one accrues from all of life's experiences, organized in a particular way and connected to everything else one knows" (Schallert, 2002, p. 557). Three characteristics of schemata are helpful for thinking about how to teach reading comprehension. The first characteristic is that the nodes making up a schema are actually variables that allow knowledge to be thought about flexibly. For example, Schallert explains,

> A reader's schema for a dog would represent a specific configuration of features capturing what a dog can look like, how it can behave, what place it can have in one's heart, or whatever aspects of dogginess an individual would have experienced. (p. 556)

For instruction, this suggests that teachers need to be aware of the possible features of a concept or idea being studied. Having thought about the range of viable features, teachers can better predict where students are likely to have gaps in their knowledge and experience or where misconceptions are likely to be lurking in students' thinking.

The second characteristic is that schemata are interembedded and dynamic—as one schema is activated, another may become the superarching structure, depending on the thinker's purpose. Schallert (2002) extends the dog example to point out that a dog schema may be overtaken by a flea structure if the thinker wishes to activate what is known about pests that bother dogs. This characteristic has many implications for instruction. For example, teachers can have a tremendous effect on student's reading comprehension when instructional time is spent helping students establish a purpose that ensures the most relevant conceptual structure is in play, or activated, during reading.

The third characteristic is that schemata are developed over time; hence, they become more elaborate and specific as an individual's experiences in particular domains increase. Those with the most elaborated schema about a given field or domain are experts. The instructional implications for this characteristic include the sorts of activities teachers provide students to extend and expand their learning, which result in elaborated schema, thereby contributing to future learning and to the ongoing development of content expertise.

The CSR also stimulated a related strand of research and practice—metacognition, which is an explanation of how one thinks about his or her thinking in order to better control and execute that thinking. Studies demonstrate that reflection on and evaluation of the quality of a reader's understanding leads to more sophisticated reading comprehension. Therefore, readers who resolve comprehension issues by using fix-up strategies are said to be metacognitive. According to Flavell, Miller, and Miller (2002), "Metacognitive territory includes both what a person knows about cognition and how she/he manages her/his own cognition" (p. 164). They later suggest that "Self-monitoring involves knowing where you are with respect to your goal of understanding and remembering the material. Self-regulation includes planning, directing, and evaluating your mnemonic activities" (p. 263).

Basic research on schema theory and metacognition generated considerable instructional research that fit well with Herber's (1978) model of before, during, and after reading instruction to support comprehension and learning in the content areas. It is possible, as shown in the discussion that follows, to make cognitive processes transparent to students by intentionally selecting instructional practices that provide opportunities to think, thereby increasing the probability that students will understand what they read.

Vintage Instructional Practices

Instructional strategies implied by schema theory and metacognition are replete in the teacher education and professional development literature. The examples that follow are offered primarily because we can explain them briefly and because more complete descriptions can be found on the Internet and in the many books and articles published about adolescent literacy. What we think is especially important, and is sometimes left out of descriptions of instructional strategies, is the linking of the strategies with the reasons for using them. Discussed next are the psychological reasons for using instructional strategies and an example of a before, during, and after reading strategy.

Before reading, students should be provided with opportunities to activate their prior knowledge related to the topic of the reading. If students lack prior knowledge, a related conceptual structure should be found or experiences should be provided to develop the needed prior knowledge. Likewise, students should have opportunities to predict what they think the reading is likely to be about and to set purposes for their reading. They should make plans for how they will accomplish the reading, basing their decisions on the quality and quantity of their prior knowledge, the organization of the text, and their purposes for reading.

One before-reading activity that accomplishes all these purposes, except making a plan for reading, is the anticipation guide (Buehl, 2001; Herber, 1978). The basic idea of the anticipation guide is that the teacher provides students with written statements that relate to the concepts in the reading assignment and that will either be confirmed or disconfirmed by the text the students will read. Before reading, each student records his or her predicted agreement or disagreement with the statements. Before reading, the teacher and students discuss the reasoning for the predictions, thereby providing the teacher with some understanding of the quality and quantity of prior knowledge students have about the ideas in the reading assignment. This prereading instructional strategy provides the teacher with insight to plan additional instruction.

During reading, students should have opportunities to organize the information being read, to pay attention to the rhetorical or story structure used by the author, to make connections between what they already know and the new information they are reading, and to confirm their predictions. The history change frame, a during-reading strategy suggested by Buehl (2001), is an example of an instructional strategy that provides these sorts of opportunities. This strategy is appropriate when the teacher expects students to read a text that has a problem-solution rhetorical structure and when groups of people being read about are confronted by problems caused by change. The teacher first asks students to survey the assignment and select the people about whom the text is written. Next, as the students silently read, the teacher directs them to discover and record on a chart the people who are involved in specific historical contexts, what problems those people faced, and what solutions guided the resulting changes in history. Students then use their charts to prepare for a discussion about how change affects people in different ways.

After-reading instructional strategies provide opportunities for students to reorganize their schemata and be metacognitive. Reorganizing the schema involves assimilating and accommodating new information with prior knowledge. This happens when students are asked to evaluate the quality of the information gained, to apply what was learned, and to reflect and respond to the reading in a personal way, asking themselves what this prose means personally. The discussions, essays, debates, labs, and similar activities typically assigned by content-area teachers provide for this sort of thinking. Reading educators suggest strategies too. For example, Harste and Short (1988) describe a strategy called Save the Last Word for Me. This strategy is employed first during reading, as each student selects quotations from the reading assignment that they find particularly important, compelling, or troubling. Each quote is written on an index card. After reading the assignment and before the class meets together again, each student writes a comment about each quote on the other side of the card. During either large- or small-group discussion, each student shares one card at a time, first reading the quote, hearing other students' comments about the quote, and then sharing his or her comment about the quote. For example, a student might choose a quote from a recent *Time* magazine editorial by Joel Klein (2006):

> In the end, the conservatives may be right: racial distinctions should not be written into law. But the embrace of our fabulous polychromatic smorgasbord has become an essential part of American society. We cherish it too much to let it slip away. (¶6)

After sharing the quote with the other students, the student would have the last word by reading his or her comment, which might be "Mr. Klein doesn't understand the depth of racism. Those in power will do anything to keep power, and laws are necessary to provide opportunities for the oppressed." No doubt, an invigorating discussion would ensue! This strategy would accomplish the psychological goals of after-reading strategies and would also serve to launch additional activities and projects.

Metacognition is enhanced when students are asked to reflect on the quality of the reading and learning experience by describing what worked well and what fix-up strategies were needed or could have helped. One teacher we know asks students to keep a metacognitive journal. She requires students in her middle school language arts and history class to select one of several graphic organizers to use as a during-reading strategy. After the reading assignment is finished, students write about how well the graphic organizer worked for them as they read the text. The teacher regularly asks students to read their journals aloud and provides opportunities for them to compare and contrast the benefits and liabilities of the various strategies.

These instructional strategies are guided by cognitive principles that are believed to influence an individual's reading comprehension before, during, and after reading. Recent research emanating from the sociohistorical-cultural perspective of teaching and learning, however, has shifted our thinking toward considering the influence of the social environment on reading and learning (González, Moll, & Amanti, 2005).

Sociocultural Perspectives

At the same time that the CSR was funded, other less well funded but nonetheless noteworthy chains of inquiry were underway. Paramount among these was the birth and development of sociolinguistic theories as promulgated by the work of Del Hymes, Courtney Cazden, John Gumperz, and their students. For example, Gilmore (1981) demonstrated how students displayed sophisticated language use outside school but were mute inside school. Denny Taylor (1983), Judith Green (1984), and David Bloome (1981) participated in research projects related to the concept that reading is a social and linguistic process. Concurrently, the widespread distribution of *Thought and Language* by Lev Vygotsky (1978) influenced scholars to theorize the relationship between a sociocultural-historical theory and the reading process (Scribner & Cole, 1981).

What are the key theoretical principles that can be gleaned by this ever-increasing literature?

The Social Nature of Learning

Sociolinguists explain that "the mind is social...human thinking is often distributed. Readers and written texts are parts of larger systems, composed of other people, other sorts of language, symbols, and tools, across which 'cognition' is distributed" (Gee, 2000, p. 198). Reading and writing are tools humans use to engage in conversations across space and time. Vygotsky, a Russian psychologist whose scholarship became readily available outside Russia in 1978, is widely credited for helping to advance ideas related to the social nature of learning, as described by Sylvia Scribner:

> Vygotsky's special genius was in grasping the significance of the social in things as well as people. The world in which we live is humanized, full of material and symbolic objects (signs, knowledge systems) that are culturally constructed, historical in origin and social in content. Since all human actions, including acts of thought, involve the mediation of such objects ("tools and signs") they are, on this score alone, social in essence. This is the case whether acts are initiated by a single agent or a collective and whether they are performed individually or with others. (as cited in Moll, 2005, p. 256)

One body of research capturing this conception of the social nature of learning is the work of Moll, Veléz-Ibáñes, and Greenberg (1989). They maintain that each human possesses funds of knowledge, which represent the material and symbolic experiences of the social groups one belongs to. The point is that students bring a system of language reflecting personal out-of-school knowledge to the classroom. If that knowledge and language are not honored, accepted, and linked to the language and learning of the classroom, students are less likely to engage in the classroom discourse community.

A discourse community—a group of people who share similar ways of communicating—is representative of certain beliefs, values, and social practices through which members constitute their identities (Gee, 2000). It is only a small inferential leap to recognize that each classroom is a discourse community and that the norms of that community govern its members' language development and use of language to negotiate ideas. This was confirmed by Sarah McCarthey's (2002) study of students' identities and literacy learning, which demonstrated the relationship between identity, language development, and learning. She analyzed students from three different settings and concluded that educators have profound influence on identity development and learning in and through the ways that language is used in the classroom. In a nutshell, then, the social nature of learning compels teachers to recognize the funds of knowledge students bring to the classroom. The teacher can then build on those funds of knowledge to create a classroom discourse community that helps students use language and engage ideas to continue to create and re-create their identities.

An Expanded Notion of Text

Another theme in this literature is related to the nature of text. A text never stands alone, rather it is part of an expanded text that involves what others have said and written about the same or related theme or topic. That is, while reading, a reader recalls other texts and experiences to construct new ideas and understandings that, in essence, create a new text. Floriani (1993), for example, used the term intercontextuality to suggest that students and their teacher negotiate the meaning of a text in ways that shape the process of using, engaging, and interacting with that text. Hence, a text is not one meaning; a text is a constructed meaning within a larger dialogue between and among language users who respond to and reflect on the text (Bakhtin, 1986). Here we see that any instruction that includes text must provide opportunities for learners to make connections with other texts, write about their reading, talk about their reading, and engage in other activities (such as role-playing and drawing) to enter the larger community of conversants around that text and the ideas it represents.

These ideas—the social nature of language, learning, and text—are radical departures from the individualistic notions of the schema theorists. Learners use reading and writing as tools not only to construct meaning but also to be participants in meaningful social networks of communication and meaning making.

Reinventing Comprehension Instruction for Adolescents

Figure 10.1 represents the morphing of theories and practices from cognitive psychology and sociohistorical-cultural theories into one model. The figure is an adaptation of the framework "Dimensions of Content Area Literacy Instruction" (Anders & Guzzetti, 2005).

In this figure, there are three circles representing context. The first, outer circle denotes the larger societal context; the second circle represents the local school context; and the third, inner circle signifies

Figure 10.1 Considerations for the Reinvention of Content Area Literacy Instruction

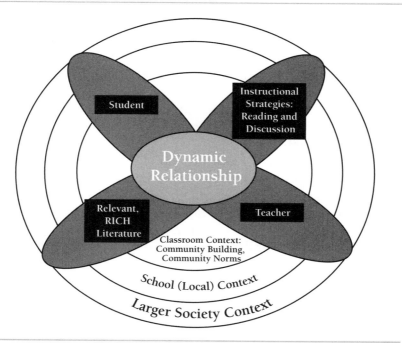

the classroom context. The placement of these circles foregrounds the social nature of teaching and learning. For example, the current culture of testing permeates the school and classroom walls and changes the principal's behavior and the teacher's instructional decision making (Anders & Richardson, 1992).

Federal policies, such as high-stakes testing, and local community norms affect the school and the teachers and students in classrooms. For example, in one of Tucson's local communities with highly educated and relatively wealthy parents, teachers are habitually the scapegoat for all that is perceived to be wrong with the community. This blame-the-teacher mentality makes it difficult for teachers in that particular district to be innovative or to step outside perceived community norms. Of course, positive examples of community norms exist too. In one town, alumni from the high school regularly visit the school, acting as mentors and sharing their expectations for the students to become alumni who are contributing members of the local community.

The first two circles influence the particular context of the classroom, but the socially aware teacher finds ways to work with students to create their own community within the larger community. Such a teacher studies the homes and neighborhoods in which students live and finds ways to take advantage of their funds of knowledge to create a unique community within their classroom.

Inside the context circles are four dimensions: the students, the teacher, the literature, and the instructional strategies to engage the ideas of the content area. In this model, the oval labeled students recognizes the funds of knowledge students bring to the classroom. Also, the language of the students and prior literacy experiences are acknowledged as resources for the developing classroom discourse community (Gee, 2000).

The teacher oval includes the roles of facilitator and conductor. The teacher guides students' discussions by ensuring that each individual is validated within the community by being a "knowledgeable other" (Lee & Smagorinsky, 2000, p. 2). A teacher in this model often makes the following types of comments: "Good job, the way you said that really stretches our thinking" or "Could you push a little harder on that idea—it seems like you are making two points that contradict each other."

Another oval in the figure is the content-area-related literature. Literature is a pivotal voice that informs the classroom community and provides a common text that the students and teacher engage with to construct meaning. The text is carefully selected to be considerate (Armbruster, 1984), to have relevant and rich content, and to have a high interest level for the students. The students read, respond in writing and artwork, discuss, and reread to engage in constructing new understandings.

They use comprehension and discussion strategies—many of which are borrowed from the instructional research emanating from schema theory and metacognition—as tools for meaning construction, which are evaluated metacognitively by students.

Creating a Dynamic Relationship

This model portrays a classroom in which the organization and activity are designed to create a space (Moje et al., 2004) where the student, teacher, text, activities, and context converge to form a dynamic relationship (the center circle) that results in students' construction of new understandings and metacognitive growth. It differs radically from what many, if not most, students experience in secondary classrooms.

In the rest of this chapter, coauthor Ellen Spitler provides a first-person account of an instructional enactment of the vintage reading comprehension research and practices with insights gleaned from the sociohistorical-cultural literature as represented in the model just discussed. Ellen is an experienced high school English teacher who teaches in a working-class school. Her students are challenging because, like many young people, they are perceived as less than successful readers and writers. Many come to her classroom with little love for reading and minimal experience composing meaningful prose. Her literacy work, presented here, began with a group of struggling 12th graders, students who were placed in her senior English class to help them reach grade-level targets in reading and writing before graduation. Our hope is that her experiences will explicate possibilities for the reinvention of comprehension instruction.

Ellen begins her account by describing the classroom community she strives to create from the first day of school. She goes on to describe the practices she employs to guide students to become literate members of the emerging discourse community by using comprehension and discussion strategies with rich relevant literature. She concludes by explaining how space is created for students' metacognitive growth. As you will read, students' testimonies as to what they learned in Ellen's class are worthy of praise—these are young people who have clearly been on a journey of reinventing themselves.

Context: Community Building in My English Class

How can teachers create a social space where students feel safe and willing to openly share their ideas? Teachers of adolescents know all too well the challenges of getting students to talk in the classroom; classroom discussions must be both interesting and academic. But, even more importantly, students must feel that they have something important to say, that they will be listened to, and that others will use what they say for developing important ideas. These conditions are met when students in a class form a community. I begin to construct the classroom community on the first day of school by reinventing classroom norms.

Reinventing Classroom Norms

On the first day of school, I do my best to throw the kids off balance so that we are free to create our own community. I greet them at the door wearing crazy sunglasses. Popular music is playing on the stereo. Students are told to choose a seat, unload their stuff, and wander the room, which is filled with art, quotes from literature, announcements, and words of encouragement. Even when the final bell rings, the music still plays.

The wackiness of my appearance and methods are designed to bust the norms of regular school, challenging students' expectations of what class should look, feel, and sound like. Early in my career, I used this first day to create a place where students felt at home. Once I recognized the importance of developing a discourse community for accomplishing the sophisticated thinking, reading, writing, and learning I expected from them, I realized that radically different classroom norms needed to be established so as to have new space for establishing community.

The next few days include several activities designed to help build personal connections. Students create colorful nameplates for their desks, take a quiz that asks questions about my life, and begin to share their lives in writing activities and interactive games. Some might think that we are just playing. In a way we are. Play is good for getting to know others and for revealing yourself to others. Play gives participants permission to let their guard down. It is good for imagination. In a playful environ-

Figure 10.2. Picasso Self-Portrait Project Student Samples

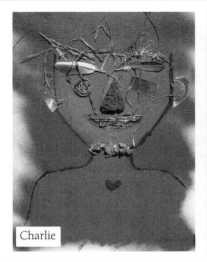

ment, risks can be taken. Through play, community is developed, and as facility with language increases, a discourse community is nurtured.

Another way we play is a Picasso self-portrait project. The project requires students to critically analyze their own lives, create a self-portrait, compose a formal piece of writing, present a speech about their portrait, and respond formally to a classmate's portrait. Here is how we do it.

First, I introduce Pablo Picasso, showing examples of his cubist portraits and sculptures made from materials found around homes. He has a cow sculpture, for example, that is made from bicycle handlebars and seat. Next, I ask each student to locate at least six materials that are representative of himself or herself. As a class we brainstorm possible materials. The list typically includes such items as gum wrappers, magazine pictures, cotton, glass, or photographs. The kids then are asked to arrange the materials in a Picasso-like self-portrait. As shown in the samples in Figure 10.2, the kids are imaginative and push themselves to illustrate their lives in multidimensional forms.

Second, I explain that the artifacts they have used to represent themselves are full of memory and I ask them to write the story of each chosen item. One of Lisa's (all student names are pseudonyms) artifacts was a poem she wrote, an excerpt of which follows:

"A simple smile, A scream inside"

There's so much that no one knows
So much that no one sees,
About the way I feel inside, my thoughts, and all my needs.

Maybe it's that they don't look,
Or the fact that I don't show,
Either way, there are things inside that no one seems to know.

…

There's a different person on the inside,
That I can't seem to show,
But maybe if you took the time that person you would know.

Lisa's willingness to share her personal adolescent angst helps to connect her to others in the class. In another portrait, Charlie explains that the rocks around his neck represent how he sees his life situation, which is demanding too much maturity from him and he is choking.

Third, students present their self-portrait to the class and also respond to each presenter. Presentation Day begins by my asking each student to record each presenter's name and to describe moments in each presentation that were particularly powerful. Next, I share my self-portrait and then students share their self-portraits. Unbeknown to the students they are "playing" with a comprehension strategy that we will use all semester—that of selecting text to which they have a personal response and building on that personal response with their peers to construct meaning.

The project culminates in more writing. Each student chooses one presenter to whom they feel most connected and writes an informal note to that person explaining the connection. We discuss who chose whom and why and pass the notes. Next I assign a formal comparative analysis. Each student uses information from his or her own presentation and their chosen person's presentation. This assignment is their first attempt at writing an academic analysis—a task they will have honed by the end of the semester.

Becoming Literate Members of the Community

Within the first weeks of school I begin a conversation about who we are as readers, and about literacy, text, and comprehension. I send home a reading questionnaire (adapted from Goodman, Watson, & Burke, 1996) asking students several questions about their personal reading beliefs and practices. For example, I ask, "Who's a good reader you know?"

"What does that person do when they struggle in their reading?" and "What do you do when struggling to comprehend?" I also ask about reading materials at home, their first memory of reading, and their own definition of literacy. As a class we analyze the results from the questionnaire, learning about the characteristics of good readers we know, sharing strategies we use when struggling with text, the quantity of reading materials in our homes, and so forth.

This analysis and discussion leads naturally to having the students write a formal essay further explicating and analyzing their individual strategy use when encountering difficult text. This writing serves as a pretest and is an introduction to our developing discourse about literacy. I score the essays using a rubric based on the number of strategies named by the student that are connected to a specific literacy context. For example, a student who lists two strategies and describes how those strategies assisted comprehension with a specific text receives a 2 out of 5 on the 5-point rubric. Getting the students to pay attention to and answer questions such as, "What do I do when I come to text I struggle to understand?" and "What strategies assist that comprehension and why?" is my primary goal.

Students don't do very well on their essays. Most of their strategies are based on those learned in elementary school, such as the following:

- "The reading strategies that you can use are probably dictionaries, or even thesaurus. You can use these to find an easier word."
- "I usually write the word on a separate piece of paper and look it up."
- "I skip the word, reread it later, or look it up in the dictionary."
- "One strategy I have thought to be most helpful is reading it over; reading difficult text over and over gets it stuck in my mind."

These responses illustrate that the kids view reading as word dependent. They seem to be saying, "If I can understand the words, then I can understand the meaning behind the sentences." I share the rubric for scoring the essays and promise them that as the year progresses they will learn about comprehension strategies they can use to be amazing students.

Having discussed the quality of their essays and explained why they were scored low, we go about the work of strategy instruction, which I teach explicitly, and include strategies that emanate from both the cognitive and social theorists. To launch the explicit instruction, I introduce the Reading Strategy Documentation Form, which is shown in Figure 10.3. As a class and through discussion, we define text, literacy, strategies, and comprehension. We record those community-developed definitions on the form, which becomes a record of the strategies we learn over the year. Comprehension and discussion strategies, samples of which are described next, are used side by side during every encounter with text, whether we are working with a nonfiction news article or a novel.

Figure 10.3. Reading Strategy Documentation Form

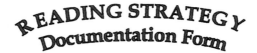

"When you encounter DIFFICULT TEXT, what
STRATEGIES do you use to assist your comprehension?"

DEFINE:

1. Text: {What is it?}

2. Literacy:

3. Reading Strategies: {What are they?}

4. Comprehension:

Reading Strategy [DETAILS!]	CONTEXT	DATE	Level of SUCCESS? [analysis]

Comprehension and Discussion Strategies: Rich, Relevant Text

We define *text* in an expanded way, as any element in life from which we can construct meaning. We formally discuss and understand that media and technology are texts, as is a mother's face, because most any child can construct meaning from just a glance at her facial expressions.

The rich texts I choose include current and controversial news and magazine articles, selections from our anthology, and literature that illustrates themes relevant to the lives of high school students in our community. For example, we read *The Bean Trees* (Kingsolver, 1988) for its thematic intensity and because it is set in familiar territory, our hometown.

We begin strategy instruction using a reading log that requires the students to select from the assigned text those ideas they find important and valuable in some way—which is the same type of "play" they experienced during the Picasso project presentations. In the nonfiction log, students document information they believe to be important and cite its location in the text, and then record at least two questions they formulated during the reading. The fiction log has an additional section for character development. Students document each character, tracking development of the characters throughout our study of the novel. The reading logs provide a text to which we refer continually while we discuss the text. This strategy serves four purposes: (1) Students learn to value each other's responses and questions. (2) Students learn to justify their impressions with quotes from the text. (3) Students begin to sense the reciprocal relationship between reading and writing. (4) Students develop the skill of citation.

When students come to class with completed logs, we use a discussion strategy such as Sketch-to-Stretch (Short & Harste, 1996) to assist the flow of ideas from the individual log to our discourse community. With the Sketch-to-Stretch discussion strategy (illustrated in Figure 10.4), each student chooses the most important idea from his or her reading log and draws a visualization of the selected idea. Additionally, each student writes about why the event was chosen, how it is important personally, and why he or she drew the image to represent that idea.

To prompt discussion of their sketches, we participate in a gallery tour. Students lay their artwork on their desks and we all wander the room, noting at least five pieces of art that grab our attention, and listing the name of the artist next to our comments. Once everyone has wandered, I ask someone to choose a most powerful piece that will lead us back to the text. The chosen artist stands and explains the drawing,

Figure 10.4. Sketch-to-Stretch Student Response to Elie Wiesel (2004, July 4), "The America I Love," *Parade Magazine.*

citing where the idea came from in the text. The class discussion is then launched, with students making connections between the art, the text, other texts, and their lives.

Another discussion strategy, the graffiti board (Short & Harste, 1996), shown in Figure 10.5, directs the students to choose several ideas from their completed reading logs to create artwork. They rely on each other to discuss the critical moments experienced in the assigned text and illustrate those chosen ideas, words, phrases, and images in graffiti fashion. Students present their boards, again requiring them to cite where the information was located in the text.

These discussion strategies are successful because they are naturally of high interest and because the students are encouraged to construct new understandings by sharing their prior knowledge and life experiences. As we continually reveal our thinking, we create a discourse community in which students are empowered to use their voices to express relevant and meaningful ideas. The classroom activity flows from

Figure 10.5. Graffiti Board Student Response to a Chapter in Barbara Kingsolver's *The Bean Trees*

individual work to small group work to the whole class and then back to the individual again. This flow provides opportunities for students to learn from each other and by doing so to become more sophisticated thinkers and, in turn, more eloquent speakers and writers.

Space for Metacognitive Growth

Each student keeps a copy of the Reading Strategy Documentation Form, which holds our definitions of literacy, strategies, and text, and a record of strategies taught and used. Twice a semester, I ask each student to write an analysis of the usefulness of the strategies used since the last time we wrote about strategies. I challenge them to expand on their notes by deeply exploring and analyzing their thinking in connection with the strategy and text. They write a formal essay, which provides another opportunity to use an analytical structure.

The essay is a graded summative evaluation, but we develop metacognition every day. Students participate in comprehension and discussion strategies, and then we reflect metacognitively every day on why particular strategies are helpful and why others don't seem to be as valuable. Through discussions and reflective activities, such as quick writes to note their evaluation of strategies, we continually engage in metacognitive practices throughout our studies together. I observe their increased confidence from learning to trust their own decisions with text, including how to talk and feeling free to do so, which creates a culture in which they regularly take the lead in classroom discussions.

My goal is to prepare young people to actively participate in the world, able to think critically within and across multiple contexts. "If unprepared to think independently, young people will seek to return to the infantile state in which there is no responsibility to make decisions; they are willing to blindly follow some 'leader' whose tools they become" (Rosenblatt, 1995, p. 123). Taking the lead on the literacy path in our classroom, being members of an academic community, and reflecting on the changes in their thinking all along the journey creates amazing growth.

Reinvented Adolescent Identities

As our year comes to an end, each student writes a posttest essay responding to the same questions about strategy use that were on the pretest. Students' responses are filled with the literacy discourse of our community, and they demonstrate their skill with the concepts and vocabulary of literacy instruction. Their writing suggests that they have reinvented their identities as literate people, as shown in the following student responses:

- "The best way to test where to find one's learning potential lies in the experimentation with a variety of reading strategies. Not only were these comprehension strategies different from anything I had ever seen, they were expecting me to think for myself with my own requirements—something I had never done in my life for a school project." (Yvonne)

- "Living is the process of building a giant puzzle of vibrant, confusing sights and experiences. To comprehend the final image of the puzzle, as well as which pieces connect, one must own a valuable tool. That tool is reading strategies. Reading strategies are instruments to aid in the comprehension of a difficult text. Difficult texts aren't just found in the pages of a book, though. They can be any event, substance, person, or idea that requires analysis, or anything that requires deep thought. In junior English, we learned about a variety of useful reading strategies. Our teacher provided us with this anti-ignorance armor to protect us from becoming victims of adult society. Without literacy and comprehension, acquired through the use of reading strategies and critical thought, people are voiceless." (Adam)

- "As a junior in high school I am in American Experience English. This class was designed to help us realize and examine who we are as individuals and as a part of the American society. In the curriculum of this class there were many pieces of literature we read and many strategies that we used to analyze and understand them on a deeper level. Through this class and the new reading strategies introduced to us, I have been looking at my life and myself on a deeper level. I am starting to notice things in the world around me. I am seeing now that reading a text, be it a piece of literature, a person, or any other element of life, is an important aspect of being an American citizen. To be able to see beyond the surface of a text is a tool I will use my entire life as an American. All of the reading strategies helped me with reading in new ways, but the greatest way they have helped me is by showing me how to analyze where I fit in America and what I attribute to my society through taking me to a deeper level helping me gain new perspectives of myself." (Brittany)

- (An unsolicited e-mail from an 11th-grade student) "Dear Spit: Hey, it's Lindsay in your third hour. I was thinking about what you said in class today and you really did transform me into a thinking warrior, this year has really gotten to me and I know I will reap the benefits in everything I go on to do. To be honest, it kind of creeps me out how much you've opened up my mind. How come I've had over 20 teachers instruct me and only one has made me, really shown me, how to think and not just how to answer questions. I appreciate what you are trying to do for me and the rest of the next generation. I just had to make sure you knew that before the year was over."

Conclusion

This chapter has reviewed the vintage strategies developed from a cognitive perspective and has recommended strategies emanating from a sociocultural-historical theory of teaching and learning. This integration suggests that creating a discourse community and supporting the development of that community with carefully selected and developed instruction makes a difference in helping students to be sophisticated and reflective students.

Ellen's students confirm for us the cognitive and social nature of teaching and learning. We have gained tremendously in our own understandings by watching what happened when Ellen's instruction opened spaces for students to express their identities and envision their future identities.

Reinventing comprehension instruction for adolescents should not be a matter of selecting between one theoretical construct and another; nor should it be viewed as an acquisition of skills and strategies void of social context or meaningful content, rather it must be taken on as a crucially important instructional responsibility across the curriculum and throughout the school. The future of our students and their academic, social, and adult lives depend on it.

Questions for Reflection

1. What are the significant differences between the vintage theories and practices and the sociohistorical-culturally influenced theories and practices?

2. Do you think the strategies suggested for reinventing reading comprehension instruction are viable for your present or future classroom? Why or Why not?

Activities

1. Create a Venn diagram analyzing the differences and similarities between the psychological, linguistic, and social theories as explained in this chapter. Choose one element of difference in each theory and one commonality, and write about the possible significance those ideas can hold for your future classroom practice.

2. Gather and choose several artifacts representing your personal literacy journey, and create a Picasso literacy self-portrait project following the same directions given to Ellen's students, as outlined in this chapter.

3. Try the Picasso self-portrait project with your students. Follow the directions provided in this chapter, and then write about your experiences as compared to Ellen's.

4. Conduct an audit of the social practices and moments in your classroom. Follow yourself for three days and record the social interactions, responses, and structures you observe. Reflect on your list and make a plan for further support of the social environment in your classroom.

Patricia L. Anders is Professor and Head of the Department of Language, Reading, and Culture at the University of Arizona, Tucson, Arizona, USA, where her teaching passion is secondary reading and content area literacy. Her original research includes investigations of interactive vocabulary strategies in the content area classroom, which has led to the links between theory and practice. She served on the Board of Directors of the International Reading Association (2000–2004), as well as on the National Reading Conference, the National Conference for the Teaching of English and Language Arts, and the American Educational Research Association. She can be reached at planders@u.arizona.edu. **Ellen Spitler** is a doctoral student at the University of Arizona, Tucson, Arizona, USA, in the Department of Language, Reading, and Culture (LRC). For the past 10 years she has taught junior high and high school language arts and English, and in the last 5 years her research interests have focused on adolescent literacy, including metacognitive reading strategy instruction. She teaches a course on content area reading in the multicultural classroom for the University of Arizona College of Education and LRC. She can be contacted at espitler@dakotacom.net.

REFERENCES

Anders, P.L., & Guzzetti, B.J. (2005). *Literacy instruction in the content areas*. Mahwah, NJ: Erlbaum.

Anders, P.L., & Richardson, V. (1992). Teacher as game show host, bookkeeper or judge? Challenges, contradictions and consequences of accountability. *Teachers College Record*, 94(2), 382–396.

Anderson, R.C., & Pearson, P.D. (1984). A schema-theoretic view of basic processes in reading comprehension. In P.D. Pearson, R. Barr, M.L. Kamil, & P. Mosenthal, (Eds.). *Handbook of reading research* (pp. 255–291). New York: Longman.

Armbruster, B.B. (1984). The problem of "inconsiderate text." In G.G. Duffy, L.R. Roehler, & J. Mason (Eds.), *Comprehension instruction: Perspectives and suggestions* (pp. 202–217). New York: Longman.

Bakhtin, M.M. (1986). *Speech genres and other late essays* (C. Emerson & M. Holquist, Eds.; V.M. McGee, Trans.). Austin: University of Texas Press.

Bartlett, F.C. (1932). *Remembering: A study in experimental and social psychology*. Cambridge, England: Cambridge University Press.

Bloome, D. (1981). *An ethnographic approach to the study of reading among black junior high school students: A sociolinguistic ethnography*. Unpublished doctoral dissertation, Kent State University, OH.

Buehl, D. (2001). *Classroom strategies for interactive learning* (2nd ed.). Newark, DE: International Reading Association.

Flavell, J., Miller, P., & Miller, S. (2002). *Cognitive development*. Upper Saddle River, NJ: Prentice Hall.

Floriani, A. (1993). Negotiating what counts: Roles and relationships, texts and contexts, content and meaning. *Linguistics and Education*, 5, 241–273.

Gee, J. (2000). Discourse and sociocultural studies in reading. In M.L. Kamil, P. Mosenthal, P.D. Pearson, & R. Barr (Eds.), *Handbook of reading research* (Vol. 3, pp. 195–207). Mahwah, NJ: Erlbaum.

Gilmore, P. (1981). Shortridge school and community: Attitudes and admission to literacy. *Reading/language arts skills in and out of the classroom* (Final report to the National Institute of Education). Washington, DC: U.S. Department of Education.

González, N., Moll, L.C., & Amanti, C. (2005). *Funds of knowledge: Theorizing practices in households, communities, and classrooms*. Mahwah, NJ: Erlbaum.

Goodman, K.S. (1976). Reading: A psycholinguistic guessing game. In H. Singer & R. Ruddell (Eds.), *Theoretical models and processes of reading* (pp. 497–518). Newark, DE: International Reading Association.

Goodman, Y., Watson, D., & Burke, C. (1996). *Reading strategies: Focus on comprehension* (2nd ed.). Katonah, NY: Richard C. Owen.

Green, J. (1984). Lesson construction and student performance. In J. Green & J. Harker (Eds.), *Multiple perspective analyses of classroom discourse* (pp. 3–23). Norwood, NJ: Ablex.

Harste, J.C., & Short, K.G. (with Burke, C.L.). (1988). *Creating classrooms for authors*. Portsmouth, NH: Heinemann.

Herber, H. (1970). *Teaching reading in content areas*. Englewood Cliffs, NJ: Prentice Hall.

Herber, H. (1978). *Teaching reading in content areas* (2nd ed.). Englewood Cliffs, NJ: Prentice Hall.

Kingsolver, B. (1988). *The bean trees*. New York, NY: HarperCollins.

Klein, J. (2006, December 10). There's more than one way to diversity. *Time*, *168*(25). Retrieved February 17, 2007, from http://www.time.com/time/mag azine/article/0,9171,1568491,00.html

Lee, C.D., & Smagorinsky, P. (2000). Introduction: Constructing meaning through collaborative inquiry. In C.D. Lee & P. Smagorinsky (Eds.), *Vygotskian perspectives on literacy research: Constructing meaning through collaborative inquiry* (p. 2). Cambridge, England: Cambridge University Press.

McCarthey, S.J. (2002). *Students' identities and literacy learning*. Newark, DE: International Reading Association.

Moje, E.B., Ciechanowski, K.M., Kramer, K.E., Ellis, L., Carrillo, R., & Collazo, T. (2004). Working toward third space in content area literacy: An examination of everyday funds of knowledge and discourse. *Reading Research Quarterly*, *39*, 38–70.

Moll, L. (2005). Inspired by Vygotsky: Ethnographic experiments in education. In C.D. Lee & P. Smagorinsky (Eds.), *Vygotskian perspectives on literacy research: Constructing meaning through collaborative inquiry* (pp. 256–268). Cambridge, England: Cambridge University Press.

Moll, L.C., Veléz-Ibáñes, C., & Greenberg, J. (1989). *Year one progress report: Community knowledge and classroom practice: Combining resources for literacy instruction* (IARP Subcontract L-10, Development Associates). Tucson: University of Arizona.

Piaget, J. (1985). *The equilibration of cognitive structures: The central problem of intellectual development* (T. Brown & K. Thampy, Trans.). Chicago: University of Chicago Press.

Rosenblatt, L. (1995). *Literature as exploration*. New York: Modern Language Association of America.

Schallert, D. (2002). Schema theory. In B.J. Guzzetti (Ed.), *Literacy in America: An encyclopedia of history, theory and practice* (pp. 556–558). Santa Barbara, CA: ABC-CLIO.

Scribner, S., & Cole, M. (1981). *The psychology of literacy*. Cambridge, MA: Harvard University Press.

Short, K., & Harste, J. (with Burke, C.). (1996). *Creating classrooms for authors and inquirers*. Portsmouth, NH: Heinemann.

Smith, F. (1971). *Understanding reading: A psycholinguistic analysis of reading and learning to read*. New York: Holt, Rinehart & Winston.

Taylor, D. (1983). *Family literacy: Young children learning to read and write*. Exeter, NH: Heinemann.

Vygotsky, L. (1978). *Thought and language* (A. Kozalin, Trans.). Cambridge, MA: The MIT Press. (Original work published 1934)

CHAPTER 11

A Professional Development Framework for Embedding Comprehension Instruction Into Content Classrooms

Doug Buehl

HIGHLIGHTS

- A content literacy framework that integrates comprehension instruction into the teaching of an academic discourse provides literacy coaches and professional development specialists with a focus for working with middle and high school teachers.

- A groundswell of influential national policy statements advocate the integration of literacy strategies into the teaching of subject disciplines.

- Reading comprehension instruction needs to be explicit and contextual, that is, taught in conjunction with the learning of meaningful content.

- Classroom teachers, as accomplished insiders in an academic discourse, must assume the central role in modeling and guiding comprehension in their academic disciplines.

The first sequence featured a touch-kick, the ball stolen from the Warwick line-out, and a subsequent encroachment as the players scrambled to retake the ball. The Newcastle team responded to make it 12–3, with a well-executed driving maul giving Nicko the space to slice through the Warwick backs and score, with Raul converting. Soon after, the referee dispatched the Warwick flanker with a yellow card when he dived into a ruck from the

---

Adolescent Literacy Instruction: Policies and Promising Practices edited by Jill Lewis and Gary Moorman. © 2007 by the International Reading Association.

side. Nicko followed up with a drop-goal for Newcastle, after the opposition team had hashed a defensive line-out.

How well would you rate your understanding of the above passage? Are you clear on what the passage is describing? Were you able to confidently visualize what the author was recounting to you? Could you accurately retell the passage in your own words? Most North American readers would have a difficult time demonstrating a deep understanding of the opening segment. Even individuals who might rank as highly proficient readers may have to concede that much of the passage was hazy and not easy to figure out. Why is the above passage so difficult for many readers?

Without question, the author is expecting that a great deal of what a reader needs to know to make sense of this passage will be provided by the reader. And most of us lack this necessary background knowledge. However, a few readers will have breezed through the opening with an immediate comprehension of the author's message. These individuals brought experiences with and knowledge about the British game of rugby to their reading.

Proficient readers, of course, would be able to deconstruct their thinking about this passage, even though they struggled to attain a satisfactory understanding. Most of us could say that we realized that we were reading an account of a sports competition, between two teams, one of which was able to score on its opponent. We could have answered some detail questions about the facts of the passage: What player scored the two goals described in this passage? Which team was ahead? What critical event set up the second score? And so on. But unless we are conversant with the game of rugby, its rules and terminology, we are still pretty much in the dark about exactly what is transpiring in this passage.

This opening example represents a dynamic intersection between two key variables in reading and learning in middle and high school classrooms: application of comprehension strategies and the discourse of a field or discipline. The example vividly demonstrates that comprehension strategies alone will not likely be sufficient to allow a reader to achieve an adequate understanding, unless the reader also possesses relevant background knowledge or is provided support with the specialized discourse of rugby.

Now imagine a group of middle and high school teachers engaged in efforts to comprehend this rugby passage. As they examine their own, likely flawed, attempts to make sense of what will be a fairly obscure text for most of them, these teachers will have the opportunity to experience first-hand several variables that have an impact on learning from content texts in their classrooms.

This chapter offers literacy coaches and professional development specialists a model for interacting with middle and high school content teachers. The chapter outlines a construct for the embedding of comprehension strategies into the academic discourse of a subject discipline as a framework for content literacy instruction. In particular, this framework emphasizes the critical importance of the nature of the content being studied—rather than merely the application of strategies—as a means for helping teachers conceptualize what effective adolescent literacy practices might look like in their daily instructional routines. Initially, the chapter stresses the necessity for building a compelling case for adolescent literacy instruction across the curriculum. The chapter then describes four stages of reflection and study for middle and high school teachers as they develop their understandings of content literacy instruction: (1) explorations of their own comprehension processes, (2) examinations of the role of academic discourse in reading comprehension, (3) experimentations with literacy strategies as instructional prototypes, and (4) teaching for metacognition.

Building the Case—Who Says I'm Supposed to Teach Reading?

In an eloquent lament in a 1998 *Journal of Adolescent & Adult Literacy* commentary, Richard Vacca, past president of the International Reading Association, decried a historic and pervasive lack of commitment to the literacy development of adolescent learners. Particularly problematic was a prevailing "mindset that literacy learning is critical only in early childhood. The faulty and misguided assumption, 'If young children learn to read early on, they will read to learn throughout their lives,' results in more harm than good" (1998, p. 606). Vacca's reflections articulated two persistent challenges for integrating literacy practices into middle and high school content instruction. First, policymakers, many educators, and the public in general have long harbored significant misconceptions about what it means to develop as a reader. Bluntly stated, these misconceptions might be summarized as follows: If students receive a solid foundation as readers in their K–3 classrooms, they will be able to continue to grow as readers without further explicit instruction. As the National Governors Association Center for Best Practices (2005) concluded in *Reading to Achieve: A Governor's Guide to Adolescent Literacy*, "Unfortunately, for too many students, literacy instruction ends in third grade" (p. 1). Second, as a result of these misconceptions, funding decisions, research initiatives, class-size reductions, literacy interventions, reading specialist support, and professional development in literacy have all disproportionately targeted younger readers.

The landscape for adolescent literacy has shifted dramatically since Vacca's 1998 somber appraisal. A flurry of significant national reports have lobbied for a redirection of literacy efforts to encompass the needs of middle and high school learners. Clearly, we are witnessing today an exciting convergence from a wide array of perspectives that literacy instruction must extend beyond the primary years, and that it must be embedded in learning within content subjects. Yet it is probably accurate to conclude that most middle and high school teachers remain unconvinced that they have a significant role in the literacy development of their students. As Kamil (2003) articulated,

> For much of the history of reading in this country, the attitude of middle and high school teachers has been that their job was not to teach reading. They view themselves as content specialists and believe that the job of teaching reading belongs to elementary school teachers. And they feel that, if only those elementary school teachers would do a better job of teaching these students to read, the problems at the secondary level would be solved. (p. 4)

Sporadic or insufficient attention to adolescent literacy only reinforced these views. The occasional inservice program on reading in the content areas or reading strategies often has been endured with a "this too shall pass" mentality from many middle and high school teachers.

Ultimately, a reinvigorated commitment to adolescent literacy must aggressively confront the knotty realm of instructional practices employed by middle and high school content teachers. As a starting point, it is important for teachers to be cognizant of the resounding chorus of high-profile adolescent literacy reports that now categorically assert that literacy instruction must become daily practice in content classrooms. Who says middle and high school subject matter teachers should teach reading? Table 11.1 presents an overview of recent policy documents that are intended to have an impact on literacy instruction in content classrooms. Sharing key statements from these documents with teachers is a crucial first step in establishing a compelling case for literacy instruction embedded within the learning of content subjects.

Table 11.1. National Policy Statements on Adolescent Literacy

International Reading Association (IRA)	"Adolescents deserve expert teachers who model and provide explicit instruction in reading comprehension and study strategies across the curriculum." (Moore, Bean, Birdyshaw, & Rycik, 1999, *Adolescent Literacy: A Position Statement for the Commission on Adolescent Literacy of the International Reading Association*, p. 7)
RAND Reading Study Report, commissioned by the U.S. Department of Education's Office of Educational Research and Improvement (OERI)	"Research has shown that many children who read at the third grade level in grade 3 will not automatically become proficient comprehenders in later grades. Therefore, teachers must teach comprehension explicitly, beginning in the primary grades and continuing through high school." (Snow, 2002, *Reading for Understanding*, p. xii)
National Council of Teachers of English (NCTE)	"In middle and high school, students encounter academic discourses and disciplinary concepts in such fields as science, mathematics, and the social sciences that require different reading approaches.... These new forms, purposes, and processing demands require that teachers show, demonstrate, and make visible to students how literacy operates within the academic disciplines." (NCTE, May 2004, *A Call to Action: What We Know About Adolescent Literacy and Ways to Support Teachers in Meeting Students' Needs, A Position/Action Statement from the NCTE's Commission on Reading*, ¶3)
Alliance for Excellent Education, a highly respected national policy and research consortium	The Fifteen Key Elements of Effective Adolescent Literacy Programs—Element 1: "Direct, explicit comprehension instruction"; and Element 2: "Effective instructional principles embedded in content." (Biancarosa & Snow, 2004, *Reading Next: A Vision for Action and Research in Middle and High School Literacy*, pp. 12).
National Association of State Boards of Education (NASBE)	"Ensure that teachers have the preparation and professional development to provide effective, content-based literacy

(continued)

Table 11.1. National Policy Statements on Adolescent Literacy (continued)

	instruction." (NASBE, 2005, *Reading at Risk: The State Response to the Crisis in Adolescent Literacy: The Report of the NASBE Study Group on Middle and High School Literacy*, p. 6)
National Association of Secondary School Principals (NASSP)	"…it becomes even more critical that secondary content area teachers better understand and teach specific literacy strategies to help students read and extract meaning from the written material used to teach the course content." (NASSP, 2005, *Creating a Culture of Literacy: A Guide for Middle and High School Principals*, p. 1)
National Governors Association (NGA)	"Students need instruction beyond third grade to learn…how to employ reading strategies to comprehend complex texts about specialized subject matter. All students need such instruction, not just those who are struggling readers and writers." (NGA Center for Best Practices, 2005, *Reading to Achieve: A Governor's Guide to Adolescent Literacy*, p. 7)
National Council of Teachers of Mathematics (NCTM), National Science Teachers Association (NSTA), National Council for the Social Studies (NCSS), in collaboration with IRA and NCTE	"Middle and high school teachers need help to understand how they can develop content knowledge at the same time that they improve student literacy; that in fact, effective teaching in their subject areas will be boosted by complementary literacy instruction related to the texts (and the other communication demands) characteristic of their subjects." (IRA, 2006, *Standards for Middle and High School Literacy Coaches*, p. 2)
U.S. Department of Education	"Improve the quality of literacy instruction across the curriculum, provide intensive literacy interventions to struggling adolescent readers, and help to build a strong, scientific research base for identifying and replicating strategies that improve adolescent literacy skills." (U.S. Department of Education, 2006, *Striving Readers*, ¶5)

Stage One: Reading Comprehension—What Are Characteristics of Proficient Readers?

Let's return to our rugby example. The rugby passage is challenging for many readers because the author assumes a background that many of us lack. Excerpts like this, from texts that are not readily accessible, can provide rich resources for working with middle and high school teachers as they investigate their own thinking processes to achieve comprehension. Because they must struggle to construct a reasonable understanding of such passages, teachers, in their role here as readers, can begin to perceive elements that contribute to comprehending a text. After reading such a demanding passage, ask teachers to reflect on their understandings of the author's message, and secondly, inventory the strategies they noticed themselves using as they attempted to make meaning. In effect, you are first focusing on their comprehension and, second, tracking their metacognition.

Literacy coaches and professional development specialists may find an interview format (see Table 11.2) an especially effective technique for guiding teachers to think about their efforts to comprehend. In their discussions of the rugby passage with their colleagues, teachers will likely comment that they did indeed employ the strategies reflected in the interview questions to help them make sense of the passage. Most revealingly, many teachers will relate that they engaged in all of these thinking behaviors and were still unable to achieve a satisfactory understanding.

Table 11.2. Comprehension Interview: Noticing Your Thinking

- Did you think about things you knew something about or had heard of before as you read?
- Did you find yourself raising questions about your reading? Were you wondering about some things (what, why, how, etc.)?
- Did you try to picture something in your head as you read?
- Did you look for clues to try to figure out what this text is describing as you read?
- Did you try to locate things that seemed particularly important or significant as you read?
- Could you condense what you have read so that you could sum it up in a few words?

In *Mosaic of Thought*, their seminal work on reading comprehension, Keene and Zimmermann (1997) focused on the following proficient-reader cognitive strategies as the foundation for the explicit teaching of comprehension: making connections to prior knowledge (schema), generating questions, visualizing and creating sensory images, making inferences, determining importance, synthesizing, and monitoring reading using fix-up strategies when necessary (see Table 11.3 for descriptions of these strategies). Harvey and Goudvis (2000), Tovani (2000), and others have adopted these specific proficient-reader characteristics as a basis for making comprehension instruction intentional and ongoing. These proficient-reader characteristics provide middle and high school content teachers with specific direction for integrating comprehension instruction into their daily practice.

Middle and high school teachers must realize that they cannot assume their students will automatically and skillfully employ these cognitive strategies to complete assignments in their classes. It is especially illuminating to engage teachers in contrasting proficient-reader strategies with three typical student behaviors that signal ineffective comprehension of content texts.

Skimming for Answers

Many classroom activities with content texts overemphasize reading for details, or a literal processing of text. Students take a cursory look at a question, skim the text for details that look appropriate (such as boldface vocabulary words), copy down definitions and relevant information, and then skip on to the next question, continuing to troll for answers. As a result, many students complete literal-level assignments with very little true comprehension of the material, handing in acceptable homework without actually having learned the material.

Surface Processing

A second typical practice is reading without thinking about what an author is trying to communicate. Students' eyes may gloss over the print as they read the words on the page, but they do not engage in an inner dialogue with the author and themselves. The lack of deep processing of a text leads students to tell their teachers: "I read it, but I didn't understand it." As a result, teachers may lose confidence in assigning independent reading and compensate with other modes of introducing new content, such as lecture, class presentations, and videos.

Table 11.3. Comprehension Strategies Characteristic of Proficient Readers

Make Connections to Prior Knowledge

Reading comprehension results when readers can match what they already know (their schema) with new information and ideas in a text. Proficient readers activate prior knowledge before, during, and after reading, and they constantly evaluate how a text enhances or alters their previous understandings.

Generate Questions

Comprehension is, to a significant degree, a process of inquiry. Proficient readers pose questions to themselves as they read. Asking questions is the art of carrying on an inner conversation with an author, as well as an internal dialogue within one's self.

Visualize and Create Sensory Mental Images

Comprehension involves breathing life experiences into the abstract language of written texts. Proficient readers use visual, auditory, and other sensory connections to create mental images of an author's message.

Make Inferences

Much of what is to be understood in a text must be inferred. Authors rely on readers to contribute to a text's meaning by linking their background knowledge to information in the text. In addition to acknowledging explicitly stated messages, proficient readers read between the lines to discern implicit meanings, make predictions, and read with a critical eye.

Determine Importance

Our memories quickly overload unless we can pare down a text to its essential ideas. Texts contain key ideas and concepts amidst much background detail. Proficient readers strive to differentiate key ideas, themes, and information from details so that they are not overwhelmed by facts.

Synthesize

Proficient readers glean the essence of a text (determine importance) and organize these ideas into coherent summaries of meaning. Effective comprehension leads to new learning and the development of new schema (background knowledge). Proficient readers make evaluations, construct generalizations, and draw conclusions from a text.

Monitor Reading and Apply Fix-Up Strategies

Proficient readers watch themselves as they read and expect to make adjustments in their strategies to ensure that they are able to achieve a satisfactory understanding of a text.

Students recognize that they really do not have to attain understanding through reading, because the teacher will tell them everything they will need to know.

Reading and Forgetting

Because many students do not use strategies that involve deep processing of the material, they do not synthesize the material, making new learning vulnerable for rapid forgetting. Consequently, many students have trouble relating reading assignments to class discussions and struggle with tests. Because new learning rarely progresses beyond what is now called "working memory," even students who manage to perform satisfactorily on exams may forget much content soon after.

Middle and high school teachers will be able to readily identify with these three descriptions of what often passes for reading in content classrooms. It is certainly arguable, from a student perspective, that these behaviors are perfectly reasonable. Given the structure of the assignments and nature of the texts, merely getting the work done can be viewed as instructionally induced behavior. It is fascinating when teachers admit to indulging in these routines themselves in their careers as secondary and college learners, and they fully admit that such mental activity does not translate into the real learning they envision in their classrooms. Instruction and classroom activities, therefore, need to be designed so that students are intentionally and mindfully engaging in the comprehension characteristics of proficient readers. Table 11.4 summarizes five issues that teachers must address with comprehension of academic texts.

Table 11.4. Comprehension Issues With Academic Texts

1. Students are best at reading to identify facts.

2. Students have significant difficulties reading at an inferential level, making generalizations, drawing conclusions.

3. Students tend to fare best with fictional literature (story form, narration).

4. Students struggle most with expository texts (nonfiction, informational texts characteristic of most academic discourse).

5. Students benefit from embedded comprehension instruction as they read to learn in science, social studies, math, and other content disciplines (scaffolding).

Stage Two: Talking the Talk—Academic Discourse

Let us revisit our rugby example one more time. As mentioned earlier, teachers will discover through their interactions with this text that proficient readers might consciously and skillfully employ comprehension strategies and still fall short with understanding this passage. What many readers are missing is appropriate background knowledge. In short, they are unable to make meaningful connections, and this inability in turn undermines their efforts to make sense of this unfamiliar text. In other words, teachers need to recognize that comprehension is contextual; sometimes even proficient readers assume the guise of struggling readers. In this case, a rugby team member, who might indeed perform like a struggling reader in many school classrooms, might achieve a far deeper understanding of what this author is saying. As *Reading Next* acknowledged: "Ensuring adequate ongoing literacy development for all students in the middle and high school years is a more challenging task than ensuring excellent reading education in the primary grades," and that "secondary school literacy skills are more complex, more embedded in subject matters, and more multiply determined..." (Biancarosa & Snow, 2004, pp. 1–2).

A second stage of reflection and study for middle and high school teachers addresses the central role of background knowledge in learning from academic texts. As Alexander and Jetton (2000) observed in their research review on "Learning from Text" in the *Handbook of Reading Research*, "Of all the factors considered in this exploration, none exerts more influence on what students understand and remember than the knowledge they possess" (p. 291). In their analysis, Alexander and Jetton distinguished between "unschooled" or informal knowledge, and "schooled" or formal knowledge. As Marzano (2004) indicated, all students arrive at school with an extensive store of informal knowledge, although because students grow up in different circumstances, the particulars of this general knowledge vary widely among individuals. However, Marzano documented a significant disparity among students in amount of "schooled," or what he termed "academic" knowledge. Academic knowledge parallels the background a person would develop when studying various academic disciplines, and it is narrower and more prescribed than general knowledge. Some students bring a wealth of academic knowledge to the learning of academic subjects, and others arrive at the classroom with very little to draw on that specifically relates to the content being studied. Some students have had experiences and access to resources outside of school that provide a solid foundation for content learning, and other students do not, necessitating the building of appropriate academic knowledge as a key component of comprehension of subject matter texts (see chapter 9).

Academic knowledge can be further subdivided into topic knowledge and domain knowledge (Alexander & Jetton, 2000). Topic knowledge represents a reader's background in and experiences with a particular idea or concept. Domain knowledge encompasses a reader's understanding of the vocabulary and thinking typical of an academic discipline. Marzano (2004) argued that academic knowledge is largely vocabulary driven; readers familiar with the language of a discipline will have deeper and more precise academic knowledge to apply to written texts in content classrooms. Readers who could "talk the talk" of rugby—*touch-kick, line-out, driving maul, ruck, hash*—brought obvious advantages to their attempts to comprehend our opening passage.

This stage of understanding content literacy is especially significant on a number of levels for middle and high school teachers. First, it reinforces that comprehension instruction cannot occur in isolation of meaningful content; students may learn effective protocols to think about texts but may still be stymied by lack of academic knowledge. Secondly, instructional strategies that build appropriate academic knowledge and encourage students to share relevant prior knowledge are essential for comprehension of subject matter texts (see chapter 9). Third, it is likely that individual students will not uniformly be proficient or struggling readers across the curriculum; they are likely to be more successful in some content environments and less successful in others. For example, they may be more proficient readers of short stories and novels in English class and less proficient readers of the science textbook in biology class. Fourth, students need to become increasingly comfortable with the insider language of academic texts; they have to develop the facility to talk the talk of an academic discipline.

Figure 11.1 offers a dynamic representation of the cognitive characteristics of proficient readers, illustrating the primary role of background knowledge. Comprehension is portrayed as emanating from a reader's schema. The questions we wonder about, the visual and sensory images we are able to create, our ability to access implicit layers of understanding, and our perceptions of the essence of a text—all involve a back-and-forth mental (and social) interaction with what we bring to a

Figure 11.1. An Interactive Model of Comprehension Strategies

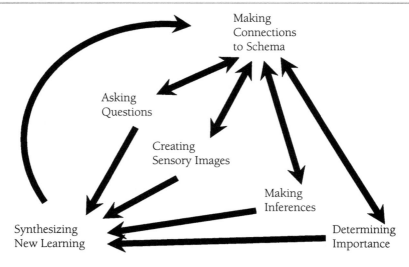

text as readers. Synthesis is what we make of a text; it is our take on it, which results in the creation of new schema.

Let's introduce a second example of a problematic text, adapted from Marvin Windows & Doors (1994):

> *Position the factory-applied nailing fin/drip cap upright for installation. Ensure drip-cap lip hangs over the head-jamb extrusion. Do not apply the nailing fin corner gaskets at this time. Install the unit into rough opening following prescribed procedures in the respective installation instructions. After the unit has been permanently secured in the dwelling, apply the four nailing-fin corner gaskets to each corner of the nailing fin.*

Again, ask teachers to examine the dynamics of their comprehension of this demanding text. They will immediately identify the insider language—the jargon, if you will—as a major impediment to their understanding. The passage is written in "contractor-speak"; home builders and construction workers would encounter little difficulty with these directions for installing a window. They can talk the talk, but the rest of us are outsiders of what Gee (1996) termed a Discourse, an accepted use of language, typically with a specialized pool of vocabulary. Insiders in a Discourse operate from a common knowledge base, exhibit a shared set of experiences and beliefs, and are expected to adhere to accepted ways of interacting. This view of comprehension mandates "that we see reading (and writing and speaking) as not one thing, but many: many different socioculturally situated reading (writing, speaking) practices" (Gee, 2000, p. 204).

Each of us is comfortable employing a wide array of Discourses. People who share a specific Discourse can be described as "discourse communities." Doctors, for example, are a discourse community, a group of people who share a common vocabulary, set of experiences, outlook, and mien. Lawyers, accountants, pharmacists, civil engineers—all exhibit the qualities of discourse communities. If you are a member, you know how to talk, you know how to act.

Our window installation excerpt is an example of academic discourse, the language one might encounter in an applied technology class. Topic knowledge in this passage includes the reader's experiences with home improvement procedures, and in particular, the process of installing doors and windows. Domain knowledge includes the Discourse of this discipline—terms such as *nailing fin*, *drip cap*, *head-jam extrusion*, and *corner gasket*—as well as the actual form of the message: very terse and straightforward language without much elaboration. Text structures within this academic Discourse contrast mightily with those expected in a literature class, a chemistry class, a math class, or a psychology class. In addition, readers expect to interact with this text and with each other in a certain way. The intention behind the window-installation reading is to do something pragmatic with one's comprehension, to follow the how-to steps to accomplish a task commonly undertaken within this domain.

Teachers will likely regard the window passage as poorly written and loaded with jargon. They will possibly offer their own examples of such inscrutable texts: the directions for wiring a ceiling fan, the assembly instructions for a product that has been purchased. People who are outsiders of a discourse need support and mentoring when encountering texts that assume insider knowledge. Teachers need to realize that subject disciplines are examples of discourse communities, and that their students, who are predominately outsiders in academic discourses, may feel overwhelmed or even alienated by all the jargon—an outsider's depiction of a Discourse— in a biology text, a math lesson, or a history passage. As a result, comprehension instruction must be embedded in the teaching of the Discourse of an academic discipline to support learners as they increasingly assume some of the attributes of insiders. As Gee (2000) explained,

> these experiences must be normed and scaffolded by "masters" and "more advanced peers" within a Discourse, and such norming and scaffolding must lead "apprentices" to build the "right" sorts of situated meanings based on shared experiences and shared cultural models. Minus the presence of masters of the Discourse, such norming and scaffolding is impossible. (p. 204)

In other words, content teachers—insiders and masters of their Discourse—are the people best positioned to mentor their students as they experiment with using comprehension strategies to learn within academic disciplines.

Stage Three: Experimentation With Classroom Strategies as Instructional Prototypes

So what exactly does it look like in math when a teacher embeds comprehension instruction into the learning of an academic Discourse? Does it look the same in chemistry? In world history? In art? In French? This third stage immerses teachers in experimenting with a variety of classroom strategies that prompt students to engage in the thinking strategies characteristic of proficient readers in specific academic disciplines. The theoretical groundwork described in the first two stages is absolutely necessary if teachers are going to be able to mine the potential of a host of promising classroom practices. This third stage of reflection and study tends to resonate with teachers, who frequently express impatience with "all the theory." Instead they await opportunities to explore ideas that can be directly transferred into their instructional practice.

This third stage is also potentially problematic for teachers representing the gamut of academic disciplines, especially if they encounter classroom strategies disproportionately modeled with language arts texts and Discourse. Teachers frequently have difficulty perceiving how a specific classroom strategy would work within their own academic discipline. In addition, middle and high school teachers do not necessarily find suggestions to seek texts outside the Discourse of their discipline— such as using more young adult fictional literature or picture books designed for younger children—especially useful when they are teaching science, math, or other academic disciplines. A common complaint among middle and high school teachers is that literacy workshops for them are usually conducted by individuals most comfortable with the English and language arts Discourse or who have elementary school backgrounds. As a result, strategies modeled with texts and goals appropriate for language arts may not seem to parallel the Discourse they teach. If comprehension instruction is to be embedded within an academic Discourse, then teachers need access to strategy models based on quality texts within that Discourse.

It is useful for teachers to regard classroom strategies as instructional prototypes, rather than ends in themselves. An instructional prototype represents an instructional application of embedded comprehension strategies that will likely assume somewhat different forms, depending on the nature of the academic Discourse. Clustering classroom strategies around the proficient-reader characteristics—making connections, questioning, visualizing, inferring, determining importance, and synthesizing—can be a helpful means for modeling instructional prototypes to teachers.

For example, consider instructional prototypes for inculcating student questioning. A generic strategy such as Questioning the Author (QtA; Beck, McKeown, Hamilton, & Kucan, 1997) can be customized for application to a mathematics text: What math concepts does this author assume I already know? Does the author use specialized math vocabulary? If so, what do I remember about these terms? Does the author introduce any new math terminology? Does what the author is describing make sense? Is the author telling me anything that is not clear at this point? What does the author expect that I will be able to do with this new information? Does the author talk about how these math concepts might appear in everyday life? And so on. In effect, math teachers, in this example, experiment with how QtA can be tailored to reinforce and prompt the types of questions that math insiders would wonder about when reading and studying math Discourse.

Math QtA questions would differ dramatically from those germane to the study of a literary work. Literature teachers might redesign QtA of a short story around questions such as these: Why would the author place this story in this setting? Why might the author have this character say or do this? What does the author's choice of words tell me about what the author might be thinking? What point might the author be making about this character's actions? How does the author use conflict in this story? What literacy devices does the author use, and what seems to be the purpose?

In contrast, an orchestra teacher in a music performance classroom might focus on QtA questions such as: When did the composer write this piece and how might the time period have influenced this music? What do we know about the composer, and was the piece characteristic of this individual's work? Why did the composer write this piece, and for whom? How does the composer use the elements of music (form, rhythm, melody, harmony, timbre, texture, and expression)? Why did the composer make these particular musical choices? What emotional responses to the music does the composer seem to be indicating? What expectations does the composer have of the musicians playing (or singing) this piece?

In this stage, a powerful strategy like QtA is investigated as an instructional prototype that represents explicit teaching of the comprehension strategy of self-questioning. The generic questions are then revised by teachers to satisfy the demands of thinking in their specific academic Discourses, to demonstrate the transcendent questions important to a biology teacher, a physics teacher, a geography teacher, an algebra teacher, and so on. The comprehension strategy is conceptualized as an instructional technique to mentor students into thinking the way an insider thinks, in this case asking the kind of questions an insider asks.

This stage represents especially fertile ground for content teachers working with literacy coaches as they collaborate to customize a generic strategy to mesh with the expectations and texts of an academic Discourse. As instructional prototypes, classroom strategies represent concrete applications that will assume a variety of forms as teachers experiment with their possible use in teaching their academic subjects.

Stage Four: Debriefing as Teaching for Metacognition

"The strategy worked so slick, the kids never knew what hit them!" This observation from a middle school teacher commenting on the effectiveness of a classroom strategy implemented in her curriculum is very revealing. On one level, the teacher is reflecting on student learning: the instructional activity led to increased student learning of the content in her classroom. But on another level, she is clearly indicating that students were unaware of what it was that worked so well for them during the lesson. This scenario demonstrates that effective learning might take place, within the structure of a well-conceived lesson that prompts comprehension strategies, but not necessarily lead to increased student independence as readers and learners.

The fourth stage of reflection and study for middle and high school teachers is the debriefing phase, which focuses on making overt the thinking elicited by the activity. Students need to recognize how an instructional routine is guiding their comprehension, or they will depart from a classroom still unduly dependent on the teacher's facility for developing well-designed lessons. As Ogle (2004) observed, "Teachers may be using effective literacy strategies but the students do not own them" (n.p.). For students to own literacy strategies, they need to develop the metacognitive awareness of the thinking they are doing, why they are doing it, and how this thinking intersects with learning within an academic Discourse.

Hence, it is imperative when literacy coaches and professional development specialists work with middle and high school teachers to include metacognitive debriefing sessions that model dialogue about an instructional practice and how the activity scaffolded comprehension. For example, when a teacher in a workshop setting makes an observation that involves an implicit understanding, model appropriate classroom conversation: "Talk about how you arrived at that idea. It sounds like you are making an inference; what does the author say that helps you make this inference? [To rest of class:] Does this seem like a justifiable inference? Are there other inferences that could also be supported?" By making one's thinking overt, teachers are modeling for learners the development of metacognitive awareness.

Metacognitive debriefing sessions with middle and high school teachers could emphasize the following phases: (1) Reflect on your thinking during this activity. How did the lesson prompt and support specific comprehension strategies? (2) What steps would you take with students to ensure that they process and share their thinking during the lesson? (3) How might this activity need to be modified to better match your academic discipline?

The debriefing stage underscores to teachers that classroom strategies are not ends in themselves, but are merely exemplars of instructional routines that engage students in the kinds of proficient thinking that add up to comprehension.

Implications

This chapter presents a four-stage framework for embedding comprehension instruction into the academic Discourse of content classrooms. No

Child Left Behind expectations are likely to promote a continuing national interest in coupling explicit comprehension instruction into the teaching of subjects across the curriculum. In particular, this framework outlines potentially effective methods for assisting middle and high school classroom teachers as they transition into literacy teachers of their subject areas. The framework suggests that professional development initiatives that focus solely on instructional strategies will be less effective than engaging teachers in truly exploring what it means for outsiders—their students—to meaningfully interact with the Discourse of their academic discipline. Teachers are asked to view themselves not as reading teachers but as teachers of an academic Discourse, who are mentoring their students' attempts to read, speak, and write the talk of this Discourse.

Questions for Reflection

1. What activities can be undertaken with middle and high school teachers to dispel misconceptions about teaching reading to adolescents?

2. How can we ensure that a metacognitive conversation is an integral component of strategy instruction?

3. What are effective ways to experiment with instructional prototypes, so that teachers can explore how explicit comprehension instruction dovetails with the academic Discourse they teach to students?

Doug Buehl is an Adolescent Literacy Support Teacher for the Madison Metropolitan School District, Madison, Wisconsin, USA. He was a member of the IRA Adolescent Literacy Commission and past President of the IRA Secondary Reading Interest Group, served on the task force that developed the *Standards for Middle and High School Literacy Coaches*, and was the 1996 winner of the IRA Nila Banton Smith Award. He is an author and a frequent presenter on content literacy topics at conferences and workshops. Buehl can be contacted at drbuehl@sbcglobal.net.

REFERENCES

Alexander, P., & Jetton, T. (2000). Learning from text: A multidimensional and developmental perspective. In M.L. Kamil, P. Mosenthal, P.D. Pearson, & R. Barr (Eds.), *Handbook of reading research* (Vol. 3, pp. 285–310). Mahwah, NJ: Erlbaum.

Beck, I.L., McKeown, M.G., Hamilton, R.L., & Kucan, L. (1997). *Questioning the author: An approach for enhancing student engagement with text.* Newark, DE: International Reading Association.

Biancarosa, G., & Snow, C.E. (2004). *Reading next: A vision for action and research in middle and high school literacy* (A report to Carnegie Corporation of New York). Washington, DC: Alliance for Excellent Education.

Gee, J.P. (1996). *Social linguistics and literacies: Ideology in discourses.* London: Taylor & Francis.

Gee, J.P. (2000). Discourse and sociocultural studies in reading. In M. Kamil, P. Mosenthal, P.D. Pearson, & R. Barr (Eds.), *Handbook of reading research* (Vol. 3, pp. 195–207). Mahwah, NJ: Erlbaum.

Harvey, S., & Goudvis, A. (2000). *Strategies that work: Teaching comprehension to enhance understanding.* York, ME: Stenhouse.

International Reading Association. (2006). *Standards for middle and high school literacy coaches.* Newark, DE: Author. Retrieved April 10, 2007, from http://www.reading.org/downloads/resources/597coaching_standards.pdf

Kamil, M.L. (2003). *Adolescents and literacy: Reading for the 21st century.* Washington, DC: Alliance for Excellent Education.

Keene, E.O., & Zimmermann, S. (1997). *Mosaic of thought: Teaching comprehension in a reader's workshop.* Portsmouth, NH: Heinemann.

Marvin Windows & Doors. (1994). *Installation instructions.* Warroad, MN: Author.

Marzano, R. (2004). *Building background knowledge for academic achievement: Research on what works in schools.* Alexandria, VA: Association for Supervision and Curriculum Development.

Moore, D.W., Bean, T.W., Birdyshaw, D., & Rycik, J.A. (1999). *Adolescent literacy: A position statement for the Commission on Adolescent Literacy of the International Reading Association.* Newark, DE: International Reading Association.

National Association of Secondary School Principals. (2005). *Creating a culture of literacy: A guide for middle and high school principals.* Reston, VA: Author.

National Association of State Boards of Education. (2005). *Reading at risk: The state response to the crisis in adolescent literacy: The report of the NASBE study group on middle and high school literacy.* Alexandria, VA: Author.

National Council of Teachers of English. (2004, May). *A call to action: What we know about adolescent literacy and ways to support teachers in meeting students' needs.* Urbana, IL: Author. Retrieved February 20, 2007, from http://www.ncte.org/about/over/positions/category/read/118622.htm

National Governors Association Center for Best Practices. (2005). *Reading to achieve: A governor's guide to adolescent literacy.* Washington, DC: Author.

Ogle, D. (2004, May). *Teaching and modeling strategies that support content learning.* Paper presented at the International Reading Association Convention, Reno, NV.

Snow, C.E. (2002). *Reading for understanding: Toward an R&D program in reading comprehension.* Santa Monica, CA: RAND.

Tovani, C. (2000). *I read it, but I don't get it: Comprehension strategies for adolescent readers.* Portland, ME: Stenhouse.

U.S. Department of Education. (2006). *Striving readers.* Retrieved December 1, 2006, from http://www.ed.gov/programs/strivingreaders/index.html

Vacca, R.T. (1998). Let's not marginalize adolescent literacy. *Journal of Adolescent & Adult Literacy, 41,* 604–609.

CHAPTER 12

Promoting Meaningful Adolescent Reading Instruction Through Integrated Literacy Circles

William E. Blanton, Paola Pilonieta, and Karen D. Wood

HIGHLIGHTS

- The reading model presented in this chapter proposes that proficient reading ability emerges as a reading system, a mental system, a set of subject matter systems, and tools are acquired, coordinated, and enacted to accomplish increasingly complex reading tasks.

- Learning-to-read and reading-to-learn instruction should occur in the Zone of Proximal Development.

- Activity in which students acquire and develop skill in coordinating and enacting reading knowledge with the assistance of others is a basic reading activity.

- Basic reading activity, such as a reading skill circle, or in the case of this chapter, the integrated literacy circle, is a way to organize the acquisition and development of skill in coordinating and enacting reading knowledge.

A ssessments continue to report that an unacceptable percentage of adolescent students are unable to read, comprehend, critically analyze, and apply information obtained by reading text (Campbell, Hombo, & Mazzeo, 2000; Donahue, Daane, & Jin, 2005; Donahue, Voelkl, Campbell, & Mazzeo, 1999). Riddle and Valencia (2002)

Adolescent Literacy Instruction: Policies and Promising Practices edited by Jill Lewis and Gary Moorman. © 2007 by the International Reading Association.

recently reported that although students could decode passages written at their reading level they could not comprehend the passages. Analysis of their strengths and weaknesses showed a variety of skill deficiencies. It was possible to place students into categories, such as struggling word callers, slow comprehenders, and disabled readers. In other words, students in the same classrooms may appear to be similar in terms of test scores; however, their strengths and weaknesses will reveal distinctly different patterns of knowledge about reading and their ability to apply it.

In the future, adolescents will be expected to regularly perform tasks requiring accessing, reading, and critically analyzing information to make important personal, professional, and political decisions. Their world will be a virtual culture of instant access to information disseminated as textual genres, such as books, essays, reviews, position papers, stock market ticker tapes, financial and medical news, and text-scrawls on television and computer monitors. Proficient reading ability, or the lack of it, will determine the extent to which they will be central participants in a world that is informationalized, symbolically represented, and virtualized.

The primary purpose of this chapter is to propose an orientation for thinking about adolescent reading instruction that is derived from cultural–historical activity theory, or CHAT (see Cole, 1996; Cole & Engestrom, 1993). Based on CHAT, we are reconceptualizing the reading circle concept common to the elementary grades and introducing what we are calling the integrated literacy circle as a teacher–peer scaffolded discussion approach to help readers develop proficiency and skill in the content areas. In order to understand the orientation to thinking about adolescent reading instruction that we are proposing, it is necessary to thoroughly examine its theoretical underpinnings in the seminal work of Vygotsky, Luria, and others. To that end, we begin with a discussion of traditional reading skill instruction. Then, we review selected principles of CHAT that we consider important to understanding proficient reading ability, followed by a CHAT model of proficient reading ability. Next, we discuss reading instruction and the development of reading skill, followed by an overview of basic reading activity, a conceptual tool for thinking about and arranging instruction that focuses on the acquisition and application of reading knowledge. Then we present a set of sample lessons for convening an integrated literacy circle. We end with comments on the transfer of reading knowledge and skill.

Traditional Basic Reading Skill Instruction and Adolescent Reading Performance

There are a number of explanations for why so many adolescents are unable to read, interpret, critically analyze, and understand text. The first explanation is that traditional basic reading skill instruction is grounded in earlier notions of mastery learning (Block & Airasian, 1971; Carroll, 1963), basal reading program management systems (Johnson & Pearson, 1975), and compendia of reading skills that are indexed to instruction, such as the Wisconsin Design for Reading Skill Development (Otto, 1977). The names of reading tasks, such as reading to determine the main idea of a text, became tagged as basic reading skills by publishers and teachers and created a serious misunderstanding. Reading to determine the main idea of a text is a basic reading task, not a basic reading skill. The completion of a basic reading task requires a student to possess skill to coordinate and enact reading knowledge. Students should acquire reading knowledge and the skill to coordinate it through engagement and participation in a basic reading activity, not decontextualized drill and practice.

Nonetheless, the notion emerged that proficient reading ability consists of a set of discrete basic reading skills that can be (a) isolated and extracted from their enactment in reading activity, (b) broken down into subcomponents, (c) organized into a valid scope and sequence, and (d) easily measured and assessed to determine level of mastery and to make decisions about review, practice, reteaching, and enrichment. Over time, classroom reading instruction began to increase the emphasis on decontextualized scripted instruction and drill and practice, while deemphasizing meaningful instruction that focuses on the enactment and coordination of reading knowledge to accomplish authentic reading tasks (Wenglinsky, 2000).

Second, the traditional approach to basic reading skill instruction continues to be sustained by administrative decision making and classroom practice, through the discourse of scientifically based reading research, No Child Left Behind, standards driven curriculum, statewide testing, and the public posting of graded school performance that is based on students' performance on high-stakes tests. As a result, a clerical approach to classroom reading instruction has emerged. Many teachers have acquired the identity of instructional clerks who view reading instruction as clerking—simply checking off reading skills as they are presented with scripted instruction to students who practice them in workbooks and other activities. Although quantitative increases in levels of reading achievement may seem to be increasing as a result of this kind of instruction, it is doubtful that significant qualitative changes in levels of literacy are being attained.

Third, basal reading programs built on the traditional skill approach continue to be the tool of choice for elementary school reading instruction. Examination of selected basal reading programs reveal that over half of their pages are allocated to narrative text, followed by approximately one-third to information text, and scant space to drama and poetry. As a result of their elementary school instructional experiences, many adolescent students come to the middle and high school classroom with insufficient opportunities to acquire, coordinate, and enact reading knowledge to accomplish reading tasks in a variety of text genres (Duke, 2000; Miller & Blumenfeld, 1993; Pilonieta, 2006).

The amount and quality of information provided in instructional manuals for teachers is another explanation. There seems to be a fuzzy continuum for helping students make the gradual transition from teacher-directed explanation, modeling, assisted practice, and enactment of reading knowledge to student-directed coordination and enactment to accomplish increasingly complex reading tasks. Basal reading manuals do not appear to offer teachers sufficient information to provide students with the quality of instruction expected by many reading professionals. Analyses of manuals and student materials continue to reveal that some reading skills are practiced but rarely introduced, introduced but rarely practiced, practiced immediately after they are introduced, practiced months later, or never practiced (Miller & Blumenfeld, 1993; Pilonieta, 2006).

The assessment provided by most basal reading programs is generally limited to lower-level cognitive tasks that require brief responses, such as circle, underline, draw a line, fill in the blank, or write a few sentences. There appears to be very little cognitive clarity in instruction on the acquisition, coordination, and enactment of reading knowledge that many students receive prior to entering upper grade levels. Very few assessment tasks focus on whether or not students have developed skill to successfully coordinate and enact reading knowledge to understand a variety of text genres. Therefore it is not surprising that the traditional reading skill instruction many students receive in elementary school may be insufficient for the shift students must make from learning to read in earlier grade levels to reading to learn in upper grade levels.

Last is the persistent belief that the proper remediation for students who experience difficulty acquiring proficient reading ability is repeated exposure to the same kind of decontextualized drill and practice contributing to their failure. Corrective reading instruction available to adolescent struggling readers is often organized as pull-out programs. Pull-out programs remove students from subject matter instruction. Consequently, students are left to participate at the periphery of instruction that focuses on reading to learn in a variety of text genres. We maintain that corrective reading instruction can be done in the classroom, by the classroom teacher, and using actual subject area material. However, it is essential that the classroom activity be organized in a way that promotes meaningful, social interaction. That is where an understanding of cultural–historical activity theory comes into play.

A Cultural–Historical Activity Theory Approach

In this section, we present four claims drawn from cultural–historical activity theory (CHAT) that are important to understanding the acquisition of proficient reading ability. Based on the theoretical insights of Lev Vygotsky (1934/1978), Alexander Luria (1932, 1973), A.N. Leont'ev (1981) and their students, CHAT refers to a family of theories that include sociocultural studies (Wertsch, 1985), distributed cognition (Resnick, Levine, & Teasley, 1991), communities of learners (Brown & Campione, 1998; Rogoff, 2003), activity theory (Engestrom, Miettinen, & Punamaki, 1999), and communities of practice (Lave & Wenger, 1991; Wenger, 1998). The focus of these theories is on how the organization of activity, including the focus of the activity, roles of participants, distribution of labor, rules and procedures, community, and instrumental and mental tools, all play a role in attaining outcomes.

The theoretical platform on which CHAT stands is that thinking is the product of the interaction among biology, culture, history, and participation in practical activity. Children begin life with a biological inheritance limited to a set of elementary mental functions, such as attention, perception, and simple memory. Adults are responsible for arranging the environment so that children acquire the cultural legacy of their forbearers and the knowledge, insight, and skill necessary to become members of their culture. Participation in everyday activities results in the acquisition of language, cultural practices, categories of thinking, general word meaning, and world knowledge (see Cole, Gay, Glick, & Sharp, 1971; Rogoff, 2003; Scribner & Cole, 1981; Tulviste, 1991). Through participation in organized educational activities, they acquire domain-specific knowledge, technical word meanings, metacognition, and the cultural form of literacy.

The first claim of CHAT is that complex systems, such as thinking, reading, writing, and subject matter systems are not stand-alone functions. Rather, they are continuously changing intercoordinated systems of knowledge and skill that emerge and unfold as one participates in culturally mediated activity (Luria, 1932, 1973). Through participation in learning activities, elementary functions that first operated independently are restructured to work together and perform more complex tasks (Vygotsky, 1987).

The next claim is that the development of complex systems, such as human thinking and reading ability, are culturally mediated. Humans cannot interact directly with their environment. Rather they interact indirectly with it by mediating their activity with both tangible and psychological tools (Vygotsky, 1934/1978). Culture enters into learning and development in that tools are artifacts produced by previous human activity and carry the cultural code for their use (Cole, 1996). For example, the invention and use of the printing press prompted changes in thinking about how to represent human knowledge, a need for instruction in writing and reading, the reorganization of the division of labor for printing and distributing text, and a need for copyright laws. Similar effects are currently being observed with computers, optic fiber, the Internet, search engines, and global conferencing platforms (see Friedman, 2005). The insertion of tools into activity can shape thinking and bring about new functions connected with their use (Vygotsky, 1981). Humans have been making tools directly available to future generations through organized education and discovery (Tomasello, 1999).

The third claim is that children develop their thinking processes and the ability to regulate themselves and others from the outside. Through the process of internalization, thinking processes come to reside on the inside (Vygotsky, 1934/1978, 1987).

Internalization does not mean making an exact copy of the outside world and placing it inside one's head. Internalization is a process that reconstructs systems, such as thinking, reading, and subject matter (Leont'ev, 1981; Wertsch, 1985, 1991). As the language mediating social activity is internalized, it is edited into a set of inner languages (Radzikhovskii, 1991). One language is a meta-language for self-regulation and the direction of personal thought. The other coordinates communication within and among systems, such as mental functions, reading, and writing.

The fourth claim of CHAT is that the Zone of Proximal Development (ZPD) explains how social structures are internalized from the outside to the inside, which results in the reconstruction of systems, such as thinking, reading, and mathematics. The ZPD is

> the distance between the actual developmental level as determined by independent problem solving and the level of potential development as determined through problem solving under adult guidance or in collaboration with more capable peers. (Vygotsky, 1934/1978, p. 86)

A ZPD is not a thing located inside the heads of children. It is the social organization for learning that occurs when children participate in activity that is motivated by and organized around their interests and goals. Children work together with adults and more accomplished peers in pairs or groups and share responsibility for accomplishing tasks leading to accomplishment of a goal. The goal is just beyond their current ability and requires the support of others to be attained. To optimize learning, guided assistance is provided, but only as much as needed, to do tasks leading to the accomplishment of the goal. Each and every participant learns from the mutual contributions of the other participants (Chaiklin, 2003; Newman, Griffin, & Cole, 1989; Wells, 1999).

A significant outcome of participation in a ZPD is learning to focus, or direct, one's attention. When left to direct their own activity, children generally attend to and interpret what they think is important. In organized activity, others (such as teachers in educational settings) may direct their attention. As participants externalize their thinking processes through language, gesture, diagrams, and other tools, implicit processes are made explicit. This lets participants "see" how the pieces of a task and its accomplishment fit together as a meaningful whole that represents a model of their future performance. Next we will see how the principles of CHAT align with proficient reading and ultimately lead to our integrated literacy circle concept described later.

A Cultural–Historical Model of Proficient Reading

Even before participating in formal reading instruction, children can observe, interpret, and think about the world around them. This provides a foundation for the acquisition of reading ability (Donaldson, 1978). Once formal reading instruction begins, children start the long journey to proficient reading so that they can accomplish increasingly complex reading tasks. These tasks include discriminating letters, learning about letter-sound correspondence, blending sounds to identify words, and retrieving the meanings to which the words refer to generate an interpretation and understanding of text about people, things, and events in their environment.

Figure 12.1 presents a model of proficient reading. This model proposes that there are three main systems that operate simultaneously in proficient reading. Beginning at the top, the reading system is a set of intercoordinated strands composed of phonemic awareness, word identification, word meaning (vocabulary), comprehension, and the knowledge of how reading works—the ability to regulate all of the previously mentioned strands to achieve meaning while reading (Adams, 1990; Crowder & Wagner, 1992; National Institute of Child Health and Human Development, 2000; Scarborough, 2001; Snow, Griffin, & Burns, 2005).

Figure 12.1. A Model of Proficient Reading

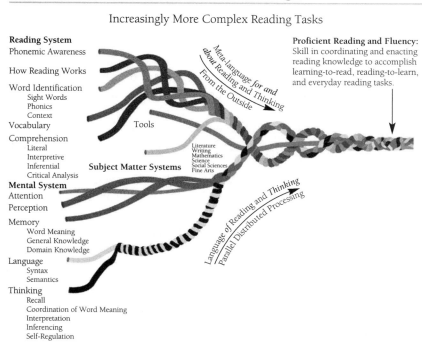

Increasingly More Complex Reading Tasks

Reading System
Phonemic Awareness

How Reading Works

Word Identification
   Sight Words
   Phonics
   Context
Vocabulary

Comprehension
   Literal
   Interpretive
   Inferential
   Critical Analysis
Mental System
Attention

Perception

Memory
   Word Meaning
   General Knowledge
   Domain Knowledge
Language
   Syntax
   Semantics
Thinking
   Recall
   Coordination of Word Meaning
   Interpretation
   Inferencing
   Self-Regulation

Tools

Subject Matter Systems
Literature
Writing
Mathematics
Science
Social Sciences
Fine Arts

Meta-language for and about Reading and Thinking From the Outside

Language of Reading and Thinking Parallel Distributed Processing

Proficient Reading and Fluency: Skill in coordinating and enacting reading knowledge to accomplish learning-to-read, reading-to-learn, and everyday reading tasks.

Next, the mental system includes the attention, perception, memory, language, and thinking strands. Third are the subject matter systems. These are composed of discipline knowledge generally thought of as subject matter that students are expected to acquire. Tools—such as discourse, books, teacher manuals, lesson plans, tests, grouping patterns, and computers—are used to conduct, or mediate, learning activities.

By participating in reading instruction and engaging in reading, these systems begin to work in unison. However, these systems are not static. They are continuously reorganized as necessary. Some knowledge disappears and new knowledge emerges, allowing students to perform increasingly more complex reading tasks, such as reading to learn from multimedia and the generation of interpretation, critical analysis, and understanding of text.

The language of reading and thinking, a form of the internalized social language, has two main functions. The first is coordination of communication within and among the reading, mental, and subject matter systems. The second function is turning experience into word meanings that are stored in memory.

Experiences are represented in memory as a network of coded relations among meanings and words that are retrieved, sampled, and integrated with the reader's world knowledge and domain knowledge to generate an interpretation and understanding of text. As an illustration, in reading the word *dog* a reader might identify it as a sight word or by coordinating knowledge of rules to decode letters and blending the sounds to spoken language representing the word. The interpretation of *dog* is limited by the experiences of the reader and the number of meanings indexed to *dog* that the reader has stored in memory. The pool of meanings may include the dog that bit me; a mongrel; Rex, my pet dog; canine; Mark Antony's angry cry in *Julius Caesar*, "Cry 'Havoc!' and let slip the dogs of war"; the slang term *dawg* as in "What's up dawg?" which is used to refer to a friend; or General George Patton's bull terrier, William the Conqueror. The coordination of these meanings mediates the generation of an interpretation and understanding of *dog*. Additional contexts might limit the number of meanings to coordinate or point to additional meanings. Words and the meanings to which they refer also link to other words, sentences, phrases, and longer text, and create expanded networks that create an infinite pool of meanings available for a reader to draw from and coordinate.

Parallel distributed processing (PDP) is a seemingly endless network of neurons that activate and deactivate in infinite combinations (McClelland, 1989; Plaut & McClelland, 1993; Rumelhart & McClelland,

1982). During engagement in reading activity, PDP coordinates the interplay within and among the reading, mental, and subject matter systems to accomplish top-down (reader-based) and bottom-up (text-based) reading processes (Rumelhart, 1994; Stanovich, 1980). The meanings words refer to are simultaneously retrieved from memory, coordinated across sentences and longer text, and integrated with world knowledge to confirm the interpretation of the text (Hagoort, Hald, Bastiaansen, & Petersson, 2004).

In terms of classroom practice, vocabulary is understood as words that refer to the meanings given to experiences, objects, events, concepts, emotional states, and procedures. Access to a large store of word meanings makes it possible for the reader to construct subtle differences of interpretation and understanding of text. Participation in discussion extends the interpretation, critical analysis, and understanding of the text and makes additional word meanings available to coordinate the continuous construction of other interpretations and understandings. Eventually, a public interpretation and understanding of the text may be negotiated with others, and the readers may integrate this interpretation and understanding with their prior knowledge.

Reading Instruction and the Development of Reading Skill

Thus far we have discussed some of the problems with traditional reading instruction, a CHAT approach to the acquisition of proficient reading, and a reading model based on key principles of CHAT. Now we turn to reading instruction. Social interactions and attention to that interaction make the reading knowledge, thinking processes, and meaning-making resources that occur implicitly during a reading lesson explicit to students. The externalization of the thinking processes and reading knowledge used by each student affects the thinking process of the reading group. In turn, every member of the group internalizes the group's thinking processes and knowledge about reading. The role of students is to participate in the group's discussion of the reading knowledge and tools used, synthesize the contributions of others, and integrate the results with their prior knowledge. It is with this premise in mind that we now present some principles for effective reading instruction.

To become proficient readers, students must acquire and develop skill in coordinating a reading system comprising declarative, procedural, and conditional knowledge of reading. Declarative knowledge (knowing what) represents knowing the tasks related to phonemic awareness, word identification, and vocabulary that are performed to construct the interpretation, understanding, and critical analysis of text. Procedural knowledge (knowing how) is composed of the steps involved in coordinating and enacting reading knowledge to perform the tasks. Conditional knowledge (knowing when and why) reflects an understanding of particular situations, text genres, problems, goals, and reading tasks that cue the need to coordinate and enact certain reading knowledge to accomplish particular reading tasks. Reading skill is demonstrated when a student can independently coordinate and enact the actions needed to apply declarative, procedural, and conditional knowledge to successfully perform reading tasks during learning-to-read, reading-to-learn, and personal reading activity.

The acquisition of proficient reading ability requires that students receive sufficient opportunity to (a) participate in systematic instruction aimed at assisting them with the acquisition of knowledge constituting a robust reading system, (b) receive assisted practice in developing skill in coordinating the knowledge comprising their reading system with other systems and tools used to accomplish increasingly complex reading tasks, (c) participate in reading-to-learn instruction that focuses on coordinating and enacting reading knowledge and tools to accomplish tasks, such as reading-to-learn subject matter presented through textbooks and other media (d) participate in substantial discussions of the interpretation, critical analysis, and understanding of material read, synthesize those discussions, and integrate the results with their world knowledge and domain knowledge, and (e) receive the long-term assistance necessary for the gradual transition from teacher-directed reading activity to student-directed reading activity.

Reading knowledge and coordinating skill to enact it to accomplish reading tasks cannot be told to or handed over to students. The role of instruction is to arrange for student participation in learning activities that facilitate the acquisition, reorganization, and intercoordination of their reading, mental, and subject matter systems to accomplish increasingly more complex learning-to-read and reading-to-learn tasks. In Vygotsky's (1926/1999) words,

> Though the teacher is powerless to produce immediate effects in the student, he is all-powerful when it comes to producing direct effects in him through the social environment. The social environment is the true lever of the educational process, and the teacher's overall role re-

duces to adjusting this lever.... Thus, it is the teacher who educates the student by varying the environment.... (p. 49)

Proficient reading ability is an outcome of the acquisition, coordination, and enactment of reading knowledge and thinking processes that are located in the social interactions of students when they participate in reading lessons and discussions. Students internalize the structure of a teacher's lesson plan, the language mediating how reading knowledge and tools are used, and the thinking processes of the reading group. Over time, the organization of reading lessons—or lack of it—is reflected in the extent to which students acquire and develop skill in coordinating their reading system with other systems to accomplish reading tasks and to regulate their participation in future reading instruction, reading-to-learn activity, and personal reading activity.

In essence, an effective reading lesson is a ZPD that is co-constructed by a teacher and students to acquire knowledge of a reading system and develop skill in coordinating that knowledge with other systems to accomplish reading tasks. It is important that the teacher is able to identify reading tasks that are just beyond students' current level of independent performance but capable of being completed with the guided assistance of others, or a true conceptual understanding will not occur.

Intervening during instruction is a major instructional decision. Teachers must be attuned to their students' strengths and weaknesses in order to anticipate patterns of behavior indicating that a task is too difficult. They must decide when to intervene and how much assistance to provide. If intervention is too soon, students may become dependent on the teacher. If intervention is too late, students may be overwhelmed by the level of difficulty of the task set for the reading lesson.

Even adolescents who have failed to acquire proficient reading ability in school regularly participate in activities they mediate with a multiplicity of tools, such as print, personal computers, advertisements, magazines, newspapers, comic books, interactive gaming, catalogues, cell phones, and instant messaging. As a result of participation in activities of this kind, many students acquire enough basic reading knowledge and skill to coordinate and enact it to read, interpret, and understand technical manuals, websites, teen magazines, and other special publications related to their interests (Moore & Hinchman, 2006). They acquire reading knowledge and skill to coordinate it to achieve personal goals, with the assistance of their peers. We have come to think of activities of this kind as basic reading activity (Griffin & Cole, 1987). With this notion that reading proficiency develops through peer interaction and meaningful activity, we introduce the integrated literacy circle, a discussion-based approach to teaching and learning content area concepts while acquiring basic reading skills.

Integrated Literacy Circle

With a little imagination, traditional drill and practice of the skills needed for proficient reading can be repurposed as basic reading activity through an integrated literacy circle. This concept is similar to the reading circles seen in many elementary classrooms in that students are assigned to groups for an instructional purpose. When applied to the middle- or secondary-level classroom, the circle concept provides a means for students to discuss the content under study while simultaneously learning how to apply a needed literacy skill. An integrated literacy circle is a way to organize the acquisition, coordination, and enactment of reading knowledge in authentic reading activity.

In this way, the integrated literacy circle provides a vehicle for teacher scaffolding of the concepts to be learned while enabling peer groups to co-construct the information through discussion. This process of co-constructing knowledge enables students to reach toward and function in their ZPD. Typically, a teacher and eight or so students form a reading skill circle. The teacher provides an explanation of a particular reading task and the reading knowledge to be used, and then models and thinks aloud when and how the knowledge is used to accomplish the task. Students are assigned a reading task to complete with the assistance of the teacher, followed by a discussion of the results. The text selected can be short or long, so long as it is of interest to students and can stimulate meaningful discussion. Students are encouraged to recruit help from the teacher and others when necessary. Students are then assigned additional material to read with the purpose of coordinating and applying the knowledge to accomplish the task independently. Instruction on the task culminates with the teacher coordinating a discussion of how the knowledge "worked," how to conduct the activity better next time, and how it might be used inside and outside school.

Through discussion, students are able to interact with each other about the task and reading knowledge they used; difficult words they needed to identify; word meanings, concepts, ideas, and content that were challenging or unclear; and their interpretation and understanding of the text. However, the focus of the discussion typically remains among the students, with the teacher monitoring from the background. In this way, reading lessons can be more meaningful and increase the likelihood that students will transfer their reading knowledge to other reading tasks.

There are seven phases of instruction in a reading skill circle: exploration, explication, translation, modeling, guided practice, application, and closure. During the exploration phase, teachers probe students' prior knowledge about a reading task to be performed. In the explication phase, the teacher explains declarative knowledge (what the task is), procedural knowledge (how the task is completed and with what knowledge), and conditional knowledge (when the knowledge can be applied and why). This is also the phase in which students take their first steps toward internalizing the meta-language of the lesson. During the translation phase students are asked to explain the task in their own words. This gives teachers an opportunity to judge how well students are interpreting and understanding the meta-language for enacting the knowledge for completing the task. The next phase requires the teacher to model how the knowledge is coordinated to complete the task. This process makes implicit thinking processes and meaning-making resources of the lesson explicit. In the guided practice phase, students work with partners or small ensembles to coordinate and enact the knowledge to accomplish the reading task. The externalization of the thinking processes of each student affects the thinking process of the group. In turn, every member of the group internalizes the thinking processes of the reading group, resulting in the transformation of their thinking processes and reading system. Afterward, students are asked to apply and enact the knowledge to independently accomplish the task in similar material. Finally, during the closure phase, students summarize what they have learned about performing the target task. The role of students is to attend to and participate in the discussion about the knowledge they used, their understanding of how it was used, synthesize the contributions of others, and revise their understanding of the task and how they might perform it better next time.

In Figures 12.2 and 12.3, we provide sample lessons that demonstrate basic reading instruction through integrated literacy circles. In Figure 12.2, the lesson focuses on text structure and sequence. In Figure 12.3, the major focus is on the understanding of context clues. Although the integrated literacy circle can be conducted with narrative texts, these examples use information texts, thereby maximizing opportunities for

Figure 12.2. Integrated Literacy Circle: Sequence and Text Structure

PHASES
Exploration
The purpose of our lesson today is to learn about a text structure called sequence. Text structure is the way an author organizes the ideas in his writing. Who can tell me what we mean by sequence? Why is it important to understand the sequence of events? What are some hints that authors give to help you follow the sequence of events?

Explication
Declarative Knowledge. The sequence text structure is the way an author writes information to show you the order in which things happen. The authors can show you the order of things in explicit and implicit ways. Sometimes they separate the steps into short paragraphs. At the beginning of each paragraph they will put a number to show which idea comes first. This is an explicit, or clear way (look for an example in *Cell to System* [Stewart, 2003], p. 12). Other times the author has statements and matching pictures in the order in which they happen. This is more implicit (look for an example in *Cell to System*, p. 15). Another way, one of the more difficult and most implicit ways, is when the author just writes all of the steps in a paragraph (look for an example in *Meet the Beetles* [Stewart, 2006], p. 7). When authors do this, it is important to look for keywords—such as *first, then, next, after*—to figure out the order of the steps.

Procedural Knowledge. The first thing you need to do to find the text structure is look at the section you are reading. Are there numbers to indicate sequence? If not, check to see if there are paragraphs with corresponding pictures. Do the pictures seem to go in order? Read the paragraphs and look for keywords (first, then, next, after, ordinal numbers). If the information is written as one big paragraph, you are going to have to read it and look for the keywords. It might be helpful to write down numbers, starting with one, over each keyword to help you better follow the order.

Conditional Knowledge. Understanding the order of events and recognizing the sequence in text are important for several reasons. First, it will help you understand how a process works or occurs. It will also help you to perform the task. Knowing about sequence text structure can help you when you're following directions for a science experiment or recipe. It can also help you understand how events occurred in your social studies textbooks. Using these keywords in your writing can also help you organize your ideas more clearly.

Translation
Using your own words, who can tell me what the sequence text structure is? How do you figure out if a text is organized in sequential order? If it's in one big paragraph, what can you do to help? When do you think it might be important to understand the sequence of something?

Modeling
Let's start with an easy example. What did you do to get ready for class today after the bell rang? To figure out the answer, let's think about what we did first. You

(continued)

Figure 12.2. Integrated Literacy Circle: Sequence and Text Structure (continued)

probably came in, sat down, and put your backpack on the floor. Then you took out your folder, and finally your pencil. What keywords did we use?

Let's look at another example (*Searching for Lost Tombs* [Granahan, 2006], p. 17). Look at page 17 where they show you how to make a mummy. The first thing I notice is the short paragraphs with numbers next to them. The numbers must tell me what happens first when you make a mummy. Now let me read the paragraphs, paying special attention to the keywords. What keywords do you notice?

Guided Practice

Read the experiment described on page 7 (*Meet the Beetles*, 2006). Work in pairs to figure out if the text structure is implicit or explicit. Work together to look for keywords that indicate order. Write a short summary describing the steps in the experiment.

Once all of the pairs are done with their summaries, they can share the keywords and summaries with the class. The teacher can then assign another passage so that students can highlight the keywords and summarize the information independently.

Application

We have been talking about the sequence text structure these past few days. Today I want you to apply this strategy as we read our social studies lesson. As you read, I want you to make a note of the keywords that indicate order. Think about how these words help you understand what is happening. Afterward, we will discuss the order of events together.

During the next week, I want you to find two examples of text written in sequence from either magazines or newspapers.

Closure

Last week you were asked to collect two examples of text written in sequence. Working in pairs, share your examples with your partner. Explain why you believe they are examples of the sequence text structure, and briefly describe the information.

Figure 12.3. Integrated Literacy Circle: Context Clues

PHASES

Exploration

The purpose of our lesson today is to learn different ways to find the meaning of an unknown word. What are some things you can do to figure out what a word means? Do you need to know the meaning of every single word you read to understand the passage? How do you know which words you definitely need to understand in your textbooks (they tend to be bold or highlighted)?

Explication

Declarative Knowledge. Vocabulary words are words you need to know to understand the passage you are reading. Vocabulary words are usually written in bold print or

(continued)

Figure 12.3. Integrated Literacy Circle: Context Clues (continued)

are highlighted in textbooks. To find the meaning of vocabulary words you can do a structural analysis of the word, look for context clues, or look at the glossary or dictionary. To do a structural analysis you need to look for prefixes, suffixes, or familiar parts of words. Context clues can be found in the sentence where the vocabulary word is or in the sentence before or after. Most textbooks have a glossary, but if it doesn't you can use a dictionary to find the meaning of the word.

Procedural Knowledge. The first thing you should do when you come across a word you don't know is do a structural analysis. That means look to see if there are clues inside the word. The clues can be prefixes or suffixes you know, or parts of words you recognize from other words. For example, look at the word *chloroplast* (*Cells to System* [Stewart, 2003], p. 6). I don't really know what *chloroplast* means, but I remember the word *chlorophyll* has something to do with plants. So maybe *chloroplast* does too. Not all words have clues inside them; there is nothing inside the word *larvae* (*Meet the Beetles* [Stewart, 2006], p. 4) to help you figure out its meaning.

The next thing to look for is context clues. Context clues are clues that help you figure out what a word means. They are usually found in the sentence where the unknown vocabulary word is, in the sentence before, or in the sentence after. Look at this example: "the beetle's 'weapon factory' is made up of two *glands*, or small organs, inside its body" (*Meet the Beetles*, p. 26). From the sentence you can tell that a *gland* is a small organ inside the beetle's body.

However, not all words have context clues to help you figure them out. Look at this example: "they are part of a foolproof system that lets the Melanophila beetle *detect* a fire from many miles away" (*Meet the Beetles*, p. 20). The sentence doesn't give you a lot of help; neither did the sentence before or after. The next thing you can do is use the glossary at the back of the book. A glossary is like a dictionary. If your book doesn't have a glossary, you can use a dictionary. When I look up the word *detect* in the glossary, it says, "notice or sense something" (*Meet the Beetles*, p. 31). So that means that the Melanophila beetle can sense fire from far away.

Conditional Knowledge. Knowing how to find the meaning of an unknown vocabulary word can help you become an independent learner. By following the three steps—using structural analysis, using context clues, or using a glossary or dictionary—you will be able to find the meaning of almost every word. You can use these three steps in any class, with any textbook, to help you find the meaning of unknown vocabulary words.

Translation
Using your own words, who can tell me how you know what the vocabulary words in your textbook are? How do you figure out what a vocabulary word means? How do you do a structural analysis? How do you use context clues? When do you use a glossary? When do you use a dictionary? When should you use these three steps?

Modeling
Let's start with an easy example: "It's made of the same hard material as a beetle's *exoskeleton*, or outer skin" (*Meet the Beetles*, p. 21). First let's do a structural analysis: *ex* in *exoskeleton* usually means out. So maybe an *exoskeleton* is a skeleton that is

(continued)

Figure 12.3. Integrated Literacy Circle: Context Clues (continued)

outside of the body. Now let's look at context clues. The sentence indicates that an exoskeleton is outer skin, and that it's made out of hard material. When I look at the glossary, it says that an *exoskeleton* is "the hard outer shell or skin of an insect and some other animals" (*Meet the Beetles*, p. 31). Mmm, that means that insects and other animals have exoskeletons.

Let's try another example:

> The team started *excavating* the tomb later that year. It was hard, hot work. They used pickaxes to pound rocks. They used shovels and hoes to remove dirt. As they dug, they discovered that the tomb had been partially destroyed. (*Searching for Lost Tombs* [Granaham, 2006], p. 10)

First we'll do a structural analysis of the word *excavating*. Again, the *ex* in *excavating* probably has to do with out. But I still don't know what the word means. Let me look for some context clues. People are using pickaxes, shovels, and hoes to remove dirt. Maybe *excavating* means to take out dirt, or to dig. Let me continue reading. "As they dug...." They are digging! Let me just check the glossary to make sure I'm right. It says, *excavate* means "dig up" (*Meet the Beetles*, p. 31).

Guided Practice

Read the section on New Arrivals (*Come to Florida!* [Vierow, 2004], p. 14). Work in a small group to do a structural analysis of the three vocabulary words. Then jot down the context clues for each word. Finally, look at the glossary and see if you were able to figure out the meaning of the words just from the context clues and the structural analysis.

Once all of the groups are done finding the meaning of the three vocabulary words, they can share their work with the rest of the class. The teacher can then assign another passage where students highlight the context clues and define the words independently.

Application

We have been talking about how to find the meaning of unknown vocabulary words. Today I want you to apply this strategy as we read our social studies lesson. As you read, I want you to make a note of the structural analysis of the vocabulary words. Then use the context clues to help you find the meaning of the word. Use the glossary if you still don't know what the word means. Think about how doing these steps helps you understand what is happening. Afterward, we will discuss the definitions of the words together.

During the next week, I want you to find three examples of vocabulary words from another class. Write down how the structural analysis helped you (if it did), write down the context clues, and then verify with the glossary to see if you were right.

Closure

Last week you were asked to find the meaning of three vocabulary words from other classes. Working in pairs, share your definitions, structural analysis, and context clues with your partner. Explain how you developed your definition.

students to acquire reading knowledge while learning subject matter. These lessons assume that students are being introduced to the particular reading task and related knowledge for the first time and are conducted over a couple of weeks.

Several texts were used for these lessons. The first text, *Cells to Systems* (Stewart, 2003), presents information about cells, DNA, cellular systems, and the relation of cells to the continuation of life. Next, *Meet the Beetles* (Stewart, 2006), explores the features and habits of arthropods, their anatomy, how they adapt to their environment, and the potential of arthropods to improve human lives. The third, *Searching for Lost Tombs* (Granahan, 2006), introduces students to archaeological investigation and the artifacts of early Egyptian and Chinese civilizations. The last, *Come to Florida!* (Vierow, 2005), discusses the diverse groups of people who come to Florida, the relation between modes of transportation and population increase, and interesting places, activities, and living styles that attract people to the state of Florida.

Simply being able to identify words and derive their meanings will not reveal the interpretation hidden in a text. As students participate in reading instruction, they need to coordinate and enact the knowledge they are acquiring in authentic reading activity. They need to think about, discuss, and argue the facts, interpretation, ideas, and understandings that can be derived from the text (Anderson et al., 2001).

Discussion is the primary way that reading knowledge, meanings, concepts, interpretations, and understandings are passed around and learned. The richer the discussion, the greater the likelihood that subject matter will be understood, integrated with prior knowledge, recalled, and applied in the future (Guthrie, Anderson, Alao, & Rinehart, 1999; Rivard & Straw, 2000).

Thus an important feature of the sample lessons is their use of discussion. Discussion occurs during each phase of a reading skill circle with the teacher providing a model and then releasing the concept to the students with scaffolding. During the explication phase of each sample lesson, the teacher introduces the meta-language to be used, through explicit modeling and thinking aloud, to enact and coordinate the necessary reading knowledge in order to accomplish the reading task. Over time, students internalize the meta-language of the teacher and use it to mediate their participation in discussions of reading tasks, reading knowledge used, how it was enacted, and its application to other reading tasks.

It is imperative that students master the academic discourse and technical vocabulary of subject matter disciplines, such as earth science, biology, physics, law, literature, and literary criticism. The understanding of subject matter is significantly enhanced through public discussion of the meanings of technical vocabulary, symbols, graphs, text structure, and other tools that specialized disciplines use. A plethora of research supports providing students with rich experiences with the technical vocabulary of subject matter areas to improve the interpretation, critical analysis, and understanding of text (Davis, 1983; Nagy, 1988).

Technical words do not frequently appear in the narrative texts that students encounter during reading instruction in earlier grade levels. However, technical vocabulary is common in information texts at upper grade levels, and it is critical to the understanding of the text. A teacher must take special care to draw students' attention to the technical vocabulary in information texts that refers to similar meanings and processes they acquired in earlier instruction focusing on narrative texts. The words *evidence*, *hypothesize*, and *record* encountered in science texts and the words *clue*, *predict*, and *write down* encountered in narrative texts point to similar meanings.

The Transfer of Reading Knowledge and Skill

The limited transfer of reading knowledge and coordinating skill to reading tasks beyond classroom instruction continues to pose problems for researchers and teachers (Beach, 1999; Bransford, Brown, & Cocking, 1999; Bransford & Schwartz, 1999; Singley & Anderson, 1989). Reading knowledge generally transfers to similar reading tasks and conditions, such as the next reading unit or the same text genre. However, it does not seem to easily transfer to significantly different reading tasks, text genres, and conditions.

The acquisition and transfer of reading knowledge and coordinating skill does not effortlessly emerge fully developed. Rather it develops incrementally, as the result of participation in well-organized reading instruction that provides explicit explanation, guided and independent practice, and the coordination and enactment of reading knowledge in authentic reading activity. When students participate in disorganized reading instruction, receive insufficient explanation, modeling, and social support, they acquire a fragmented and incomplete reading system. Consequently the transfer and application of the target knowledge is limited.

Skill in coordinating basic reading knowledge to accomplish basic reading tasks has two levels. The first is the independent level of skill performance. At this level, a student has achieved the ability to coordinate and enact particular declarative, procedural, and conditional knowledge to independently accomplish a particular reading task. The second is the assisted level of skill performance. At this level, a student can be expected to gradually acquire, coordinate, and enact particular declarative, procedural, and conditional knowledge to accomplish a particular reading task, with the explicit instruction of a teacher and the guided assistance provided by a teacher or accomplished others. Although a student may reach the independent level of performance, a change in conditions, such as reading an unfamiliar genre or engaging in a more complex text, may cause a student to drop back a level and require assistance. When this occurs, it is important to give the student as much assistance as needed, but only as much as needed.

Understandably, when new reading knowledge is initially used to perform a task, students require frequent opportunities to coordinate and enact that knowledge to accomplish the task, with the support of the teacher or others. To be sustained and transferred, the new knowledge must be coordinated and enacted with similar tasks and discussed repeatedly over a long period of time. The more opportunity students have to coordinate and enact new knowledge in different reading activities and to engage in reflective conversations about the outcomes, the more likely they will be able transfer it to new tasks and contexts.

Summary

In this chapter, we discussed the problems we consider important to the acquisition of proficient reading ability. We also discussed a set of principles derived from CHAT to develop a model of proficient reading ability. Then we offered basic reading activity as an alternative approach to traditional basic reading skill instruction and presented this concept through a set of model lessons we termed the integrated literacy circle. We ended with some comments about the transfer of basic reading knowledge and coordinating skill to accomplish basic reading tasks.

Questions for Reflection

1. Based on your own experiences as a teacher, why do you believe many adolescents are struggling readers?

2. Given your experience as a classroom teacher, what seem to be the main differences between students who experience success in reading to learn from text and students who experience difficulty?

3. How does the model of proficient reading ability presented in this chapter differ from models of reading you have studied?

4. How does an integrated literacy circle differ from the skill lesson you normally teach?

5. What do you see as the advantages and disadvantages of using an integrated literacy circle? How can the disadvantages be overcome? Explain how you could adapt this concept to your classroom.

William E. Blanton teaches undergraduate courses on reading in the content areas and educational psychology and doctoral seminars in reading education at the University of Miami, Coral Gables, Florida, USA. His work currently focuses on the application of cultural-historical activity theory to problems of literacy. For the last two decades, he has directed research on the acquisition of literacy in the 5th Dimension, a project of the Laboratory of Human Cognition at the University of University of California at San Diego, California, USA, and the University Community Links at Berkeley, California, USA. He may be contacted at blantonw@miami.edu. **Paola Pilonieta**, an Assistant Professor at the University of North Carolina at Charlotte, North Carolina, USA, previously taught first grade in Coconut Grove, Florida, USA. She recently received her PhD in reading from the University of Miami, Florida, USA. Her research interests are in the areas of informational text, early literacy, reading comprehension, and English-language learners. She may be contacted at pilonieta13@yahoo.com. **Karen D. Wood** is a Professor at the University of North Carolina at Charlotte, North Carolina, USA, and a former middle school teacher and K–12 literacy coordinator in the public schools. She has authored over 175 articles, chapters, and books, all of which involve translating research and theory into middle and high school classroom practice. She may be contacted at kdwood@email.uncc.edu.

REFERENCES

Adams, M.J. (1990). *Beginning to read: Thinking and learning about print.* Cambridge, MA: MIT Press.

Anderson, R.C., Nguyen-Jahiel, K., McNurlen, B., Archodidou, A., Kim, S., Reznitskaya, A., et al. (2001). The snowball phenomenon: Spread of ways of talking and ways of thinking across groups of children. *Cognition and Instruction, 19*(1), 1–46.

Beach, K. (1999). Consequential transitions: A socio-cultural expedition beyond transfer in education. In G.P. Baxter, A. Iran-Nejad, & P.D. Pearson (Eds.), *Review of research in education* (Vol. 24, pp. 101–140). Washington, DC: American Educational Research Association.

Block, J.H., & Airasian, P.W. (Eds.). (1971). *Mastery learning: Theory and practice.* New York: Holt, Rinehart, & Winston.

Bransford, J.D., Brown, A.L., & Cocking, R.R. (Eds.) (1999). *How people learn: Brain, mind, experience, and school*. Washington, DC: National Academy Press.

Bransford, J.D., & Schwartz, D.L. (1999). Rethinking transfer: A simple proposal with multiple implications. In G.P. Baxter, A. Iran-Nejad, & P.D. Pearson (Eds.), *Review of research in education* (Vol. 24, pp. 61–100). Washington, DC: American Research Association.

Brown, A.L., & Campione, J.C. (1998). Designing a community of young learners: Theoretical and practical lessons. In N.M. Lambert & B.L. McCombs (Eds.), *How students learn: Reforming schools through learner-centered education* (pp. 153–186). Washington, DC: American Psychological Association.

Campbell, J.R., Hombo, C.M., & Mazzeo, M. (2000). *NAEP 1999 trends in academic progress: Three decades of student performance*. Washington DC: OERI, U.S. Department of Education.

Carroll, J. (1963). A model for school learning. *Teachers College Record, 64,* 723–733.

Chaiklin, S. (2003). The Zone of Proximal Development: Vygotsky's analysis of learning and instruction. In A. Kozulin, B. Gindis, V.S. Ageyev, & S.M. Miller (Eds.), *Vygotsky's educational theory in cultural context* (pp. 39–64). Cambridge: Cambridge University Press.

Cole, M. (1996). *Cultural psychology*. Cambridge, MA: Harvard University Press.

Cole, M., & Engestrom, Y. (1993). A cultural-historical approach to distributed cognition. In G. Salomon (Ed.), *Distributed cognitions: Psychological and educational considerations* (pp. 1–46). Cambridge, England: Cambridge University Press.

Cole, M., Gay, J., Glick, J.A., & Sharp, D.W. (1971). *The cultural context of learning and thinking*. New York: Basic Books.

Crowder, R.G., & Wagner, R.K. (1992). *The psychology of reading: An introduction* (2nd ed.). New York: Oxford University Press.

Davis, F.B. (1983). Fundamental factors of comprehension in reading. In L.M. Gentile, M.L. Kamil, & J.S. Blanchard (Eds.), *Reading research revisited* (pp. 235–245). Ohio: Charles E. Merrill.

Donahue, P.L., Daane, M.C., & Jin, Y. (2005). *The nation's report card: Reading 2003* (NCES 2005-453). U.S. Department of Education, Institute of Education Sciences, National Center for Education Statistics. Washington, DC: U.S. Government Printing Office.

Donahue, P.L., Voelkl, K.E., Campbell, J.R., & Mazzeo, J. (1999). *NAEP 1998 Reading report card for the nation and the states* (NCES 1999-500). Washington, DC: U.S. Department of Education, Office of Educational Research and Improvement, National Center for Educational Statistics.

Donaldson, M. (1978). *Children's minds*. New York: Norton.

Duke, N.K. (2000). 3.6 minutes per day: The scarcity of informational texts in first grade. *Reading Research Quarterly, 35,* 202–225.

Engestrom, Y., Miettinen, R., & Punamaki, R.L. (Eds.). (1999). *Perspectives on activity theory*. Cambridge, England: Cambridge University Press.

Friedman, T.L. (2005). *The world is flat: A brief history of the twenty-first century*. New York: Farrar, Straus and Giroux.

Granahan, S. (2006). *Searching for lost tombs*. New York: Newbridge.

Griffin, P., & Cole, M. (1987). New technologies, basic skills, and the underside of education: What's to be done? In J. Langer (Ed.), *Language, literacy, and culture: Issues of society and schooling* (pp. 199–231). Norwood, NJ: Ablex.

Guthrie, J.T., Anderson, E., Alao, S., & Rinehart, J. (1999). Influences of concept-oriented reading instruction on strategy use and conceptual learning from text. *The Elementary School Journal, 99*, 343–366.

Hagoort, P., Hald, L., Bastiaansen, M., & Petersson, L.M. (2004). Integration of word meaning and world knowledge in language comprehension. *Science, 304*, 438–441.

Johnson, D., & Pearson, P.D. (1975). Skills management systems: A critique. *The Reading Teacher, 28*, 757–764.

Lave, J., & Wenger, E. (1991). *Situated learning: Legitimate peripheral participation.* Cambridge, England: Cambridge University Press.

Leont'ev, A.N. (1981). *Problems of the development of mind.* Moscow: Progress.

Luria, A.R. (1932). *The nature of human conflicts: An objective study of disorganization and control of human behavior* (W.H. Gantt, Ed. & Trans.). New York: Liveright.

Luria, A.R. (1973). *The working brain.* New York: Basic Books.

McClelland, J.L. (1989). Parallel distributed processing: Implications for cognition and development. In R. Morris (Ed.), *Parallel distributed processing: Implications for psychology and neurobiology* (pp. 8–45). New York: Oxford University Press.

Miller, S.D., & Blumenfeld, P.C. (1993). Characteristics of tasks used for skill instruction in two basal reader series. *The Elementary School Journal, 94*(1), 33–47.

Moore, D.W., & Hinchman, K.A. (2006). *Teaching adolescents who struggle with reading: Practical strategies.* Boston: Allyn & Bacon.

Nagy, W. (1988). *Teaching vocabulary to improve reading comprehension.* Newark, DE: International Reading Association.

National Institute of Child Health and Human Development (2000). *Report of the National Reading Panel. Teaching children to read: An evidenced-based assessment of the scientific research literature on reading and its implications for reading instruction* (NIH Publication No. 00-4769). Washington, DC: U.S. Government Printing Office.

Newman, D., Griffin, P., & Cole, M. (1989). *The construction zone: Working for cognitive change in school.* Cambridge, England: Cambridge University Press.

Otto, W. (1977). The Wisconsin design: A reading program for individually guided education. In H.J. Klausmeier, R.A. Rossmiller, & M. Saily (Eds.), *Individually guided elementary education: Concepts and practices* (pp. 216–237). New York: Academic Press.

Pilonieta, P. (2006). *Genre and comprehension strategies presented in elementary basal reading programs: A content analysis.* Unpublished Dissertation, University of Miami.

Plaut, D., & McClelland, J.L. (1993). Generalization with componential attractors: Word and nonword reading in an attractor network. In *Proceedings of the 15th annual conference of the Cognitive Science Society* (pp. 824–829). Hillsdale, NJ: Erlbaum.

Radzikhovskii, L.A. (1991). Dialogue as a unit of analysis of consciousness. *Soviet Psychology, 29*(2), 8–21.

Resnick, L.B., Levine, J.M., & Teasley, S.D. (Eds.). (1991). *Perspectives on socially shared cognition*. Washington, DC: American Psychological Association.

Riddle, M.R., & Valencia, S.W. (2002). Below the bar: Profiles of students who fail state reading assessments. *Educational Evaluation and Policy Analysis, 24*(3), 219–239.

Rivard, L.P., & Straw, S.B. (2000). The effect of talk and writing on learning science: An exploratory study. *Science Education, 84*(5), 566–593.

Rogoff, B. (2003). *The cultural nature of human development*. New York: Oxford University Press.

Rumelhart, D.E. (1994). Toward an interactive model of reading. In R.B. Ruddell, M.R. Ruddell, & H. Singer (Eds.), *Theoretical models and processes of reading* (4th ed., pp. 864–894). Newark, DE: International Reading Association.

Rumelhart, D.E., & McClelland, J.L. (1982). An interactive activation model of context effects in letter perception: Part II. The contextual enhancement effect and some tests and extensions of the model. *Psychological Review, 89*, 60–94.

Scarborough, H.S. (2001). Connecting early language and literacy to later reading (dis)abilities: Evidence, theory, and practice. In S. Neuman & D. Dickinson (Eds.), *Handbook for research in early literacy* (pp. 97–110). New York: Guilford Press.

Scribner, S., & Cole, M. (1981). *The psychology of literacy*. Cambridge, MA: Harvard University Press.

Singley, M.K., & Anderson, J.R. (1989). *The transfer of cognitive skill*. Cambridge, MA: Harvard University Press.

Snow, C., Griffin, P., & Burns, S.M. (Eds.). (2005). *Knowledge to support the teaching of reading: Preparing teachers for a changing world*. San Francisco: Jossey-Bass.

Stanovich, K.E. (1980). Toward an interactive-compensatory model of individual differences in the development of reading fluency. *Reading Research Quarterly, 16*, 32–71.

Stewart, M. (2003). *Cells to systems*. New York: Newbridge.

Stewart, M. (2006). *Meet the beetles*. New York: Newbridge.

Tomasello, M. (1999). *The cultural origins of human cognition*. Cambridge, MA: Harvard University Press.

Tulviste, P. (1991). *The cultural-historical development of verbal thinking*. Commack, NY: Nova Science.

Vierow, W. (2005). *Come to Florida!* New York: Newburg.

Vygotsky, L.S. (1978). *Mind in society: The development of higher psychological processes* (M. Cole, V. John-Steiner, S. Scribner, & E. Souberman, Eds. & Trans.). Cambridge, MA: Harvard University Press. (Original work published 1934)

Vygotsky, L.S. (1981). The genesis of higher mental functions. In J.V. Wertsch (Ed. & Trans.), *The concept of activity in Soviet psychology* (pp. 144–188). Armonk, NY: M.E. Sharpe.

Vygotsky, L.S. (1987). *The collected works of L.S. Vygotsky: Vol.1, Problems of general psychology. Including the volume thinking and speech* (N. Minick, Trans.). New York: Plenum.

Vygotsky, L.S. (1999). *Educational psychology*. Boca Rotan, FL: St. Lucie Press. (Original work published 1926)

Wells, G. (1999). The Zone of Proximal Development and its implications for learning and teaching. In G. Wells (Ed.), *Dialogic inquiry: Towards a socio-cultural practice and theory of education* (pp. 313–334). Cambridge, England: Cambridge University Press.

Wenger, E. (1998). *Communities of practice: Learning, meaning, and identity.* New York: Cambridge University Press.

Wenglinsky, H. (2000). *How teaching matters: Bringing the classroom back into discussions of teacher quality.* Princeton, NJ: Educational Testing Service.

Wertsch, J.V. (1985). *Vygotsky and the social formation of mind.* Cambridge, MA: Harvard University Press.

Wertsch, J.V. (1991). *Voices of the mind: A socio-cultural approach to mediated action.* Cambridge, MA: Harvard University Press.

CHAPTER 13

Teaching the Language of School to Secondary English Learners

Janice Pilgreen

HIGHLIGHTS

- To participate fully and successfully in school, English learners must develop academic language—the basic terms used to communicate tools and tasks across content areas.
- Teachers can make the development of language proficiency for English learners more interactive and engaging by using content area literacy strategies such as detail questions, visual support, scanning, cloze, main idea questions, the Herringbone Technique, test practices, sequence questions, and sentence strips plus timelines.
- Content area literacy strategies help both English learners and fluent English speakers handle content in the core curriculum with higher levels of comprehension and retention.

I t is a challenging task to meet the needs of all students. After all, learners are so diverse. Not only do they come to the classroom with varying degrees of educational experience, different cultural perspectives, and a broad continuum of developmental abilities, but they also arrive with an entity that is difficult to conceptualize and even less possible to assess adequately: *language*.

Language is what enables us to communicate, language is what makes collaboration possible, and using language is a way of transmit-

---

Adolescent Literacy Instruction: Policies and Promising Practices edited by Jill Lewis and Gary Moorman. © 2007 by the International Reading Association.
This chapter is adapted and updated from Pilgreen, J. (2006). Supporting English learners: Developing academic language in the content area classroom. In T.A. Young & N.L. Hadaway (Eds.), *Supporting the literacy development of English learners: Success in all classrooms* (pp. 41–60). Newark, DE: International Reading Association.

ting and negotiating knowledge. But language is precisely the barrier that English learners face when they sit in the classroom.

I have been a classroom teacher for more than 22 years, and for most of those years, I was an English as a second language (ESL) teacher. I cannot tell you how many community members, social acquaintances, and even colleagues and administrators from my own school and district offered words of sympathy to me as they watched me interact with classroom after classroom of students who came from more than 53 language groups. Lucky they were, they thought, that they didn't have to work with "those kids."

Yet when we think about what English learners bring to the table, it is quite amazing. Many of them have had interesting and varied experiences in other countries. Some, as young as they are, have experienced the trauma of war, hunger, and family crisis. Most of them have developed a reservoir of knowledge that is unlike what children in the United States have developed—and this can even include literacy in multiple languages other than English.

Nieto (2004) remarks that linguistic diversity can be a "great asset to learning" (p. 216), noting that teachers' attitudes toward and expectations of English learners can have a huge impact, both positively and negatively, on student achievement. To help English learners in the context of the content area classroom, teachers must recognize the challenges these learners face and use methods that give them the greatest access to the core curriculum. Teachers need to build on what students know—and to see them as capable, contributing members of the school community.

Goals for English Learners

A primary goal for English learners is to gain enough English proficiency to carry out school tasks about as well as their fluent English-speaking peers (Peregoy & Boyle, 2005). In kindergarten and first grade, "the linguistic performance gap" between English learners and their English-speaking contemporaries is relatively small (Peregoy & Boyle, 2005, p. 62). But in the later grades, school presents increased challenges for English learners because they have more to achieve and less time in which to achieve it. Also, English learners are typically competing with fluent English speakers in the classroom. Cummins and Schecter (2003) point out that "English as a first language speakers are not standing still waiting for ESL students to catch up. Every year their literacy skills are expanding and, thus, ESL students must catch up with a moving target" (p. 8).

There is a discrepancy, too, between the challenges confronting an English learner who is beginning first grade and one who is entering seventh. When students are in the early stages of language acquisition, their main objective is to understand their teachers and peers and to make themselves understood. Much of the language they use is for social purposes, such as interacting on the playground (Peregoy & Boyle, 2005). However, especially as they proceed into the upper grades, English learners are asked to engage in higher level thinking and problem solving; they have to work diligently to acquire the formal-language competence that they need for more advanced instruction in the content areas.

English learners must maneuver their way through complex social and cognitive interactions in English, not only orally, but also in reading and writing (Peregoy & Boyle, 2005). As Cummins (1980) has shown, in order to become fully proficient, English learners need to progress beyond the level of basic interpersonal communication skills (BICS) to achieve ever-deepening levels of cognitive academic-language proficiency (CALP).

This is a distinction that is sometimes difficult to assess, particularly when students are highly verbal and seem more proficient in the target language than they really are. English learners may speak fluently (and frequently!) and appear to have a native-like command of oral language, but still be unable to read and write at grade level. Teachers must "be aware of the differences between conversational fluency and academic language proficiency," so that they can "continue to provide the academic support that ESL students may need" (Cummins & Schecter, 2003, p. 8).

Educators need a repertoire of techniques to support English learners in the goal of full English language and literacy development—development that is at the same level of proficiency as that of fluent English-speaking peers. If students are to become capable of using both oral and written language in formal ways for academic purposes, their teachers must believe and expect that they can meet this aim and "provide social and academic support at every step along the way" (Peregoy & Boyle, 2005, p. 64). The techniques described in the rest of this chapter are part of such a repertoire. They are especially appropriate for secondary teachers who want to arm their students with a toolbox of strategies for developing CALP.

Explicit Development of Academic Language

A separate vocabulary is used by people who have been formally educated, and we sometimes refer to this category of words as "the language of school." Most educated people take for granted that such language just develops naturally. In fact, the concepts and word meanings may well be learned inductively—but in a very specific context: school.

I am speaking of such words as *title, chapter, paragraph, table, caption,* and *excerpt* and of such concepts as *note-taking, summarizing, tracing events, outlining,* and *comparing and contrasting,* to name only a few. Such terms constitute the language of school, or what is referred to as *academic language.*

Many teachers who work with English learners are familiar with Krashen's (1995) seminal work on comprehensible input. Educators first need to make their messages understandable to English learners. Only when they understand the instruction do English learners have access to what is being taught. As Krashen maintains, it is incumbent upon teachers to make lessons clear and fully comprehensible for English learners, regardless of students' level of competence in English.

Making content comprehensible is best done by providing linguistic and nonlinguistic support. Some of the linguistic aspects of simplified input that appear to be effective for promoting comprehension are slower speech rates, clear articulation, less slang, fewer idioms, and a greater use of high-frequency vocabulary (Krashen, 1995). Nonlinguistic elements include objects, visuals, videos, storyboarding, movement, role-plays, and collaborative learning (Cary, 2000).

However, English learners also need to learn the academic terms that accompany the concepts they are learning, for this is part of the knowledge that propels them over the BICS hurdle and lands them solidly in the world of CALP. Teachers can use an explicit approach to teach academic concepts and their related terms that, fortunately, can be as beneficial for fluent English-speaking students as it is for English learners.

A Confession

I did a disservice to my English learners when I was teaching developmental reading classes. I certainly demonstrated many vocabulary, comprehension, and metacognitive strategies that I'm sure they used throughout each day at school. These approaches may even have transferred to higher grade-level applications as their schooling continued. But I made a huge mistake. I did not explicitly teach the academic language that English learners need to internalize in order to manage the wide variety of reading tasks related to previewing text, understanding organizational structures, and highlighting specific chunks of text. For example, when talking about the "little title" under the "big title," I didn't mention the word *subtitle*. I frequently moved my body and arms in a sideways position as I referred to "the slanted letters" of a text (*italicized print*) or used my forefinger to punctuate "the dark letters" (*boldface print*). I never talked about *illustrations* either, only "the pictures."

In trying to make the concepts easy enough, to use language that was comprehensible, I failed to introduce many technical terms—labels that are critical for negotiating the academic pathways of school. What I did not recognize then is that the explicit teaching of academic language is crucial; students do not just "'pick it up' along the way" (Alvermann & Phelps, 2005, p. 9).

How to Start: Introducing Academic Language

In California I frequently work with teachers at various schools to provide them with practical, hands-on literacy strategies to use in their language arts and content area classes. I also direct a literacy center at the University of La Verne, where graduate-level reading-specialist candidates (who are typically full-time teachers) tutor students in grades 1 through 12. Many of these students are English learners who face challenges when reading grade-level texts. The tutors help English learners approach expository reading selections that at first may appear quite intimidating. Usually, the very first step a tutor takes is to analyze the kinds of terms that students need to know in order to maneuver through and talk about texts. A tutor typically starts with a list of terms like those presented in the first column of Table 13.1.

Many of the tutors look at the list, shrug, and say "of course" they use these vocabulary words on a daily basis in their own classrooms. But when I ask if there are any terms that they might be hard-pressed to define if students were to ask, the tutors usually admit that at least some of their responses might be a bit vague. This is primarily because it is rare for people to stop to consider definitions of terms that they have used most of their lives. The words in Table 13.1 represent the kind of school talk that educators engage in regularly. But these words are not part of the listening or speaking (not to mention the reading and writing) vocabulary of many students.

Let's take a look at three of the most commonly confused terms: *paragraph*, *passage*, and *excerpt*. Many fluent English-speaking students

Table 13.1. Academic Terms for Book Parts and Corresponding Definitions

Academic Term	Definition
author index	a list of the authors referred to in a book or other text
bibliography	a list of books, articles, etc. (containing author and publisher information) referred to in a book, article, or chapter
boldface type	type that is printed in a thick, black style, or "face"
caption	a title or brief description appended to an illustration
chapter	a main division of a book or text
chart	a sheet of information in the form of a table, graph, or diagram
column	a vertical division of a page, chart, etc., containing a sequence of figures or words
conclusion	a summing up of any kind of text material
diagram	a drawing showing the general scheme or outline of an object and its parts; may also indicate processes related to an object or phenomenon
excerpt	a short extract from a book, text, article, motion picture, piece of music, etc.
figure	a diagram or other illustrative drawing
font size	a set of type of one size; can be any style or "face"
font/print	a set of type of one style or "face"
glossary	an alphabetical list of terms, with definitions, relating to a specific subject or text, typically placed at the end of a book
graph (line, bar)	a diagram showing a relationship, usually between two variables, each measured along one of a pair of axes
graph (pie)	a circular diagram, typically showing the relationships among specific variables
handbook	a short manual or guidebook
illustration/picture	a painting, drawing, photograph, cartoon, etc., that illustrates a book, magazine article, text, etc.
indentation	space preceding a line of type, so that the type begins farther from the margin than other lines; used to mark a new paragraph
index	an alphabetical list of names, subjects, etc., with references, typically placed at the end of a book
introduction	an explanatory section at the beginning of a book, text, etc.
italicized type	type that is printed in a style, or "face," that has sloping letters (like early Italian writing)

(continued)

Academic Term	Definition
map	typically a flat representation of the earth's surface, or part of it, showing physical features, cities, etc.
page	a leaf of a book, periodical, etc.; what is written or printed on this
paragraph	a distinct section of a piece of writing, typically beginning on a new indented line; contains one primary (main) idea and other related ideas
passage	an extract from a book or other text piece; may consist of one or more paragraphs
preface	an introduction to a book, stating its subject, scope, etc.; the preliminary part of a speech
quotation	a passage or remark which represents a specific statement (or part of a statement) by another person
section	a subdivision of a book, article, text, etc.
selection	may be used interchangeably with *passage* when used to indicate an extract; or a complete piece of text that has been chosen as the topic of reading and/or discussion
subtitle/subheading	secondary or additional title of a book, work of art, piece of music, text, chapter, article, poem, document, etc.; secondary or additional heading within these works to indicate a new section
table	a set of facts or figures, systematically displayed, especially in columns
table of contents	a set of topics, listed with corresponding page numbers, indicating the different sections of a book or text
title page	a page that precedes the main part of a book or text; contains the title, author's name, date (or copyright), and, if appropriate, publisher information
title/heading	the name of a book, work of art, piece of music, text, chapter, article, poem, document, etc.
transition	a word or phrase that signals a change from one idea (or set of ideas) to the next

would have problems differentiating among the three definitions—so an English learner would have an even greater challenge dealing with such technical language. Unless these terms are taught explicitly by the teacher—that is to say, as a lesson focus and with planned repetition—

students may not retain and use them correctly. Worse, they may not even understand them in the first place.

Let's say *paragraph* means "a collection of sentences that revolve around one central, or main, idea" (in expository text in particular). The main idea is contained in the paragraph's topic sentence. The topic sentence is supported by details (or reasons, or examples). How is *paragraph* different from *passage*?

A *passage* is a set of sentences, divided into paragraphs (or contained in one long paragraph). Each paragraph has its own main idea. If a passage has three paragraphs, then each paragraph has its own main idea, and the passage itself, as a whole, has a large main idea: four main ideas in all. If the passage has a title, the title most likely reflects the main idea of all three of the paragraphs put together.

Consider how *excerpt* is different from *paragraph* and *passage*. An excerpt is a section of text, which can be taken from the beginning, the middle, or the end of a larger text. An excerpt may be confusing because a good deal of the context may be missing. Readers have to use critical reading skills to make sense of an excerpt, to fill in the missing information around the edges.

One might conceivably wonder why such specificity of language is important. The fact is, in order to read, comprehend, analyze, and talk about text, readers have to be able to use these terms and see how they function. These terms help students talk about how text is organized and to see how the ideas relate to one another.

Directions such as "Please read the following passage and identify the main idea of paragraph two" are common in classrooms, usually starting as early as third grade. They are also common on standardized tests. Such directions reflect the academic language used in school.

But how do students respond to directions such as this? Do they ask what is meant by the term *passage*, and how it is different from a *paragraph*? Do they ask what a *main idea* is, how it is different from a fact, or, even more important, how to identify it?

No. They do what people in general do when they don't really know what is being asked of them: they guess. Many students, especially those who are learning English, are genuinely perplexed by reading assignment questions. They struggle hard to grasp the basic content of the text while simultaneously being asked to internalize and manipulate academic concepts and terms they probably haven't been introduced to, except perhaps indirectly.

Yet if teachers spent some time with students analyzing paragraphs and looking at *passages* that are made up of one, two, four, six, or more *paragraphs*, students would understand these terms. They would "get it." Even better, they would be able to read pieces of text for the big ideas, for the details, or for both. We know that "explicit instruction with regard to the structure of a text facilitates the development of important comprehension strategies" (Droop & Verhoevan, 2003, p. 101).

The same holds true for other aspects of text, such as the use of boldface or italic fonts. Not addressing these explicitly may not seem like a major transgression—until students come across words that are italicized for a reason and are unable to comprehend their significance. It is absolutely critical that we teach students—and especially English learners, for whom English poses a specific challenge—the text terms that they need to understand in order to approach text in thoughtful and meaningful ways and to develop a common vocabulary that will serve them throughout their schooling.

Table 13.1 (see page 243) provides basic definitions for the academic terms listed. These terms need to become a part of every teacher's classroom vocabulary. Teachers have to remember, though, that just giving students the definitions is not enough. As Harvey and Goudvis (2000) assert, "For too many years we have been telling students what to do without showing them how" (p. 12).

Teachers need to show examples of captions and illustrations and model how to find important information embedded in them; choose excerpts from texts, magazine articles, diary entries, etc., and talk about what can be learned from them, both in and out of context; use the information in pie, bar, and line graphs to quantify the general information given in a chapter; and repeat academic terms over and over, bringing them up explicitly in different situations using a "think-aloud process" (Daniels & Zemelman, 2004). In short, it is necessary to provide comprehensible input—and then add the academic terms that match the concepts.

Keys to Comprehension

If we view the comprehension process as a transaction between reader and text, in which readers construct mental representations of the text by using their existing knowledge, along with the application of flexible strategies (Rupley & Willson, 1997), then it becomes very clear that the reason people read—and the way in which they read something—

will determine what they get out of it. That is to say, readers set a purpose for reading and then read strategically with that purpose in mind.

For example, if I am interested in getting the overview, or the big picture, of a magazine article that interests me, I may choose to read the title, the subtitles, and perhaps even the first sentence of each paragraph—before I decide whether or not I want to read the whole article. In the same way, teaching strategies should focus on reading as an authentic process, keeping in mind that readers highlight different information for themselves as they read, based on their individual purposes for reading.

The goal is to teach English learners the processes that enable them to access many different kinds of information, including (but not limited to) *main ideas, details, sequences of events, implications* that authors make, and vocabulary that is defined through textual *context clues.*

For most students, these terms are abstract. I often hear teachers tell pairs of students to "read the paragraph and then tell your partner the main idea." If students ask what that means, they reply, "You know, what it's mostly about." Those directions seem pretty simple, but for an English learner who is foraging through a maze of new words, figuring out what the paragraph is "mostly about" results in a retell of every point that the student can remember—which generally consists of a mishmash of details and very rarely even approaches the main idea.

English learners need tools for figuring out the big picture, not just prompts that use other words to ask the same question. For each reading strategy that can be taught, there are identifiable keywords that match—labels that come from the pool of academic language. Generally, the kind of information readers look for in their reading is determined by the questions they ask. Sometimes the questions are posed by teachers, sometimes they are listed at the ends of chapters, and, ideally, they are asked by readers who are reading actively.

Detail Questions

When asking students the most basic recall questions about stories and texts, teachers take for granted that students know what kind of information is needed to answer the questions. Detail questions, which begin with WH words (words that start with *w* or *h*, such as *who, what, when, where, why,* and *how*), are frequently posed during class and are often listed at the ends of chapters. Teachers sometimes forget that English learners may confuse the WH words, having not had as much time to acquire them as their fluent English-speaking counterparts.

Visual Support. One technique that I adopted, suggested by a group of teachers in our University of La Verne graduate reading program, is to use illustrations of answers that match the detail questions. For example, if the question starts with *who*, the icon is a stick figure, illustrating a person; if the question begins with *when*, the icon is a clock (see Figure 13.1). English learners are then able to visualize what the answer looks like, as soon as they see the question. The link between the exact WH word and an appropriate answer is made much faster and with a higher degree of correctness when students first practice answering questions using the WH words with icons for support.

Scanning. Along with using this pictorial aid, I taught students how to *scan* effectively. Teachers frequently assume that students know the procedure for scanning; after all, it is second nature to adults. Scanning is not really reading, in the true sense of the word; it is searching quickly (running your eyes over the page) to locate target information. For example, if you want to look up someone's telephone number in a telephone directory, you first recognize that you will be looking for a set of numbers and then you think about how the information is organized—in this case, alphabetically by name. So you think about what the per-

Figure 13.1. Detail Keywords With Icons

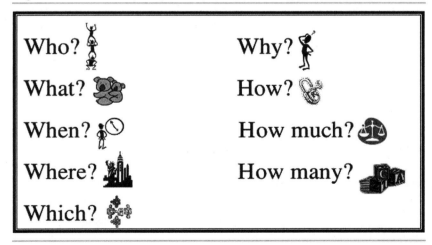

son's last name is and search until you finally zero in on the exact name and number.

I have found that many English learners do not scan effectively because they don't know the procedure for getting the specific information they need. I model the following scanning procedure for them in class:

1. Identify the target information needed.
2. Look at the WH word in the question.
3. Visualize what the answer looks like.
4. Find other keywords in the question.
5. Think about how the reading is organized.
6. Scan for the target information, using keywords and the visualized answer.

Next, the students do the procedure in groups, then in pairs, and finally individually, Vygotskian-style (1934/1986). The teacher and the students collaborate until the students have internalized the task and can carry it out on their own. Once students feel comfortable, the teacher raises the bar and, as Valencia and Riddle Buly (2004) recommend, asks students to apply the procedure often, using different types and levels of materials throughout the school year.

Students might utilize the scanning procedure with the excerpt in Figure 13.2 and answer the following questions:

1. *How much* could a fortunate miner earn a year?
2. *What* activities were common in boomtowns?
3. *Why* did citizens sometimes take the law into their own hands?
4. *When* was Virginia City a mining camp?

To answer the first question, students look at the WH words (*how much*), visualize what the answer looks like (an amount), find keywords in the question (*fortunate, miner, earn, year*), notice that the writing is organized in a list format (topic sentence followed by details), and scan the text for the answer ($2,000). In the same way, to answer the second question, students look at the WH word (*what*), visualize what the answer looks like (things), find keywords in the question (*activities, common, boomtowns*), recall that the writing is organized in a list format, and scan for the answer (cheating and stealing). Students follow the scanning procedure again to answer questions 3 and 4.

Figure 13.2. Excerpt for Scanning Exercise

The Mining Frontier

The gold strikes created boomtowns—towns that grew up almost overnight around mining sites. The Comstock boomtown was Virginia City, Nevada. In 1859 the town was a mining camp. Two years later it had a stock exchange, hotels, banks, an opera company, and five newspapers.

Boomtowns were lively, untamed places filled with people from far-off regions. Gold and silver strikes attracted eager prospectors from Mexico, China, and other countries.

Money came quickly—and was often lost just as quickly through extravagant living and gambling. A fortunate miner could earn as much as $2,000 a year, about four times the annual salary of a teacher at that time. Still, food, lodging, clothing and other goods cost dearly in boomtowns, draining the miners' earnings.

Violence was a part of everyday life in boomtowns, where many people carried large amounts of cash and guns. Cheating and stealing were common. Few boomtowns had police or prisons so citizens sometimes took the law into their own hands. These vigilantes dealt out their own brand of justice without benefit of judge or jury, often hanging the accused person from the nearest tree.

Text selection from *The American Journey: Building a Nation* (Appleby, Brinkley, & McPherson, 2000, p. 526). Copyright 2000 by the McGraw-Hill Companies. Reprinted by permission.

Having a handle on how to locate specific information in their reading is very important for English learners who are overwhelmed by large pieces of text. Focusing on important details, through the use of the scanning procedure, gives students a concrete way to learn about detail questions and to practice finding target information. The scanning procedure is also useful for answering detail questions on standardized tests when students cannot recall specific facts they have just read.

Cloze Procedure. Another method that helps students to highlight important detail information in reading selections is the cloze procedure. Originally, this technique was developed in 1950 as an assessment tool for determining what grade levels of text students could handle (Reutzel & Cooter, 2000). After reading a story or passage at a predesignated readability level, students were asked to fill in specific blanks within a "cloze" version of the same text. In this way, educators determined if students comprehended the text at the prescribed reading level. In the original version, blanks replaced original text at intervals of every 5th or 10th word, and generally the first and last sentences were left intact.

However, a type of modified cloze procedure is now being used frequently by teachers for emphasizing content details that are especially important to the reader's understanding of a particular text. Students read a selection or passage first, and then they are given the same passage with words that have been deleted. The students' job is to fill in the missing information from memory or by using a word bank as support. Of course, the words that have been deleted (typically by whiting out words and inserting lines with a ruler on a photocopy) are those that the teacher has selected as being the most important vocabulary for the lesson, based on what is known about the students' background knowledge and the content focus.

The cloze procedure can also be used to help students learn parts of speech and grammatical forms. One effective way of highlighting life in boomtowns on the western frontier (based on the passage shown in Figure 13.2) would be to delete many of the verbs and then have students replace them (Figure 13.3). In doing so, students focus on recall of the text and also pay attention to the correct verb forms.

Figure 13.3. Paragraphs for Cloze Exercise

The gold strikes _____ boomtowns—towns that _____ up almost overnight around mining sites. The Comstock boomtown was Virginia City, Nevada. In 1859 the town _____ a mining camp. Two years later it _____ a stock exchange, hotels, banks, an opera company, and five newspapers.

Boomtowns were lively, untamed places _____ with people from far-off regions. Gold and silver strikes _____ eager prospectors from Mexico, China, and other countries.

Money _____ quickly—and was often _____ just as quickly through extravagant living and gambling. A fortunate miner could _____ as much as $2,000 a year, about four times the annual salary of a teacher at that time. Still, food, lodging, clothing and other goods _____ dearly in boomtowns, draining the miners' earnings.

Violence was a part of everyday life in boomtowns, where many people _____ large amounts of cash and guns. Cheating and stealing were common. Few boomtowns had police or prisons so citizens sometimes _____ the law into their own hands. These vigilantes _____ out their own brand of justice without benefit of judge or jury, often _____ the accused person from the nearest tree.

Word Bank

took	came	carried
grew	created	lost
earn	was	dealt
cost	hanging	attracted
had	filled	

Text selection from *The American Journey: Building a Nation* (Appleby, Brinkley, & McPherson, 2000, p. 526). Copyright 2000 by the McGraw-Hill Companies. Reprinted by permission.

Readers not only strive to re-create the meaning of the text as they fill in the blanks with specific verbs from the word bank, but they also enjoy the challenge of trying to recall the specific answers on their own. The activity can easily be scaffolded as well, as the teacher moves from doing most of the work in the initial demonstration phase (along with a think-aloud process, "showing kids how smart readers think") to having groups and pairs work collaboratively (Daniels & Zemelman, 2004, p. 102). Eventually, the word bank component can be completely discarded when learners feel that they can do it without the extra support.

Main Idea Questions

The easiest questions to answer are detail questions, which are at the recall level of Bloom's taxonomy (Bloom, Englehart, Furst, Hill, & Krathwohl, 1956). They are the questions that English learners find the least intimidating because a tangible answer can be found directly stated in the text. I have worked with students of all ages, and I believe that they are uncomfortable with some of the other kinds of questions that they are asked to answer, such as main idea questions, because they have not been explicitly taught how to find the information to answer them. They also do not recognize the benefits of comprehending main ideas as they read.

When teachers talk about the "big idea" in a paragraph (or the "gist of it"), they are speaking of the main idea. A reader who can identify the main idea of each paragraph in a passage or selection will come away with what I think of as "the jigsaw puzzle picture on the top of the box."

This may seem like a strange analogy, but if you think about trying to put together pieces of a jigsaw puzzle without knowing what the picture looks like ahead of time, you will have a very difficult time placing all the little parts in the right places. If you know what the picture will look like, it's a much easier matter to fit in each of the components. Of course, this is an issue of having a schema—a framework in your head on which to hang the new information that you acquire as you read. Schema allows a reader to make links between what is known already and the text content.

Reading a paragraph to identify the main idea—and then rereading it to assimilate all of the details—is an authentic practice. I do it when I read new text, I'm sure that many other proficient readers do it, and it would be an effective strategy for English learners to utilize as well. Students should begin by identifying the keywords of questions. The following main idea key phrases tell students that they are being asked to find the "big picture":

- Main idea
- Main point
- Mainly about
- Mostly about
- Has to do mainly with
- Has to do mostly with
- Contains information about
- Good title
- Possible title
- Alternative title

Herringbone Technique. By teaching strategies for "getting the big picture," especially strategies that students can practice in pairs or at table groups, teachers help students grasp the abstract concept of the main idea. One such strategy is the Herringbone Technique (Tierney, Readence, & Dishner, 1990). It consists of a short graphic organizer and is a concrete way of helping students find the comprehensive idea in a paragraph or passage. Students answer the questions listed in the fishbone graphic organizer (see Figure 13.4). This leads to the synthesis of all the information in one newly created sentence, which becomes the main idea statement.

The excerpt in Figure 13.5 shows how threatening it might be to any student, much less an English learner, to be asked to identify the main idea. After all, there is a good deal of information in the text, along with some difficult vocabulary words. One student's attempt to answer such a main idea question clearly shows that he was not certain about what information was appropriate to share (see page 254):

Figure 13.4. Herringbone Technique

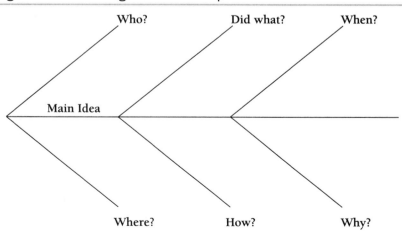

Source: Tierney, Readence, and Dishner (1990).

Figure 13.5. Excerpt for Herringbone Technique Exercise

Boom and Bust

Many mining "booms" were followed by "busts." When the mines no longer yielded ore, people left the towns. At its peak in the 1870s, Virginia City had about 30,000 inhabitants. By 1900 its population had dropped below 4,000. Many boomtowns turned into ghost towns—deserted as prospectors moved on to more promising sites or returned home. Some can still be seen in the West today, relics of the glory days of the mining frontier.

Text selection from *The American Journey: Building a Nation* (Appleby, Brinkley, & McPherson, 2000, p. 526). Copyright 2000 by the McGraw-Hill Companies. Reprinted by permission.

This is about mining and the booms that were followed by busts when people left the towns, and there were only 4,000 people left from the 30,000 to start with, so the towns became ghost towns. Many prospectors moved to more promising sites or returned home, and some ghost towns from the West can still be seen today, and they are relics from the glory days.

This student did his best to assimilate the information but ended up simply including it all. He was not able to identify one main idea. However, when I modeled my own thinking as I read the text and then asked the students to help figure out the information that went into the graphic organizer, the class came up with the information in Figure 13.6. (Note that students write the main idea below the middle line, rather than on it.)

By putting all the detail pieces together, students get a main idea sentence such as "Prospectors caused boomtowns to turn into ghost towns in the 1870s in Virginia City by moving on to more promising sites or returning home because the mines no longer yielded ore." If the word order doesn't sound right or make sense, students move the words around for a clearer message, such as "Because the mines no longer yielded ore in the 1870s in Virginia City, prospectors moved on to more promising sites or returned home, causing this boomtown to turn into a ghost town."

The work these students did is a clear indication that "visual structures are powerful tools for comprehension instruction because they offer concrete, memorable representations of abstract thinking processes" (Barton & Sawyer, 2004, p. 338). The next step for learners, as Alvermann and Phelps (2005) suggest, is to "give them occasional follow-up passages and [have them] read for the specific task" (p. 200). Students used the Herringbone Technique with many different selections throughout the year and became more successful with it over time. They also became ex-

Figure 13.6. Class Herringbone Organizer

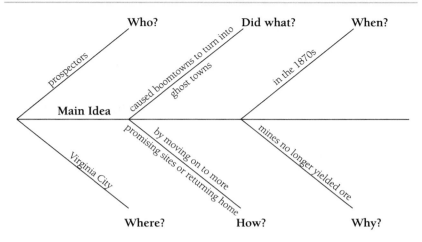

First try: Prospectors caused boomtowns to turn into ghost towns in the 1870s in Virginia City by moving on to more promising sites or returning home because the mines no longer yielded ore.

Revised version: Because the mines no longer yielded ore in the 1870s in Virginia City, prospectors moved on to more promising sites or returned home, causing this boomtown to turn into a ghost town.

tremely capable of recalling the details associated with the big picture, as they had a schematic structure within which to connect the pieces.

Test Practices. Once students have begun to use comprehension strategies such as the Herringbone Technique, it becomes a simple matter to transfer their competencies to test practice situations. McCabe (2003) notes that reading scores often "reflect test anxiety to a large degree, rather than true reading ability" (p. 12). He adds that some students have had more opportunities to experience mastery in test-taking and that careful selection and use of test-like material are critical. Teachers can use easy test material (authentic pieces from class readings) and highlight short, manageable sections. As success with short portions is achieved, teachers gradually increase the length of the selections.

Taking the final main idea sentence created with the Herringbone Technique, students can now apply the information to the question "What is the main idea of the paragraph?"

A. At its peak in the 1970s, Virginia City had about 30,000 inhabitants.

B. Some ghost towns can still be seen in the West today, relics of the glory days of the mining frontier.

C. Prospectors left Virginia City when the mines no longer yielded ore, causing it to turn into a ghost town.

D. By 1900, Virginia City's population had dropped below 4,000 people.

It is not difficult for students to identify the correct answer as *C*, as it most closely matches the sentence written with the aid of the fishbone graph. The other possible answers are either too general or represent very specific details.

Talking about such choices not only helps English learners to articulate their views on the big idea of the text piece, but it also helps them to become familiar with the way in which such concepts arise in the context of standardized tests. It is not burdensome for the teacher to provide multiple-choice practices every once in awhile, keeping in mind that the primary purpose of teaching these strategies is to boost comprehension, not simply to develop testwiseness. Most important is the "explicit modeling and discussion of the components of comprehension...on a routine basis" in order to help students become metacognitive thinkers (Barton & Sawyer, 2004, p. 338).

Sequence Questions

Another understanding that is critical to comprehension is that events have a prescribed order in which they happen, and that writers achieve cohesion by using clues, such as sequence words (which can also operate as transition words; e.g., *after, at the same time as, before, during, finally, first, in conclusion, last, next, second, then, to begin with*).

Questioning is a strategy that "propels readers forward"—when students ask themselves ongoing questions as they read, they are less likely to abandon the text (Harvey & Goudvis, 2000, p. 22). Confusion about the order of events is a roadblock that keeps English learners from moving ahead with confidence; they may ask themselves about the relationships among events but not be able to see them clearly. What many students do not understand is that the events may be told by the author in an order that is different from the way in which they actually occurred. When a writer tells the first event first and the second event second, there is not much of a problem identifying what was first and what was second (though the keywords, like those listed, still need to be taught explicitly). But when a writer describes the events in a convoluted way, students often do not see that the events are not being told chronologically. If they are trying to comprehend the order in which the events truly happened for the purpose of understanding the story, or if they are being asked sequence questions by a teacher (or on a test), then they usually go by the order of the *telling*.

Sentence Strips + Timeline. One interactive and effective strategy to use with all students—and especially English learners, who may not be familiar with the specific discourse patterns and conventions of the English language—is called Sentence Strips + Timeline.

When utilizing an excerpt such as the one in Figure 13.7, if the teacher used an overhead transparency and sentence strips to list the events in the order in which they occur in the text, the strips would typically appear as they do in Figure 13.8. However, by analyzing the text carefully, it becomes evident that the Figure 13.8 strips do not represent chronological order. Therefore, readers must reorder the events to make sense of the selection.

In this activity, as the teacher puts the strips on the overhead projector, students write the same information on sticky notes, which they can move around on a sheet of paper containing a simple hand-drawn timeline. The teacher models, and the students follow, the process (Figure 13.9). After much discussion and collaboration, the strips are in the correct order, and the students can then rewrite the text chronologically. Later, using another part of the same text—or even a different text altogether—students can tell the teacher the order in which to put the strips, this time without as much assistance.

Figure 13.7. Excerpt for Sentence Strips + Timeline Exercise

Government and the Railroads
Railroad construction was made possible by large government subsidies, financial aid and land grants from the government. Railroad executives argued that their companies should receive free public land on which to lay track because a rail network would benefit the entire nation.

The national government—and states, too—agreed. In all, the federal government granted more than 130 million acres of land to the railroad companies. Much of the land was purchased or obtained by treaty from Native Americans.

Text selection from *The American Journey: Building a Nation* (Appleby, Brinkley, & McPherson, 2000, p. 526). Copyright 2000 by the McGraw-Hill Companies. Reprinted by permission.

Figure 13.8. Order of the "Telling"

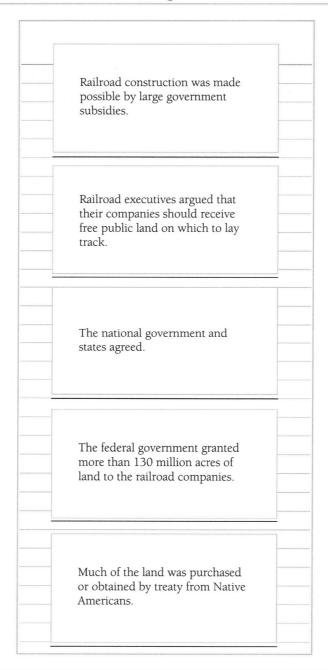

Railroad construction was made possible by large government subsidies.

Railroad executives argued that their companies should receive free public land on which to lay track.

The national government and states agreed.

The federal government granted more than 130 million acres of land to the railroad companies.

Much of the land was purchased or obtained by treaty from Native Americans.

Figure 13.9. Determining Chronological Order Using Sticky Notes

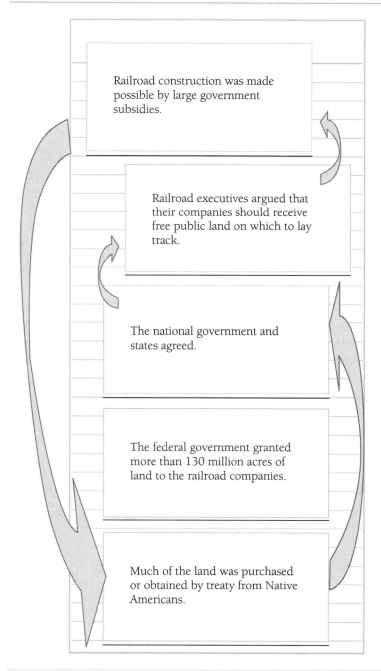

Railroad construction was made possible by large government subsidies.

Railroad executives argued that their companies should receive free public land on which to lay track.

The national government and states agreed.

The federal government granted more than 130 million acres of land to the railroad companies.

Much of the land was purchased or obtained by treaty from Native Americans.

As they approach new readings in the future, they are much more likely to recognize when writers choose to introduce information in a nonchronological way, such as in flashbacks. Being able to identify the correct sequence of events is a skill required of standardized-test takers, so this strategy, which supports better comprehension during reading, can be transferred to testing contexts as well.

Conclusion

Pressley (2002) laments that "there is little comprehension strategy instruction in primary-level classrooms" (p. 181), but I hope that trend is changing, for the primary grades are where it should begin. However, secondary teachers must continue throughout the middle and high school years to provide effective instruction that supports their students in accessing the core curriculum. There are numerous sources available now that provide interactive, engaging methods for making comprehension instruction motivational and successful, not only for English learners, but for all students.

In this chapter, I've suggested that students need to recall details, find main ideas, and determine the sequence of events. Beyond this, students also need to learn to make inferences, differentiate between facts and opinions, figure out vocabulary definitions through context clues, identify causes and effects, and much, much more. In addition, as I hope I've emphasized, we must teach the academic language associated with concepts and strategies explicitly, not rely on students to pick them up inductively or in passing.

For English learners, the linguistic task is clearly a more difficult one than it is for other students, so the importance of teaching academic language is exacerbated. As Pransky and Bailey (2003) put it, "The challenge for teachers is to accommodate these students' needs in mainstream classrooms where, in the end, all students must learn to work confidently, productively, and successfully" (p. 382).

Questions for Reflection

1. How many of your colleagues regularly (and explicitly) teach academic language terms to the English learners in their secondary classrooms? If only a few do it, why do you think this is the case? What might you do to encourage your colleagues to focus on the "language of school" more explicitly?

2. How can you incorporate the use of content area literacy strategies into your own teaching? What would be the benefit of having everyone in your department teach the same strategies, using the same or different texts?

3. Which of the strategies presented in this chapter appeal to you the most? Explain why—and discuss your answers with others in a group.

Activities

1. Observe a content area classroom and note examples of academic text terms being used. Jot down notes about the teacher's role in emphasizing academic language and the students' comfort and proficiency levels with using it.

2. Choose one strategy presented in this chapter. Select a text piece that would lend itself well to the introduction of this strategy. Explain how you would develop the strategy, based on this text piece, and describe how you would model it for your students.

Janice Pilgreen is Chair of the Graduate Reading Program and Director of the Literacy Center at the University of La Verne, La Verne, California, USA. A secondary teacher of English, reading, and ESL for 18 years prior to her doctoral work, her research interests include approaches to content area literacy and sustained silent reading. She teaches a variety of graduate reading courses at ULV and works with candidates who tutor K–12 children in the surrounding community. She also consults widely to help language arts, ESL, and content area teachers to incorporate literacy strategies and independent reading practices into their curricula. She may be contacted at pilgreen@ulv.edu.

REFERENCES

Alvermann, D., & Phelps, S. (2005). *Content reading and literacy: Succeeding in today's diverse classrooms.* Boston: Pearson Education.

Appleby, J.O., Brinkley, A., & McPherson, J.M. (Eds.). (2000). *The American journey: Building a nation.* New York: Glencoe/McGraw-Hill.

Barton, J., & Sawyer, D. (2004). Our students are ready for this: Comprehension instruction in the elementary school. *The Reading Teacher, 57,* 334–347.

Bloom, B.S., Englehart, M.B., Furst, E.J., Hill, W.H., & Krathwohl, D.R. (1956). *Taxonomy of educational objectives: The classification of educational goals. Handbook I: Cognitive domain.* New York: Longman.

Cary, S. (2000). *Working with second language learners: Answers to teachers' top ten questions*. Portsmouth, NH: Heinemann.

Cummins, J. (1980). The construct of language proficiency in bilingual education. In J.E. Alatis (Ed.), *Georgetown University roundtable on languages and linguistics* (pp. 76–93). Washington, DC: Georgetown University Press.

Cummins, J., & Schecter, S. (2003). School-based language policy in culturally diverse contexts. In S. Schecter & J. Cummins (Eds.), *Multilingual education in practice: Using diversity as a resource* (pp. 1–16). Portsmouth, NH: Heinemann.

Daniels, H., & Zemelman, S. (2004). *Subjects matter: Every teacher's guide to content-area reading*. Portsmouth, NH: Heinemann.

Droop, M., & Verhoevan, L. (2003). Language proficiency and reading ability in first- and second-language learners. *Reading Research Quarterly, 38*, 78–103.

Harvey, S., & Goudvis, A. (2000). *Strategies that work: Teaching comprehension to enhance understanding*. York, ME: Stenhouse.

Krashen, S.D. (1995). *Principles and practice in second language acquisition*. London: Phoenix ELT/Prentice Hall International.

McCabe, P. (2003). What reading teachers should know about ESL learners. *The Reading Teacher, 57*, 12–20.

Nieto, S. (2004). *Affirming diversity: The sociopolitical context of multicultural education*. Boston: Pearson Education.

Peregoy, S., & Boyle, O. (2005). *Reading, writing, and learning in ESL: A resource book for K–12 teachers*. Boston: Pearson Education.

Pransky, K., & Bailey, F. (2003). To meet your students where they are, first you have to find them: Working with culturally and linguistically diverse at-risk students. *The Reading Teacher, 56*, 370–383.

Pressley, M. (2002). Effective beginning reading instruction. *Journal of Literacy Research, 34*(2), 165–188.

Reutzel, D.R., & Cooter, R.B., Jr. (2000). *The essentials of teaching children to read*. Upper Saddle River, NJ: Pearson Education.

Rupley, W.H., & Willson, V.L. (1997). The relationship of reading comprehension to components of word recognition: Support for developmental shifts. *Journal of Research and Development in Education, 30*, 255–260.

Tierney, R., Readence, J., & Dishner, E. (1990). *Reading strategies and practices: A compendium* (3rd ed.). Needham Heights, MA: Allyn & Bacon.

Valencia, S., & Riddle Buly, M. (2004). Behind test scores: What struggling readers REALLY need. *The Reading Teacher, 57*, 520–531.

Vygotsky, L.S. (1986). *Thought and language* (A. Kozalin, Trans.). Cambridge, MA: The MIT Press. (Original work published 1934)

CHAPTER 14

Millennials and How to Teach Them

Gary Moorman and Julie Horton

HIGHLIGHTS

- Reading and writing can be viewed as technological tools with a 5,000-year history.

- Today's adolescents are members of the Millennial generation, the first generation born into the digital world; they are "digital natives"—fluent in the language, customs, and values of the digital world—and members of all other generations are "digital immigrants."

- Millennials live in a wired world: 87% use the Internet, 90% of these use e-mail, 45% own cell phones, and 57% have contributed online content to the Internet.

- Because Millennials think and process information in fundamentally different ways, educators must recognize and value these differences.

- Educators need to adjust their instruction to take advantage of the unique skills, abilities, and knowledge adolescents bring to the classroom.

More than 2,400 years ago, Socrates wandered the streets of Athens bemoaning the youth of his day, claiming that they lacked discipline and the basic knowledge necessary for successful citizenship. Throughout history, it has been typical for adults to criticize the academic achievement and work ethic of their own children,

Adolescent Literacy Instruction: Policies and Promising Practices edited by Jill Lewis and Gary Moorman. © 2007 by the International Reading Association.

and this criticism tends to intensify during times of rapid social change. Berliner and Biddle (1995) have dubbed this the "Socrates legacy." In this tradition, there is currently a high level of national concern about adolescents' abilities to read and write.

Indeed, there is much that can be improved in terms of adolescent literacy achievement and instruction. Every chapter in this book addresses problems and suggests solutions for improving secondary schooling. We agree with Blanton, Wood, and Pilonieta (see chapter 12) that there are shortcomings in basic reading instruction. Lewis (see chapter 9) is correct in her assessment of the need for explicit instruction in academic literacy. And Bean and Harper (see chapter 17) are on target with their call for democratic reform in secondary schools. In our view, adolescent literacy achievement in America can best be described as not good enough.

Nonetheless, the high level of national concern does not accurately reflect the current reality. For example, the latest National Assessment of Educational Progress indicates that in the last decade and a half, the overall reading test scores at both the fourth- and eighth-grade levels have improved:

> The national results from the assessment showed a 2-point increase between the average fourth-grade reading score in 2005 and the score in 1992. The average eighth-grade reading score also was 2 points higher in 2005 than in 1992. Of the 42 states and jurisdictions that participated in both the 1992 and 2005 fourth-grade reading assessments, 20 showed higher average scores in 2005 and 3 showed lower scores. Of the 38 states and jurisdictions that participated in the 1998 and 2005 eighth-grade assessments, 3 showed higher average reading scores in 2005 and 8 showed lower scores. (National Center for Education Statistics, 2005, ¶1).

Certainly, we should not settle for a gradual increase in achievement, but still the crisis mentality that accompanies much of today's political rhetoric and media coverage is unwarranted.

This chapter begins by examining the relatively rapid evolution of the technologies that have made literacy possible, from the earliest writing systems through the current digital technologies. We then will argue that, despite real concerns that must be addressed, the central tendency of the current generation is extremely positive. Those born after 1982 or so are members of what is now termed the "Millennial Generation" (Howe & Strauss, 2000). Millennials bring to school a unique set of skills, knowledge, and attributes unlike any other in history. We will make the case that today's adolescents read and write more, have a more realistic and broader view of the world, are more accomplished socially, and process information in fundamentally different ways than previous generations. Based on this perspective, we will suggest ways that teachers can adapt instruction to build on the strengths that Millennials bring with them to school. We strongly believe that taking a more positive, realistic, and embracing attitude toward today's adolescents can have only positive academic outcomes.

Literacy in Historical Perspective

It is important to put current controversies about the level of adolescent literacy skill into a historical perspective. To begin, it is useful to view literacy as a technology. The definition for technology in Wikipedia (Technology, n.d.) refers to entities created by the application of mental and physical effort to achieve value. In this use, technology is the current state of our knowledge of how to combine resources to produce desired products, solve problems, meet needs, or satisfy wants. This view of technology includes technical methods, skills, processes, tools, and raw materials, for example, as used in computer technology, construction technology, or medical technology.

This definition implies two important components of any technology: the physical tool and the cultural knowledge necessary to utilize the tool. For any technology to become part of culture, it must evolve in terms of the sophistication of the physical tool and the distribution of the knowledge necessary to utilize the tool. There must be a social demand for the tool (or for the product the tool creates). The technology of literacy appeared in Western culture because it solved socially relevant problems, and it expanded in response to additional social needs. The evolution of literacy is marked by the introduction of three technological tools: writing systems, the printing press, and information communication technology (ICT).

Literacy is a relatively new invention in humankind, and the changing demands on today's adolescents are mind-blowing in this context. A little more than 5,000 years ago, communities moved from hunter–gatherer tribes into socially stratified and politically complex societies, and the first technological tool emerged (Diamond, 1999). These writing systems developed because they made the transmission and storage of information easier and more efficient. However, literacy remained in the hands of a small number of professional scribes directly under the control of royalty, priests, or other politically powerful individuals (Manguel, 1996). Jumping forward about 4,000 years, the second technological tool emerged with the invention of the printing press. This invention was the result of the demand for text created by the Reformation and the Renaissance (Smith, 1965). For the first time in history, a vision of universal literacy began to emerge. As societies continued to evolve from agrarian to industrial economies, and toward increasingly democratic forms of government, the need for written texts, and for more workers and citizens who were literate, gradually increased.

The third tool appeared in the second half of the 20th century: ICT and the rapid emergence, growth, and use of the Internet and the World Wide Web. In the early 1960s, the idea of a decentralized, computer-based communication system first emerged. About the same time, researchers at MIT began to conceptualize a system for social networking, particularly among scientists (Leiner et al., 1999). Initially, supercomputers were linked together to provide more power, speed, and capacity. As personal computers became increasingly sophisticated, even more powerful computers joined the Web. By 1992, the Web was so large and the potential so great that the first Web browser, Mosaic, was invented. Therefore, as of this writing, the Web as it is known and used today is arguably only 15 years old. Given how pervasive (and invasive) the Internet is in today's world, the speed and impact of this technology is truly dramatic, especially for the adolescents who are well versed in this new world.

Millennials: The Wired Generation

Children who have grown up since the emergence of the World Wide Web and the assortment of related digital technologies (cell phones and instant messaging, for example) are sometimes termed "Generation Y," but now are more commonly called Millennials, as noted previously. Millennials is a term that they, as well as most people in the United States, seem to prefer (Howe & Strauss, 2000). This generation, as any teacher of adolescents will tell you, is different in important ways from previous generations (see Howe & Strauss, 2000, for an excellent primer). In this section, we will review what is known about the Millennials, particularly in terms of their use of ICT.

Generational Theory

Let us begin with a brief description of generational theory. A generation is a socially comprised group that shares a historical time and place;

metaphorically, the group creates a shared social biography. A generation is usually thought to encompass approximately 20 birth years; for example, the Baby Boomer generation is generally defined as individuals born between 1943 and 1960. According to Howe and Strauss (2000), there have been 18 American generations, beginning with the Puritan generation born from 1588 to 1617. There are currently five living generations, GI (1901–1924), Silent (1925–1942), Baby Boomers (1943–1960), Gen Xers (1961–1980), and Millennials (1982–2002).

Each rising generation is shaped by interactions with other generations, and seems to follow an evolutionary pattern (Coomes & DeBard, 2004). First, it refuses to define itself as an extension of the previous generation; Millennials see themselves in clear contrast to Gen Xers. Rules, values, and constructs that were previously useful are rejected as the new generation begins to redefine its social context. Second, the new generation reacts to perceived faults of the midlife generation. Attempts are made to correct excesses, faults, or shortcomings; Millennials entering college seem to be replacing the iconoclastic and free-spirited values of Baby Boomers in the 1960s with a traditional and structured perspective. Finally, the newest generation seeks to associate with the departing elder generations, often assuming many of their values and perspectives; Millennials hold in high esteem the cooperative, upbeat, and patriotic viewpoint of the GI Generation. In a survey of students in the High School Class of 2000, Howe and Strauss (2000) found that Millennials held Generation Xers in the lowest esteem and the GI Generation in highest esteem. Their views of the Silent Generation and Baby Boomers were mixed.

DeBard (2004) argues that the rewards and sanctions provided by Baby Boomer parents have led Millennials to a set of normative characteristics. Howe and Strauss (2000) identify seven traits that define the Millennial persona:

- **Special**: Millennials have been raised to believe that they are vital to the nation (a perception reinforced by pervasive advertising) and to their parents' sense of self-esteem.

- **Sheltered**: Baby Boomer parents have made great efforts to shelter Millennials from harm's way; note the child safety laws, zero tolerance policies, and constant encouragement to follow the rules.

- **Confident**: Millennials display a sense of optimism about their lives and futures; trust in an authority that has been successful in protecting and providing for them has led to expectations that awards and rewards await.

- **Team-oriented**: Fueled partially by advances in communication technology (cell phones, e-mail, text messaging and instant messaging) and an educational trend of cooperative learning, Millennials show a sense of community and a desire to collaborate.

- **Achieving**: Accountability and standards-based education, along with ICT's ability to provide easy access to information and instruction, have led Millennials to be the most informed generation ever.

- **Pressured**: There can be no doubt that Millennials have felt the pressure to perform and be successful; Baby Boomer parents have created a "hurried child syndrome" that places a high emphasis on success in school as well as other structured activities, such as sports and music.

- **Conventional**: Millennials have come to accept the social rules imposed on them out of respect for the authority figures who have imposed them; Millennials seem to take pride in good behavior.

Millennials and the New Literacy Technologies

One of the most important factors leading to the Millennials' distinctive characteristics is that they are the first generation to have been immersed in ICT. Computers have generally been part of their home and school lives and they have always had access to the Internet. As we shall see, they live in a wired world. Prensky (2005–2006) refers to today's adolescents as "digital natives," and those of us born earlier are "digital immigrants." Digital natives are fluent in the language and culture of ICT. They adjust easily to changes in technology and are adept at utilizing it in creative and innovative ways. Digital immigrants, on the other hand, always "speak with an accent," struggling to learn and apply new ICT. One of this chapter's authors watched in awe as a Millennial friend easily and seemingly intuitively wired and programmed a new HDTV/Surround Sound stereo/cable networked/DVD/Videotape system that the author had worked hours on, and the Millennial did not bother to look at the instruction manual. Oblinger (2003) identifies these technology-related attitudes and aptitudes among Millennials:

- Computers are not new technology; for Millennials ICT has always been a part of their personal and social environment.

- The Internet is preferred over television; Millennials spend less time watching television than other generations, and more time on the Web.

- Knowing is less important than doing; Millennials believe that knowledge is constantly changing and relative, and that experience is of equal or greater value.

- Learning is more trial and error than sequential problem solving; Millennials view mistakes as a valuable part of the learning process.

- Handwriting is being replaced by typing; computers and other digital communication require typing skills, which Millennials find faster and more efficient.

- Immediacy is expected; Millennials have a low tolerance for delay and a high expectation for immediate access to information, communication, and response.

- Distinctions between creator and consumer, between owner and borrower, are blurring; Millennials operate in a cut-and-paste world where ownership, and in academics, plagiarism, are not clearly defined.

For a clear, research-based look at the wired world today's adolescents live in, let's turn to the Pew Internet and American Life Project (2005). This project systematically researches the impact of the Internet on American society: work, home, families, daily life, education, health, and so forth. Pew researchers produce 15 to 20 reports per year. The reports are based on well-designed national surveys using digital telephone technology and online surveys. These data sets are supplemented with current research from governmental agencies and other expert venues, observations of what people do when online, and in-depth interviews. Overall, this project and its website are a highly respected resource for information on Internet use.

In a 2004 telephone survey (Lenhart, Madden, & Hitlin, 2005), a national random sample of 1,100 twelve- to seventeen-year-olds and a parent or guardian were interviewed. Highlights of this study include

- 84% of the teenagers reported owning one or more personal media devices (computer, cell phone, personal digital assistant).

- 87% used the Internet, up from 73% in 2000; in comparison, 66% of adults used the Internet.

- 51% of the adolescent Internet users went online daily.
- 76% of the adolescent Internet users got news online, 41% had made online purchases, and 31% relied on the Internet to get health information.
- 90% of the online teens used e-mail, but instant messaging (IM) was beginning to be the preferred method for personal communication. Teens commented that e-mail was for sending messages to many recipients, for complex messages, and (disturbingly) for "old people."
- 45% of the teens reported owning cell phones, and 33% used their cells for text messaging.

These data portray Millennials as highly engaged in ICT. Their use of telecommunications exceeds other generations in virtually every way. There are qualitative differences as well. For example, older users are more likely to turn to the Internet for money-related activities such as banking and making travel arrangements; in other words, as a better tool to solve existing problems. Adolescents, in contrast, are more likely to use the Internet for social, creative, and communicative purposes; in other words, to use the technology in innovative ways.

This research clearly showed that teens live in a wired world. For example, 83% indicated that "most" of the people they knew used the Internet. But despite this extensive use, the teens in this survey also led active social lives offline. They reported regular social contact with an average of 20 friends, and 83% belonged to some sort of social group, such as a club, sports team, or band. The teens also reported spending more time doing social activities with friends (an average of 10.3 hours per week) than communicating via technology (7.8 hours per week).

In a second report, Lenhart and Madden (2005) observed that teens in the previously discussed survey were not just consumers of Internet content but were actively engaged as Internet content creators. More than half of the online teens (57%, or a remarkable 12 million) reported engaging in activities that placed their work on the Internet. This includes sharing creations such as artwork, photos, stories, and videos (33%); working on webpages or blogs for others (32%); creating and maintaining their own websites (22%); and creating their own online journals or blogs (19%).

Blogs. Blogs (short for "Web log") are a particularly interesting phenomenon. A Google search for "blogs" provides 1.3 billion hits. Typically, blogs combine text, images, and links, offering commentary on news and other subjects. Easy to create at a variety of commercial and free spots (myspace.com and msn.spaces, for example), the blog owner contributes regular entries, which are presented in reverse chronological order. Particularly popular among teen girls (25% of online 15- to 17-year-old girls are bloggers), blogs are commonly created by teens as online, multimedia journals. A current concern, and an issue that can be addressed by teachers, is privacy related to posting on the Internet.

Video games. A final distinctive characteristic of Millennials is the large number that play games online; those figures are 81% of online teens and only 32% of online adults. Around noon on July 5, 2006, one of the chapter authors logged on to http://www.bungie.net, an online gaming community. According to their online statistics, during the previous 24 hours, 263,705 unique players had logged 614,952 games; in total, 30,940 players worldwide had been online at this site. The number of players on Microsoft's online gaming site, Xbox Live (http://www.xbox.com), doubled from 2004 to 2005, adding a new player on average once every 30 seconds (Microsoft, 2005). An emerging form of online gaming, massively multiplayer online games (MMOGs) are highly graphical virtual interactive worlds. Players create their own digital characters, known as avatars, and interact not only with the game's software, but other avatars. It is worth noting that the video game industry now makes more money than Hollywood box office movies (Steinkuehler, 2004). For Millennials, video games and online games are a principle form of entertainment.

But video games do more than entertain. Gee (2003, 2005) argues that video game designers use learning principles well founded in current educational theory and research, and that the best of the video games generally adhere to these principles better than instruction in school (particularly in the skill and drill atmosphere of high stakes competency testing). There is much to be learned by playing the games. Prensky (2001) believes that developing expertise at computer-based games leads to the development of a large number of higher-order thinking skills

> including reading visual images as representations of three-dimensional space (representational competence), multidimensional visual–spatial skills, mental maps, "mental paper folding" (i.e., picturing the results of various origami-like folds in your mind without actually doing them), "inductive discovery" (i.e., making observations, formulating hypotheses and figuring out the rules governing the behavior of a dynamic

representation), "attentional deployment" (such as monitoring multiple locations simultaneously), and responding faster to expected and unexpected stimuli. (p. 4)

Interestingly, the computer games, particularly when played online, develop skills in demand in today's high-tech workplace (such as complex problem solving, collaborative problem solving, use of multimedia, learning by trial and error, and rich meaning making) better than schools (Steinkuehler, in press).

Instructional Implications

In order for Millennials to be literate in the 21st century, they must develop literacy skills beyond what was required of adolescents from previous generations. These new literacies build on the traditional skills of reading and writing print, but also require students to read and produce texts representative of the information and multimedia eras (Leu, 2001, 2002). As the world changes, education must adapt to the unique skills and knowledge that Millennials bring to school in order to teach the new literacies. To date, education has failed to do so. Digital immigrants seem to have a more difficult time dealing with technological change than the Millennials.

Because of ICT, today's adolescents are immersed in a rich educational environment. In this environment, they think and process information in fundamentally different ways than earlier generations (Alvermann & Eakle, chapter 4; Prensky, 2005–2006). Outside school, learning is ongoing, interesting, and seamless. The Internet provides instant access to information. E-mail, instant messaging, cell phones, and text messaging provide instant communication. To adapt to this high-speed environment, Millennials have learned to multitask, network, and learn through trial and error. However, they are often undisciplined and are not reflective in their learning. The unstructured digital environment generally fails to help adolescents develop critical evaluation and higher-order thinking skills. Unfortunately, as Lewis (see chapter 9) points out, schooling is apparently failing to provide today's adolescents with the skills necessary to be academically literate. The question facing adolescent educators is how to take advantage of the considerable skills and knowledge that Millennials have developed outside school to help them develop the more structured, higher-order academic skills that are crucial to their success in subsequent schooling and later in their adult lives. At the risk of overstating the importance of our task, the well-being of our communities, nation, and world are at stake.

Clearly, there is a disconnect between how adolescents learn outside school and what is expected in classrooms. As educators, we have the historical opportunity to adapt our instruction to the rich knowledge and high-tech skills that Millennials bring with them to school. Learning inside and outside school should interact: Teachers need to build on the skills and knowledge Millennials bring from outside school, and they also need to use out-of-school learning opportunities to extend and enrich in-school learning.

The need for systematic educational change in response to rapid changes brought about by ICT is clear. Classroom teachers and reading specialists should view this process of change as evolutionary rather than revolutionary. Integration of digital technology into the classroom should proceed as a measured and thoughtful process. A good beginning point is to establish a baseline of exactly how technologically literate your students are. The Student Technology Inventory (see Figure 14.1) provides an overview of where to begin. Results of the inventory provide a view of the technical background knowledge and skills that students bring with them to class. You can use this to begin considering appropriate instructional changes. There are two broad tactics that you can take to begin the evolutionary process: expanding the concept of text, and integrating the Internet into your classroom.

Expanding the Concept of Text

One clear mismatch between in-school and out-of-school learning is text. Outside school, Millennials' lives are filled with electronic text. They have instant access to massive amounts of printed information through the Internet and regularly write e-mails, instant messages, and text messages. In contrast, at the middle and high school level, the use of a single textbook dominates instruction, and writing is limited to assessment and reports (Alvermann & Moore, 1991).

The need to reform classroom text and textbooks is long overdue. Wade and Moje (2000) argue that current approaches to instruction emphasize a "transmission approach" to learning, in which texts and teachers serve as the ultimate authority, and the role of students is to acquire the knowledge presented through instruction. In such a model, textbooks are often not read by the student; the textbook serves more as a curriculum and pacing guide for the teacher. Other texts, especially those written

Figure 14.1. Student Technology Inventory

1. Do you have a computer at home?   Yes _____   No_____
2. Where is it located? _____
3. Do you have Internet access at home?   Yes _____   No_____
   If yes, is it high speed?   Yes _____   No_____
4. Estimate how much time you spend on the computer daily. _____
5. Do you use the computer for the following?
   a. Word processing   Yes _____   No_____
   b. Spreadsheets   Yes _____   No_____
   c. PowerPoint presentations   Yes _____   No_____
   d. Creating webpages   Yes _____   No_____
6. Have you used the World Wide Web to find more information about a topic
   of interest?   Yes _____   No_____
7. What search engine do you prefer (e.g., Yahoo, Google)? _____
8. Do you have your own television?   Yes _____   No_____
9. How many televisions are in your house? _____
10. Estimate how much time you spend watching television daily. _____
11. What is your favorite program? _____
12. Why is this your favorite program? _____
13. Do you play video games?   Yes _____   No_____
14. Do you play video games played online? Yes_____   No_____
15. How much time do you spend playing games video games daily? _____
16. What is your favorite video game? _____
17. Why is this your favorite game? _____
18. Do you use e-mail?   Yes _____   No_____
19. How much time do you spend e-mailing daily? _____
20. Do you have a Web log (e.g., myspace.com)? Yes _____   No_____
21. Do you have a cell phone?   Yes _____   No_____
22. Do you use text messaging?   Yes _____   No_____
23. How much time do you spend daily communicating using:
    a. E-mail
    b. Instant messaging
    c. Cell phone
    d. Text messaging
24. Do you have a Blackberry?   Yes _____   No_____
25. Do you have an iPod?   Yes _____   No_____
26. Do you download music to your cell phone,
    computer, or iPod?   Yes _____   No_____
27. Do you burn your own CDs? DVDs?   Yes _____   No_____

for students by students, are unacknowledged and unsanctioned. Information in today's schools is a limited commodity (King & O'Brien, 2004), dominated by textbooks and other published materials, controlled by teachers and, more problematically, by powers outside the classroom.

As an alternative, we would encourage teachers to consider a socio-cultural view of learning (see e.g., Anders & Spitler, chapter 10; Blanton, Wood, & Pilonieta, chapter 12). Such a view suggests that learning occurs through participation and cannot occur in isolation. Learning requires active discussion and other social activity. Learning is ongoing and occurs as a result of the active participation of multiple contributors. From this perspective, teachers and students engage in a learning process that grows from interactions among printed text, technology, and social dialogue.

For this process to be successful at this point in history, it is crucial to alter how classroom texts are viewed and used. Two approaches are possible. One is to use the textbook as one of several sanctioned texts. Internet resources—as well as other traditional texts, including books, newspapers, journals, and magazines—can supplement information from the textbook. It is also important to accept what have previously been unsanctioned texts (Wade & Moje, 2000). These are the texts that students themselves generate, which have always been a powerful and largely ignored resource (we remember notes passed among our friends when we were adolescents). Today's unsanctioned texts, particularly in the form of student generated e-mails, websites, and blogs, can be a valuable addition to the body of classroom text. Teachers should take advantage of the substantial amount of text that students construct and read outside the classroom. This can serve as a bridge to academic literacy skills.

A second approach is to teach students how to locate quality educational texts. This alternative builds on a skill most adolescents already possess—searching the Internet. One of the teacher's roles with this approach is to provide students with more sophisticated skills in Internet searching. Instruction in the use of a variety of search engines, how they differ, and when to use each will provide understandings not usually acquired outside school. Instruction in how to refine searches using Boolean logic is also valuable.

Evaluation of Websites

One critical skill teachers can develop with their students is the evaluation of the quality of websites. Many students have little experience or skill in determining the reliability or accuracy of Internet resources. The common strategy is to type a word into a search engine (Google is the current favorite) and click on the first site. One excellent resource for assisting students in evaluating websites is Kathy Schrock's Guide for Educators website evaluation page (http://school.discovery.com/schrockguide/eval.html), which is part of Discoveryschool.com (http://school.discovery.com), the Discovery Channel's Education website. Schrock provides an excellent series of evaluation surveys for students at every level, as well as teachers. In addition, many research library websites have resources for evaluating websites. For example, the Appalachian State University library has a quick reference guide (http://www.library.appstate.edu/reference/howTo/evaluating.html). Finally, a Google search using "website evaluation" produced 73.6 million hits, so the information is readily available.

Media Literacy

Another valuable skill to develop with Millennials is broader media literacy. Students must be able to evaluate not only Internet sites but any type of media formats they encounter, such as textbooks, advertising, magazines, television, and newspapers. Considine (Media Literacy Workshops and Consulting, n.d.) defines media literacy as "the ability to access, analyze, evaluate and create information" (¶1). Teachers must teach students to understand the context of the programs they watch and how to evaluate their individual experiences. It is necessary for our new wave of media consumers to make intelligent decisions about the written and electronic messages they are flooded with daily both inside and outside the classroom. Once again, this change in technology has outpaced our pedagogy, curricula, and what it means to be literate in a multimedia society (Semali, 2001).

There is a real danger that adolescents worldwide are developing a standardized set of values and opinions put forward by large, multinational corporations (Gee, 2004). It is interesting to travel to foreign countries and see adolescents dressed exactly like U.S. or Western European teens. Although the issue of dress is relatively trivial, the worldwide adoption of a sense of entitlement and mass consumption is more problematic. Certainly, values related to consumerism and advertising on the Web are worth exploring in class.

Educational Websites

The Internet is a valuable but massive resource for teachers: A Google search for "education" returns 1.8 billion sites. In addition to the problem of sorting through the large number of sites available for teachers, there are problems when listing websites in a text such as this one. First and foremost, the Internet is constantly changing, and any website listed here may quickly become obsolete or unavailable. With that said, we will provide teachers with a short list of valuable technology tools for teachers' use (see Table 14.1).

With the same caveats about teacher websites, we provide a list of instructional websites for students in Table 14.2. These websites are valuable learning resources for adolescent learners, and include tutorial assistance in reading, writing, and Internet usage, homework help lines, and reading groups. It should also be pointed out that many Millennials are expert at Internet searching, and in fact may be capable tutors for other students and even teachers. This creates the possibility, a positive one from our perspective, for teachers to become students and students to become teachers.

Table 14.1. Helpful Internet Sites for Teachers

Educational Websites for Teachers	http://www.camden.rutgers.edu/~wood/edwebsites.htm
Sites for Teachers	http://www.sitesforteachers.com/index.html
Scholastic Teachers	http://teacher.scholastic.com
PBS Teachers	http://www.pbs.org/teachersource
The Teacher's Corner	http://www.theteacherscorner.net
Education World	http://www.education-world.com
Teaching Tolerance	http://www.tolerance.org/teach/index.jsp
Council for Exceptional Children	http://www.cec.sped.org

Table 14.2. Helpful Internet Sites for Students

Google Directory for Kids & Teens	http://www.google.com/Top/Kids_and_Teens
Pandia	http://www.pandia.com/kids/index.html
Teen Web LA Library	http://www.lapl.org/ya/homework/directories.php
A+ Research & Writing Info Search	http://www.ipl.org/div/aplus/skills.htm
Teen Web: Homework Help	http://www.library.nashville.gov/teens/tee_homework.asp
Yahooligans	http://yahooligans.yahoo.com

Although there are far too many instructional Internet resources to review, this section will present three: Thinkfinity, formerly known as MarcoPolo; ReadWriteThink; and the Webquest Page.

The Thinkfinity website (http://www.thinkfinity.org) is designed to provide high-quality Internet content for teachers and students as well as professional development for teachers throughout the world. The website houses collections from seven standards-based Content Partners, each with lesson plans and student Web resources. All lesson plans and Web resources are peer reviewed, and many are aligned with state standards. The Content Partners include ArtsEdge, John F. Kennedy Center for the Performing Arts; EconEdLink, National Council on Economic Education; EDSITEment, National Endowment for the Humanities; Illuminations, National Council of Teachers of Mathematics; ReadWriteThink, International Reading Association and the National Council of Teachers of English; Science NetLinks, American Association for the Advancement of Science; and Xpeditions, National Geographic Society.

ReadWriteThink (http://www.readwritethink.org) is one of the Thinkfinity websites for teachers, and it is maintained in conjunction with the standards from the International Reading Association and the National Council of Teachers of English. The site includes K–12 lessons in reading and language arts as well as instructional resources, student materials, and a literacy calendar. ReadWriteThink lessons can be sorted by grade band and type of literacy engagements, including learning language, learning about language, and learning through language. A collection of student materials supplements a variety of lessons available for educational purposes. The site's calendar highlights significant literary events during the year, and each entry provides a brief description, multiple lesson plans, and activities for student engagement. For example, September 21 is the International Day of Peace. By clicking on this day, teachers may find a 9th- to 12th-grade lesson titled The Peace Journey: Using Process Drama in the Classroom. In this lesson, students work in small groups to create and perform skits that reflect their developing notions of peace. Teachers can access the full peer-reviewed lesson, which includes strategies for integrating the Internet and other technology.

A webquest is an inquiry-oriented activity designed for teachers to support the interests and ideas of the students. The model was developed by Bernie Dodge in 1995 at San Diego State University. The Webquest Page (n.d.) at http://webquest.sdsu.edu hosts a wealth of knowledge about webquests, including excellent examples in multiple grade levels and a discussion forum. Readings and training materials are available to guide teachers through the process of creating webquests for their classrooms. Webquests usually emphasize group activities and can focus on a single discipline or be interdisciplinary. According to Dodge (1997), a webquest should contain the following six parts: (1) an introduction that sets the stage for the upcoming work ahead; (2) a task that is both attainable and appealing; (3) information sources, which can be embedded within the webquest; (4) a process description, explaining what the learner should do to accomplish the task; (5) guidance describing how to organize information gained during the webquest; and (6) a conclusion, which brings closure to the webquest. One example, Webquest: The Truth...and Nothing but the Truth! Evaluative Persuasive Reading may be found at http://www.pampetty. com/persuasivestudent.htm. In this webquest, students are asked by the Secretary of Education to serve as a panel of experts and solve some problems affecting schools all over the country. They are expected to take a pro or con stand on a controversial topic affecting education. Students are required to read a persuasive text and then analyze and synthesize the information, write a narrative in response to the text, and create a PowerPoint presentation summarizing their findings. Students are graded individually and as a group, using a rubric.

The following three websites offer teachers some strategies for providing students with the new learning and literacy skills required for success in the highly technological work and social environments of the 21st century. Teachers can also engage their classes in collaborative instructional projects with children around the world through the Internet. The following sites will aid teachers who are looking for international projects for their classes. With any activity or project, teachers must remember that the Internet is only an instructional tool; good teaching can never be replaced by a machine.

- The Global Virtual Classroom, at http://www.virtualclassroom. org, is a collection of free, online educational activities and resources. According to the site, students in the 21st century need three essential skills: cross cultural communication, collaboration, and computer skills. The Global Virtual Classroom has two projects underway: (1) a contest for school websites; and (2) a clubhouse for schools to come together to communicate and work on topics of mutual interest.

- Global Dimension, at http://www.globaldimension.org.uk, is a searchable website based in the United Kingdom. It provides multimedia resources focusing on global perspectives, including links to books, videos, posters, and websites, and information on partnerships with schools in other countries.
- The International Education and Resource Network (iEARN), at http://www.iearn.org, offers 35 to 40 structured projects—each with a teacher–facilitator—in social studies, science, environment, math, arts, literature, and interdisciplinary areas.

Teachers must always consider issues of diversity throughout their classrooms, and equity issues in technology may sometimes prove challenging. The websites listed below offer alternatives for students as well as teachers to address educational inequities.

- Young women may visit sites such as Club Girl Tech (http://www.girltech.com) or the GirlTECH site on getting girls interested in computers (http://math.rice.edu/~lanius/club/girls.html).
- Teaching Tolerance (http://www.tolerance.org/teens/index.jsp) offers students activities that create more inclusive environments in their schools and communities. There is also a space in the teen section where students can sign up to receive an e-newsletter.
- The American Library Association recommends that sites be compliant with the Americans with Disabilities Act as much as possible. Teachers who want to evaluate how well their classroom websites meet standards of accessibility, quality, and privacy can visit the CAST website (http://www.cast.org).

Building Classroom Websites

It is easy to be overwhelmed by the Web. One problem Millennials may have (but not be aware of) is that they are not intimidated by the massive amount of information currently available and do not always critically evaluate the reliability and quality of the information on websites. As of January 2005, one study said there were 11.5 billion webpages on the publicly indexable Web (Gulli & Signorini, 2005). Teachers can help by developing a classroom website that serves as a clearinghouse for quality sites that are useful to the students and teacher.

Although constructing a webpage may seem like a daunting task, it is really quite easy. Anyone with basic word processing skills can apply them to webpage design. One way to start is to use a common Web browser. Mozilla, for example, has a built in Web editor. When the user clicks on the File pull-down menu, there is an Edit Page option. This allows the user to create a page, either by starting with another similar page or beginning with a blank page. Once a teacher or student designs the webpage for the class, a district or school technology specialist should be able to help put it online. If this assistance is not available, on-line Web construction programs can help. For example, Geocities (http://geocities.yahoo.com), part of the Yahoo website (http://www.yahoo.com), provides free space, an online editor, and easy to follow directions. However, the free space is limited (currently 15 megabytes) and probably inadequate for the long term.

Two other resources may be useful. One is the Internet itself. Online searches using terms such as "website design," "webpage design," and "designing websites" yield sites that will walk you through the process and provide useful hints on construction. For example, Designing School Websites to Deliver (http://www.fno.org/webdesign.html) provides extensive suggestions about the design process. Designing Websites (http://www.rcs.k12.va.us/csjh/webpages.htm), from the Cave Springs Middle School in Roanoke, Virginia, gives step-by-step instructions.

Your second readily available resource is the students. The Pew Internet and American Life Project (Lenhart & Madden, 2005) points out that more than half of American teens have placed material on the Internet. Most middle and high school classes will have some students familiar with Internet design. Engaging students in the ongoing design, re-finement, and maintenance of the classroom website can build a sense of community and lead to more active student engagement. In addition to serving as a resource for useful Internet sites, a well-organized classroom homepage can provide lessons, instructional aids, helpful study tips, and upcoming events in the class. The website also can serve to bring parents into the instructional program by providing access to homework assign-ments and displaying student work, schedules, a calendar of upcoming events, and other useful information. Overall, the classroom websites can be a valuable tool in developing the classroom learning community.

The following are examples of classroom webpages:

- Mrs. DeCosa's seventh-grade English class website (http://oswego.org/staff/jdecosa/web) has links to short- and long-term assign-ments, current topics, samples of student work, resources for students and parents, and class assignments for students who have been absent. A handy Parents' Page includes answers to frequently asked questions about helping students succeed.

- Mrs. Gogas's page (http://members.tripod.com/dscorpio/index. htm) shares information for an eighth-grade English class. This webpage illustrates the teaching objectives for the class and for the current unit that the students are working on. Some of the topics available on this site are the class syllabus, ideas for book reports, notebook guidelines for students, and a virtual tour of topics explored in class such as the Diary of Anne Frank and Edgar Allen Poe.

Questions for Reflection

1. Based on your observations, how do today's adolescents differ from previous generations in their experiences with media and technology?

2. How do e-mail, instant messaging, and text messaging affect student writing? In what ways do students' experiences with these technologies enhance the quality of their writing? In what ways are they detrimental?

Activities

1. Develop a set of interview questions that explore students' use of technology and their learning styles. You can use the Student Technology Inventory for ideas (Figure 14.1, page 274). Interview several adolescents and share your findings.

2. Identify what you consider to be ethical issues related to technology use (e.g., plagiarism; downloading music, art, photos, or pornography; privacy issues). Discuss your views on these issues and how your views might differ from a typical Millennial.

Gary Moorman is Professor of Education at Appalachian State University, Boone, North Carolina, USA. He is past Chair of the American Reading Forum and served as the Online Communities Director for *Reading Online* and as an editor of the Yearbook of the American Reading Forum. He has served on the editorial review boards for ReadWriteThink.org, *Journal of Educational Research*, *Reading Research and Instruction*, *Reading Psychology*, and *Teaching and Teacher Education*. His scholarly interests include adolescent literacy, technology and literacy, and sociocultural theory. He also serves as a volunteer consultant for the Secondary Education Reform Activity program in Macedonia and has also worked on a faculty development project in Qatar. He may be contacted at moormangb@appstate.edu. **Julie Horton** is an Assistant Professor at Appalachian State University, Boone, North Carolina, USA. Her research interests center on issues of White identity and multicultural teacher education. She has written numerous articles and co-edited a book on diversity and technology. She may be contacted at hortonjk@appstate.edu.

REFERENCES

Alvermann, D.E., & Moore, D.W. (1991). Secondary school reading. In R. Barr, M.L. Kamil, P.B. Mosenthal, & P.D. Pearson (Eds.), *Handbook of reading research* (Vol. 2, pp. 951–983). White Plains, NY: Longman.

Berliner, D.C., & Biddle, B.J. (1995). *The manufactured crisis: Myths, fraud, and the attack on America's public schools*. Reading, MA: Addison-Wesley.

Coomes, M.D., & DeBard, R. (2004). A generational approach to understanding students. *New Directions for Student Services, 106*, 5–16.

DeBard, R. (2004). Millennials coming to college. *New Directions for Student Services, 106*, 33–45.

Diamond, J.M. (1999). *Guns, germs and steel: The fates of human societies*. New York: W.W. Norton.

Dodge, B. (1997). *Some thoughts about webquests*. Retrieved March 6, 2007, from San Diego State University website: http://webquest.sdsu.edu/about_webquests.html

Gee, J.P. (2003). From video games, learning about learning. *Chronicle of Higher Education, 49*, B13.

Gee, J.P. (2004). Millennials and bobos, Blues Clues and Sesame Street: A story of our times. In D. Alvermann (Ed.), *Adolescents and literacies in a digital world* (pp. 40–50). New York: Peter Lang.

Gee, J.P. (2005). The classroom of popular culture: What video games can teach us about making students want to learn. *Harvard Education Letter, 21*, 8.

Gulli, A., & Signorini, A. (2005). The indexable Web is more than 11.5 billion pages. Retrieved March 6, 2007, from http://www.cs.uiowa.edu/~asignori/websize/size-indexable-web.pdf

Howe, N., & Strauss, W. (2000). *Millennials rising: The next great generation*. New York: Vantage Books.

King, J., & O'Brien, D. (2004). Adolescents' multiliteracies and their teachers' needs to know: Toward a digital detente. In D. Alvermann (Ed.), *Adolescents and literacies in a digital world* (pp. 40–50). New York: Peter Lang.

Leiner, B., Cerf, V., Clark, D., Kahn, R., Kleinrock, L., Lynch, D., et al. (1999, January 23). *A brief history of the Internet.* Retrieved June 27, 2006, from arXiv.org website: http://arxiv.org/html/cs.NI/9901011

Lenhart, A., & Madden, M. (2005, November 2). *Teen Content Creators and Consumers.* Retrieved March 7, 2007, from Pew Internet & American Life Project: http://www.pewinternet.org/index.asp

Lenhart, A., Madden, M., & Hitlin, P. (2005, July 27). *Teens and technology: Youth are leading the transition to a fully wired and mobile nation.* Retrieved July 3, 2006, from the Pew Internet & American Life Project: http://www.pewinternet.org/pdfs/PIP_Teens_Tech_July2005web.pdf

Leu, D.J., Jr. (2001). Internet project: Preparing students for new literacies in a global village [Electronic version] . *The Reading Teacher*, 54(6). Retrieved March 7, 2007, from http://www.readingonline.org/electronic/elec_index.asp?HREF=rt/3-01_column/index.html

Leu, D.J., Jr. (2002). The new literacies: Research on reading instruction with the Internet and other digital technologies. In A.E. Farstrup & S.J. Samuels (Eds.), *What research has to say about reading instruction* (3rd ed., pp. 310–336). Newark, DE: International Reading Association.

Manguel, A. (1996). *A history of reading.* New York: Viking Press

Media Literacy Workshops and Consulting. (n.d.) Retrieved September 29, 2006, from http://www.gailehaley.com/considine/media-literacy.htm

Microsoft. (2005, July 20). *Xbox Live online gaming community doubles in just one year, new member added every 30 seconds* [press release]. Retrieved July 5, 2006, from http://www.microsoft.com/presspass/press/2005/jul05/07-20XboxLiveCommunityPR.mspx

National Center for Education Statistics. (2005). *The Nation's Report Card: Reading 2005* [online summary overview]. Washington, DC: Author. Retrieved April 16, 2006, from http://nces.ed.gov/pubsearch/pubsinfo.asp?pubid=2006451

Oblinger, D. (2003). *Boomers, Gen-Xers & Millennials: Understanding the new students.* Retrieved July 5, 2006, from http://www.educause.edu/ir/library/pdf/ERM0342.pdf#search=%22Oblinger%22

Pew Internet and American Life Project. (2005). Retrieved July 3, 2006, from http://www.pewinternet.org/index.asp

Prensky, M. (2001). *Digital natives, digital immigrants.* Retrieved July 5, 2006, from http://www.marcprensky.com/writing/Prensky%20-%20Digital%20Natives,%20Digital%20Immigrants%20-%20Part1.pdf

Prensky, M. (2005–2006). *Listen to the natives.* Educational Leadership, 63(4), 8–13.

Semali, L.M. (2001, November). Defining new literacies in curricular practice. Reading Online, 5(4). Retrieved March 6, 2007, from http://www.readingonline.org/newliteracies/lit_index.asp?HREF=semali1/index.html

Smith, N.B. (1965). *American reading instruction: Its development and its significance in gaining a perspective on current practices in reading.* Newark, DE: International Reading Association.

Steinkuehler, C.A. (2004). *Learning in massively multiplayer online games*. In Y.B. Kafai, W.A. Sandoval, N. Enyedy, A.S. Nixon, & F. Herrera (Eds.), Proceedings of the sixth international conference of the learning sciences (pp. 521–528). Mahwah, NJ: Erlbaum.

Steinkuehler, C.A. (in press). *Cognition and literacy in massively multiplayer online games*. In D. Leu, J. Coiro, C. Lankshear, & K. Knobel (Eds.), Handbook of research on new literacies. Mahwah, NJ: Erlbaum.

Technology. (n.d.). Retrieved June 19, 2006, from Wikipedia website: http://en.wikipedia.org/wiki/Technology#Definition_of_technology

Wade, S.E., & Moje, E.B. (2000). *The role of text in classroom learning*. In M.L. Kamil, P.B. Mosenthal, P.D. Pearson, & R. Barr (Eds.), Handbook of reading research (Vol. 3, pp. 609–627). Mahwah, NJ: Erlbaum.

The webquest page. (n.d.). Retrieved September 28, 2006, from http://webquest.sdsu.edu

CHAPTER 15

Fostering Literate Academic Identities During the First Days of School

David W. Moore and Karen A. Onofrey

HIGHLIGHTS

- Youth who identify themselves as literate academic individuals, who assert membership in particular classroom literacy communities, can be expected to benefit academically.
- Fostering adolescent academic identities when launching the school year is imperative.
- The many excellent strategies for stimulating and nurturing literate academic identity include the following:
  - Riveting invitations
  - Shoebox autobiographies
  - Literacy resumes
  - Literary connections
  - Peer interviews
  - Guest book talks
  - Informing internal dialogues
  - Identity maps and mini-ethnographies

According to Holland, Lachicotte, Skinner, and Cain (1998), identities are enacted when "People tell others who they are, but even more important, they tell themselves and then try to act as though they are who they say they are" (p. 3). The claims people make about themselves connect with their actions.

Adolescent Literacy Instruction: Policies and Promising Practices edited by Jill Lewis and Gary Moorman. © 2007 by the International Reading Association.

Students who enact claims as insiders to classroom reading and writing, who assert membership in particular classroom literacy communities, have an academic advantage. For instance, students who consciously ask and answer questions about texts in concert with teachers' expectations have been shown to experience success in those classrooms (Moje & Dillon, 2006). Students who consciously complete assignments, read independently, and study for tests in line with academic expectations tend to accomplish school-related goals (Jackson, 2003). Students who identify themselves as literate academic individuals can be expected to arrange their mental habits and proficiencies accordingly. Consequently, fostering such identities is important instructional work.

Conceptual Base

Our recommendations for fostering youths' academic identities are based on several fundamental concepts. First, individuals exhibit various identities that can be distinguished along a continuum of core and socially situated identities (Gee, 2001). Core identities are relatively fixed, enduring across time and condition, expressing people's predictable responses. Individuals who claim to generally act decisively, industriously, or honestly are claiming somewhat stable and continuous core identities. On the other hand, individuals' socially situated identities are adaptable, changing according to circumstances. The term *socially situated* expresses the idea that people act according to the circumstances of different societal conditions, enacting identities amid certain environments and not others (McCarthey & Moje, 2002). For instance, students might act disengaged and defiant in one classroom yet involved and obliging in another. Acknowledging flexible, socially situated identities is important because it opens the door to youthful modifications and transformations according to the classroom circumstances teachers create.

Individuals also exhibit clusters of identities that can be distinguished along a continuum of collective and individual (Simon, 2004). Collective identities emphasize a few common characteristics of particular groups in which people claim membership. Identifying oneself as a backpacker, biker, gardener, lowrider, scrapbooker, skateboarder, or social activist means aligning oneself with the primary features that unite members of these groups. Conversely, individual identities emphasize personal characteristics that distinguish people from others in a group. A person might identify himself or herself as a backpacker but then particularize this identification by noting that, unlike others, he or she is a traditional backpacker who prefers relatively primitive equipment and solo hikes in canyons. Adolescent literacy teachers who appreciate collective identities work to develop classroom communities of readers and writers, and include all class members in these communities. Additionally, these teachers realize that individuals will stake out different positions within the communities, demonstrating preferences for different reading materials and response styles.

A third essential point addresses the ways individuals' identities are positioned, or determined. Social positioning occurs when community members interact, jointly producing story lines for one another (Davies & Harré, 1990). For instance, teachers who are convinced that students are competent learners often treat them that way, and over time the students come to see themselves and act like competent learners. Common sayings about how youth who live with criticism learn to be critical, how those who live with hostility learn to be hostile, and how those who live with security learn to be secure are grounded in the concept of social positioning.

Along with social positioning, youth independently exert agency to determine their identities (Moore & Cunningham, 2006). Youth bring agency into play through internal mental dialogues, silently talking to themselves about who they are and who they want to be, and acting accordingly. Indeed, many youth fall short of academic expectations because they willfully decide to not learn course content rather than actually miss content due to a lack of ability (Kohl, 1994). For instance, many students in a language arts class might be able to learn to share visualizations of literary settings, but they choose not to for personal reasons. Educators who embrace this perspective seek ways to inform youthful decisions because they believe young people ultimately decide the extent to which they see themselves reading, writing, and participating in school. Recognizing the roles of social positioning along with self-positioning can help balance instructional planning relative to identity formation.

Our final key concept about academic identities involves the first few days of school. The expectations that are communicated, the tone that is set, and the momentum that is initiated during the very first days of the school year tend to persist through all the remaining days (Marzano, Marzano, & Pickering, 2003). Adolescent literacy educators who recognize the importance of getting off to a good start directly address students' integral beliefs and mental habits during this time (Fielding, Schoenbach, & Jordan, 2003). Consequently, fostering academic identities when launching classes with adolescent readers and writers is important. The rest of this chapter describes instructional practices designed to accomplish this.

Instructional Practices

Riveting Invitations

Riveting invitations presented during the first few days of school are meant to result in students thinking something like, "Cool! Looks like I'm going to do interesting things and learn interesting stuff in this class!" Riveting invitations entice youth to become members of classroom communities. Chemistry teachers present a classic example of a riveting invitation on the first day of class when they fill different colored balloons each with different gases, note the chemical reactions such as a burst of flame when they puncture each balloon, then guide students through scientific analyses of the reactions. Such a compelling activity is designed to fascinate students, absorbing them in course content right from the start.

Adolescent literacy teachers might not burst balloons during the first few days of class to invite student membership in their learning communities, but they have other devices. They might share book excerpts that have thrilled them and spoken to them personally and forcefully. For instance, during the first day of his classes, David regularly displays a copy of John McPhee's *Basin and Range* (1990) and shares the following quotation from that text: "If by some fiat I had to restrict all this writing to one sentence, this is the one I would choose: The summit of Mt. Everest is marine limestone" (p. 183). David then explains why he finds this sentence so profound, how it so elegantly expresses the essence of geology (the content area in which he teaches literacy skills), and how it has made the look of the world different for him. Along this line, some teachers have students produce bookmarks that contain compelling excerpts—such as the one McPhee shares—along with their sources, making the bookmarks available to class members as a way to publicize especially engaging reading materials.

Playing brief spoken-word recordings at the beginning of the course is another way to invite membership to a literate community. Most libraries and bookstores house recordings of texts spoken by the authors themselves, by celebrities, or by spoken-word professionals. The teacher can show video clips of time-honored scenes, such as the communication breakthrough when Annie Sullivan pumps water over Helen Keller's hand in *The Miracle Worker*, or George shooting Lenny before a vengeful mob captures him in *Of Mice and Men*. Such practices invite youths to enter communities that appreciate the wonder and power of print.

Shoebox Autobiographies

Shoebox autobiographies (Whitmore & Goodman, 1996) are a powerful and engaging venue for students to express their identities in and out of school. These autobiographies demonstrate how reading and writing fit students' lives, providing glimpses of their world outside the classroom. Students are asked to fill a shoebox with objects or artifacts that best represent them as readers and writers. Karen has started her first week of school for years by sharing her own shoebox autobiography with students. In it, she shares different types of reading material, a piece of writing, cherished photos, objects representing hobbies, favorite CDs, and a brownie mix to defend her title of "the worst brownie maker in the world."

Placing minimal demands on the contents of the boxes makes sense, although you might consider two stipulations. One, the artifacts must fit in the shoebox, though backpacks or simple brown bags will work if shoeboxes aren't available. And two, youth need to mind school regulations about what is appropriate to share.

Students spend a few days collecting artifacts and typically share their shoebox autobiographies within the first week of school. The informal sharing takes only a few minutes and can take many forms. As Karen models the process, she takes the intended artifacts out of the shoebox in support of her statements. Students can sit on the floor in a large circle, allowing each one to share with the entire class. When time is more demanding, students can share in small groups and then choose one artifact to share with the rest of the class.

Shoebox autobiographies create opportunities for you to make personal connections with students and welcome them into a classroom community where multiple forms of reading and writing are valued. You can suggest specific books and writing projects to individual students after learning about them through their shoebox autobiographies. You can use artifacts to group students throughout the year. For example, similar interests in music or sports may lead to a quick impromptu grouping for an assignment.

Literacy Resumes

Having youth celebrate their reading and writing experiences goes far in promoting their identities as readers and writers. Launching the school year with literacy resumes is a useful step in this direction (Rief, 1992).

Similar in style to a professional resume, or vita, literacy resumes chronicle students' life experiences with reading and writing. Collect resumes from willing teachers and former students (minus identifying information) and distribute them to students in small groups. Ask students to collectively decide which categories are needed and which are personal choices. Then have students brainstorm all literary experiences from their early school years to the present, considering all their actions inside and outside school as readers and writers. Are they avid comic book readers, poets, or song lyricists? What magazines and websites do they frequent? What literacy-related projects have they completed in the lower grades? Other informative items include educational background, work experience, favorite pastimes and hobbies, and other outside interests. Compiling such information helps students analyze their identities in general and their academically literate identities in particular.

After students produce their literacy resumes, they can honor their past accomplishments. What have they enjoyed the most? What have they taken the most pride in accomplishing? What have they done that they would recommend to others? Students also can reflect on any correlations between their hobbies and literacy experiences. Do they like to move around and write about their experiences? Do they enjoy craftwork and reading about such crafts as well? Finally, many teachers have students consider literacy goals. What would they like to continue doing as readers and writers? What would they like to do differently or improve? Would they like to explore a particular genre or author? Would they simply like to find enjoyment in reading and writing? Goal setting can result from group discussions as well as internal dialogues, helping youth continually build on their literate academic identities.

Literary Connections

With thousands of young adult books available, students have access to quality texts that provide opportunities to form literary connections that can help them identify with others as readers and writers. A key part of our jobs as teachers is to get the right books into the right students' hands.

The young adult books presented here focus on literary characters who are examining their academically literate identities, making these resources good springboards for youth to examine their own identities. The books are divided into three sets: (1) writing to understand the world, (2) reading toward change, and (3) constructing identities as readers and writers. We have hesitantly divided the books into middle-school and high-school subgroups based on interest, knowing that interests vary.

In Figure 15.1, Writing to Understand Your World, the characters use writing as a tool for understanding the world around them. They write to explore truth and to make sense of their lives. For example, *Don't You Dare Read This, Mrs. Dunphrey* (Haddix, 1996) is a provocative book that readily launches readers into examining their own decisions. Gum-smacking 16-year-old Tish is asked to keep a journal by her sophomore English teacher. Before long the journal becomes more than an assignment; it becomes a therapeutic escape from Tish's stressful life where she can contemplate responses to her problems. In line with Trelease's (2000) statement that "reading aloud is the most effective advertisement for the pleasures of reading" (p. 235), we have found read-alouds to be effective tools for getting books such as *Don't You Dare Read This, Mrs. Dunphrey* into students' hands. One of the many benefits of reading this book aloud is its journal format. You needn't wait for a chapter break or the build up of a cliff hanger to stop reading. The read-aloud can reasonably take just a few minutes and maintain students' interests from day to day.

Another top pick for triggering reflections on literate identities is the nonfiction piece, *The Freedom Writers Diary* (Gruwell, 1999). This

Figure 15.1. Writing to Understand Your World

Title	Author	Middle School	High School	Focus
Nothing but the Truth	Avi	X		Writing, speaking
The Freedom Writers Diary	The Freedom Writers with Erin Gruwell		X	Writing, reading
Don't You Dare Read This, Mrs. Dunphrey	Margaret Peterson Haddix	X		Writing
Daphne's Boo	Mary Downing Hahn	X		Writing
The Year of Secret Assignments	Jaclyn Moriarty	X	X	Writing

book is written by Erin Gruwell and 150 of her high school students from the inner city of Long Beach, California. To protect anonymity, the journal entries are not attributed to specific individuals, but they nonetheless capture attention with riveting tales of death, danger, and despair. Using Gruwell's book as a launching point, students can learn to read critically with and against the grain of the text (Hynds, 1997), forming connections with the Freedom Writers. Students could respond to various journal entries in *The Freedom Writers* in both written and oral formats. Have students record the pace at which they read. Did they increase or decrease their speed with certain entries? After careful examination, have students synthesize their own reading process. This book serves as a great example of a piece that can be used to examine literacy processes as well as identities.

The role of reading becomes a vehicle for characters to explore their academic identities, as in the books listed in Figure 15.2, Reading Toward Change. *Speak* by Laurie Halse Anderson (1999) is widely acclaimed. Main character Melinda has morphed into a decidedly different person during the summer prior to her freshman year. As she stumbles through her academic classes each day, she creates barriers, keeping the outside world at bay. When students read this text, invite them to keep an ongoing map of Melinda's feelings. What do they predict is the reason for her sudden change in affect? Have they ever seen this happen to someone they know? Are there similarities to their own lives? Are there preventive measures to keep it from happening? If this main character were in the students' peer group, how might they develop a plan to

Figure 15.2. Reading Toward Change

Title	Author	Middle School	High School	Focus
Speak	Laurie Halse Anderson	X	X	All content areas
"The Gift of Reading" from *Better Than Life*	Daniel Pennac		X	Reading
Guys Write for Guys Read	Edited by Jon Scieszka	X	X	Writing, reading (selected pieces)
The Library Carxd	Jerry Spinelli	X		Reading

Figure 15.3. Constructing Identities as Readers and Writers

Title	Author	Middle School	High School	Focus
P.S. Longer Letter Later	Paula Danziger and Ann Martin	X		Writing
Taming the Star Runner	S.E. Hinton	X		Writing
Nightjohn	Gary Paulsen	X		Reading
Hard Love	Ellen Wittlinger		X	Writing

help her begin to recover from her deep depression? These types of activities and questions help students move toward considerations of Melinda's—and perhaps their own—school-related actions and beliefs.

Some books we reviewed had compelling characters and could speak to academically literate identities in a global manner, as depicted in Figure 15.3, Constructing Identities as Readers and Writers. The characters in these books address their identity as writers and readers mainly outside school. They include *Taming the Star Runner* (Hinton, 1988), *P.S. Longer Letter Later* (Danziger & Martin, 1998), *Hard Love* (Wittlinger, 1999), and *Nightjohn* (Paulsen, 1993). The first three all successfully deal with different forms of writing, from creating a novel to letter writing to the construction of a magazine. *Nightjohn* has a secondary theme, which is learning how to read. All the texts are suitable for middle school, with the exception of *Hard Love* because of its sophisticated content.

Peer Interviews

Having students interview one another provides entry into a classroom community, initiating the construction of collective identities as readers and writers. The following peer interview formats are promising practices for launching your school year.

Semi-structured interviews. Students who conduct semi-structured interviews prior to introducing one another to the class incorporate reading, writing, listening, and speaking. To begin, students brainstorm a list of written questions that are open ended and invite conversation, knowing that more questions can be asked once the interview has started. Questions might address favorite reading materials, music, courses, and pastimes. To mix the dynamics of a classroom, have students interview only someone who sits at least 6 feet away. This requires students to physically move about the room and seek out someone rather than just be resigned to whomever is in the immediate vicinity.

Students interview each other in pairs, recording the answers to their questions. Given a brief amount of time, students then organize their findings and introduce the interviewee to the class. The challenge is that students cannot ask their partner for any clarifying information during the introduction, so they must be active listeners and recorders during the interview.

Twenty literacy questions. Modifying the traditional 20 questions game to target books or short stories is another way to initiate peer interviews about literacy. Have students work in groups and collectively brainstorm and record questions beginning with open-ended ones and becoming more specific as the process goes along. Beginning questions might include: Is the book fiction or nonfiction? Did you read it in school or out of school? Was it an award-winning book? Was it made into a movie? Would you recommend it?

Once a skeletal list has been formulated, one group selects one piece of print, then the other groups take turns asking no more than 20 total questions to identify the selection. Whole-class discussions about youths' experiences with specific printed items often result from this practice. Be sure to record the selected titles so you can refer to them later during class.

The yes–no name game. Like semistructured interviews, the yes–no name game is a social mixer involving literacy and is devoted to building community and developing a collective identity. Students often report that they welcome this activity because it is personalized, calming, and reveals how much they have in common with others. The goal is to find something in common with each person in the class.

To begin the yes–no name game, provide each student with a class list, including your name. Use only first names and last initials. Be sure to collect the lists at the close of class, in keeping with privacy requirements. On the back of the list, have students brainstorm as many yes–no questions as possible that they could truthfully answer "yes" to when asked. Examples include, do you like sports? Do you like chocolate? Do you like to read?

After explaining and modeling the practice, have students form temporary pairs and introduce themselves by name to one another. Then one student asks a question designed to elicit a "yes" answer. If the partner does not answer yes, then more questions need to be asked until a yes is received and both parties find something in common. When a student receives a yes, then he or she crosses that question and the respondent's name off his or her list. The second student then follows the same procedure, asking his or her questions until receiving a yes. You can participate in this interview process, too. Set a time limit of about 10 minutes for this practice so students move along expeditiously, making contact with one another early in your class.

Two truths—one lie. A modified version of the popular party game, two truths—one lie can be adapted for peer interviews. In the traditional version, participants share three statements about themselves. Two statements are true, and one is false. Have students write their statements, allowing time for creativity and deception. Model an example for students by introducing yourself and sharing your two truths and one lie. Together as a class, students will try to identify which statement is the lie. The student that correctly guesses the lie proceeds next.

Guest Book Talks

Classroom guests who talk about their favorite books and other reading materials enlarge classroom communities to include schools, businesses, and neighborhoods. Having people from outside your classroom share their reading and writing inside your classroom provides students unmatched opportunities to access new ideas, perspectives, and role models. Talking about print with people from outside classrooms can position youth as literate academic individuals.

Scheduling a book talk with a guest speaker during the first few days of school signals your intention to create a widespread community of readers. You can be responsible for bringing the first few guests to class, although you might share this responsibility later on with students. You might schedule a regular time—perhaps 15 minutes every second Monday—to routinize this practice over the long haul. However, you may need to vary the periods when visitors come to your classes to accommodate busy schedules. It is best for students to experience guest book talks live, but making video recordings is a useful option.

Be creative in seeking out guests, and try to involve multiple and diverse groups of adults. Teachers, administrators, and school staff are nearby yet often underutilized (Morley, 1996). Older students, parents, and individuals from the business and local neighborhood communities are other possible guests. Have the visitor begin the book talk by sharing a favorite book or set of books with the class. For instance, David has witnessed ex-military personnel captivate entire classrooms with the exploits of Louis L'Amour, Zane Grey, and Tony Hillerman's characters that were read during some of the lengthy down times common in the service. Guests often explain how they first became acquainted with the particular books they bring to class, read aloud a stirring portion of each book, then describe what else they tend to read and why. When all goes well, students initiate spontaneous conversations, share related experiences and titles, and develop collective identities as readers and writers amid an extensive community.

After a visitor leaves, display a book talk record such as a photograph of the person and a list of the materials shared for reminders and motivation. You might create a family tree of past guests with branches representing their different specializations (e.g., academic disciplines for teachers, types of companies for business partners). You also might record the talks on audio or video for airing on school or community-access stations or for individual showings to other class periods.

Informing Internal Dialogues

Learners tend to deepen insights into their efforts when they engage in a verbal give and take, or dialogue, with others about those efforts (Palincsar & Herrenkohl, 2002). And readers who dialogue about their reading tend to become more aware and in control of their reading processes. In a well-regarded form of dialogue called "metacognitive conversations" (Schoenbach, Greenleaf, Cziko, & Hurwitz, 1999), teachers and students discuss topics such as the cognitive strategies they use when reading, the connections they make when encountering new ideas, and the complexities of different genres.

Unlike the external dialogue of typical metacognitive conversations, internal dialogue consists of what students say to themselves in the form of self-talk (Purkey, 2000). Such dialogue includes individuals' own original thoughts as well as those of persuasive others. Students orchestrate multiple voices and ideas during internal dialogues.

A productive use of internal dialogues involves youths' literate academic identities, and you might begin to inform these dialogues during the first days of school. To start, you might have youth brainstorm thoughts they have (or questions they ask themselves) when they don't see themselves reading or writing (Ortiz, 1996). These thoughts, called "shut-downs" or "avoidance talk," consist of items such as the following:

- Why should I read?
- Reading isn't for me.
- What else could I be doing?
- I'll skip reading for now and probably get back to it later.

Then have students brainstorm thoughts they have (or questions they ask) when they want to convince themselves to be readers and writers. These thoughts, called "open-ups" or "approach talk," might consist of the following:

- I can do this.
- Literacy is going to open doors for me, so I better get after it.
- Reading is for everyone.
- This is important.

Additionally, you might talk about strategies such as the following that are useful for beginning unwelcome tasks:

- Divide tasks into portions, and do one portion at a time.
- Make and stick to bargains with yourself (e.g., As soon as I finish this, I'll reward myself with a snack).

You also might have students generate common inspirational sayings and advice such as the following that get them going:

- Just do it.
- A journey of 1,000 miles begins with a single step.
- If not me, who? If not now, when?
- Work first, play later.

Display these strategies and affirmations and discuss them occasionally during the beginning of school. Ongoing discussions about how items such as these might contribute to internal dialogues can enable youth to direct their agency, their personal decision making, toward literate identities.

Identity Maps and Mini-Ethnographies

Students sometimes do not identify themselves as readers and writers in classrooms because they lack the fine points of acting like academic readers and writers (Rex, 2001). They lack particular academic discourses; they are unaware of the expectations established for success and the language customs that are sanctioned in particular classroom settings. For instance, some language arts teachers might expect students to engage in writing conferences as a sign of being a serious writer. Students who prefer a solitary approach or are unaware of the importance of writing conferences in this particular classroom then are at risk of being considered second-rate. Other language arts teachers might expect students to keep in mind multiple interpretations of deliberately ambiguous passages as a sign of being a serious reader. Students who do not realize this expectation and prefer puzzling through, then holding a single interpretation, are at risk of being considered inferior in this class. These students could benefit from deep insights into the social situations of their classrooms. They could profit from being fully informed of their teachers' subtle and often invisible expectations and preferred language customs.

Clarifying what is needed to succeed in particular classroom situations might begin by showing students how to examine any social situation (Skarin, n.d.). During the first days of school, you might present an identity map that depicts the different social situations people inhabit, such as family member, sports fan, church member, and gourmet cook. Then select one situation you regularly inhabit—perhaps family member—and explain the expectations held for you there and the special language customs you follow. Describe what your spouse, siblings, children, and parents anticipate from you, and role-play your face-to-face verbal interactions with them. Next, compare and contrast your actions and language as a sports fan, for example, with those as a church member. Then have students create their own identity maps and highlight selected expectations and language customs. For instance, if a student includes music, friends, and weekend employee on his or her map, have the student portray the actions and language of someone who would be the ideal musician, friend, and employee. Finally, have individuals compare and contrast the social expectations and language among these various situations.

Once your class members begin to recognize the expectations and language customs of social situations, focus attention on academics. What are the subtle and often invisible expectations and language customs of their classes? What does it take to succeed in their class with you as well as in their mathematics, science, social studies, and other classes? What would perfect students do in each situation? You might have students conduct mini-ethnographies in order to answer these questions. Have students conduct and compare interviews of you, their other teachers, and older successful students. Have students collect and compare course artifacts such as syllabi, reading materials, and completed assignments. Have students record and compare detailed observations of all classroom activities, concentrating on successful and unsuccessful interactions between students and their teachers.

Identity maps and mini-ethnographies help clarify social situations, enabling students to define what is needed to participate as members of particular communities. These strategies allow students to act and see themselves more fully as readers and writers in school.

Implications for Practice

Acknowledging adolescents' identities leads to instructional practices that invite students to view themselves as readers and writers. By using many, varied, and versatile practices, you allow students to position themselves in school communities while maintaining ownership in other outside-of-school communities. This pathway provides the groundwork for a literacy-rich learning environment that ultimately can lead to student achievement and academic success.

Questions for Reflection

1. Are you a reader? Have you always been a reader? Were you ever a struggling reader or limited in your areas of proficiency? What influenced change?

2. Reflect on your writing identity in the same manner. How has your literacy identity influenced your teaching?

Activities

1. Form small groups and explore this chapter's description of identity. What are additional examples of identities not presented in this

chapter? How does identity differ from related concepts such as resilience, engagement and motivation, interest, attitude, and self-efficacy? You might write a reflection on the concept of identity after exploring it in small groups.

2. Remain in your small groups and explore this chapter's conceptual base for developing identities. How important is the distinction between core and socially situated identities? How important is the distinction between collective and individual identities? How else can educators point social positioning and agency toward identity? How do this chapter's recommendations for the first few days of school compare with other recommendations for this time period?

3. Create your own internal dialogue about the various instructional practices presented in this chapter. Begin by brainstorming thoughts, statements, or questions about why the suggested activities will not work in your classroom. Next, brainstorm statements you would use to convince yourself that the suggestions may work for your students. Do the positive statements outweigh the negative statements? How can you use the positive statements as a skeleton plan for the launch of your next school year?

David W. Moore is a Professor of Education at Arizona State University, Phoenix, Arizona, USA, where he specializes in adolescent literacy. His vita shows a 25-year publication record that balances research reports, professional articles, book chapters, and books. He co-chaired the International Reading Association's Commission on Adolescent Literacy (2000–2004). Moore can be reached at david.moore@asu.edu. **Karen A. Onofrey** is an Assistant Professor of Education at Arizona State University, Phoenix, Arizona, USA. Her primary interests include the role of humor in middle school literacy and developing practical classroom strategies that promote literacy. She currently has more than seven publications in these areas. She can be contacted at karen.onofrey@cox.net.

REFERENCES

Anderson, L.H. (1999). *Speak*. New York: Farrar Straus, and Giroux.

Avi. (1991). *Nothing but the truth: A documentary novel*. New York: Orchard Books.

Danziger, P., & Martin, A.M. (1998). *P.S. Longer letter later*. New York: Scholastic Press.

Davies, B., & Harré, R. (1990). Positioning: The discursive production of selves. *Journal for the Theory of Social Behaviour, 20*(1), 43–63.

Fielding, A., Schoenbach, R., & Jordan, M. (Eds.). (2003). *Building academic literacy: Lessons from reading apprenticeship classrooms, grades 6–12*. San Francisco, CA: Jossey-Bass.

Gee, J.P. (2001). Identity as an analytic lens for research in education. In W.G. Secada (Ed.), *Review of research in education* (Vol. 25, pp. 99–125). Washington, DC: American Educational Research Association.

Gruwell, E. (1999). *The Freedom Writers diary: How a teacher and 150 teens used writing to change themselves and the world around them*. New York: Doubleday.

Haddix, M.P. (1996). *Don't you dare read this, Mrs. Dunphrey*. New York: Simon & Schuster.

Hahn, M.D. (1983). *Daphne's book*. New York: Clarion Books.

Hinton, S.E. (1988). *Taming the star runner*. New York: Delacorte Press.

Holland, D., Lachicotte, W., Jr., Skinner, D., & Cain, C. (1998). *Identity and agency in cultural worlds*. Cambridge, MA: Harvard University Press.

Hynds, S. (1997). *On the brink: Negotiating literature and life with adolescents*. New York: Teachers College Press.

Jackson, D.B. (2003). Education reform as if student agency mattered: Academic microcultures and student identity. *Phi Delta Kappan*, 84, 579–585.

Kohl, H.R. (1994). *"I won't learn from you": And other thoughts on creative maladjustment*. New York: The New Press.

Marzano, R.J., Marzano, J.S., & Pickering, D.J. (2003). *Classroom management that works: Research-based strategies for every teacher*. Alexandria, VA: Association for Supervision and Curriculum Development.

McCarthey, S.J., & Moje, E.B. (2002). Identity matters. *Reading Research Quarterly*, 37, 228–238.

McPhee, J. (1990). *Basin and range*. New York: Noonday Press.

Moje, E.B., & Dillon, D.R. (2006). Adolescent identities as mediated by science classroom discourse communities. In D.E. Alvermann, K.A. Hinchman, D.W. Moore, S.F. Phelps, & D.R. Waff (Eds.), *Reconceptualizing the literacies in adolescents' lives* (2nd ed., pp. 85–106). Mahwah, NJ: Erlbaum.

Moore, D.W., & Cunningham, J.W. (2006). Adolescent agency and literacy. In D.E. Alvermann, K.A. Hinchman, D.W. Moore, S.F. Phelps, & D.R. Waff (Eds.), *Reconceptualizing the literacies in adolescents' lives* (2nd ed., pp. 129–146). Mahwah, NJ: Erlbaum.

Moriarty, J. (2004). *The year of secret assignments*. New York: Arthur A. Levine Books.

Morley, S. (1996). Faculty book talks: Adults sharing books and enthusiasm for reading with students. *Journal of Adolescent & Adult Literacy*, 40, 130–132.

Ortiz, R.K. (1996). Awareness of inner dialogues can alter reading behaviors. *Journal of Adolescent & Adult Literacy*, 39(6), 494–495.

Palincsar, A.S., & Herrenkohl, L.R. (2002). Designing collaborative learning contexts. *Theory into Practice*, 41(1), 26–32.

Paulsen, G. (1993). *Nightjohn*. New York: Delacorte Press.

Pennac, D. (1994). The gift of reading. In D. Pennac, *Better than life* (pp. 121–207). Toronto: Coach House Press.

Purkey, W.W. (2000). *What students say to themselves: Internal dialogue and school success*. Thousand Oaks, CA: Corwin Press.

Rief, L. (1992). *Seeking diversity: Language arts with adolescents*. Portsmouth, NH: Heinemann.

Rex, L. (2001). The remaking of a high school reader. *Reading Research Quarterly, 36*, 288–314.

Schoenbach, R., Greenleaf, C., Cziko, C., & Hurwitz, L. (1999). *Reading for understanding: A guide to improving reading in middle and high school classrooms*. San Francisco, CA: Jossey-Bass.

Scieszka, J. (Ed.). (2005). *Guys write for guys read*. New York: Viking.

Simon, B. (2004). *Identity in modern society: A social psychological perspective*. Malden, MA: Blackwell.

Skarin, R. (n.d.). *Generation 1.5 in Hawaii: Gaining critical tools for reading the world*. Retrieved April 5, 2006, from the Center for Second Language Research website: http://www.hawaii.edu/cslr/community_college.htm

Spinelli, J. (1997). *The library card*. New York: Scholastic.

Trelease, J. (2000). Jim Trelease speaks on reading aloud to children. In N.D. Padak, T.V. Rasinski, J.K. Peck, B.W. Church, G. Fawcett, J.M. Hendershot, et al. (Eds.), *Distinguished educators on reading: Contributions that have shaped effective literacy instruction* (pp. 234–240). Newark, DE: International Reading Association. (Original work published in 1989)

Whitmore, K.F., & Goodman, Y.M. (1996). *Whole-language voices in teacher education*. York, ME: Stenhouse.

Wittlinger, E. (1999). *Hard love*. New York: Simon & Schuster Books for Young Readers.

CHAPTER 16

Helping Boys Find Entry Points to Lifelong Reading: Book Clubs and Other Strategies for Struggling Adolescent Males

William G. Brozo

HIGHLIGHTS

- Adolescent males continue to perform less well than their female peers on standardized assessments of reading and writing.
- Boys are capable of developing skillful and lifelong reading habits when teachers and other adults with whom they interact view them as a resource.
- Strategies are effective when they honor boys' outside-of-school interests and literacy practices and link those interests and practices to academic literacy and learning.

> And then the whining schoolboy
> With his satchel and shiny morning face
> Creeping like a snail
> Unwillingly to school.
>
> —William Shakespeare

For as long as there have been schools, there have been boys who would rather be absent from them. Male youth mentally absent from school and disengaged academically are, more often than not, disaffected and struggling readers (Brozo, 2002). And these are the

---

Adolescent Literacy Instruction: Policies and Promising Practices edited by Jill Lewis and Gary Moorman. © 2007 by the International Reading Association.

students contributing to one of the most persistent and ubiquitous achievement gaps found in America.

Numerous suggestions and initiatives have been tried to close the reading achievement gap, particularly for male youth in dire urban school settings, including such controversial approaches as same-sex classrooms (Logsdon, 2003) and massive male teacher recruitment (Canada, 1998). Although these initiatives have met with varying degrees of success, they suggest the lengths school personnel are willing to go to address the serious academic and literacy shortcomings of boys. In this chapter I assert that teachers and schools do not have to take extraordinary measures but can employ feasible and effective practices to entice boys to read and to keep reading. I begin with a brief overview of what we know about boys and reading achievement. I then develop the concept of entry points to reading and make the case for why teachers of youth should be doing all they can to help adolescent males find texts that capture their imagination and sustain their attention. The chapter concludes with the description of practical lessons gleaned from my experiences in a middle school boys book club, as well as other proven ways to increase male youths' engagement and ability by discovering and tapping their existing interests and competencies.

What We Know About Boys' Reading Achievement

That girls read better than boys is a notion that has become embedded in the popular consciousness. But it's not a myth. The facts are that boys in elementary through high school score significantly lower than girls on standardized measures of reading achievement (Grigg, Daane, Ying, & Campbell, 2003; Mullis, Martin, Gonzalez, & Kennedy, 2003; Organization for Economic Co-operation and Development, 2001) and writing achievement (Applebee, Langer, Mullis, & Jenkins, 1990), and boys dominate the rolls in corrective and remedial reading programs (Bae, Choy, Geddes, Sable, & Snyder, 2000). This same gender imbalance holds true in programs for the learning disabled, emotionally impaired, and speech and language impaired. Furthermore, boys are far more likely to be retained at grade level. These same patterns favoring girls over boys in verbal ability and academic achievement have been documented in Australia, Canada, the United Kingdom, and more than 40 countries around the globe (Mullis, Martin, Gonzalez, & Kennedy, 2003; Organization for Economic Co-operation and Development, 2001).

In spite of recent attention the gender-based reading achievement disparity has received in the media, it's not a new phenomenon. In 1961, Arthur Gates's landmark study of 13,000 U.S. elementary students popularized the idea of female reading superiority when he reported that girls significantly outscored boys on tests of comprehension and vocabulary. And at least 30 years earlier, evidence for boys far outnumbering girls in remedial reading classes had been accruing (Holbrook, 1988). It is perhaps this long, well-documented history of male underachievement that has helped contribute to an entrenched, popular perception and, indeed, an expectation that many boys simply will not become thoughtful, accomplished readers (Brozo, 2002).

Reversing perceptions of boys as weak readers and addressing the complex problems facing those who have turned off to reading or are striving to improve their reading abilities will challenge educators for years to come. Today, several prominent advocates (Brozo, 2002; Newkirk, 2002; Smith & Wilhelm, 2002) are urging teachers to take more seriously the literate behavior and attitudes of male students and to design special language schemes to honor their unique male imaginations. Teachers who see potential in their male students discover ways of teaching and reaching them that are personally meaningful, culturally responsive, and capitalize on the resources they bring to the classroom (Alloway, Freebody, Gilbert, & Muspratt, 2002).

Viewing boys as a resource in the classroom holds great promise for helping them overcome literacy and learning difficulties (Alvermann, 2003). Male youth care about many things and have passions, hobbies, aspirations, and experiences rife with opportunities for genuine curricular links (Brozo, 2002). Exploring these links and inviting boys to find connections between their lifeworlds and school-based literacy may be the key to helping them find entry points to lifelong reading while reducing achievement disparities with their female peers (Brozo, 2005a; Brozo & Schmelzer, 1997).

The Importance of Finding Entry Points to Reading for Boys

An entry point is the text or reading material that first captures one's imagination and propels one to seek and read more. For me it was the exhilaration of finding the novels of Stephen Meader, a writer of typical boy fare in the 1930s, 1940s, and 1950s, in a branch of the Detroit Public Library on a rainy summer morning at age 10. His tales of adventure kept me spellbound for hours and served admirably as my entry point to a pastime that would become my life's work.

These book encounters were identity-affirming and even life-altering experiences for me, as similar encounters with print have been and will always be for countless adults who found their own points of entry into literacy as children or youth. And this leads me to the crucible of my point in this chapter. Where we begin our literate journeys may have little resemblance to where we find ourselves at some future place on that journey. What is important is that all adults who interact with male youth need to support them in their search for a point of entry to reading.

Helping boys find entry points to reading means we will need to respect their discourses of desire (Emerson, 1983), specifically the texts they want to read and write, regardless of what those might be when we encounter them. This is critical because we simply don't know where boys' first exciting experiences with text will take them. What we do know, however, is that their chances for expanded consciousness and for widening life and career options are sharply diminished without that first step down a path of active literacy.

Respecting boys' discourses of desire is to avoid demeaning their lives by suppressing their reading choices because they fail to match our current ideal. In this connection, I strongly urge tolerance of students' discourses even though their desires for celebratory narratives of popular culture and stereotypical gender behavior may leave some educators uncomfortable. I think it's important to bear in mind that we all begin modestly down our own literate paths. So it's not where we begin, but what we develop along the way on our literate journeys that's important. The rewards of staying on that path of years of traditional print explorations are sophisticated and flexible linguistic abilities. Acquiring these abilities with language may only be possible if youth first become engaged with reading. And this engagement would only seem likely if they are sanctioned to begin their literate journeys with text that interests them, that captures their imaginations. Thus, it's important not to prejudge what boys ought to be reading, especially those who may be filled with disaffection toward books.

Addressing the needs of failing boys and reversing the trend of lower reading achievement for them will require creative programs and instruction that honor their discourses of desire (Tatum, 2005). One promising approach finding growing support among teachers and librarians is the establishment of student book clubs.

Forming Boys' Book Clubs as Contexts for Literacy Engagement

Book clubs and book discussion groups designed to increase reading engagement and time for male youth are occurring in middle schools, classrooms, and libraries around the country. Greater critical discourse about books, improvement in reading and writing skills of linguistically diverse learners, elevation of self-esteem, greater leadership and independence, and tolerance of diversity are just some of the important benefits of book club membership documented in the literature (Brozo, 2005b).

From my participation as an electronic member of a middle school book club for boys who had failed the reading portion of their state test, and based on conversations with several middle school teachers running clubs for striving male readers, here are three important lessons learned for ensuring their success.

Link book club selections to members' interests. The boys in these clubs should determine selection of reading material solely on the basis of what they like (Brozo, 2005b). The quickest way to undermine enthusiasm is to set up a book club context but use the same texts and skill instruction from the regular reading curriculum. The material really does matter and can make or break a successful book club experience. Students who are disaffected readers in part because of the kinds of books and other print material they're required to read in class will need free rein (Brozo, 2005b) on all matters related to what will be read in a book club context.

For example, in the boys book club I participated in, members indicated a strong interest in playing on the computer. Armed with this knowledge, their teacher identified various books that would match their strong interest in computers, finally introducing them to *ChaseR: A Novel in E-Mails* (Rosen, 2002), with which they had an enjoyable reading experience.

Allow book club members multiple modes of expression. Typically, middle school youth are allowed a limited range of response options based on what they read. Answering the teacher's or the anthology's questions is most common. To help reluctant male readers become more engaged with text, creative response formats should be made available to them. These might include reinterpretations with song lyrics, electronic presentations, art, and various real-world connections. For example, a young man in the club I was in completed a project on the book *Death Walk* (Morey, 1991) using computer animation to show the route the main character, Joel, takes from Seattle to Alaska and then his 100 mile trek to the nearest link to civilization, a cabin of a ham radio operator.

Make having fun with books a high priority in book clubs. When reading is difficult and unappealing for boys, one of the best antidotes is to immerse them in experiences with simply-told stories that are very funny (Scieszka, 2005). To make sure boys never grow too weary of the selections for the book club, even when they are related to their interests, make humorous books available throughout the year. For instance in the club where I participated, books by Jon Scieszka from his Time Warp Trio series reinvigorated interest and kept the boys laughing.

Six of the eight boys in the club passed the reading portion of the state achievement test in May of that year. Because book club was employed in lieu of the boys' regular reading curriculum, their teacher was convinced it made all the difference.

Bridging Boys' Competencies With Familiar Texts to Academic Literacy

Linking boys' out-of-school literacies with academic literacy is a practice that honors who they are in all their diversity and demonstrates the value we place on youths' lifeworlds beyond the classroom walls (Sturtevant et al., 2006). There is a growing realization of the importance of creating spaces in schools for striving and listless readers' everyday literacies so they can showcase and build on their strengths with the print and digital media they use on their own (O'Brien, 2003).

Martin's eighth-grade self-contained English class included eight boys and three girls. Flashcards and workbooks as the basis for word study were yielding nothing but complaints and despondency from the students. As he observed his students enter the classroom each day, Martin became inspired by an obvious way vocabulary and word families could be linked to their real-world interests and desires. Many had hip-hop music pulsing from their headsets, which led Nathan to consider how the lyrics from songs and raps his students were listening to could form the basis of a fun and meaningful experiences for learning word families.

After getting a few of the most popular titles of tunes from his students, he tracked down the lyrics on the Internet and found they possessed a variety of words that could be studied as families. With these words they created and studied a particular word family, then expanded on the words from the family to generate new words for their individual vocabulary notebooks. His students then used the word families as models for decoding other similar words in school texts and in their own writing.

For example, with the rapper Snoop Dogg's lyrics for "I Love to Give You Light," Nathan's class of mostly boys found numerous examples of words with /ck/ and /ch/ blends. These words were written into a t-chart in their vocabulary notebooks, as shown in Figure 16.1.

Nathan then had students work with a partner to think of new words with the /ch/ and /ck/ sounds and add them to the t-chart. When finished, he asked student pairs to write their own rap lyrics that would contain all or some of the new words they generated for the two word patterns. Renard read the rap he and Hugo wrote, while Hugo kept rhythm on his desktop. It went like this:

I put my socks in my backpack when I go to school.

I put my backpack in my locker or I look like a fool.

I get my socks from my backpack when I go to gym.

Where I catch a ball then I kick it to him.

Figure 16.1. Chart of /ch/ and /ck/ Words in "I Love to Give You Light"

ch	ck
choir	background
such	jackers
alchemist	glock
preach	block
chuuch	locked
teachin	black
watchin	
each	
preachin	
reach	
purchase	
Beach	
child	

Nathan's students never had such fun doing word study work as when they used song lyrics for analyzing related vocabulary. For his male students in particular, their enthusiasm translated into genuine learning. He noticed their ability to recognize many of the same words in other texts, and many of these students obtained higher end-of-year reading test scores in vocabulary and comprehension. By eliminating barriers to his students' competencies with outside-of-school texts and classroom practices, Nathan was able to increase engagement in learning and literacy abilities for his striving male readers.

Matching Boys With Reading Material Based on Outside-of-School Interests

Eighth grader Claude had a genuine passion for hockey, but none of his teachers seemed to take notice. One day, however, his fervor for the game was revealed to his history teacher, who found him standing outside the classroom before the bell talking animatedly with his mates about a picture in the daily tabloid of a referee who had been hit by a puck. The teacher had played hockey in his youth and passed on to Claude *The Leafs vs. the Canadiens* (Duplacey, 1996). Claude, an early teen who had never read an entire book, came to experience for the first time the unique pleasures of reading, and it seemed there was no turning back from there. "It's the first book I ever read all the way through," he told his teacher, and then he asked for other similar ones. For Claude, books about hockey served as his entry point to reading.

Although the history teacher just happened to learn about Claude's interest in hockey, teachers do not have to rely on chance encounters to discover students' outside-of-school interests. Using a strategy such as My Bag, teachers can learn a great deal about individual students' hobbies, dreams, and experiences, which provide important clues to finding reading material to match. Not unlike the shoebox autobiographies discussed in the Moore and Onofrey chapter in this book (see chapter 15), the My Bag strategy involves placing items in a bag that symbolize different aspects of one's life and then revealing them to classmates and the teacher. For example, Delfino, a young man I worked with in a university reading center, shared with me a photograph from his bag that showed him and some friends standing on the beach with their sailboards. After asking him some questions about his hobby, I learned that in spite of his intense attraction to windsurfing, he was not reading about it from books, magazines, or the Internet. He became very enthusiastic, however, when

I introduced him to Tim Winton's (1991) *Lockie Leonard, Human Torpedo*. Lockie became Delfino's entry point to literacy (Brozo, 2005a) when he confided "I still don't like to read much...but after Lockie Leonard, I like it more than I used to" (Brozo, 2002, p. 81).

Through a My Bag activity, a sixth-grade science teacher found out that Armondo, one of his weakest readers, developed a fascination about the U.S. space program after seeing the movie *Apollo 13*. Even though books on the topic were very limited in his school, the teacher found numerous interesting and easy-to-read passages and articles about rockets, space shuttles, and the space station on the Internet that he made available in an electronic folder for Armondo. The folder also contained links to photos, audio, and video clips. The young man discovered for perhaps the first time that he could enjoy reading in school about something that captured his imagination outside school.

For both Delfino and Armondo, discovering strengths and interests led to encounters with texts that heightened reading engagement. Increasing Delfino's print experiences translated into significant improvement on measures of reading comprehension at the end of his tutorial sessions in the reading center as compared to his pretutorial test scores. Armondo's teacher continued to make available to him high-interest material throughout the remainder of the school year, which resulted in a greater level of participation in class activities and a significant improvement in Armondo's course grade.

Using Community Mentors as Reading Buddies

A teacher at a local middle school received a state-funded grant to organize a mentoring program for the most seriously struggling readers. The program used high-achieving peers and community volunteers to read to and with the low-ability students. The primary goal of the program was to find ways to motivate struggling readers to read on a daily basis with a mentor and more often on their own. With an increase in time spent reading came the expectation that reading achievement test scores also would increase.

One mentoring pair included Rickey, a recently retired Naval pilot and instructor, and Marcus, a 13-year-old seventh grader with a reading achievement level of fourth grade and a special education label. Marcus had spent the previous year in a juvenile detention facility after a conviction for auto theft. During the current school year, his mother was working closely with teachers and counselors to find ways of keeping this tall, soft-spoken boy in school and improving his reading skills. Rickey was an ideal mentor for Marcus because gender-matched role models have the most positive effect on educational outcomes (Zirkel, 2002) and are sorely needed in the lives of many boys (Brozo, 2002).

Soon after they were introduced, Marcus recounted his experience in the juvenile justice system and expressed a great deal of confusion and curiosity over his legal rights. Armed with this knowledge, Rickey actively searched for reading materials and planned meaningful activities around the topic of juvenile crime, courts, and penal facilities. He correctly reasoned Marcus's inquisitiveness would motivate him to exert sustained effort to read about others with similar experiences to his own and explore related social policy and law in a critical way.

To build reading fluency, Marcus and Rickey read *The House That Crack Built* (Taylor & Dicks, 1992). A somber redux of the house that Jack built, this is a tale with pictures of the depths to which one can sink when trafficking in and addicted to drugs. Rickey read it aloud, while Marcus repeated the refrain "This is the house that crack built." Eventually, after repeated readings, Marcus was able to complete the entire book on his own.

The House That Crack Built instigated conversation about who and what are responsible for drug addiction and drug-related crimes, which led to another rewarding mentoring experience for Marcus and Rickey, reading the young adult novel *Monster* (Myers, 2001). Rickey found the novel in the middle school's library and realized shortly into it that virtually all of the issues of juvenile crime and justice were embodied in the experiences of the main character and narrator, Steve Harmon. Marcus was drawn in from the very first page.

As they read *Monster* together, Rickey and Marcus kept a journal of their reactions to critical questions that arose during conversation and discussion. For example, Rickey asked Marcus to compare and contrast how the U.S. legal system is portrayed in the novel with his own experiences. To do this, Marcus devised a split-page approach, putting direct quotes and brief descriptions in one column and what he remembered about his treatment in juvenile court and detention in the other. Another interesting activity they tried while reading *Monster* was to assume the identities of different figures in the courtroom and argue the scenes of the trial and details of the case from those points of view.

At the conclusion of *Monster*, Marcus felt so strongly about what he believed was the unfair treatment of minors in the criminal justice system that he urged Rickey to help him express his feelings in some way that might influence lawmakers. This led to further research, taking them online to find information on their state representatives' policy positions related to youth crime. Their search uncovered some interesting facts. Although both representatives had cosponsored a youth advocacy task force, they also had voted in favor of trying minors as adults. One had even supported legislation to make the death penalty an option for minors found guilty of capital murder. Rickey suggested Marcus compose an e-mail letter to make his case to their legislators. The composition process itself necessitated discussion and work on form, punctuation, and grammar, as well as finding statistics and quotes from the various articles and books they had accumulated during their exploration of the topic. Rickey observed a level of enthusiasm for this effort unlike any he had seen from Marcus before. And even though Marcus's sense of empowerment was diluted once he received a perfunctory reply from the representatives, stating that they appreciated his input and asking him to continue to remain engaged in the political process, he remained proud of himself for expressing his views.

The mentoring relationship was a confirmed success for Marcus. Not only did his attitudes toward reading improve but his test scores did as well, showing a grade-level increase of two years on the Nelson-Denny Reading Test. Although Marcus still lagged behind his seventh-grade peers, his progress in reading had buoyed his confidence and gave him the determination to continue to improve.

Humble First Steps on Literate Journeys: A Final Story About Entry Points

I got to know Daniel, a youth center volunteer in Corpus Christi, Texas, while doing research for my book, *To Be a Boy, To Be a Reader* (Brozo, 2002). I became intrigued by this 30-year-old Mexican American during my first visit to the center. It was a cool winter Saturday, with wind and occasional rain. The center had a TV, shelves of board games, and several portable tables. Daniel made certain there were plenty of paperback books on hand, as well. Although there was only one rickety bookcase, crammed with books, he stored others in cardboard boxes and plastic crates. "I lose 10 or so books a month," Daniel told me, "but I consider that to be a good problem.... It usually means kids are taking the books home and reading them. I buy them for almost nothing at garage sales and goodwill stores. The library has donated discard books to the center, too...so most of them are give-aways anyway. Some of the kids will ask me if they can have a book, and I always say it's okay."

Daniel proceeded to describe to me how he encourages but never forces the kids who come into the center to read. Part of what he hopes to accomplish is to connect boys who are trying to make good choices with others, younger and older, doing the same.

"We got a donation from a local bookstore," Daniel went on, "and I picked up this terrific book called *Trino's Choice*" (Gonzalez Bertrand, 1999). This young adult novel focuses on adolescent Latinos and blacks from poor neighborhoods in San Antonio, the author's hometown. Daniel, too, was born in San Antonio. He remembered having many of the same home and street troubles as those Trino experiences in the story, such as growing up in the absence of adult male guidance, living in poverty, constantly threatened by gangs, and dropping out of school.

When Daniel was 18 he enlisted in the army, and shortly after was sent to Saudi Arabia, where he saw action in the Gulf War. While there he met a fellow Mexican American from California who read all the time and was always giving Daniel books and magazines to read. Daniel told me he turned down most of the offers because he always thought of himself as a poor reader and read only what he absolutely had to for the army. His inchoate journey began by accepting motorcycle and low-rider magazines from his army buddy. Then, after some weeks of goading, he finally agreed to try reading a book, although he was sure he hadn't read one from cover to cover on his own until that time. This was no ordinary book, however, this was Rudolpho Anaya's (1972), *Bless Me, Ultima*. Daniel was transformed. This story of curanderismo (folk healing) and Mexican American folkways brought him back to his own childhood in San Antonio, where his grandmother from Monterrey came to live with them. The book helped him relive her strange customs of egg-sweeping and home altars, mal ojo (evil eye), and charismatic Catholicism. More critically, the book became Daniel's point of entry into literacy.

Talking about *Trino's Choice*, Daniel said, "It was easy for me to sell this book because I lived the life, and it was hard getting out. These kids around here, especially the teenagers, all have problems at home and at school. Most don't have dads living with them. They can barely pay the bills. They live in projects that are crowded, noisy, and not the best place for young kids to feel good about themselves."

"What's special about the story," Daniel explained, "is it's realistic but shows how a kid living in many ways just like these guys around here live can decide to stay out of trouble and make something of himself. I tell these kids that even if they feel they were born with bad luck they can give themselves a chance for something better...but they gotta know how to read if they ever want to get to college and get a good job."

While monitoring the center, Daniel spends as much of his time as feasible reading, because as he terms it, he is a "born-again" reader, and he wants the kids to see him enjoying books. That winter day I visited him he was reading Ignacio Garcia's (1990) scholarly though highly penetrable *United We Win: The Rise and Fall of la Raza Unida Party*.

Daniel's dedication to trying to improve the lives of youth from the "hood" is laudatory in itself, but what makes his story even more special is what we learn from his own literate journey. As an adult male and active reader, his attitudes of compassion and concern for young boys and girls have been shaped by and are bound up in his literate consciousness. Reading for Daniel has been what all of us believe it can be—an emancipatory journey of self-discovery and possibility. For Daniel, the journey began at the age of 20 with magazines about customized cars from the barrio. Ten years down the road we find a sophisticated literate sensibility at a distance so far from its point of entry that little similarity remains.

Daniel's story reminds us that finding entry points to literacy with engaging practices and texts is the highest goal when working with struggling and disaffected adolescent male readers. The interests and experiences uncovered in book clubs, during reading buddy relationships, through strategies such as My Bag, and even through careful day-to-day observations resulted in the selection of engaging texts and enactments of responsive literacy practices for boys. Once engaged by text, regardless of the particular material that initially captures their imaginations, boys are likely to become regular and lifelong readers.

Questions for Reflection

1. Have you been fortunate enough to help an adolescent boy find an entry point to reading? If so, how was this accomplished? What text served as his entry point?

2. How would you set up a boys' book club in your school? Who would you ask among your colleagues for support? Which boys would be invited to participate in the club?

3. Assuming adolescent boys you teach are in need of adult male role models who can demonstrate the personal and professional value of literacy, what strategies could you use to connect your students with these role models?

William G. Brozo is Professor of Literacy in the Graduate School of Education at George Mason University, Fairfax, Virginia, USA. He is the author of numerous articles on literacy development for children and young adults. His research focuses on the intersection of cultural, political, gender, and strategic variables in adolescent literacy. He can be reached at wbrozo@gmu.edu.

REFERENCES

Alloway, N., Freebody, P., Gilbert, P., & Muspratt, S. (2002). *Boys, literacy and schooling: Expanding the repertoires of practice.* Sydney, NSW, Australia: Department of Education, Science and Training.

Alvermann, D. (2003). *Seeing themselves as capable and engaged readers: Adolescents and re/mediated instruction.* Naperville, IL: Learning Point.

Anaya, R. (1972). *Bless me, Ultima.* New York: Warner Books.

Applebee, A., Langer, J., Mullis, I.V.S., & Jenkins, L.B. (1990). *The writing report card, 1984–1988.* Princeton, NJ: National Assessment of Educational Progress/Educational Testing Service.

Bae, Y., Choy, S., Geddes, C., Sable, J., & Snyder, T. (2000). *Trends in educational equity of girls and women* (NCES 2000-030). Washington, DC: National Center for Education Statistics.

Brozo, W.G. (2002). *To be a boy, to be a reader: Engaging teen and preteen boys in active literacy.* Newark, DE: International Reading Association.

Brozo, W.G. (2005a). Helping students find entry points to literacy. *Thinking Classroon/Peremena, 6,* 45–46.

Brozo, W.G. (2005b). It's okay to read, even if other kids don't: Learning about and from boys in a middle school book club. *The California Reader, 38,* 5–13.

Brozo, W.G., & Schmelzer, R.V. (1997). Wildmen, warriors, and lovers: Reaching boys through archetypal literature. *Journal of Adolescent & Adult Literacy, 41,* 4–11.

Canada, G. (1998). *Reaching up for manhood: Transforming the lives of boys in America.* Boston: Beacon Press.

Duplacey, J. (1996). *The Leafs vs. the Canadiens.* Toronto, ON: Kids Can Press.

Emerson, C. (1983). The outer word and inner speech: Bakhtin, Vygotsky, and the internalization of language. *Critical Inquiry, 10,* 245–264.

Garcia, I. (1990). *United we win: The rise and fall of la Raza Unida Party.* Tucson: University of Arizona Press.

Gates, A. (1961). Sex differences in reading ability. *The Elementary School Journal, 61,* 431–434.

Gonzales Bertrand, D. (1999). *Trino's choice.* Houston, TX: Piñata Books.

Grigg, W.S., Daane, M.C., Ying, J., & Campbell, J.R. (2003). *The nation's report card: Reading 2002, national assessment of educational progress.* Washington, DC: National Center for Education Statistics.

Holbrook, H.T. (1988). Sex differences in reading: Nature or nurture? *Journal of Reading, 31,* 574–576.

Logsdon, E.C. (2003). "No Child Left Behind" and the promotion of single-sex public education in primary and secondary schools: Shattering the glass ceilings perpetuated by coeducation. *Journal of Law & Education, 32,* 291–296.

Morey, W. (1991). *Death walk.* Hillsboro, OR: Blue Heron.

Mullis, I.V.S., Martin, M.O., Gonzalez, E.J., & Kennedy, A.M. (2003). *PIRLS 2001 international report: IEA's study of reading literacy achievement in primary schools in 35 countries.* Chestnut Hill, MA: Boston College.

Myers, W.D. (2001). *Monster.* New York: HarperCollins Children's Books.

Newkirk, T. (2002). *Misreading masculinity: Boys, literacy, and popular culture.* Portsmouth, NH: Heinemann.

O'Brien, D. (2003, March). Juxtaposing traditional and intermedial literacies to redefine the competence of struggling adolescents. *Reading Online, 6*(7). Retrieved October 13, 2006, from http://www.readingonline.org/newliteracies/lit_index.asp?HREF=obrien2

Organisation for Economic Co-operation and Development. (2001). *Knowledge and skills for life: First results from PISA 2000.* Paris: Author.

Rosen, M.J. (2002). *ChaseR: A novel in e-mails.* Cambridge, MA: Candlewick Press.

Scieszka, J. (2005). *Guys write for guys read.* New York: Viking.

Smith, M.W., & Wilhelm, J.D. (2002). *Reading don't fix no Chevys: Literacy in the lives of young men.* Portsmouth, NH: Heinemann.

Sturtevant, E., Boyd, F., Brozo, W., Hinchman, K., Moore, D., & Alvermann, D. (2006). *Principled practices for adolescent literacy: A framework for instruction and policy.* Mahwah, NJ: Erlbaum.

Tatum, A.W. (2005). *Teaching reading to black adolescent males: Closing the achievement gap.* Portland, ME: Stenhouse.

Taylor, C., & Dicks, J.T. (1992). *The house that crack built.* San Francisco: Chronicle.

Winton, T. (1991). *Lockie Leonard, human torpedo.* Boston: Little, Brown.

Zirkel, S. (2002). Is there a place for me? Role models and academic identity among white students and students of color. *Teachers College Record, 104,* 357–376.

CHAPTER 17

Literacy Education in Democratic Life: The Promise of Adolescent Literacy

Helen Harper and Thomas Bean

HIGHLIGHTS

- Although democracy is sometimes thought of as a detached subject, literacy and democracy are closely linked.
- It is easy to dismiss adolescents in social and democratic life.
- Adolescents want voice and will act on issues of significance to them; therefore, teachers need to pay more attention to adolescents' interests and activism.
- There are four different literacies reflecting the needs and emphases of democratic life: (1) basic literacy, (2) national literacy, (3) communicative literacy, and (4) critical literacy.

D
emocracy is a powerful and privileged concept in American society and indeed in many countries throughout the world. The establishment or restoration of democracy has provided sufficient, and indeed almost inarguable, reason to go to war, as evident in the recent and ongoing involvement of American, British, Australian, and other troops in Iraq and Afghanistan. Despite the powerful call to defend or establish democracy literally to the death, it is not an easy concept to name and consider, particularly as it applies to one's everyday life. Democracy is sometimes taught as if it is a detached subject to be

---

Adolescent Literacy Instruction: Policies and Promising Practices edited by Jill Lewis and Gary Moorman. © 2007 by the International Reading Association.

studied and forgotten. However, literacy and democracy are closely linked, with literacy practices the major vehicle for the communication and deliberation that democracy is built on. Thus, in this chapter we explore four literacy foundations for democratic practices and offer concrete teaching strategies teachers can apply in the classroom to integrate literacy and democracy in action.

As part of an institute held in 2006 at the Annual Conference of the International Reading Association (IRA) in Chicago, we asked teachers to take on this task by identifying moments in their lives as educators when they did or did not feel democracy in action. Initially there was some struggle to take on this question, in part because democracy proved difficult to define for various reasons, and perhaps for some because the task seemed distinctly uninteresting. But when pressed, the teachers generally wrote and spoke of moments when they had voice (or not) in the decisions affecting school and classroom curricular materials, practices, and policies. Some named union and staff meetings, study groups, and strategic planning committees as sites where democratic principles were overtly in play. Some indicated that principals, senior administrators, and government officials explicitly suppressed democratic decision making in their schools and districts by mandating policy and practice, particularly in the area of assessment.

When asked about how their students might respond to a similar question and to students' interest in democracy more generally, the teachers indicated that most students would want more voice in the decisions affecting their lives as students. The teachers suggested that with so many rules students often feel imposed upon and that too often they have no choice in the materials they read and the school and classroom rules they follow. Oddly enough, one lone teacher indicated that students want an authoritarian teacher. Despite speaking of their own need for voice and the desire of students to have voice in school decision making, several teachers described their own classrooms as dictatorships, with the teacher in control. We suspect this is a common notion in teacher discourse. When she taught high school, one of the authors remembers using the term "benevolent dictatorship" to describe her own classroom, which for her meant that the teacher had the final say in what occurred in the classroom, once students' opinions had been aired.

There were varied opinions about whether students cared about democratic life. Some teachers thought that students were definitely not interested, but in direct contrast, other teachers believed that students definitely were interested in democracy and current politics. Other teachers indicated that interest varied across students and that some students were just confused. One teacher wrote that many students were disengaged in democratic life unless it had something to say to them about issues of interest to them.

At the time of our institute this last comment seemed to be particularly insightful. Before, during, and after the conference, large numbers of students across the United States were actively participating in immigration protests and walkouts on the issue of immigration reform and undocumented workers. Initially organized by students using text messaging, demonstrations in Southern California alone garnered 40,000 middle and high school student participants (Crary, 2006). In conjunction with the nationwide Day Without Immigrants on May 1, 2006, nearly 72,000 students were absent in protest from the Los Angeles Unified School District (Planas, 2006). Such numbers suggest that many students are deeply committed to issues of social justice and wish to be and can be active in democratic life. Although the whole notion of thinking about democracy in the context of school life was largely unfamiliar ground for our participants and, we would argue, for many of us, evidently adolescents are or can be engaged in issues facing the country and the global community.

Certainly we also know that young Americans are willing to defend democratic life and serve their country through military service. Particularly after September 11, 2001, many young Americans signed up. Some have paid the ultimate price. As of September 23, 2006, 169 eighteen- and nineteen-year-old American soldiers have been killed in Iraq (http://www.fallenheroesmemorial.com).

It is also apparent that students have interests and commitments not only to extending democracy and defending their country, but also in a citizenship that extends beyond their own borders. A study of 194 secondary students in Japan and Alberta, Canada, found that over 90% agreed that in the 21st century it is more important to understand the nature of being an active and responsible member of the world community than being a member of a particular country (Blades & Richardson, 2006). If this study is any indication, then adolescents are indeed interested not only in national but also in global citizenship.

Still, it is easy to dismiss adolescents in social and democratic life. It is Henry Giroux's (2003) contention that democracy, particularly since September 11, has become even more fragile and that this fragile democracy devalues children and youth in the public sphere: "Increasingly, children seem to have no stranding in the public sphere as citizens, and thus are denied any sense of entitlement and agency" (p. xiv). Moreover, it has been more customary to align democratic citizenship with adults and thus to see adolescents as citizens-in-waiting rather than as citizens in and of themselves. However such a position is in violation of the United Nations Convention on the Rights of the Child (CRC) (see http://www.un.org), which recognizes all children and young people under the age of 18 years as citizens who have the right of participation (Banks et al., 2005; Verhellen, 2000). In addition, youth have the right, as do adults, to have their voices heard in decisions that affect their lives (Banks et al., 2005). Clearly from the participants' comments cited at the outset of this chapter, teachers and students evidently want more voice in the decisions that impact school practice and policy.

If adolescents, as a group, are emotionally and intellectually invested in global and national citizenship and in democratic life, if they do want and are entitled to voice, if they can and will act on issues of significance to them, and have a right to do so, it would seem important for those of us who work with them to pay attention to their interests and activism. The relevancy and significance of our lessons are at stake. Most importantly, as educators in the public system, we bear a heavy responsibility to provide democratic education in our classrooms, and literacy teaching practices can model democratic deliberation.

In the United States, democracy and public schooling have been aligned since the time of Thomas Jefferson. Jefferson argued that free, compulsory education was important in order to ensure that the nation had an electorate who could make informed, rational decisions and a voting public who could be trusted with matters of the state. Schools were expected to create these kinds of citizens. Notions of democracy and literacy have been expanded and modified—and many would claim buried under the pressure to improve tests scores—yet more than two centuries later public schools still find themselves charged with the task of creating democratic citizens (Michelli & Keiser, 2005).

As cited previously, the United Nations Convention on the Rights of the Child recognizes young people as citizens who have the right to an education that allows for the development of respect for human rights and fundamental freedoms (Article 29). These rights and freedoms, according to the Universal Declaration of Human Rights (see http://www.un.org), entail democratic principles of free elections, peaceful association and protest, freedom of speech, and fair hearings. American scholars James Banks, Cherry Banks, and their colleagues (2005) at the Center for Multicultural Education suggest in their text *Democracy and Diversity:*

Principles and Concepts for Educating Citizens in a Global Age that, "all students should be taught knowledge about democracy and democratic institutions and provided opportunities to have "authentic experience and engagement in democratic activities" (p. 13).

These scholarly and policy documents, among a host of other local and national mandates, require or encourage democratic lessons for all children and all youth. Clearly there are solid grounds for teachers to offer such lessons, providing for students opportunities to think about, articulate, and experience democratic principles in the classroom. In doing such work, we encourage teachers to work with and cite these documents in their discussions with students, parents, and administrators.

Democracy, Literacy, and Literacy Teachers

Of course it may be argued that it is the civics teachers or social studies teachers who bear the brunt of teaching citizenship, but we maintain that all teachers carry this responsibility, including and perhaps most particularly literacy teachers. As a form of collective life, democracy (1) demands that all voices be heard and respected; (2) requires active participation and critical deliberations; (3) seeks to expand equity, fairness, and compassion for all; and (4) is committed to ensuring and creating greater freedom, which entails choice and possibility. In short, democracy is a noisy way of life, demanding active participation and critical deliberation in ongoing efforts to establish and expand human dignity, rights, and freedoms. Communication is of critical importance to collective democratic life. It is in print and nonprint media that positions and issues are raised, forwarded, and debated. It is in language that democratic rights, freedoms, and ideals are articulated and constrained. Literacy is therefore necessary and directly connected to active, critical democratic participation.

Over the history of the United States and many other countries, democratic principles have been understood and articulated in varying ways or with varying emphasis. Each emphasis ultimately affects the kinds of literacy lessons expected. We have identified four different literacies, each reflecting a different need or emphasis in democratic life.

1. Basic literacy (to encode and decode print) to ensure the electorate is able to make rational, informed voting decisions. Basic literacy refers to the ability to read documents, including voting

flyers, and other instrumental print (e.g., a map to the polling place).

2. National literacy that ensures powerful identification with a standard narrative (some might add proficiency in the "national" language) in the reproduction of patriotic citizens who will name and defend the American way of life and its democratic values. Values such as individual freedom, freedom of speech, and so on underpin national literacy and affiliation with the nation state. Such an education ensures the development of citizens who can transcend individual, local, or regional affiliations, literacies, and languages.

3. Communicative literacy that is flexible and supports dialogue and inquiry across groups, ensuring understanding and empathy, and an acknowledgment or acceptance of social difference in order to name and secure the common good, solve problems, and to arrive at some degree of consensus. This form of literacy supports careful deliberation and compromise over stubborn inflexibility.

4. Critical literacy that seeks to produce, foster, and critique social thought and social difference from a perspective that views plurality and dissent as engines of growth, renewing and expanding democracy while providing choice or options in everyday life.

There is across these four forms (and possibly more) a tension between unity and diversity, between individuality and commonality, between freedom and restriction. The first form of literacy assumes that an effective democracy can be achieved by ensuring a basic, standardized, overarching literacy for all citizens. According to Thomas Jefferson, basic literacy—critical for the new republic—would ensure an electorate who could read and understand the arguments of a "natural aristocracy" who would be running the country. At a time when the commoners (albeit initially referring only to white, propertied males) were not entirely or immediately trusted, Jefferson argued that through public (common) schooling, an educated and literate electorate could be assured and thus trusted with decisions of importance to the country (Edelsky, 2004; Shannon, 2001).

The second form, national literacy, ensured that despite increasing immigration and an expanding population of divergent homegrown interests across the country, a basic American literacy would transcend difference and ensure a sense of unity and that the common good would prevail in the deliberations of the state. In effect, this literacy would ensure that Americans would literally and figuratively speak the same language in public life (Hirsch, 2006; Hirsch, Kett, & Trefil, 1987). For many citizens this form of literacy education requires a dual consciousness (that is, national and local), a degree of bilingualism, and biculturalism or multiculturalism. Moreover, because a singular national public literacy is privileged over all others in collective public life, the state is defined largely through a single literacy and single culture, which public schools are responsible for instilling.

The third form, a communicative literacy, acknowledges social difference and plurality in democratic life and seeks a literacy that allows us to speak to and hear others on their own terms. It is a literacy that emphasizes multiple perspectives, allowing for the personal and linguistic skills that make possible discussion, negotiation, deliberation, and consensus building across groups. Such literacy demands lessons that allow for the development of empathy and understanding, as well as powerful and flexible communication skills. This is the form of literacy promoted by Louise Rosenblatt (1938/1968) and John Dewey (1916).

Critical literacy, the last form, encourages both the performance and critique of social difference. It is a literacy education that focuses on the abilities of citizens to formulate and express their particular perspectives, and to think critically about the various readings of the world, their own included, within a frame that values freedom, equity, and democratic life. Critical literacy calls for learning to deconstruct all forms of texts through questioning and discussion (Cherland & Harper, 2007; Stevens & Bean, 2007). Such literacy lessons examine the limits of language and thought in how we individually and collectively name the self, the other, and the world. For example, such lessons would include questions about the source, perspectives, and values available and missing from various real or fictive accounts of society. Knowing the limits of thought and language suggest the possibility of alternative meanings, thoughts, and actions, and with alternatives there is the possibility of choice. And ultimately choice is key to the expansion of freedom and opportunities. This is the literacy suggested in the work of Paulo Freire (1998) and Henry Giroux (2003), and the early scholarship of Peter McLaren (1995).

Considering the differences among these four relationships, it is no wonder that Patrick Shannon (2001) suggested that literacy teachers experience the connections between democracy and literacy as "hostile contradictions rather than working dialectics" (p. 10). Fortunately, we believe there is hope. In the remainder of this chapter we explore what research in the field of adolescent literacy offers to literacy teachers in their efforts to support the renewal of democratic life in their schools and communities. It is our contention that the field of adolescent literacies is deeply implicated in the project of democracy as the central vehicle for the communication and deliberation of ideas, policies, and social practices. Research and scholarship in adolescent literacy reveal a complex and dynamic picture of adolescent communicative life that educators can use to formulate and intensify classroom literacy lessons that work with and beyond the four relationships of democracy and literacy that teachers are contending with in school curricula. In particular, we believe that the research and scholarship occurring in the field of adolescent literacy support and extend the literacy-democracy relationship of communicative and critical literacy. We will discuss this support and then describe and discuss examples of pedagogical practice that would seem to articulate the intersection of democracy and adolescent literacy in such promising ways.

Adolescent Literacy and Democracy

The field of adolescent literacy in the United States has only recently been established. Of course, education researchers and teachers have always been interested in the reading practices of youth, but concentrated and distinct study can be said to have started formally with the publication of the IRA position statement from the Commission on Adolescent Literacy published in 1999 (Moore, Bean, Birdyshaw, & Rycik, 1999; Sturtevant et al., 2006). Researchers in this field are concerned with the number of adolescents who have not yet attained basic literacy, with minority youth and their literacies, with the new and emerging techno-literacy practices of youth, and with the growing genre of contemporary young adult literature.

Over the last decade, largely ethnographic research on the literacy practices of adolescents has revealed many unexpected results including the following:

- The multiple and changing texts and textual practices, in particular the new and digitally mediated literacies that are now constituting the out-of-school lives of many teens (albeit often Western and affluent youth).
- The difference and plurality among adolescents as a group. There are many voices of youth, and it is evident that race, social class,

ethnicity, gender, and language infuse the category of youth in dynamic and changing ways.

- The multiple and fluid local and potentially global affiliations and identifications of individual adolescents, largely as a result of new technologies and the ubiquitous world of pop culture.
- Youths' concerns about local and global issues and their abilities to critique the policies and issues that impact their lives.

Compared to previous generations, adolescents as a group are showing greater complexity, intensity, and diversity in their literacy practices. Despite efforts to narrow the scope of literacy performance with a singular notion of literacy through the use of standardized testing, adolescents' own out-of-school literacies are diverse and complex (O'Brien, 2006). Their literacy education needs to reflect that diversity and complexity; together with a democracy that also embraces the diversity and complexity of their lives in the articulation of its principles. We consider efforts of adults to narrow school literacy education as the effects of fear, most particularly the fear that society, democracy, and adolescents themselves are in jeopardy from plurality, difference, and the increasing complexity of the new literacies and of 21st century life more generally. Whatever the reason, educators and researchers need to seize rather than fear the possibilities and, in our estimation, ask the question: How do we utilize the new literacies of youth in ways that intensify democratic life in their times and in ours?

Promising Practices

Creating Voice and Communicating Across Difference

The wider and potentially more diverse audiences possible in the digital world of teens can be used to heighten literate democratic citizenship. The Japan-Alberta Science/Social Studies Project for Educational Reform (JASPER) demonstrates how students can be keen to expand their social and school-based networks to include other students in other countries (Blades & Richardson, 2006). JASPER was designed to bring together students, teachers, and academics from Shizuoka Prefecture in Japan and in Alberta, Canada, to investigate contemporary issues related to global citizenship.

Students conversed on e-mail about world issues and world citizenship, particularly related to science as a double-edged sword of change. They discussed the advances science has afforded humanity but also critiqued its downside—namely the degradation of our environment, particularly global warming (Blades & Richardson, 2006). Students also felt that talking with other adolescents was not enough. They also sought action aimed at ameliorating global problems. Blades and Richardson (2006) noted,

> The sophistication of student comments about actually addressing world issues reminded us that developing a global imaginary [or vision] must include the voices of this generation. These voices, when invited to participate in public discourse on the common good, interrupt received or preexisting notions of global citizenship. (p. 120)

The opportunities afforded by the new communication technologies to engage across geographical, social, and cultural boundaries create a need to develop a literacy that encompasses the knowledge and skills to communicate across difference. This entails the capacity to communicate meaning (and potentially translate) across context and language ability and requires the extensive development of English language competencies. It intensifies the importance of multilingualism or at least the knowledge of how other languages work (Young & Hadaway, 2006). It also requires linguistic and related cultural protocols and conventions in cyberspace and elsewhere.

Content is also important. Although there may be many topics of common interest to youth, a worldwide audience as suggested by the JASPER collaboration would be seen to provide a forum to discuss and act on global issues of interest to youth. Pedagogical attention to developing literacy skills, basic and beyond; to enhancing global, cultural, and linguistic knowledge; and to recognizing the limits of one's immediate context and perspective, can be embedded in lessons with real-life engagement with worldwide audiences. These are audiences that many adolescents are already connected to or would like to be. Such knowledge and skills and real-life engagements can well serve national and democratic practices.

For adolescents who are not particularly or immediately motivated to engage in international or national issues or events, nor interested in communicating with a global audience, there are increasing numbers of young adult novels and other literary forms that may help to motivate students, even struggling readers, to think about social and political issues of importance to them (Bean & Harper, 2006; Harper & Bean, 2006). For example, Graham Salisbury's (2005) award-winning novel *Eyes of the Emperor*, offers an insider's view of the other (in this case, Japanese American soldiers). Protagonist Eddy Okubo was a Japanese American soldier in WWII shipped off to isolated Cat Island in Mississippi to serve as dog bait in training K-9s so Japanese soldiers could be detected. Through a series of critical literacy questions, students in U.S. history can examine differential treatment and social difference in light of democratic principles of equality and freedom. For example:

- How is Eddy Okubo like or not like U.S. Mexican American soldiers serving in Iraq when their families are targeted for deportation?
- In what ways is democracy depicted in the novel and in news articles about Hispanics in uniform?

The JASPER Project and the young adult literature studies suggest that providing opportunities for students to engage global and national issues in text and the real-life global audience of cyberspace may support and indeed intensify the development of a more powerful democratic communication. However, besides stronger communication and cultural/linguistic knowledge, critical literacy is also necessary for expanding freedom and democracy.

Creating Critical Literacy and Agency

In order to develop critical, astute citizens in a global community, Banks et al. (2005) argue that students must be "provided opportunities to practice democracy in schools" (p. 13). This is a difficult but important task to undertake, despite the fact that schools are not often in and of themselves democratic structures for students or teachers. Nevertheless, within the range of possible forms of participation and citizenship actions, schools can be sites of democracy.

Westheimer and Kahne (2004) distinguish three forms of citizenship that vary in the degree to which they help ameliorate society's ills and injustices. Many middle and secondary schools seek to participate in the first two forms of citizenship and democracy.

1. The personally responsible citizen takes individual action to contribute to society. For example, contributing cans of food to a food drive involves at least some effort at the individual level.

2. The participatory citizen goes a step beyond the personally responsible citizen. For example, organizing a food drive entails greater effort and commitment than simply bringing cans of food to a pre-established food drive.

3. The justice-oriented citizen goes beyond the first two levels, seeking systemic change in the conditions that produce hunger.

Each of these forms of citizenship is important. Westheimer and Kahne (2004) recommend that teachers investigate school curriculum with an eye toward the degree to which programs support civic participation aimed at critical analysis and social change. Issues surrounding immigration, war and peace, global warming, nuclear arms, and a host of other problems call for careful reasoning, deliberation, and critical literacy. We offer two strategies, structured academic controversy (Parker, 2003) and resident critic (Stevens & Bean, 2007), aimed at developing adolescents' skills in reading about, discussing, and acting on issues of social justice.

Structured academic controversy. Walter Parker (2003) is a well-known scholar in social studies and the teaching of democracy. In his years of experience working with adolescents, he has developed a step-by-step process for moving students into deliberation and decision making on difficult topics. The goal of structured academic controversy is to develop learners who can listen actively and be comfortable with difference, as well as think critically. The steps involved in structured academic controversy are as follows:

1. Students in groups of four read background material (e.g., immigration policy reform).

2. Each group breaks into two pairs and each pair is assigned a different position on the issue along with primary and secondary sources to consider.

3. Each pair plans and gives a presentation on its position and arguments.

4. The pairs then reverse positions and present again.

5. The pairs dissolve into a group of four to form one deliberative body.

6. The pairs are asked to drop the positions to which they were assigned and forge consensus on the issue or clarify the nature of the disagreement.

It is important to note the high profile of literacy in this process. Policy documents and background material must be read and critiqued before deliberation can occur. Thus, basic literacy, national literacy, communicative literacy, and critical literacy processes discussed earlier in the chapter all play important roles in structured academic controversy.

We suggest reading Walter Parker's (2003) book *Teaching Democracy* to gain a complete understanding of this process and others aimed at developing astute, critical citizens. In many cases, adolescents are already engaged in critical deliberation on the Internet or in their working lives (Bean, 2006). However, learning to listen to arguments that may run counter to one's hard-held beliefs is crucial for informed, collective democratic action. Toward that end, we offer one other critical literacy strategy, resident critic.

Resident critic. Resident critic is designed to engage students in an examination of how the media treats an issue or topic such as immigration, adolescence, family life, war, politics, or any number of other topics (Stevens & Bean, 2007). In addition to media text, resident critic can be adapted for more conventional print texts, film, blogs, and so on. Indeed, there is some evidence that bloggers are likely to include adolescents who create video clips and other multimedia designed to influence voting behavior (Cohen, 2006). For example, at a bloggers' convention, 15-year-old Ava Lowery created a homegrown video aimed at dishonesty in politics (YouTube.com). Thus, "the breakout commercial in the next presidential cycle could be one produced on a teenager's computer and e-mailed from friend to friend" (Cohen, 2006, p. 2).

The steps involved in resident critic are as follows:

1. Create a series of questions or an observation survey provoking a critical stance.

2. Ask students to provide written responses to the question or observation survey and be able to defend their responses in a classroom discussion.

3. Engage students in a follow-up discussion and debriefing, giving them an opportunity to raise additional questions.

Figure 17.1. Resident Critic Guide

1. Describe the similarities and differences you noted in the blog site discussion of immigration reform and the news account.
2. What political positions are represented in the two accounts?
3. How are immigrants portrayed in the two accounts?
4. In your view, which text accurately represents the issues?
5. If you were going to rewrite either of these texts, what would you change?

For example, the Resident Critic Guide in Figure 17.1 was designed to compare and contrast two articles on the issue of immigration reform, one published on an open-forum Internet blog site, and the other published in a small-town newspaper.

The two strategies introduced, structured academic controversy (Parker, 2003) and resident critic (Stevens & Bean, 2007), entail slowing down the pace of curriculum delivery to read, analyze, discuss, and deliberate collectively. If we are truly to develop citizens capable of moving beyond the confines of narrow literacy assessments into the realm of active, democratic citizenship, then this form of knowledge is absolutely essential. Moreover, it is likely to connect with democratic action that adolescents are already engaged in, ranging from organizing immigration rallies via text messaging on cell phones to participating in global Internet blogging communities with multiple participants. Simply put, while our literacy curriculum may be centered on issues of basic literacy, there is a clear need to prepare students for more expanded forms of literacy, including international participation and critical literacy as a foundation for democratic citizenship.

Other possibilities. We asked participants at the end of our session on democracy and literacy at the IRA Institute described at the outset of this chapter about the potential places or spaces in literacy education where democratic sensibilities might be infused or heightened. They provided many ideas. In general, participants indicated that more student choice (particularly choice of literary texts) and more diverse perspectives needed to be infused into the curriculum. With enthusiasm, some indicated the possibilities of extending the perspectives offered on topics and readings in class; the importance of reader-response, literature circles, and inquiry methodology; and the possibilities of wider student publication, possibly on the Internet, and in student newspapers. Others suggested organizing curriculum by thematic units on democratic or social-justice issues rather by genre units, using appropriate young-adult novels, providing opportunities for students to work on social-justice projects and initiatives (e.g., letter writing), and in general for teachers and students to make greater connections between their school work and global or national events.

A few participants reiterated the point that teachers first need to experience democratic principles in their working lives as teachers before they can articulate such practices and principles in their own classrooms for their own students.

Sharing Experiences Joining Literacy and Democracy

The studies and suggestions discussed here provide tantalizing possibilities for teachers and their students to consider, to modify, and to extend in their own context. Certainly there are many other pedagogical strategies possible that can engage the literacies and lives of 21st century youth that enhance democratic sensibilities. The authors of this chapter would like to hear about any effort, small or wide-reaching, successful or not, by literacy educators who take this work further (helen.harper@unlv.edu and beant1@unlv.nevada.edu). And, considering the comments of some of our participants, we are also interested in the efforts of teachers to find their own voices, agency, and democratic life in their work experiences through literacy projects, broadly defined. We will welcome your responses and applaud any effort that speaks to new modes of and possibly new energies for the renewal of democratic life in our schools.

Questions for Reflection

1. How are we utilizing the new literacies of youth in ways that intensify democratic life in their experiences, in these times?

2. What are the spaces, places, or moments in our curriculum that exist now or might be created for developing a literacy that embraces a more powerful and expanded sense of democratic life?

3. How can and how are teachers, individually and collectively, intensifying democratic principles in their own working lives?

Helen Harper is Professor of English Education and Cultural Studies in the College of Education, University of Nevada, Las Vegas, Nevada, USA. She taught secondary English and language arts in small, rural communities in northern and central Alberta, Canada, for a number of years. Throughout her school and academic career, her work has focused on the politics of literacy and literary education. She may be reached at helen.harper@unlv.edu. **Thomas Bean** is Professor of Literacy/Reading in the College of Education, University of Nevada, Las Vegas, Nevada, USA. Considered a leading scholar in the area of content literacy, with more than 30 years of experience, he has published extensively and has worked with teachers and school districts in Hawaii, California, Illinois, Nevada, Oregon, South Dakota, and Australia. He may be contacted at bean1@unlv.nevada.edu.

REFERENCES

Banks, J.A., Banks, C.A.M., Cortes, C.E., Hahn, C.L., Merryfield, M.M., Moodley, K.A., et al. (2005). *Democracy and diversity: Principles and concepts for educating citizens in a global age.* Seattle: WA: Center for Multicultural Education, University of Washington. Available: http://depts.washington.edu/centerme/home.htm

Bean, T.W. (2006). A scholar's response. In E.G. Sturtevant, F.B. Boyd, W.G. Brozo, K.A. Hinchman, D.W. Moore, & D.E. Alvermann (Eds.), *Principled practices for adolescent literacy: A framework for instruction and policy* (pp. 138–141). Mahwah, NJ: Erlbaum.

Bean, T., & Harper, H. (2006). Exploring notions of freedom in and through young adult literature. *Journal of Adolescent and Adult Literacy, 50*(2), 96–104.

Blades, D.W., & Richardson, G.H. (2006). Restarting the interrupted discourse of the public good: Global citizenship education as moral imperative. In G.H. Richardson & D.W. Blades (Eds.), *Troubling the canon of citizenship education* (pp. 115–123). New York: Peter Lang.

Cherland, M.R., & Harper, H.J. (2007). *Advocacy research in literacy education: Seeking higher ground.* Mahwah, NJ: Erlbaum.

Cohen, A. (2006, June 21). Bloggers a growing force in politics. *Las Vegas Sun*, p. 2.

Crary, D. (2006, May 4). Young drawn to immigrant rights rallies: Hispanic students embrace activism. *Las Vegas Review Journal*, pp. 7A, 13A.

Dewey, J. (1916). *Democracy and education: An introduction to the philosophy of education.* New York: MacMillan.

Edelsky, C. (2004). Democracy in the balance. *Language Arts, 82*(1), 8.

Freire, P. (1998). *Pedagogy of freedom: Ethics, democracy, and civic courage.* Lanham, MD: Rowman & Littlefield.

Giroux, H. (2003). *The abandoned generation: Democracy beyond the culture of fear.* New York: Palgrave-MacMillan.

Harper, H., & Bean, T. (2006). Fallen angels: Finding adolescents and adolescent literacy(ies) in a renewed project of democratic citizenship. In D. Alvermann, K. Hinchman, D. Moore, S. Phelps, & D. Waff (Eds.), *Reconceptualizing the literacies in adolescents' lives* (2nd ed., pp. 147–160). Mahwah, NJ: Erlbaum.

Hirsch, E.D. (2006). *The knowledge deficit: Closing the shocking education gap for American children*. Boston: Houghton Mifflin.

Hirsch, E.D., Kett, J.F., & Trefil, J.S. (1987). *Cultural literacy: What every American needs to know*. Boston: Houghton Mifflin.

McLaren, P. (1995). *Critical pedagogy and predatory culture: Oppositional politics in a postmodern era*. New York: Routledge.

Michelli, N.M., & Keiser, D.L. (2005). *Teacher education for democracy and social justice*. New York: Routledge.

Moore, D.W., Bean, T.W., Birdyshaw, D., & Rycik, J.A. (1999). *Adolescent literacy: A position statement for the Commission on Adolescent Literacy of the International Reading Association*. Newark, DE: International Reading Association.

O'Brien, D. (2006) "Struggling" adolescents' engagement in multimediating: Countering the institutional construction of incompetence. In D.E. Alvermann, K.A. Hinchman, D.W. Moore, S.F. Phelps, & D.R. Waff (Eds.), *Reconceptualizing the literacies in adolescents' lives* (2nd ed., pp. 29–46). Mahwah, NJ: Erlbaum.

Parker, W.C. (2003). *Teaching democracy: Unity and diversity in public life*. New York: Teachers College Press.

Planas, A. (2006, April 18). Immigration gets personal for students: Stories of separation, legal hurdles. *Las Vegas Review Journal*, pp. 4B–5B.

Rosenblatt, L.M. (1968). *Literature as exploration*. New York: Modern Language Association of America. (Original work published in 1938)

Salisbury, G. (2005). *Eyes of the emperor*. New York: Laurel-Leaf Books.

Shannon, P. (2001). *Becoming political, too: New readings and writings on the politics of literacy education*. Portsmouth, NH: Heinemann.

Stevens, L.P., & Bean, T.W. (2007). *Critical literacy: Context, research, and practice in the K–12 classroom*. Thousand Oaks, CA: Sage.

Sturtevant, E.G., Boyd, F.B., Brozo, W.G., Hinchman, K.A., Moore, D.W., & Alvermann, D.E. (Eds.). (2006). *Principled practices for adolescent literacy: A framework for instruction and policy*. Mahwah, NJ: Erlbaum.

Verhellen, E. (2000). Children's rights and education. In A. Osler (Ed.), *Citizenship and democracy in schools: Diversity, identity, equality* (pp. 33–43). Stoke, England: Trentham.

Westheimer, J., & Kahne, J. (2004). What kind of citizen? The politics of educating for democracy. *American Educational Research Journal, 41*, 237–270.

Young, T.A., & Hadaway, N.L. (Eds.). (2006). *Supporting the literacy development of English learners: Increasing success in all classrooms*. Newark, DE: International Reading Association.

CHAPTER 18

Adolescent Literacy: Australian Approaches to Teaching and Learning

Nea Stewart-Dore

HIGHLIGHTS

- Literacy embraces understandings about processes and practices that vary according to context and to individuals' interpretations of its uses and applications.

- In Australia, critical literacy has been the focus of much press criticism and professional defense; teachers and professional associations defend it as providing opportunities to pose essential questions about democracy and civil life.

- To succeed academically, students must be able to coordinate several multiliteracies simultaneously.

- Models of multiliteracies can help teachers select and implement strategies that engage students' learning and develop their literacy competencies across the curriculum.

- Boys' disparate in- and out-of-school literacies could be integrated in classrooms in order to improve boys' literacy performances.

- Teachers of adolescents in the United States and Australia face similar challenges and obstacles. They also enjoy the same privilege of being in a position to empower students through the literacies that adolescents must master if they are to realize satisfying public and personal lives.

Adolescent Literacy Instruction: Policies and Promising Practices edited by Jill Lewis and Gary Moorman. © 2007 by the International Reading Association.

Authors of prior chapters in Part II have defined adolescent literacy in various ways. Lewis, for example, employs a functional definition in locating literacy as a situated practice within Discourses (see chapter 9), and Moore and Onofrey (see chapter 15) contextualize literacy practice in academic communities. Further, Buehl (see chapter 11) argues the need to integrate literacy within academic disciplines, thereby supporting the views of Lewis and Moore and Onofrey. On the other hand, Moorman and Horton (see chapter 14) deploy metaphor to establish literacy as technology and, hence, as a tool requiring sociocultural knowledge in order to use it. Likewise, Anders and Spitler (see chapter 10) regard literacy as a tool but from the perspective of conversing across space and time. Pursuing concepts of civics and democracy, Harper and Bean (see chapter 17) recognize the need to develop not only basic literacy to participate fully in sociopolitical life, but also a critical literacy and agency in multiple ways. Meanwhile, Pilgreen (see chapter 13) adopts the stance that literacy equates to English-language learners' basic comprehension, with emphasis on written (academic) language proficiency. As evidenced, then, in all its myriad complexities, literacy is very much a contested construct in out-of-school and in-school sites at all levels of formal and informal education. Indeed, the ways in which literacy is qualified and represented in different forums attest to its variety and diverse characteristics.

In the current context, we are concerned primarily with the broad concept of adolescent literacy, which I define as the literacy skills, abilities, practices, and knowledge of adolescents, including English-language learners, in a range of social contexts. Such skills, abilities, practices, and knowledge are juxtaposed most commonly in Western cultures with those of adult literacy, child literacy, family literacy, and intergenerational literacy. There are also expressions that define literacy according to certain behaviors when practicing "it": performing, doing, thinking, speaking, listening, writing, viewing, visualizing, demonstrating, and interacting socially in diverse contexts. Further, there is a tendency to name various domains of literacy and that tendency categorizes their context of occurrence, yielding a vast array of labels such as cultural literacy, scientific literacy, computer literacy, financial literacy, visual literacy, graphic literacy, and so on. Such terms recognize the increasing importance of text forms, purposes, and practices and beg the question as to the nature of multiliteracies, their functions, modes and channels of representation and communication, and the way multimodal texts influence the literate practices necessary to be critically active citizens. As can be seen, the term literacy embraces understandings about processes and practices that vary not only according to context, but also according to individuals' interpretations of its uses and applications.

Multiliteracies: An Umbrella Term

In Australia over the past decade or so, three descriptors of literacy have entered the educational lexicon, namely, in chronological order: critical literacy (Freebody & Luke, 1990), multiliteracies (New London Group, 1996), and curriculum literacies (Wyatt-Smith & Cumming, 1999). It is the term multiliteracies that becomes a useful, overarching one because it embraces critical and curriculum (or academic) literacies. In their book published recently by the International Reading Association, Australian authors Anstey and Bull (2006) draw on a range of conceptions to identify the characteristics of a multiliterate person as one who "can interpret, use, and produce electronic, live, and paper texts that employ linguistic, visual, auditory, gestural, and spatial semiotic systems for social, cultural, political, civic, and economic purpose in socially and culturally diverse contexts" (p. 41). Further, literacies are constructed by sociocultural experiences and expectations. As Gee (2000) suggests,

> A Discourse-based, situated, and sociocultural view of literacy demands that we see reading (and writing and speaking) as not one thing, but many: many different socioculturally situated reading (writing, speaking) practices. It demands that we see meaning in the world and in texts as situated in learners' experiences—experiences which, if they are to be useful, must give rise to midlevel situated meanings through which learners can recognize and act on the world in specific ways. (p. 6)

The notion of situated literacy practices (see chapter 9) gives rise to generalized definitions such as that adopted in 2000 by the Department of Education in Queensland, an Australian state:

> Literacy [or multiliteracy] is the flexible and sustainable mastery of a repertoire of practices with the texts of traditional and new communications technologies via spoken language, print, and multimedia. (Queensland Department of Education, 2000, p. 9)

Critical Literacies

Lankshear (1997) suggests that there are three ways that critical literacy becomes part of literacy and literacy practices. A critical literacy might involve any or all of the following:

1. Knowing literacy in general, or particular literacies, critically; that is having a critical perspective on *literacy* or *literacies per se*.
2. Having a critical literacy perspective on particular *texts*.
3. Having a critical perspective on—i.e., being able to make "critical readings" of—wider *social practices, arrangements, relations, allocations, procedures*, etc., which are mediated by, made possible, and partially sustained through reading, writing, viewing, transmitting, etc., texts. (p. 44, italics in original)

Although definitions of critical literacy vary, generally they make some reference to power relations among textual participants (author, readers, and subject of the textual content), and to ways of interrogating the ideologies of texts.

In their four roles and resources model, Freebody and Luke (1990) and Luke and Freebody (1999a, 1999b) hypothesize that when reading, the critically literate person is simultaneously a code breaker, a text participant, a text user, and a text analyst. As code breakers, readers identify and use the code in which a text is composed; it may be alphabetic in the case of written English, nonlinear as in electronic texts, or symbolic as in graphic texts. They further note or take account of the text's grammatical structure and how the text is organized structurally according to certain conventions for sequencing and otherwise organizing and linking ideas.

In the role of text participants, readers draw on background knowledge, understandings about genres, visual information if provided in illustrative material, and syntactic and semantic resources to make sense of whatever kind of text confronts them. As text users, readers need to know that different kinds of texts are designed to realize different purposes, which in turn influence the way the text is constructed, as is the case in everyday contexts (including schooling). Finally, in the role of text analysts, readers are concerned with examining how texts of different kinds are composed and consumed and to what effect. Thus, readers draw on resources about power and influence to determine whose interests are served by a text and the nature and purposes of gaps and silences. In doing so, they need to draw on their evaluative capacities as well as on the other roles and resources of the four roles and resources model simultaneously.

Critical literacy as a curriculum practice in Australia has recently been the focus of much press criticism and professional defense. Whereas some educational commentators who are outside the school system assert that deconstructing texts and adopting a range of reading positions is the practice of "trendy, left wing...ideologues applying theories dreamt up by the education faculties of our universities" (Ridd, 2006, p. 30), teachers and spokespersons for professional associations defend critical literacy practices as providing opportunities to pose essential questions about democracy and civil life. Thus, students—even in primary classes—are encouraged to interrogate texts by asking such questions as the following: What beliefs underpin this text? For whom and why was this text composed? Who or what is favored by this text? What are the implications of that? What social action can I take in response to this text? How does the text composer view the world? How am I positioned in relation to the composer's stance? How is age, gender, or ethnicity depicted in the text? Who is not mentioned in the text? Why not? Such an interrogative stance is regarded by some as being appropriate also for English-language learners (Alford, 2001, 2005).

Curriculum Literacies

Another dimension of multiliteracies relates to language, texts, and text structures of academic subject areas. Termed "academic literacies" by Lewis (see chapter 9), "academic language" by Pilgreen (see chapter 13), and "academic discourse" by Buehl (see chapter 11), the term "curriculum literacies" (Cumming & Wyatt-Smith, 2001; Cumming, Wyatt-Smith, Ryan, & Doig, 1999; Wyatt-Smith & Cumming, 1999) would be the Australian equivalent representing the language and literacy demands made on students as they engage with content area subject matter.

The range of literacies for different curriculum areas in secondary school subjects is considerable, requiring the extension of participants' knowledge of the technical vocabulary and the linguistic forms and structures of different curriculum areas. These need to be taught explicitly in the context of content learning because literacy and curriculum (or academics) are interrelated and dynamic in nature, embracing semiotic, visual, and textual practices. In a comprehensive Australian study involving numerous academics who analyzed videotapes of the delivery of curriculum in grade 11 and 12 classes, it was found that to succeed academically students must be able to coordinate a number of multiliteracies simultaneously (Cumming et al., 1999). Yet there was little evidence of explicit teaching of how to read classroom materials. Further, it was found that there was a mismatch between the language of the classroom and that of tests. As a result of the study, it was recommended that further investigation be undertaken into "the multimodality and complexity of the literacy demands for students as they undertake each subject and as they move from subject to subject" (p. 133). This research remains to be done.

Australian Frameworks for Developing Adolescent Literacy

Most of the authors of prior chapters have considered the nature of teaching and learning frameworks or learning strategies. For example, Buehl (see chapter 11) explored notions of explicit comprehension instruction through the use of Questioning the Author (Beck, McKeown, Hamilton, & Kucan, 1997) as a principal literacy teaching strategy and by working within a four-stage framework that includes teacher reflection, and teaching for metacognition. Anders and Spitler (see chapter 10), on the other hand, use the traditional before, during, after framework to discuss instruments that help students understand difficult text. Blanton, Pilonieta, and Wood (see chapter 12) offer three conceptions of literacy instruction before providing a seven-phase reading Skill Circle to support learners. For Brozo (see chapter 16), identifying entry or bridging points is crucial for engaging boys in the reading enterprise, and Lewis explicated guiding principles and strategies to address the demands of "situated practice within Discourses" (see chapter 9). With respect to developing English-language learners' literacy, Pilgreen (see chapter 13) identified a number of discrete strategies that serve to support students' learning to identify and distinguish main ideas and supporting details, and to sequence information gleaned from texts.

Over the past 25 years, much effort has been expended in the different Australian states in providing professional development programs and courses for middle and high school teachers that address the needs of adolescent literacy learners in all subjects. The earliest program, Effective Reading in the Content Areas (ERICA), was developed by two academics (Morris & Stewart-Dore, 1984) working with a team of experienced, practicing teachers, many of whom were heads of subject departments.

Influenced by the work of Herber (1978) and his colleagues at Syracuse University as well as the practices of subject teachers assigning reading as a teaching and learning strategy, the ERICA development team met one afternoon weekly for six months to address teacher concerns about students' literacy performances. They did this by sharing teaching and learning strategies gleaned from personal experience, an extensive literature review, and the results of classroom action research.

As work progressed, a bank of units of work in a range of subject areas at different high school grade levels was built up around what came to be known as ERICA strategies based on printed material—principally grade-level textbooks—used regularly in classrooms. These strategies had been reported in the professional literature but were mostly unfamiliar to Australian high school teachers.

The strategies were organized into four stages according to purpose: preparing for reading, thinking through information, extracting and organizing information, and translating information. Preparing for reading involved tapping into what students already knew about the subject matter to be learned in the content area classroom and recording that by means of a class-developed word map or structured overview (tree diagram); previewing and surveying texts for their organizational and graphic features, such as headings, subheadings, captions, and diagram labels; developing a graphic outline of the text content to indicate what information was given priority and emphasis; and identifying new vocabulary and word meanings in context. Thinking through information focused on developing comprehension using three-level guides (Herber, 1978) and teacher-prepared cloze passages (cf. cloze tests) derived from classroom texts of significance. Extracting and organizing information made use of the top-level structure of texts to help students identify main ideas and distinguish them from supporting details by using charts, diagrams, and other graphic organizers to select and record information for later use. Translating information required readers either to engage in group discussion or to write reports, essays, scripts, explanations, narratives, and other genres in their own words based on the notes, outlines, diagrams, and charts they made earlier. Reinforcement activities in the form of board and word games were encouraged as follow-up as well. Around the same time, complementary work was developed to support English-language learners' needs through the English Language Development Across the Curriculum Project (Houston, 1989).

Because of advances in literacy research and theory since the ERICA model was first conceived, Stewart-Dore (2002) developed a revised version called "learning to learn" and now termed "developing multiliteracies." It incorporated new thinking, especially about multiple literacies and their uses in and beyond the classroom. The revised model was based on notions of what successful learners (and productive users of multiliteracies) do to realize learning goals. For example, successful learners control their learning by using language to define their goals, determine how to achieve them, and correct performance if necessary. Successful learners also choose and use various strategies to develop plans to guide their learning. These plans help learners solve problems and construct, organize, reflect on, and communicate new knowledge in different forms and media.

Many teachers wonder, however, what they can do to show students how to become successful learners. Such teachers benefit from adopting a pedagogical framework for developing multiliteracies, including critical and curriculum literacies. The developing multiliteracies model helps teachers select and implement strategies that engage students' learning and develop their literacy competencies across the curriculum. Like the ERICA model, this framework consists of four interconnected phases following the pattern, "i.link; i.think; i.know; i.show." The framework draws on a range of theories to support its various phases and general configuration. Included are schema theory (Anderson, 1977), scaffolding and the Zone of Proximal Development (Vygotsky, 1934/1978), reflective practice (Schon, 1996), multiliteracies (New London Group, 1996; Stewart-Dore, 1994a, 1994b), and the four roles and resources model (Freebody & Luke, 1990). A description of the purposes of each of the four facets follows.

Phase 1: i.link. The first phase engages students in using language to learn by having them access and enhance their prior knowledge of the content to be learned and of the codes, signs, and symbols used in the source material. This material includes print, visual, or media texts to be used in a course of study. Insofar as the function of headings, subheadings, and the nature of link words are concerned, the top-level structure of those texts is also considered. New vocabulary is introduced together with links to known word parts and concepts. Selected strategies for i.link, which accords with the four roles and resources model's code-breaker role, include brainstorming; developing word and concept maps (Novak & Gowin, 1984), and completing a vocabulary definition map (Schwartz & Raphael, 1985). The code-breaker role is essentially about decoding the codes and conventions of written, spoken, and visual texts.

Phase 2: i.think. In Phase 2, learners are in the role of text participants according to the four roles and resources model. They think through their content material (mostly of a nonfiction, information kind), using language to interrogate possible meanings and reflect critically on their understanding of whole text. Their fundamental task is to comprehend texts, whatever their mode and medium. Strategies employed during this phase include responsive elaboration (Duffy & Roehler, 1987); three-level guide (Herber, 1978), and making entries in a reflective dialogue journal (Atwell, 1987; Bean & Zulich, 1989; Peyton & Staton, 1991; Stewart-Dore, 1996).

Phase 3: i.know. The third phase is designed to help students connect understandings—especially within and across different texts used in and out of school. They use language to analyze, select, and organize information in the role of text analyst (Freebody & Luke, 1990), which requires readers to uncover how texts position consumers. Strategies used include the development of a variety of graphic organizers such as retrieval charts and Venn diagrams to identify and record organizational patterns in and top-level structures of diverse text (Meyer, 1975; Meyer, Brandt, & Bluth, 1980; Rhoder, 2002) for note-making purposes.

Phase 4: i.show. The final phase of the strategic learning enterprise, representing knowledge (synthesizing learning), involves using language to synthesize, represent, and evaluate what has been learned in functional and critical ways. This goal is achieved by assuming the role of text critic and designing and creating new structures and forms of information presentation, including word and concept maps (Murdoch, 1998; Novak & Gowin, 1984). This phase also involves developing procedures for constructing artifacts and composing a range of written, visual, and media texts appropriate to the subject area and focus of study.

Helping Teachers Implement Strategies in Classrooms

A feature of the developing multiliteracies pedagogical model is its attention to explaining to teachers precisely how to teach students a learning strategy. The reason for this focus is that very often teachers will say, "Oh, yes, I use this (or that) strategy all the time." However, the real question (to which there is often no response) is, Do your students use this (or that) strategy all the time as well and do they know how, when, where, and why they should use it? For effective learning, teachers need to follow up on students' adoption and regular use of specific strategies.

The three-step procedure adopted for teaching students a learning strategy within the developing multiliteracies model derives from the work of McLaughlin and Allen (2002). Step 1 is teacher directed in a whole-class situation. Here, the teachers name the strategy and explain its purpose. They then show how the strategy works with a text by thinking aloud. Next, students practice the strategy by applying it to another text of similar type while the teachers provide support as required. Finally, students are asked to reflect on and write about the nature of the strategy and how it could be used with other texts they are required to study.

Step 2 requires students to work in small groups under teacher guidance. First, the class reviews the strategy, and students are asked to name it, identify its purpose, and enumerate procedural steps. Next, teachers guide students' use of the strategy by having them apply it to a new text. Peer collaboration is encouraged. The final aspects in Step 2 involve students reflecting on their success or otherwise in using the strategy with a new text in their reflective dialogue journals before engaging in whole-group discussion on how the strategy helped them work with and understand text. Steps 1 and 2 should be revisited frequently to ensure students' understanding and regular use. Step 3, individual reflection, involves asking students to review their experiences using the strategy by reflecting critically in reflective dialogue journal entries. This reflection may be framed by posing questions such as,

1. How does (name of strategy) help you to learn?
2. What problems did you have learning to use (name of strategy) and how did you overcome them?
3. When will you most likely use (name of strategy) and why?

As well, teachers implementing this three-step procedure should monitor students' strategy learning progress. They can do that by identifying students' stages of strategy use and recording judgments about them for reporting to parents and other staff. Stewart-Dore (2002) noted that students' "mastery of learning strategies is critical to being able to engage cognitive, affective and regulative processes and to construct new knowledge effectively" (p. 24). In identifying the extent to which students have mastered a strategy, teachers note each student's (a) degree of focus, attention, motivation, and interest; (b) participation in various kinds of learning activities; (c) willingness to reflect on the strategy use in reflective dialogue journals; (d) preparedness to articulate his or her thinking and provide reasons for the method of working; and (e) ability to identify the steps that are required to use a strategy effectively.

Other Frameworks for Developing Adolescent Literacy in Australia

Two other frameworks available to Australian teachers focus on helping them enhance adolescent literacy. Stepping Out is a professional development program and resource developed initially by the Western Australian Department of Education (see http://www.ecurl.com.au). Influenced by the ERICA model, it is now marketed through Pearson Education outside Australia. Stepping Out is organized around study modules labeled according to traditional language modes, namely, reading and viewing, writing, and listening and speaking, and requires two days' seminar attendance by teachers for training. The program provides teachers with tools to help students meet the literacy demands of school subjects (cf. curriculum literacies and academic literacy). Materials accompanying the professional development program offer a rationale for the program and sponsor the idea of a whole-school approach to improving adolescent literacy performance.

Literacy and Learning Strategies (Education Department of Western Australia, 1997), a supplement to the Stepping Out professional development program, is the major program resource, a result of teachers wanting a procedural handbook of strategies modeled in the professional development workshops. The book comprises two parts: the first details the theoretical underpinning of the Stepping Out program, and the second describes more than 50 strategies. Each strategy is accompanied by an explanation of its purpose; steps for implementation, including conditions for use such as independent, pair, group, and whole-class activities that are suitable for a wide age and ability range; and ideas for evaluation.

The second resource is titled *MyRead* (Vervoorn & van Haren, 2004). It is the outcome of a collaborative project developed by members of the Australian Association for the Teaching of English and the Australian Literacy Educators' Association. Underlying principles and beliefs of the material outcome of the project are that all students can learn to become literate; teachers can make a difference; monitoring and assessment of literacy growth inform teaching; and to be successful, teachers need a repertoire of strategies and practices.

Sixteen strategies are accompanied by implementation guides and guideposts for each strategy. The latter are outcomes-based assessment rubrics at beginning, developing, and achieving levels, and the indicators are useful for monitoring student learning formatively. The guides explain how teachers can be empowered by employing effective literacy and learning strategies, and how, in turn, students can become engaged in purposeful social practices based on the four roles and resources model. Ideas for monitoring and assessment also form part of the strategy guides.

In terms of the specific needs of students, teachers are concerned about the nature, especially for boys, of in- and out-of-school literacies in Australia. In previous chapters, few authors have addressed explicitly an alleged plight of adolescent boys regarding either literacy practices or performances. Although it is well known that adolescent boys' literacy performances lag behind those of adolescent girls, the precise nature of their literacy practices is perhaps less well known. There have been numerous Australian studies that have explored these issues. One in particular helped to address the shortcomings noted.

The study reported in *Boys, Literacy and Schooling: Expanding the Repertoires of Practice* was undertaken in 2002 by Alloway, Freebody, Gilbert, and Muspratt. One aspect of the research was the training for 24 teachers in 12 schools to understand better the links between gender and literacy, review and redevelop current classroom activities, and develop an action plan that they would monitor and evaluate. Of three kinds of interventions undertaken as well, two have pertinence here. One intervention aimed to make classroom literacy a very active process, providing opportunities for boys especially to exercise choice and draw on personal experience while enhancing their sense of self worth. The second intervention engaged students in negotiating repertoires of practice that extended beyond the classroom to include the use of materials from popular and commercial youth culture and various modes of expression (including electronic, musical, visual, and multimodal work). Several recommendations emerged from the study. They included the need for schools to adopt a practical and futures-directed approach to literacy and for teachers to use strategies that will "promote an active, purposeful and democratic learning environment" (Alloway et al., 2002, p. 8). Thus, there is disparity between boys' in- and out-of-school literacies that could be integrated in classrooms to improve boys' literacy performances.

Envisioning a Futures Perspective on Adolescent Literacy

The New London Group (1996) asserts that we should re-vision litera-cy for the future. The group's members reason that becoming literate is an active process of designing the future. The future that I am concerned with creating here is one in which students study literacy from three per-spectives: as a construct or object, as an everyday practice, and as a tool or technology for learning. That is to say, by using their current literacy skills, processes, knowledge, and practices, students will learn about literacy as they develop their literacy by using it. This concept is akin to that of Halliday's (1978) children's language development triptych: Students learn language, learn through language, and learn about lan-guage simultaneously. Such study would extend necessarily across the curriculum and have students engaged in examining the language and texts that they use to construct knowledge in different curriculum ar-eas. The focus here is on students using literacy to learn about it.

A literacy study of this kind could begin by asking students to iden-tify what they think are the characteristics of a good reader. Such ques-tionnaires abound. A popular one is the Burke Reading Interview (Burke, 1987). Some questionnaires are designed to discover students' attitudes toward literacy as well as their literacy practices. They may require stu-dents to respond by completing sentences such as the following:

- The best book that I ever read was...
- Reading is hard when...
- Draw a picture of what reading looks like...
- I like/don't like reading because...
- When I go to the public library,...

Other available surveys pose questions such as Where do you read? When do you read? What do you read? Do you ever have more than one book in progress at a time? What kinds of books are they? What books do you reread? What reading do you do on the computer? Are you a good reader and writer? Why do you think that? Which classroom materials are the hardest and easiest to understand? Why is that? No doubt there are other statements and questions that you could develop. The purpose is to probe students' thinking about their understanding of reading and writing as literate practices that they engage in personally.

To tap into students' literate interest and practices with electronic media, discussion would revolve around the following kinds of questions:

What are your favorite websites? What is it that attracts you to them? What do they teach you? Who is the audience for these websites? How do you know? How did you locate them? What electronic, digital, and telephonic devices do you use at home, at school, and with your friends? Does texting lead to spelling laziness or confusion? Why or why not? How are reading from a computer or personal digital assistant screen and viewing television or a video like or unlike reading conventional print (e.g., a book, newspaper, magazine)? Consider your everyday life. What uses do you make of the components of multiliteracies, that is, oral and print language, images, aural and gestural texts, and the spatial arrangement of text information?

Other activities that students could explore include studying the history of printing (and an exploration of the life and times of Gutenberg), of reading, and of writing, and then drawing up comparative timelines for each. In each instance, students would be encouraged to audit their own neighborhood practices in relation to each area of study. For example, they might visit a local printing operation that publishes a local newspaper or a commercial outfit that specializes in particular kinds of social printing such as specialized brochures, flyers, cards, and newsletters. Another focus could be on a local sign writer: What kinds of signs does he or she prepare? Who commissions the signs? What is the nature of the signs? Where are they written? Why do they take the form that they do?

Further, students could explore the world of texts and their nature from the earliest times to the present day, which would include more than paper or bound print texts. Among those of later times could be chapbooks, broadsides, newspapers, comic books, magazines, and a range of electronic texts developed by using multimedia. Included in this kind of study would be the language of printing and text production such as stereotyping, diazotyping, phototypesetting, and more. Such study might lead to an examination of the use of print as an artistic device incorporated into visual displays of paintings in galleries and other art exhibitions.

Arguably, a focus on community or public print in one or more of these ways could yield opportunities to heighten students' understanding of literacy, its uses, and its manifestations. These types of activities could also provide adolescents with the chance to study ways in which their literacies—of mostly an out-of-school nature—are inexorably linked to traditional and developing literacies. Certainly, many opportunities would arise from such a study of literacy to intrigue boys interested in the mechanics of operations and the means of production of artifacts. Through work experience placements in printing industry businesses, there is also the chance for some students to entertain the possibility of a future trade or profession.

None of these ideas, however, has touched on myriad topics of interest to boys in relation to information and communication technology, albeit electronic and video games. Gee (2000) and others extol the virtues of some electronic games in advancing literate competences. Further, all students need to share with their teachers—ironically, as teachers themselves—their understandings about out-of-school literacy practices that could help teachers relate curriculum content more readily to adolescent interests and activities. Until there is a meeting of minds between teachers and students about the kinds of knowledge they have about the literacies of new times, little advance is likely in developing adolescent literacies.

Conclusion

Teachers of adolescents in the United States of America and Australia face similar challenges and obstacles. They also enjoy the same privilege of being in a position to empower students through the literacies that adolescents must master if they are to realize satisfying public and personal lives as lifelong learners, workers, citizens, community volunteers, and possibly parents or caretakers. As Harper and Bean explain (see chapter 17), contemporary literacies are complex and diverse. As a result, today's adolescents must practice various literacies daily, as Buehl recommends (see chapter 11), while being helped to focus explicitly on ways to make meaning—to comprehend—as a tool for communicating across space and time, as Anders and Spitler note (see chapter 10). Guiding principles for recognizing literacies as situated practices, as Lewis describes (see chapter 9), must be incorporated into instructional repertoires that explore, explicate, translate, model, guide, apply, and effect closure in ways that Blanton, Pilonieta, and Wood (see chapter 12) describe. In preparation for futures experience and study, it is useful to conceive 21st century literacies as new technologies, as Moorman and Horton do (see chapter 14). Consciously connecting through everyday literacy practices will permit, as Moore and Onofrey imply (see chapter 15), membership in literate communities of practice. With increasing numbers of students whose mother tongue is not English entering our classrooms, it behooves us to heed and adopt Pilgreen's (see chapter 13) strategies for supporting English-language learners' literacy development through intentional, strategic teaching. And that summation leaves the issue of boys and literacy open for further research, discussion, and debate not only in light of that research, but also in response to teachers' observations, knowledge, and understandings. But let's not ignore what adolescent boys themselves can contribute to deliberations about how they learn literacy in and out of school. Today's students may well be our best teachers of what's best for them!

Questions for Reflection

1. How do you and your colleagues prepare adolescents for the demands of contemporary multiliteracies in and out of the classroom?

2. What advice would you offer to an adolescent who eschewed the need for a wide repertoire of literacy practices?

3. How are you preparing, both personally and professionally, to meet your likely future literacy needs?

Nea Stewart-Dore is Adjunct Associate Professor in the Faculty of Arts, Humanities and Education, Central Queensland University, Rockhampton, Australia, where her principal role is the supervision of higher degree research candidates. She is a Fellow of the Australian College of Educators, and has played a key role in realization of the 2005 Rotary International/International Reading Association Memorandum of Understanding that focuses on fostering and developing collaborative literacy development projects worldwide. She may be contacted at colnea@byterocky.net.

REFERENCES

Alford, J. (2001). Learning language and critical literacy: Adolescent ESL students. *Journal of Adolescent & Adult Literacy, 45*(3), 238–242.

Alford, J. (2005). Critical literacy in high school preparation language programs: Challenges and possibilities. *Curriculum Perspectives, 25*(3), 44–50.

Alloway, N., Freebody, P., Gilbert, P., & Muspratt, S. (2002). *Boys, literacy and schooling: Expanding the repertoires of practice.* Canberra, Australia: Department of Education, Science, and Training.

Anderson, R.C. (1977). The notion of schemata and the educational enterprise: General discussion of the conference. In R.C. Anderson, R.J. Spiro, & W.E. Montague (Eds.), *Schooling and the acquisition of knowledge.* Hillsdale, NJ: Erlbaum.

Anstey, M., & Bull, G. (2006). *Teaching and learning multiliteracies: Changing times, changing literacies.* Newark, DE: International Reading Association.

Atwell, N. (1987). *In the middle: Writing, reading, and learning with adolescents.* Portsmouth, NH: Heinemann.

Bean, T.W., & Zulich, J. (1989). Using dialogue journals to foster reflective practice with preservice, content area teachers. *Teacher Education Quarterly, 16*(1), 33–40.

Beck, I.L., McKeown, M.G., Hamilton, R.L., & Kucan, L. (1997). *Questioning the Author: An approach for enhancing student engagement with text.* Newark, DE: International Reading Association.

Burke, C. (1987). Burke Reading Interview. Available: http://www.sonoma.edu/users/n/nickle/463/burke.reading.interview.pdf

Cumming, J.J., & Wyatt-Smith, C.M. (Eds.). (2001). *Literacy and the curriculum: Success in senior secondary schooling.* Melbourne, Victoria, Australia: ACER.

Cumming, J.J., Wyatt-Smith, C.M., Ryan, J., & Doig, S.M. (1999). The literacy-curriculum interface: Literacy demands of the curriculum in post-compulsory schooling. *Queensland Journal of Educational Research, 15*(1), 133–139.

Duffy, G.G., & Roehler, L.R. (1987). Improving reading instruction through the use of responsive elaboration. *The Reading Teacher, 40,* 514–519.

Education Department of Western Australia. (1996). *Literacy and learning strategies.* East Perth: Author.

Freebody, P., & Luke, A. (1990). "Literacies" programs: Debates and demands in cultural context. *Prospect: A Journal of Australian TESOL, 5*(3), 7–16.

Gee, J. (2000, September). Discourse and sociocultural studies in reading. *Reading Online, 4*(3). Available: http://www.readingonline.org/articles/art_index.asp?HREF=handbook/gee/index.html

Halliday, M.A.K. (1978). *Language as social semiotic: The social interpretation of language and meaning.* London, England: Edward Arnold.

Herber, H.L. (1978). *Teaching reading in content areas.* Englewood Cliffs, NJ: Prentice-Hall.

Houston, C. (1989). *English language development across the curriculum.* Brisbane, Queensland, Australia: Immigrant Education Services, Division of Special Services, Department of Education.

Lankshear, C. (1997). Critical social literacy for the classroom: An approach using conventional texts across the curriculum. In C. Lankshear (with J.P. Gee, M. Knobel, & C. Searle), *Changing literacies* (pp. 40–42). Buckingham, England: Open University Press.

Luke, A., & Freebody, P. (1999a). A map of possible practices: Further notes on the four resources model. *Practically Primary, 4*(2), 5–8.

Luke, A., & Freebody, P. (1999b). Further notes on the four resources model. *Reading Online.* Available: http://www.readingonline.org/research/lukefreebody.html

McLaughlin, M., & Allen, M.B. (2002). *Guided comprehension in action: Lessons for grades 3–8.* Newark, DE: International Reading Association.

Meyer, B.J.F. (1975). *The organization of prose and its effects on memory.* Amsterdam: North-Holland.

Meyer, B.J.F., Brandt, D.M., & Bluth, G.J. (1980). Use of the top-level structure in text: Key for reading comprehension of ninth-grade students. *Reading Research Quarterly, 16,* 72–103.

Morris, A., & Stewart-Dore, N. (1984). *Learning to learn from text: Effective reading in the content areas.* North Ryde, New South Wales, Australia: Addison Wesley.

Murdoch, K. (1998). *Classroom connections: Strategies for integrated learning.* Armadale, Victoria, Australia: Eleanor Curtain.

New London Group. (1996). A pedagogy of multiliteracies: Designing social futures. *Harvard Educational Review, 66*(1), 60–92.

Novak, J.D., & Gowin, D.B. (1984). *Learning how to learn.* Cambridge, England: Cambridge University Press.

Peyton, J.K., & Staton, J. (Eds.). (1991). *Writing our lives: Reflections on dialogue journal writing with adults learning English.* Englewood Cliffs, NJ: Regents Prentice Hall and Center for Applied Linguistics.

Queensland Department of Education. (2000). *Literate futures: Report of the literacy review for Queensland State Schools.* Brisbane, Queensland: The State of Queensland.

Rhoder, C. (2002). *Mindful reading: A framework for adolescent literacy.* Paper presented at the 19th World Congress on Reading, International Reading Association, Edinburgh, United Kingdom, August 2002.

Ridd, P. (2006, October 11). Ideologues hijack education. *The Courier Mail.* Retrieved March 12, 2007, from http://www.news.com.au/couriermail/story/0,23739,20563092-27197,00.html

Schon, D.A. (1996). *Educating the reflective practitioner: Toward a new design for teaching and learning in the professions.* San Francisco: Jossey-Bass.

Schwartz, R.M., & Raphael, T.E. (1985). Concept of definition: A key to improving students' vocabulary. *The Reading Teacher, 39,* 198–205.

Stewart-Dore, N. (1994a). Different literacies for different knowledge areas: Some post-Wiltshire reflections. *Words' Worth, 27,* 4.

Stewart-Dore, N. (1994b). Literacy across the curriculum: Much more than the written word. Reading 6 in *Helping students to learn.* A professional development program for subject teachers. Literacy and Learning Program, Directorate of School Education, Victoria. Melbourne, Victoria, Australia: DEET and the Victorian Ministry of Education.

Stewart-Dore, N. (1996). *Literacy learning across the curriculum.* LINC Module: National Professional Development Program. Toowoomba, Queensland, Australia: Commonwealth Department of Education and Training, Australian Literacy Educators' Association & the University of Southern Queensland.

Stewart-Dore, N. (2002). *Learning to learn strategy pack.* Bald Hills, Queensland, Australia: St. Paul's School.

Vervoorn, J., & van Haren, R. (2004). *MyRead: Strategies for teaching reading in the middle years.* Canberra: Department of Education, Science and Training.

Vygotsky, L.S. (1978). *Mind in society: The development of higher psychological processes* (M. Cole, V. John-Steiner, S. Scribner, & E. Souberman, Eds. & Trans.). Cambridge, MA: Harvard University Press. (Original work published 1934)

Wyatt-Smith, C.M., & Cumming, J.J. (1999). Examining the literacy demands of the enacted curriculum. *Literacy Learning: Secondary Thoughts, 7*(2), 19–30.

AUTHOR INDEX

G

Garcia, I., 316
Gates, A., 306
Gay, J., 217
Geddes, C., 305
Gee, J.P., 146, 173–174, 176, 204–206, 271, 276, 287, 338, 350
Gilbert, P., 306, 347
Gilmore, P., 173
Giroux, H., 321, 325
Glick, J.A., 217
Goff, L.S., 101
Goffman, E., 78
Gonzales Bertrand, D., 315
Gonzalez, E.J., 305–306
González, N., 172
Goodman, K.S., 168
Goodman, Y.M., 180, 290
Goodwin, A.L., 148
Gose, B., 144
Goudvis, A., 199, 246, 256
Gowin, D.B., 343–344
Granahan, S., 227, 229–230
Green, B.F., 8
Green, J., 173
Greenberg, J., 173
Greenleaf, C., 297
Griffin, P., 4, 218–219, 224
Grigg, W.S., 305
Grossman, K.N., 147
Gruwell, E., 292
Guattari, F., 67, 77
Gulli, A., 280
Guth, N.D., 113, 115
Guthrie, J.T., 230
Guzzetti, B.J., 175

H

Hadaway, N.L., 328
Haddix, M.P., 292
Haertel, G.D., 85, 136
Hagood, M.C., 73
Hagoort, P., 221
Hahn, C.L., 322, 329
Hahn, M.D., 292
Hald, L., 221
Halliday, M.A.K., 348
Hamilton, R.L., 207, 341
Hargis, C., 97
Harper, H.J., 325, 329
Harré, R., 288
Harris, D.E., 113

Harste, J.C., 171, 183–184
Harvey, S., 199, 246, 256
Havens, L., 89
Hemphill, F.C., 8
Herber, H.L., 168, 170, 342, 344
Herman, N., 113
Heron, A., 73
Herrenkohl, L.R., 297
Hiebert, E.H., 4
Higher Education Act, 26, 32
Hill, W.H., 252
Hinchman, K.A., 223, 309, 326
Hinton, S.E., 294
Hirsch, E.D., 325
Hitlin, P., 269
Holbrook, H.T., 306
Holland, D., 286
Holland, P.W., 8
Hombo, C.M., 212
Houston, C., 342
Howe, N., 264, 266–267
Hughes, P., 73
Hull, G.A., 65
Hurwitz, L., 297
Hynds, S., 293

I

International Reading Association, 10, 23, 25–30, 32, 35–36, 41, 113, 116, 197
Ivey, G., 96, 98–99

J

Jackson, D.B., 287
Jacobson, L., 148
Jenkins, L.B., 305
Jensen, J.M., 97
Jetton, T., 147, 202–203
Jin, Y., 212
Johnson, D.W., 152, 214
Johnson, R.T., 152
Jones, L.R., 4
Jordan, M., 10, 288

K

Kahn, R., 266
Kahne, J., 329–330
Kame'enui, E.J., 6, 150
Kamil, M.L., 112, 148, 195
Keene, E.O., 199
Keiser, D.L., 322
Kennedy, A.M., 305–306

SUBJECT INDEX

Note. Page numbers followed by *f* and *t* indicate figures and tables, respectively.

A

K–L

KUMASAKA, JOANN, 105
LANGUAGE. *See* academic language/discourse; talk
LEADERSHIP: in Alabama Reading Initiative, 59–60; loose-tight style, 86; for schoolwide literacy initiative, 98
LEARNING: social nature of, xi, 173–174, 275
LEARNING OPPORTUNITIES: for collaboration, 151–152; for critical thinking, 150; for development of academic literacy, 153–162; for integrating reading and writing, 151; for prior knowledge, 150–151; for responsibility, 152
LEARNING STRATEGIES: immature adolescents and, 83–84, 88–89; for schoolwide literacy initiative, 99–100, 100t–101t
LEARNING STYLES: and academic literacy, 152; museums and, 69
LEWIS, JILL, ix–xiii, 20–45, 143–166
LIBRARY(IES): boundaries of, 72–75; circulation, reading and, 52; escaping boundaries of, 75–76; literacy of, 78–79
LINES OF ESCAPE, 72; definition of, 65
LITERACY: boundaries of, 67; and democracy, 323–326; historical perspective on, 265–266; social nature of, xi, 173–174
LITERACY CIRCLES, INTEGRATED, 212–237; characteristics of, 224–231; sample lessons in, 226f–229f
LITERACY COACHES: in Canada, 137–138; definition of, 110; keys to success for, 114–115; need for, 111–112; role of, 112–114; in secondary schools, 110–123; strategies for, 115–121, 116t; websites for, 120t
LITERACY LEADERSHIP TEAM: literacy coaches and, 117; for schoolwide literacy initiative, 98
LITERACY PRACTICES: for academic identities, 300; challenging, 64–81; definition of, 65; for democracy, 327–333; metacognition and, 170–172; school, outside and, 77–79
LITERACY RESUMES, 280–291

LITERACY THEORIES: challenging, 64–81; complicating, 78; for immature adolescents, 89–92; vintage, 168–172
LITERATURE CLASSROOM: QtA in, 207
LONG, RICHARD, 21
LOOSE-TIGHT LEADERSHIP STYLE, 86
LYON, REID, 6, 13–14

M

MAIN IDEA QUESTIONS, 252–256
MALE ADOLESCENTS. *See* boys
MANITOBA: curriculum development in, 126–131
MAPS: identity, 299–300
MASSIVELY MULTIPLAYER ONLINE GAMES (MMOGs), 271
MATERIALS: for academic literacy, 149; IRA reflections on, 29–30
MATHEMATICS CLASSROOM: QtA in, 207
MEDIA LITERACY, 276
MEMORY: in reading model, 220
MENTAL SYSTEM, 219
MENTORS: for boys, 312–314
METACOGNITION, xi; and academic literacy, 150; growth in, space for, 185–186; for immature adolescents, 89–92; and instructional practices, 170–172; teaching for, debriefing as, 208–209; theory on, 169–170
MILITARY: adolescents and, 321
MILLENNIALS, xi–xii, 263–285; characteristics of, 266–268; instruction for, 272–280; and new literacy technologies, 268–272
MINI-ETHNOGRAPHIES, 299–300
MISSION: for schoolwide literacy initiative, 97–98
MITCHELL, KATHERINE, 47
MMOGs, 271
MODELING PHASE: in reading skill circle, 225
MONTANA ACADEMY, 82–94
MOORE, DAVID W., 286–303
MOORMAN, GARY, ix–xiii, 263–285
MULTILITERACIES, 338–341; developing, 343–344
MULTIPLE LITERACIES, 64–66, 146; assessment in, 144–145; versus boundaries, 67; and democracy, 326; future of, 213; Millennials and, 268–272; in museums, 68–69; and

reading knowledge and skill, 223–224; term, xi

MULTIPLE PERSPECTIVES: learning activity on, 154–156

MUSEUMS: boundaries of, 68–71; escaping boundaries of, 71–72; literacy of, 78–79

MUSIC CLASSROOM: QtA in, 208

MYSPACE, 68

N

NATIONAL ASSESSMENT OF EDUCATIONAL PROGRESS (NAEP), 4–5, 7–8, 145, 264; Alabama scores, 47

NATIONAL ASSOCIATION OF SECONDARY SCHOOL PRINCIPALS: on adolescent literacy, 197t

NATIONAL ASSOCIATION OF STATE BOARDS OF EDUCATION: on adolescent literacy, 196t–197t

NATIONAL COUNCIL FOR TEACHERS OF ENGLISH: on adolescent literacy, 196t

NATIONAL COUNCIL FOR THE SOCIAL STUDIES: on adolescent literacy, 197t

NATIONAL COUNCIL OF TEACHERS OF MATHEMATICS: on adolescent literacy, 197t

NATIONAL EDUCATION ASSOCIATION: Alabama chapter, 48

NATIONAL GOVERNORS ASSOCIATION: on adolescent literacy, 197t

NATIONAL JOINT COMMITTEE ON LEARNING DISABILITIES, 21

NATIONAL LITERACY, 324–325

NATIONAL SCIENCE TEACHERS ASSOCIATION: on adolescent literacy, 197t

NEW LITERACY: assessment in, 144–145; Millennials and, 268–272

NO CHILD LEFT BEHIND ACT, x, 5; IRA and, 22, 29–30; and teacher morale, 41

O

OGLE, DONNA, 132

ONOFREY, KAREN A., 286–303

OPEN-UPS, 298

OUTSIDE: challenging literacy theories and practices from, 64–81; definition of, 65; digital resources and, 66–67; literacy coaches and, 118–119; perspective of, 66–68; and text selection for boys, 311–312

P

PAN-CANADIAN ASSESSMENT PROGRAM, 129

PARAGRAPH: definition of, 245

PARALLEL DISTRIBUTED PROCESSING (PDP), 220–221

PARTNERSHIP: and academic literacy, 151–152

PASSAGE: definition of, 245

PEER INTERVIEWS, 294–296

PERSISTENCE: for immature adolescents, 91

PICASSO SELF-PORTRAIT PROJECT, 179–180, 179f

PILGREEN, JANICE, 238–262

PILONIETA, PAOLA, 212–237

PISA. See Programme for International Student Achievement

PLAGIARISM: Millennials and, 269

PLAY, 178–179

POETRY: libraries and, 74–75

POLICY ACTORS, 9–11; in Canada, 128; versus policy entrepreneurs, 13–14

POLICY ENTREPRENEURS, 13–14

POLICYMAKING, xii; agenda-setting for adolescent literacy, 3–19

POLICY WINDOW, 5

POPULAR CULTURE: and adolescent literacy, 71–72, 77; and texts for boys, 309–311, 310f

PORTFOLIO ASSESSMENT: electronic, 145

POSTSECONDARY OCCUPATIONS: lack of preparation for, 9

POWER: relations of, 67

PRINCIPAL. See administration

PRINTING PRESS, 266

PRIOR KNOWLEDGE: and academic literacy, 150–151; Australian approach to, 343–344; and comprehension, 170, 202; for immature adolescents, 91

PROCEDURAL KNOWLEDGE, 221–222

PROCESS-ORIENTED INSTRUCTIONAL APPROACHES: and academic literacy, 150

PROFESSIONAL DEVELOPMENT, xii; in Canada, 133–134; for comprehension instruction, 192–211; framework for, 89; IRA reflections on, 31–32; literacy coaches and, 113–114; for schoolwide literacy initiative, 101–102; white paper on, IRA and, 37

PROFICIENT READERS: characteristics of, 198–201, 203–204, 204f;

cultural–historical activity theory on, 218–221, 219*f*; strategies of, 200*t*
PROGRAMME FOR INTERNATIONAL STUDENT ACHIEVEMENT (PISA), 128, 145
PUBLIC LIBRARY: boundaries of, 72–75; escaping boundaries of, 75–76; literacy of, 78–79

Q

QUALITY UNDERGRADUATE ELEMENTARY & SECONDARY TEACHER EDUCATION IN READING (QUESTER) PROJET, 35
QUESTIONING THE AUTHOR (QTA), 207–208
QUESTIONS: detail, 247–252; main idea, 252–256; sequence, 256–260; twenty literacy, 295. *See also* reflection questions

R

RAND READING STUDY REPORT: on adolescent literacy, 196*t*
READ-ALOUDS, 100*t*; for schoolwide literacy initiative, 105
READING: entry points to, for boys, 306–316; and forgetting, 201; language of, 220; and writing, 151
READING ACHIEVEMENT: attention to, 4–6; by boys, 305–306; poor, 8–9
READING BUDDIES, 312–314
READING EXCELLENCE ACT, 5
READING FIRST, 5–7, 15; IRA on, 36
READING KNOWLEDGE: transfer of, 231–232
READING LOG, 183
READING QUESTIONNAIRE, 180–181
READING STRATEGY DOCUMENTATION FORM, 181–182, 182*f*
READING SYSTEM, 219; coordination of, 221–222
READWRITETHINK, 278
RECIPROCAL TEACHING, 100*t*
RECOGNITION: accurate, 86–88
REFLECTION: on comprehension instruction, for content teachers, 198–209; definition of, 22
REFLECTION QUESTIONS: on academic identities, 300; on academic literacy, 162; on agenda-setting, 16; on Alabama Reading Initiative, 62–63; on boys, 316; on content-area comprehension instruction, 210; on democracy, 333; on ELLs, 260–261;

on in- and out-of-school literacies, 79; on international perspectives, 139; on IRA and federal policies, 41–42; on literacy circles, 232–233; on literacy coaches, 121; on Millennials, 282; on multiliteracies, 351; on reinventing comprehension instruction, 188; on schoolwide literacy initiative, 107; on struggling adolescent readers, 93
REMEDIAL INSTRUCTION: problems with, 216
RESIDENT CRITIC, 331–332; guidelines for, 332*t*
RESPONSIBILITY: and academic literacy, 152
RESUMES: literacy, 280–291
RIGOR: scientific, 11
RIVETING INVITATIONS, 289–290
RUGBY, 192–193, 198, 202–203

S

SALINGER, TERRY, 3–19, 46–63
SANTA, CAROL M., 82–94, 132
SAVE THE LAST WORD FOR ME, 171–172
SCALABILITY, 11, 14
SCANNING: instruction in, 248–250, 250*f*
SCHEMA, x–xi; reorganizing, 171–172; theory on, 168–169
SCHOOL-BASED LITERACY PRACTICES: outside and, 64–81
SCHOOL COMMUNITY, xii; Alabama Reading Initiative and, 56–57
SCHOOL CONTEXT, 175, 175*f*
SCHOOLWIDE LITERACY INITIATIVE, 95–109; in Canada, 135–137; components of, 97–104; in Hawaii, 104–106
SCIENTIFIC RIGOR, 11
SEAGULL CONSULTING, 102
SECONDARY SCHOOL LITERACY INSTRUCTION. *See* adolescent literacy instruction
SELF-ESTEEM: academic, survey of, 154, 155*f*–156*f*
SELF-MONITORING, 170; and academic literacy, 150
SELF-REFLECTION: IRA and, 22–33
SELF-REGULATION, 170
SENSEMAKING, 59
SENTENCE STRIPS + TIMELINE, 257–260, 258*f*–259*f*
SEQUENCE: questions on, 256–260; reading skill circle on, 226*f*–227*f*
SHARED READINGS, 100*t*; for schoolwide literacy initiative, 105

UNITED STATES DEPARTMENT OF
EDUCATION, 12–13; on adolescent
literacy, 196t–197t; models from,
IRA and, 35–36

V

VIDEO GAMES, 271–272
VISION: for schoolwide literacy initiative,
97–98
VISUAL MESSAGES: learning activity on,
157–158
VISUAL SUPPORT, 248, 248f
VOCABULARY DEVELOPMENT: strategies for,
100t
VOCATIONAL EDUCATION SUBJECTS:
academic literacy and, 147; literacy
and, IRA on, 38
VOICE: creating, 327–329
VYGOTSKY, LEV, 173, 222–223

W

WEBQUEST, 278–279
WEBSITES: classroom, 280–282;
educational, 276–280; evaluation of,
275–276; learning activity on, 158,

159f–160f; for literacy coaches, 120t;
for students, 277t; for teachers, 277t
WESTERN AND NORTHERN CANADIAN
PROTOCOL (WNCP), 124–140
WH WORDS, 247–248, 248f
WIDE READING OPPORTUNITIES: for
schoolwide literacy initiative, 98–99,
105; text selection for, 99t
WILLIAMS, DOUG, 103–104, 104f
WIRELESS COMMUNICATION TECHNOLOGIES
(WIFI), 64–65
WNCP. See Western and Northern
Canadian Protocol
WOOD, KAREN D., 212–237
WORLD WIDE WEB, 266
WRITING: immature adolescents and, 92;
to learn, for schoolwide literacy
initiative, 101t, 105; and reading, 151
WRITING SYSTEMS, 265–266

Y–Z

YES-NO NAME GAME, 295–296
YOUTH GROUPS, 67–68
ZONE OF PROXIMAL DEVELOPMENT, xi, 212,
218, 223–224, 343